Exceptionalism and Industrialisation

This book explores the question of British exceptionalism in the period from the Glorious Revolution to the Congress of Vienna. Leading historians examine why Great Britain emerged from years of sustained competition with its European rivals in a discernible position of hegemony in the domains of naval power, empire, global commerce, agricultural efficiency, industrial production, fiscal capacity and advanced technology. They deal with Britain's unique path to industrial revolution and distinguish four themes on the interactions between its emergence as a great power and as the first industrial nation. First, they highlight growth and industrial change, the interconnections between agriculture, foreign trade and industrialisation. Second, they examine technological change and, especially, Britain's unusual inventiveness. Third, they study her institutions and their role in facilitating economic growth. Fourth and finally, they explore British military and naval supremacy, showing how this was achieved and how it contributed to Britain's economic supremacy.

LEANDRO PRADOS DE LA ESCOSURA is Professor of Economic History at Universidad Carlos III, Madrid, and Prince of Asturias Distinguished Visiting Professor at the Georgetown University.

Exceptionalism and Industrialisation

Britain and Its European Rivals, 1688–1815

Edited by

Leandro Prados de la Escosura
Professor of Economic History at Universidad Carlos III, Madrid

CAMBRIDGE
UNIVERSITY PRESS

PUBLISHED BY THE PRESS SYNDICATE OF THE UNIVERSITY OF CAMBRIDGE
The Pitt Building, Trumpington Street, Cambridge, United Kingdom

CAMBRIDGE UNIVERSITY PRESS
The Edinburgh Building, Cambridge, CB2 2RU, UK
40 West 20th Street, New York, NY 10011–4211, USA
477 Williamstown Road, Port Melbourne, VIC 3207, Australia
Ruiz de Alarcón 13, 28014 Madrid, Spain
Dock House, The Waterfront, Cape Town 8001, South Africa

http://www.cambridge.org

First published 2004

Printed in the United Kingdom at the University Press, Cambridge

Typeface Plantin 10/12 pt. *System* LaTeX 2ε [TB]

A catalogue record for this book is available from the British Library

Library of Congress Cataloging in Publication data
Exceptionalism and industrialisation : Britain and its European rivals, 1688–1815 / edited by Leandro Prados de la Escosura.
p. cm.
"This volume originated in a conference held in March 26–27, 2001 in Madrid, on 'Britain and Its Rivals' . . . to honour . . . Patrick Karl O'Brien, . . . [and] sponsored by Fundación BBVA" – P..
Includes bibliographical references and index.
ISBN 0-521-79304-1 (hb.)
1. Industrial revolution – Great Britain – History – Congresses. 2. Great Britain – Economic conditions – Congresses. 3. Technological innovations – Great Britain – History – Congresses. 4. Industrial revolution – Europe – History – Congresses. 5. Europe – Economic conditions – Congresses. 6. Technological innovations – Europe – History – Congresses. I. Prados de la Escosura, Leandro. II. O'Brien, Patrick Karl.
HC254.5.E95 2004
330.941′07 – dc22 2003049546

ISBN 0 521 79304 1 hardback

For Patrick K. O'Brien

Contents

List of tables and figures

Tables

Figures

List of contributors

ROBERT C. ALLEN is a Fellow of Nuffield College and Professor of Economic History at the University of Oxford. He is the author of *Enclosures and the Yeomen, The Agricultural Development of the South Midlands 1450–1850*, Oxford: Clarendon Press, 1992. His latest book is *From Farm to Factory. A Reinterpretation of the Soviet Industrial Revolution*, Princeton University Press, 2003.

DANIEL A. BAUGH is Professor Emeritus of Modern British History, Cornell University. His principal works are *British Naval Administration in the Age of Walpole*, Princeton University Press, 1965, and *Naval Administration, 1715–1750*, London: Navy Records Society, 1977. He has also written on governmental, social and economic aspects of England, 1660–1830, especially on poor relief. His published essays of the past two decades mainly concern eighteenth-century British maritime and defence policy.

RICHARD J. BONNEY is Professor of History at Leicester University. He is author of *The Limits of Absolutism in Ancien Régime France*, Aldershot: Edward Elgar, 1995, and the editor of *The Rise of the Fiscal State in Europe, c.1200–1815*, Oxford University Press, 1999.

FORREST CAPIE is Professor of Economic History at the Cass Business School, City University, London. He was co-editor of the *Economic History Review* (1993–1999). He has written widely on money, banking and trade and commercial policy. Recent publications include: *Policy-makers on Policy*, London: Routledge, 2001 (co-edited with G. E. Wood) and *Capital Controls*, IEA, 2002. He is currently working on financial stability and regulation.

NICK CRAFTS has been Professor of Economic History at the London School of Economics since 1995. He is the author of *British Economic Growth during the Industrial Revolution*, Oxford: Clarendon Press, 1985. He is currently co-editor of the *Economic History Review*.

JAVIER CUENCA ESTEBAN is Professor of Economics at the University of Waterloo, Ontario. For three decades he has worked on the quantitative aspects of international trade during the late eighteenth and early nineteenth centuries. Published case studies include Spain, France, the United States and Britain. He is currently finishing a detailed account of net India transfers to Britain in 1757–1812.

STANLEY L. ENGERMAN is the John H. Munro Professor of Economics and Professor of History at the University of Rochester. He is co-author (with Robert W. Fogel) of *Time on the Cross*, Boston: Little and Brown, 1974 co-editor (with Robert E. Gallman) of the *Cambridge Economic History of the United States*, Cambridge University Press, 1996–2000 and co-author (with Lance E. Davis) of the forthcoming *Blockades in Peace and War*.

RAINER FREMDLING is Professor of Economic and Social History at Groningen University. He is the author of *Eisenbahnen und deutsches Wirtschaftswachstum1840–1879*, Dortmund: Gesellschaft für Westfälische Wirtschaftsgeschichte, 1975, 2nd edn 1985, and *Technologischer Wandel und Internationaler Handel im 18. und 19. Jahrhundert: Die Eisenindustrien in Großbritannien, Belgien, Frankreich und Deutschland*, Berlin: Duncker & Humblot, 1986.

KNICK HARLEY is Professor of Economics at the University of Western Ontario, Canada. In April 2004, he will become a Fellow of St Antony's College and University Lecturer in Economic History at the University of Oxford. He has worked extensively on the Industrial Revolution and on nineteenth-century globalisation. He is currently co-editor of the *Journal of Economic History*.

CHRISTINE MACLEOD is Senior Lecturer in Economic and Social History, University of Bristol. She is the author of *Inventing the Industrial Revolution: the English Patent System, 1660–1800*, Cambridge University Press, 1988, and is completing a book on the cultural history of invention and its influence on the historiography of the Industrial Revolution, *Heroes of Invention: Constructing Reputations in Nineteenth-Century Britain*.

LARRY NEAL is a Professor of Economics at the University of Illinois at Urbana-Champaign and a Research Associate of the National Bureau of Economic Research. He served as President of the Economic History Association and of the Business History Conference. He is the author of *The Rise of Financial Capitalism: International Capital in the Age of Reason*, Cambridge University Press, 1990.

LEANDRO PRADOS DE LA ESCOSURA has been Professor of Economic History at Universidad Carlos III, Madrid, since 1990. He served as President of the *European Historical Economics Society*. He edited (with Patrick O'Brien) *The Costs and Benefits of European Imperialism*, *Revista de Historia Económica* XVI, 1, 1998. His latest book is *El progreso económico de España, 1850–2000*, Madrid: Fundación BBVA, 2003.

JAMES SIMPSON is Professor of Economic History at the Universidad Pablo de Olavide, Sevilla. His publications on Spanish agriculture include *Spanish Agriculture: The Long Siesta, 1765–1965*, Cambridge University Press, 1995, and (with Juan Carmona) *El laberinto de la agricultura española. Instituciones, contratos y organización entre 1850 y 1936*, Zaragoza: PUZ, 2003. He currently is working on the wine market in nineteenth-century Europe.

JAMES THOMSON is Reader in History at the University of Sussex. Specialising in Mediterranean history, he has published *Clermont-de-Lodève, 1633–1789. Fluctuations in the Prosperity of a Languedocian Cloth-Making Town*, Cambridge University Press, 1982, *A Distinctive Industrialization: Cotton in Barcelona, 1728–1832*, Cambridge University Press, 1992, Catalan edn 1994 (Catalan Economics prize, 1992), and *Decline in History, The European Experience*, Cambridge Polity, 1998; Portuguese edn 2001.

GIANNI TONIOLO is Professor of Economic History at the University of Rome 'Tor Vergata', Research Professor of Economics at Duke University, and Research Fellow at CEPR. His books include: *An Economic History of Liberal Italy*, London, Routledge, 1990, *Economic Growth in Europe since 1945*, Cambridge University Press, 1996 (edited with N. Crafts), *The European Economy Between the Wars*, Oxford University Press, 1997 (with C. Feinstein and P. Temin).

Acknowledgements

This volume originated in a conference held on 26–7 March, 2001 in Madrid, on *Britain and Its Rivals: The Struggle for Hegemony: 1688–1815*, to honour the fecund academic career both as a teacher and a researcher of Professor Patrick Karl O'Brien, currently Centennial Professor of Economic History at the London School of Economics. The wide intellectual interests of Patrick O'Brien and his distinguished position in British and continental European economic history made the choice of topic and the selection of contributors difficult. Finally, we decided to focus on recurrent questions, such as: When was Britain's superiority within Europe acquired? and: What differentiated Britain from its rivals and led on to the First Industrial Revolution? A group of his friends and specialist colleagues accepted the challenge to contribute not to the usual *festschrift* but to a '*textschrift*', which would make the ongoing debates accessible to a larger audience of university students and non-specialist readers.

The Conference was sponsored by Fundación BBVA and took place in the most pleasant environment of the early twentieth-century small palace that was, at the time, the headquarters of the Fundación. The editor and the contributors to the volume are most grateful to its Adjunct Director General, José Ángel Moreno Izquierdo, who did everything to make the conference a successful event. We are also obliged to François Crouzet, Juan Pablo Fusi, Antonio Gómez Mendoza, Regina Grafe, Stefan Houpt, Alan S. Milward, Pablo Martín Aceña, Jordi Palafox and Blanca Sánchez Alonso, who attended the conference and made most valuable contributions as discussants and chairs. Antonio Gómez Mendoza provided an affectionate account of his memories as Patrick's student at Oxford.

Finally, we owe a special debt to Richard Fisher, the then history editor at Cambridge University Press, for his enthusiastic response to the project and his constant encouragement, and to his successor, Michael Watson, who has helped us in the final stage of the book and has shown much patience with this volume's editor.

Introduction: Was British industrialisation exceptional?

Leandro Prados de la Escosura

Between 1688 and 1815 Great Britain entered into sustained competition with its European rivals while simultaneously initiating an irreversible process of economic modernisation known as the Industrial Revolution. At the time of the Treaty of Vienna, Britain had achieved a hegemonic position in terms of naval power, international commerce, agricultural efficiency, industrial production, fiscal capacity and advanced technology. In 1820 the British enjoyed the highest per capita income in Europe (one-third higher than the French and one-fifth more than the Dutch) and its primacy persisted down to 1914 (Prados de la Escosura, 2000).

For more than a century the British Industrial Revolution has been perceived, in Max Hartwell's (1971) words, as one of the great discontinuities in history. It exhibited fast growth rates for aggregate economic activity that stemmed from increasing rates of capital formation, but above all from technological innovation (Feinstein, 1978). As depicted by David Landes (1969), British industrialisation was the paradigm for modern economic growth, so the diffusion of its best practice techniques of production and institutions became the yardstick for the assessment of the success or failure of subsequent national development.

The last two decades have witnessed a systematic challenge to the British paradigm. Nowadays, the idea of industrialised Britain's superiority above other regions of Europe based on more efficient institutions, cultural values and economic performance is seriously questioned. The publication a quarter of a century ago of Patrick O'Brien and Caglar Keyder's book *Economic Growth in Britain and France, 1780–1914: Two Paths to the Twentieth Century* represented the departure from a long-standing tradition that goes back to nineteenth-century economics, and to post-World War II development economists and economic historians (Rostow, 1960; Landes, 1969; Hartwell, 1971, among others). Simply being first to experience modern economic growth, asserts O'Brien, does not necessarily imply the achievement of the 'best practice', and no optimal path for growth can be identified in Britain's pioneering path and pattern of industrialisation.

More recent research on European development has pointed to the fact that Britain did not fit the modes of accumulation and resource allocation that prevailed in continental Europe (Crafts, 1985). Nicholas Crafts and Knick Harley (1992) point out that Britain was a country growing at a slow pace in per capita terms while experiencing a deep structural transformation and localised technological innovation. This precocious structural change paralleled by an acceleration in both output and population growth allowed Britain to maintain average income per head while feeding a much larger number of people. The stylised facts presented by Crafts (1985: 62–3) depict Britain's industrialisation as virtually unique among historical cases of economic development in terms of low dependence on agriculture (both as an employer of resources and a contributor to output), high urbanisation, openness and low investment in both human and physical capital. Private consumption in industrialising Britain defies the suggestion, so often expressed in the literature on economic development, of a generational sacrifice as the price to be paid for economic progress. Public consumption in eighteenth-century Britain was, in turn, below that of nineteenth-century Europe except at time of war.

Specific facets of British industrialisation that make it unique and exceptional include:

- slow pace of growth accompanied by deep but prolonged industrial transformation,
- distinctive technological change that allowed society to escape from the Malthusian trap,
- favourable natural endowments including coal, mineral ores and fecund soils,
- high exposure to foreign goods and ideas,
- low investment demand derived from limited opportunities to invest,
- weak dependence on agriculture,
- high rural–urban migration,
- high defence expenditure as a precondition for economic success in overseas trade and commerce,
- uniquely permissive institutions for growth.

All these features taken together portray Britain's Industrial Revolution as a singular case study of economic development and question the relevance of a diffusion model for the spread of British industrialisation across Eurasia.

Nevertheless, the now persuasive contention that British industrialisation was an unique phenomenon does not imply that each of its features was unmatched by present-day developing countries or by the nineteenth-century economies of continental Europe. For example, the accepted view of eighteenth-century Britain as a developing country where savings systematically exceeded investment so that the country became, consequently, a net foreign investor at levels of income at which most nations are still net debtors, has been put to an empirical test by Elise Brezis (1995). She rejected this view. Her data suggest that, as would be expected of a developing economy, industrialising Britain had an investment demand larger than its domestic supply of savings and foreign capital played a part in British industrialisation. Her view has, however, been disputed by Norris Nash (1997) and Javier Cuenca Esteban (2001). The latter reinstated the view that, after 1776, Britain became a net creditor.

A second, and more important, issue is the role of technological change in the advance of the British economy. Computations of total factor productivity (TFP) growth, as the residual obtained by subtracting growth contributed by land, labour and capital (in which each factor's growth rate is weighted by its share in national income) from the aggregate rate of economic growth, are taken as a measure of efficiency or (disembodied) technological change. The results from these exercises suggest that TFP provided not more than one-fifth of British economic growth during the First Industrial Revolution (Crafts and Harley, 1992; Antrás and Voth, 2003), a proportion that increases slightly with the new growth accounting approach that takes embodied technological change into account (Crafts, 2003). Factor accumulation prevailed over efficiency gains. Such a statement is at odds with McCloskey's (1981) dictum that 'ingenuity rather than abstention' was the dominant element in British industrialisation. This unique feature of the British Industrial Revolution stems from comparisons with twentieth-century experience (Crafts, 1998). A closer examination of the evidence assembled in Crafts (2000) reveals that, although the finding of slow TFP growth is confirmed when the comparison is carried out with western European economies during the Golden Age (1950–73), this is not the case when Britain is compared with the economies of the United States in the nineteenth century, or with East and South Asian countries in the 1960–90s period, or with China during the last decade. In all these historical experiences TFP contributed less than a quarter to the overall rate of growth. The implications are a) that slow (fast) TFP growth cannot be equated to low (high) TFP contribution to output growth, and b) that the suggestion of a unique TFP behaviour during the British Industrial Revolution should be reconsidered. Meanwhile, the position that growth appears to derive largely from increased factor inputs rather than from improvements in their efficiency during the first stages of industrialisation can be maintained. Once industrialisation is well under way (and when, perhaps, growth rates are no longer at peak levels), TFP plays a more significant role. Why would this pattern appear? Is it because improving efficiency implies a more complex learning process than allocating additional capital and labour to production, or is it just the result of a composition effect due to the fact that, in the early stages of industrialisation, traditional economic sectors exhibiting lower TFP growth are predominant and, hence, condition aggregate factor productivity performance? Crafts (2003) points out that steam, like other major technologies, had a mild impact in its early years, as it took time to realise its potential. Crafts also argues that small market size, low R and D investment and extended rent-seeking activities all help to explain the reduced role of TFP in British growth during the Industrial Revolution (Crafts, 1996).

All in all, the gradualist approach to the Industrial Revolution cannot evade the fact that Britain moved ahead of continental Europe and even those regions that had already found, in Gerschenkron's words, substitutes for the prerequisites of modern industrialisation. By 1851 Britain was recognised as the 'workshop of the world' and the achievements of industrial Britain as compared to the rest of Europe by the mid-nineteenth century were reflected in:

- higher income per capita (coupled with a widening inequality over previous decades), with levels often above those that obtain in developing countries at the present time,
- higher standards of welfare, as measured by life expectancy or literacy, than most of Western Europe,
- greater civil and political liberties,
- confined rent-seeking activities,
- an urbanised society,
- more rapid diffusion of technical knowledge,
- better integrated commodity and factor markets,
- higher shares of world trade in manufactured goods and services.

An attempt to rehabilitate the Industrial Revolution emerges from the recent work by Berg and Hudson (1992) and Cuenca Esteban (1994, 1997), among others, and finds support in the contributions of global historians, such as Kenneth Pomeranz (2000), who argues that the discontinuities in growth associated with the Industrial Revolution were more pronounced and that technological and organisational changes were more pervasive and significant than revisionists are ready to accept. Natural endowments (including accessible deposits of coal at home and extensive land overseas) plus defence expenditure (which led to the acquisition of naval and military power) are, for global historians, crucial elements behind British success.

When was Britain's superiority within Europe acquired? What differentiated Britain from its rivals and led on to the First Industrial Revolution?

Were endogenously created institutions behind British growth and technical progress what eventually promoted overseas expansion? These are some of the questions explored in this volume, which includes twelve essays in comparative history that will elaborate upon the unique path to modernisation followed by Britain.

The first part of the book, comprising parts I to III, looks at the immediate determinants of British success. Part I investigates the origins of British primacy, which can traced back into the early modern period, when Britain appeared as a relative latecomer that experienced intensive and pervasive Smithian growth before the rest of Europe. The welfare of London workers, for example, was already above those of other capital cities, including Paris and Amsterdam, by 1600 and the gap widened over time (Allen, 2001). In chapter 1, 'Britain's economic ascendancy in a European context', Robert Allen concludes that the exceptional British wages and per capita income levels maintained despite exceptionally rapid population growth emanated from high levels of urbanisation and agricultural productivity. Allen underlines suggestions made by O'Brien that the basic impetus to change in agriculture came from the extension of proto-industrial and urban economies, rather than a peculiar set of 'capitalist' institutions. In his view, the keys to Britain's early success were the artisans and merchants who made the new draperies – a crucial sector in the 'industrious revolution' – yeomen farmers who actively responded to shifts in demand by increasing yields and Britain's effective mercantilist state, which defeated rival powers and seized a world empire to the benefit of its trade and industry.

The role of trade in the rise of Britain to a hegemonic position in the early nineteenth century has been extensively discussed by economic historians, who have opposed a *Smithian* vent-for-surplus interpretation (that is: trade providing employment opportunities for otherwise idle resources) (O'Brien and Engerman, 1991) to *Ricardian* comparative advantage (improving resource allocation through trade) (Thomas and McCloskey, 1981; Harley, 1994) as explanations for the British experience. The question of whether colonies overseas made a substantial, if qualitative, contribution to the emergence of disparities between Britain and other European powers (the Netherlands, France and Spain) is central to an explanation for Britain's unique performance during the 'long' eighteenth century and has been recently addressed by Acemoglu, Johnson and Robinson (2002). They suggest that expansion overseas promoted (*pace* Braudel) political leverage among commercial groups with interests in the colonial trade and thereby contributed to pro-business institutional changes in maritime and parliamentary countries such as Britain and the Low Countries.

The distinctive and permanent role played by Britain's transcontinental and imperial trade in promoting economic growth as compared to domestic forces is stressed by Javier Cuenca Esteban in chapter 2, 'Comparative patterns of colonial trade: Britain and its rivals'. He finds that a substantial share of British export growth was exogenous to the home economy, in the sense that exports were sold to Britain's more prosperous trade partners with independent sources of wealth, and increased at the margins of her pre-existing networks of commodity flows and payments. In particular, Cuenca Esteban argues for the significance of 'windfall' British exports to the Iberian empires that significantly added to autonomous expenditure by the United States on British manufactures, particularly during times of war.

Part II addresses the connections between agriculture and industrialisation. A large labour productivity differential between Britain (and the Low Countries) on the one hand and Western European economies on the other, has been traced back to the seventeenth century and persisted up World War I (Allen, 2000; O'Brien and Prados de la Escosura, 1992). By 1600 Britain was at a similar level of output per worker as France (and Spain), but by 1700 it was one and a half times higher than French labour productivity and by 1750 almost twice the French level (Allen, 2000). Why such a gap appeared is discussed in chapter 3, 'European farmers and the British "agricultural revolution"', by James Simpson, who argues that differences in the rate of capital formation provide a powerful reason for Britain's superior performance, and greater incentives existed for investment in British agriculture between 1650 and 1750. Large, capital-intensive farms in England (and also northern France) were more efficient in utilising factor inputs than either the small family farms in north-western Europe or the large estates of Mediterranean regions. In addition, more intense rural–urban migration and relatively lower physical and institutional barriers to trade led to a greater commodity and factor market integration and, consequently, to larger efficiency gains in Britain.

In chapter 4, 'Precocious British industrialisation: a general-equilibrium perspective', Nicholas Crafts and Knick Harley examine the structural transformation over 1770–1840 in response to changes in factor endowments and productivity in the context of an open economy. With the help of a computable general equilibrium model, they analyse the implications of a shift from traditional, small-scale family farming, prevailing in continental Europe, to capitalist farming. Their model and data indicate that such a move enabled Britain to raise labour productivity, to release labour and, at the same time, to promote industrialisation. Crafts and Harley conclude that agriculture's conversion to capitalist farming was a key feature of the national economy's exceptional employment structure.

The extent to which capitalist farming explains British unique allocation of resources can also be assessed with the help of Chenery and Syrquin's (1975) exposition of patterns of development. Britain deviated from the 'European norm' (that is, the predicted behaviour of the average European economy at similar per capita income and population levels), as it allocated less labour and derived a lower share of output from agriculture while the opposite happened in industry and services (Crafts, 1985). Crafts and Harley's new simulations provide the counterfactual shares of employment and output for agriculture and industry that could flow from the absence of capitalist farming, and they also allow for its impact on the openness of the British economy. When their counterfactual estimates (table 4.6) are placed beside those predicted by the 'European norm' for the levels of income per head achieved by the British economy (Crafts, 1985: 62–3), the degree of coincidence is striking. The implication of this rigorous exercise in cliometrics is that the early move to capitalist farming appears to be the prime explanation for Britain's exceptional resource allocation.

Another and surprising result derived from the model is the hypothetical increase by almost one-fifth in the capital stock (and by 8 per cent in per capita income) that could counterfactually have occurred in the event of an even higher level of protection for domestic agriculture that would have resulted in the contraction of agricultural imports in 1841 to the level of 1770 (see column 3 of table 4.2). The notion that an increase in the relative size of the agricultural sector could provide extra incentives for capital accumulation appears counter-intuitive and seems to be in contradiction with the process of industrialisation associated with the introduction of capitalist farming. The explanation for the paradox offered by Crafts and Harley is that the decline in the share of wages in national income that would accompany an expansion of agriculture under protection would have been paralleled by an increase in the share of income accruing to property. Given that savings rates by workers were negligible, the outcome could be overall higher savings and investment rates. An increase in landowners' wealth would indeed be a feature of a more rural economy. However, higher wealth cannot necessarily be identified with an increased capital stock, as the latter only includes reproducible assets and excludes unimproved land (and even less with an increase in the productive capital, that is, when dwellings are excluded). Nonetheless, if the results from Crafts and Harley's counterfactual were accepted as they stand, investment rates would increase and narrow the British deviation from the 'European norm'.

Part III examines Britain's exceptional inventiveness and innovation and its determinants, in particular, the two macro-technologies that together first revolutionised industrial production: the network of coal, iron and steam power and the mechanisation of cotton textiles. In chapter 5 Christine MacLeod addresses 'The European origins of British technological predominance' and the paradox of why it was that Britain, a peripheral nation in terms of European technical progress, took the technological lead. She suggests that the paradox cannot be solved by looking at Britain in isolation, for its Industrial Revolution drew on techniques accumulated across Europe (Mokyr, 2002). Population density reduced (*pace* Boserup) transaction costs, facilitating the exchange of ideas and promoting competition. In that context, the returns to innovation were growing and inventions were attracted from Europe and, as an outcome, new products and ideas were successfully adapted and improved.

In the case of the cotton industry, mechanisation occurred as an outcome of European technological developments which came on stream at a time when only the British had a modern cotton industry. Patrick O'Brien's analysis of innovation in that industry is deepened by James Thomson's 'Invention in the Industrial Revolution: the case of cotton' (chapter 6). He argues that the improvement in technical abilities of Lancashire's cotton workers, the larger supply of different sorts of raw cotton and a better understanding of their qualities for different uses, in conjunction with the great increase in the demand for labour, played a major role in the explanation of the sequence of 'macro-inventions' in cotton textiles.

Although the British government offered patents for invention, they were expensive and hard to enforce, and the state's main contributions to inventive activity can be located in the combination of tariffs and prohibitions on imported cotton goods from India and in the expansion and effectiveness of the Royal Navy, which safeguarded commerce overseas. Thus, the emergence of large-scale textile production in the metropolis can be closely associated with Asian trade conducted by the East India Company and public expenditure in sea power.

In Britain a long-standing scarcity of wood coexisted with rich and accessible coal deposits and other ores (especially iron). MacLeod argues that coal abundance was fortuitous and Pomeranz (2000) has pointed to coal as a felicitous ingredient of British supremacy. Historical evidence suggests, however, that coal should be represented as an endogenous rather than an exogenous phenomenon. Other regions of the world (including India, China and Eastern Europe) also possessed regular coal deposits. Only the British exploited the new source of energy intensively and systematically. Like mineral resources in the United States in the nineteenth century (David and Wright, 1997), the exploitation of natural endowments on a large scale was an endogenous phenomenon that resulted from Britain's own economic progress.

Nevertheless, coal had both land- and labour-saving effects in substituting for wood and agricultural land (Wrigley, 1988). Moreover, overcoming the constraints of an organic economy was a prerequisite for the occurrence of the First Industrial Revolution (Wrigley, 1994: 28). Overseas expansion provided Britain with additional primary produce and the economy's ability to import resource-intensive goods helped to relax the natural resource constraint that restrained the development of Asian regions; this is a distinctive feature of British industrialisation.

The relative shortage of wood and building timber and the abundance of coal triggered an early transition to coal-burning technologies, while iron replaced timber in construction. Britain was actually the first country to substitute coal for the scarce resource of charcoal for smelting, refining and processing metals on a large scale. This early eighteenth-century British breakthrough in metallurgical technology was closely observed in continental Europe but the transfer to hard-coal technology in smelting, refining and processing iron did not take hold in iron-producing regions of continental Europe before the nineteenth century. Why were they unable to adopt British technology? Why did technological differences persist up to the mid-nineteenth century? These are questions that David Landes raised in his classic work *The Unbound Prometheus* (1969). In chapter 7, 'Continental responses to British innovations in the iron industry during the eighteenth and early nineteenth centuries', Rainer Fremdling provides an answer by analysing the evolutionary transition from techniques using vegetable fuel to those using mineral fuel, a process which transformed the British iron industry from a small and costly sector at the end of the seventeenth century into a large and efficient industry and the world's largest exporter by the end of the Napoleonic Wars. These results confirm Wrigley's view (1988) that growth was carried forward by the early changeover to a fossil fuel energy base.

The second part of the book deals with institutional and geopolitical determinants of Britain's exceptional industrialisation and concentrates on the roles played by financial and monetary institutions (part IV) and by the Royal Navy (part V) in facilitating modern economic growth.

For more than a century after the Peace of Westphalia Europe's modern nation states experimented with financial and monetary regimes to fund their engagements in warfare and colonisation overseas. Larry Neal notes in chapter 8, 'The monetary, financial, and political architecture of Europe, 1648–1815', that institutional innovations that relied on private financial markets (e.g., British and Dutch institutions) proved their superiority and governments refrained from interfering in capital markets, a difficult restraint, especially in times of war.

How did the British government manage to raise the stock of national debt with each successive war and, then, to raise sufficient taxes to service the public debt? Part of the answer is, according to Neal, provided by the increasing value of public debt as an insurance against the risks incurred in other markets. Widening opportunities for risk sharing contributed to British success.

The steady rise of central government taxation in Britain throughout the eighteenth century, already one of the highest-taxed economies in Europe, stands in sharp contrast with the historical experience of, for example, France, where the proportion of commodity output extracted in taxation remained unaltered and the tax revenue per head failed to increase significantly in real terms throughout the 'long' eighteenth century (Mathias and O'Brien, 1976; White, 2001). France never mobilised sufficient financial resources to defeat Britain at any time during the second Hundred Years War. Special interest groups constrained the ability to finance war by obstructing reforms to improve fiscal efficiency in Bourbon France and Spain. In Britain, conversely, privileges and fiscal exemptions and regional local tax quotas were removed and a universal taxation was the norm. In chapter 9, 'Towards the comparative fiscal history of Britain and France during the "long" eighteenth century', Richard Bonney argues that public opinion remained sceptical or hostile to Bourbon financial and fiscal policy and distrustful of government contracts. Furthermore, the efficiency of the fiscal system was discernibly lower in France than in Britain, and the French domestic credit market was less sophisticated and enjoyed much less government support. Such striking contrasts lend credence to the view that only governments backed by strong representative institutions were able to extract revenues and to borrow in substantial amounts of money for warfare (Hoffman and Norberg, 1994). A conclusion that is confirmed by Forrest Capie in Chapter 10, 'Money and Economic Development in Eighteenth-Century England'. His analysis reveals that a well established monetary economy and a sophisticated financial system along with trust and the rule of law were already in place before the industrialisation accelerated in the late eighteenth century.

Nonetheless the unsolved question remains, How were the tax increases approved by a parliament dominated by landowners? Mathias and O'Brien (1976) suggest that the state relied increasingly upon indirect taxes. O'Brien (1988) observes that excises (that is, indirect taxes on domestic consumption goods) were levied on price-inelastic and income-elastic goods, and paid mostly by the 'middling' social groups, while the upper classes, well represented in parliament, diversified their portfolios into public debt. Excise taxes and a regressive fiscal tool, were required to service that long-term debt, without which the British government could not have raised funds for the finance of the wars (Brewer, 1989; O'Brien, 2001). Capie adds that the tax collection was facilitated by the extensive circulation of cash and credit in Britain, in contrast to France's persistent shortage of money.

In other words, efficient macroeconomic policy allowed the British government to raise revenues while minimising inter-temporal distortions to the growth of the economy (White, 2001). Its fiscal and financial strategies reinforced each other over the eighteenth century. Increased expenditure in times of war was financed by growing debt, rather than inflation, funded by future taxes. The public debt enabled the financial sector to withstand the demands of war finance over the eighteenth century more effectively than any other country in continental Europe (including Holland) (Neal, chapter 8 of this volume). The transparency of its budget and debt policies was crucial for the government's reputation and credibility and was the precondition for a successful fiscal military state.

The long-term economic effects of higher taxes and an ever-increasing national debt are now perceived to be positively associated with Britain's extension of its empire and commerce overseas. The ratio of national debt to gross domestic product rose with each successive war while the economy continued to expand (O'Brien, 1988). But how much larger might private investment have been without these budget deficits? Growing defence expenditures in Britain led to higher taxes and promoted protectionism over the eighteenth century (Crafts, 1996). Williamson (1984, 1985), and more recently Crafts (1996), have associated government borrowing with the crowding out of private investment during the Revolutionary and Napoleonic Wars, 1793–1815. Contrary to this thesis, O'Brien (1989) and Harley (1992) point that the substantial increase in the ratio of stock of national debt to domestic product did not have a negative impact on the investment/GDP ratio. It seems that public deficit, or negative government saving, in wartime was offset by a rise in private saving and by foreign capital inflows so domestic capital formation was little affected (Brezis, 1995; Neal, 1990). The debate is unresolved but the counterfactual of the British state and economy delinked from mercantilist and imperial warfare over 1689–1815 is perhaps too unreal to contemplate.

Were the benefits of the British 'blue water' policy, then, worth the costs? In chapter 11, 'Naval power: what gave the British navy superiority?', Daniel Baugh contends that the particularity of the British navy during the eighteenth century was to remain in large part and constantly at sea to defend the realm and guarantee the stability of overseas trade. This strategy provided British commerce with significant advantages over France, whose trade suffered far more from wartime disruptions. An Atlantic commercial system and British competitiveness was safeguarded by the Royal Navy. There is a growing (if unquantified) consensus among historians that suggests that the economic benefits accruing from the heavy expenditure in naval power leading to the final defeat of France outweighed losses from crowding out and high taxation.

From the contributions to the present volume a view emerges that depicts Britain over the 'long' eighteenth century as a fiscal military state that succeeded in developing stable fiscal, financial and monetary institutions. This view associates the mercantilist state's contribution with British industrialisation, at least as regards the provision of public goods (particularly, the navy) and its promotion of efficient institutions. As Stanley Engerman states in his concluding assessment, 'Institutional change and British supremacy, 1650–1850: some reflections', free private initiative backed by a strong government that enforced property rights and resorted to naval and military power to protect foreign trade and shipping led to the British victory in the mercantilist struggle for world-economy and geopolitical hegemony.

The exceptional nature of Britain in the context of European industrialisation is a conclusion shared by all the chapters in this book. Such a departure from what until recently was the paradigm of modern economic growth owes a great deal to distinguished and pioneering contributions by Patrick O'Brien. As a modest homage this book is dedicated to him.

Part I

The origins of British primacy

1 Britain's economic ascendancy in a European context

Robert C. Allen

In 1815, Britain was the leading economy of Europe. The Industrial Revolution was two generations old, the breakthrough technologies in cotton, iron and steam were blossoming into large industries, more and more production was mechanised, urbanisation was far advanced, the railway was in sight. Britain's economic ascendancy was at hand.

It had not always been so. In 1500, Britain was a peripheral economy far from the economic core of Europe, which was still the Mediterranean. Most of the British population lived in the countryside, and most depended on agriculture. Productivity and incomes were low. Much of the rest of Europe was similarly backward. In the sixteenth and seventeenth centuries, the Dutch Republic pulled ahead and became the economic wonder of the age. British advance was slower but steady. By the seventeenth century, British incomes pushed past those of its chief continental rivals – France and the Habsburg Empire. By the eighteenth century, Britain extended its lead and overtook the Dutch. The Industrial Revolution was the capstone to this advance.

This book documents Britain's ascent in its many dimensions and examines the causal factors at work. These were both economic and political. Britain's economic progress cannot be separated from the establishment of her military hegemony. We begin by charting the dimensions of Britain's emergence as the leading economy.

Economic structure

Economic backwardness and advance show up dramatically in economic structure. Table 1.1 divides the population of the leading economies of Europe into three groups: agricultural, urban and rural non-agricultural. Countries are defined in terms of modern boundaries.

In 1500, most Europeans lived in backward economies. This is indicated, in the first instance, by the fraction of the population engaged in agriculture. About three-quarters of the population was agricultural in England, Austria-Hungary, Germany, France and Poland. This

Table 1.1 *Distribution of the population by sector, 1500–1800*

	1500			1800		
	urban	rural non-agriculture	agriculture	urban	rural non-agriculture	agriculture
most successful over the period						
England	.07	.18	.74	.29	.36	.35
moderately successful over the period						
Netherlands	.30	.14	.56	.34	.25	.41
Belgium	.28	.14	.58	.22	.29	.49
small advance over the period						
Germany	.08	.18	.73	.09	.29	.62
France	.09	.18	.73	.13	.28	.59
Austria/ Hungary	.05	.19	.76	.08	.35	.57
Poland	.06	.19	.75	.05	.39	.56
little change over the period						
Italy	.22	.16	.62	.22	.20	.58
Spain	.19	.16	.65	.20	.16	.64

Source: Allen, 2000: 8–9.

proportion was also characteristic of the less-developed countries of Asia, Africa, Latin America and eastern Europe early in the twentieth century (Kuznets, 1971: 203, 249–55). In terms of economic structure, western Europe was at a similar – low – level of development at the end of the Middle Ages.

The consequence of having a large fraction of the population in agriculture was small cities, which included less than 10 per cent of the population. In 1500, for instance, only 50,000 people lived in London; other English cities were much smaller and little more than market towns. Non-agricultural employment in the countryside was also limited, especially in comparison to later developments.

The leading economies of Europe in 1500 were Italy, Spain and present-day Belgium. The Dutch economy also showed advanced proportions, but its population was so small that its figures are more a portent of the future than an indicator of economic importance at the time. The urban fraction ranged from 19 to 30 per cent in these economies, and those cities housed the great manufacturing industries of the Middle Ages. The agricultural fraction was correspondingly reduced to about 60 per cent.

The economies of Europe followed a variety of trajectories between 1500 and 1800, and the countries in table 1.1 are grouped to emphasise these divergences. England was the most successful country by far. The fraction of its population in agriculture dropped to 35 per cent – this was the biggest decline and the lowest value reached in Europe. The drop in the agricultural share was matched by rises in both the urban and the rural non-agricultural proportions.

The growth in 'rural non-agricultural' employment corresponds to the 'proto-industrial' revolution. This was a phenomenon of the early modern period. In many parts of Europe, manufacturing industries developed in the countryside. Production was carried out either in workshops or in people's homes. Merchants signed up rural residents as piece-rate workers, brought them raw materials and collected the finished products. These were often sold in large market halls to other merchants, who shipped them across Europe. Regions were intensely specialised. Woollen cloth industries developed around Norwich and in the West Riding of Yorkshire; metal buttons, fittings and implements were made in Birmingham; stockings were knit in Leicestershire; blankets were woven near Oxford and shipped to Canada by the Hudson Bay Company. Rural industries were found in many parts of Europe, but they were particularly dense in England.

The Low Countries were the second most successful economies in the early modern period. Less than half of their populations were engaged in agriculture, and the urban and rural non-agricultural shares were also very high. Flanders in present-day Belgium had been highly urbanised and a leading manufacturing centre in the Middle Ages. Its economy failed to grow as rapidly as the leaders in the early modern period, but it still retained a more modern structure and higher incomes in 1800 than most of the continent. The Netherlands were lightly settled in the Middle Ages but developed a highly urbanised and successful economy in the seventeenth century. Indeed, it was so successful that the main question in economic policy was how to emulate the Dutch. Trade was critical to the progress of the Netherlands. Amsterdam was the great wholesale market in Europe, but manufacturing and rural industry were also formidable.

The third group was the rest of the continent of Europe north of the Alps and Pyrenees. France and Austria were major military powers, Poland was united in 1500 but dismembered in the next three centuries, and Germany remained divided into many states throughout the period. Prussia, however, was an actor on the international stage.

These countries showed modest development in the early modern period. Their agricultural shares dropped to about 60 per cent – rather like Italy and Spain in 1500. This decline was matched by a rise in the share of people in proto-industry. These countries developed important rural manufacturing industries that rivalled those of the leading economies in terms of the fractions of the population employed. Their urban shares, however, scarcely increased, and that sets them apart from England and the Low Countries.

Italy and Spain comprise the final group. What is remarkable about these economies is the absence of structural change between 1500 and 1800. They had larger urban shares and smaller agricultural shares than most of the continent at the end of the Middle Ages, and these shares hardly budged. A corollary is the absence of growth in rural manufacturing. The proto-industrial revolution did not extend south of the Alps or the Pyrenees.

Wages and prices

The changes in economic structure correlate with changes in the income of the working majority of the population. Price histories are an indispensable source of data. In these works, the historian finds an institution like a college or hospital with accounting records extending over hundreds of years. The price and quantity of all the goods bought and sold are used to compute the price paid or received for each item every year. These data can often be supplemented with the records of prices in organised markets and the regulated prices of basic commodities like bread. Thorold-Roger's *A History of Agriculture and Prices in England* (1866–92) and Hanauer's *Etudes économiques sur l'Alsace ancienne et moderne* (1878) were the first comprehensive price histories. Since then, many other cities have been studied. Much work was done in the 1930s under the auspices of the International Price History Commission, and more histories have been written since.

The price histories also record wages. Every institution hired building craftsmen and labourers. The local currencies in which their wages are recorded must all be converted to an international standard for cross-country comparisons. Since silver coins were the common medium of exchange, converting all units of account to grams of silver is a common approach. Figure 1.1 shows the wage of daily building labourers in London, Antwerp, northern Italy, Valencia, Krakow and Vienna expressed in this way.

England's exceptional performance stands out in the graph. Silver wages were fairly similar across Europe late in the fifteenth century. During the Price Revolution (1550–1620), wages rose in western and southern Europe, but remained at a low level in the east (as in Krakow and Vienna in figure 1.1). Early in the seventeenth century, there was a three-way split in western European wages. Italian and Spanish silver wages slowly declined, wages in Amsterdam and Antwerp continued

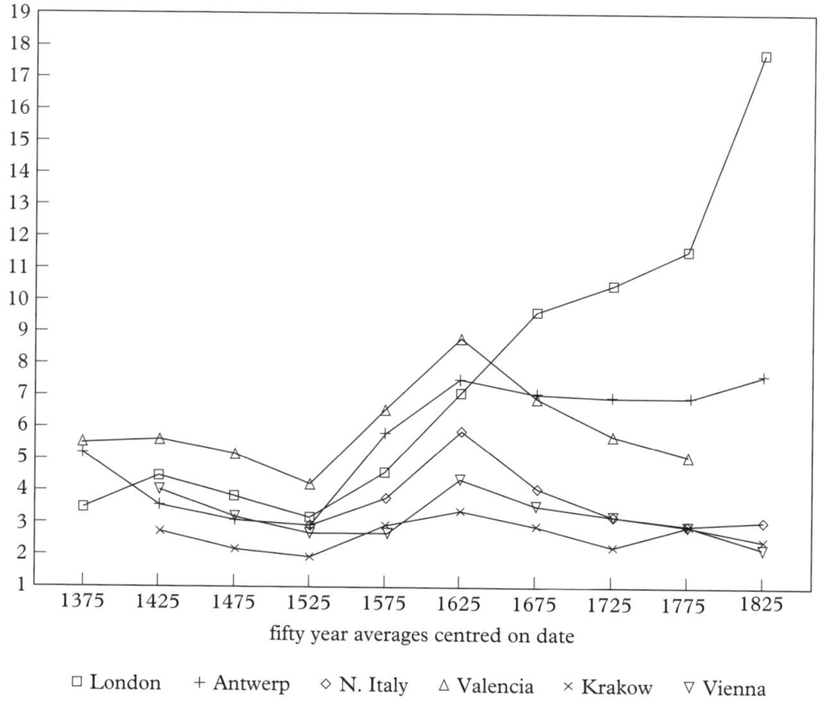

Figure 1.1 Labourers' nominal wages, 1375–1825 (grams of silver wages per day)

unchanged, and English wages inflated to even higher levels. England was also exceptionally successful in exporting in this period. High wages combined with great competitiveness imply high productivity. England's lead over the rest of the continent emerged before the Industrial Revolution.

High silver wages do not imply a high standard of living since they might be offset by high prices. That was the case in England where food prices were considerably higher than those elsewhere in Europe. Prices recorded in price histories can be used to measure these inflation differentials. To make international comparisons, the prices must be converted to grams of silver and the weights and measures must be converted to metric equivalents. To assess their purchasing power – and thus the standard of living of workers – it is necessary to specify a 'basket' of consumer goods and compute its cost across Europe. Figure 1.2 shows the real wage of building labourers defined in this way.

All across Europe, the fifteenth century marked a peak in the standard of living of workers. After 1500, population growth drove down the real

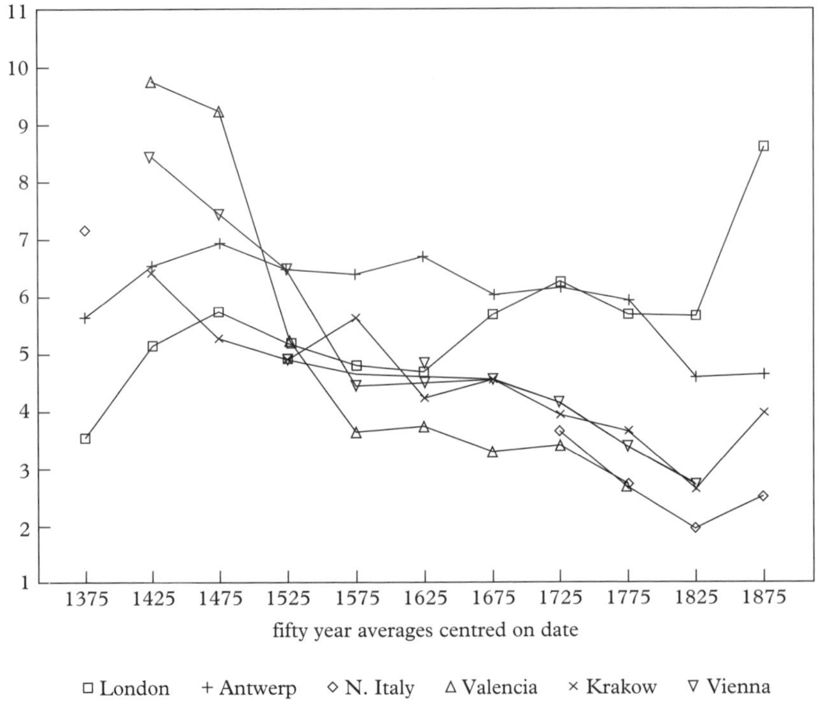

Figure 1.2 Labourers' real wages, 1375–1875 (silver wages deflated by cpi)

wage in the parts of Europe that experienced little or no structural change. In the successful countries, however, particularly in their larger cities, wages remained more or less constant. In no case did workers realise real wages above medieval levels, but it was still a singular achievement to maintain a constant real wage in the face of rapidly growing population (North and Thomas, 1973). English workers enjoyed real wages that were 50 per cent higher than those elsewhere in Europe on the eve of the Industrial Revolution, and that premium was maintained throughout the nineteenth century.

GDP per head

In modern economies, performance is usually measured by Gross Domestic Product (GDP) per head of the population. Historians have tried to reconstruct this indicator for earlier times. The task is fraught with difficulty since there is so little information about production. Attempts

Table 1.2 *GDP per head, 1500–1820 (1990 international dollars)*

	1500	1600	1700	1820
most successful over the period				
United Kingdom	714	974	1250	1707
moderately successful over the period				
Netherlands	754	1368	2110	1821
Belgium	875	976	1144	1319
small advance over the period				
Germany	676	777	894	1058
France	727	841	986	1230
Austria/Hungary	585	677	780	927
Poland	462	516	566	636
little change over the period				
Italy	1100	1100	1100	1117
Spain	698	900	900	1063

Note: Maddison did not report values for Poland, so the values shown are those he assigns to eastern Europe (excluding the former USSR) generally. The value I show for Austria/Hungary is the simple average of Maddison's values for Austria and for eastern Europe.
Source: Maddison, 2001: 264.

have nevertheless been made, and they are worth examining, although they must be approached with caution.

Table 1.2 summarises Maddison's (2001) recent estimates of GDP per head in early modern Europe. These are obtained by extrapolating 1990 per capita incomes back to 1500 using national indices of the growth in GDP and population. Maddison's reconstructions show Italy with the highest income in Europe in 1500 but realising little growth from then until 1820. In contrast, the Dutch Republic and the UK showed considerable growth between 1500 and 1820, when they were the two richest economies. More problematic reconstructions include Spain. Maddison's figures portray it as a rapidly growing economy in this period – a far more optimistic assessment than one based on structural transformation or real wages. Discrepancies like this emphasise that GDP estimates for the early modern period must be regarded with scepticism. Even for the early nineteenth century, the calculation of GDP per head is beset with difficulties. Thus, Maddison (1995) and Prados de la Escosura (2000) agree that Britain had the highest income in Europe in 1820, but they disagree significantly about the income of the USA. Maddison puts it below Britain's, while Prados puts it above. The differences in ranking reflect difficulties in deflation, for which there are no simple solutions.

Comparing the per capita GDP and the real wage series raises some interesting possibilities. In Italy, the wage fell and GDP per head grew very little; in north-western Europe, GDP rose rapidly, while the wage remained constant. Why was there a growing gap? It may have been filled by a rise in profits – Hamilton's (1929) profit inflation thesis – or by an increase in the number of hours worked – de Vries' (1994) 'industrious revolution'. A rise in rents, however, was probably a major explanation of the growing gap. In England, for instance, nominal rents rose by a factor of thirty-two and real rent by a factor of seven between 1450 and 1800 (Allen, 1992: 172, 285). In Italy, the rise in real rent was probably the result of population growth in the face of diminishing returns to labour. In England, the rise was due to productivity growth in farming. Whatever the explanation, the early modern period saw a large increase in inequality as the income of landlords rose with respect to that of workers.

The rise in rent raises a further question about sectoral links: was capital accumulation in the urban and manufacturing sectors financed by the savings of the landlords? In all likelihood the answer is no in this period. The classical economists never regarded the gentry and aristocracy as a source of savings (Crouzet, 1972), and Crafts' (1985: 122–5) calculations support that conclusion. Landlords spent their incomes on lavish living and luxury accommodation.

The agricultural revolution

Economic growth in early modern Europe had both an agricultural and a non-agricultural component. Labour productivity in agriculture had to rise so that each farm worker could support more and more workers in manufacturing. Releasing labour from agriculture was not enough, however. Jobs in rural industry and the cities had to be created so that the former farm workers could be re-employed outside of agriculture instead of remaining unemployed rural paupers. I begin with the release of labour from agriculture before taking up its absorption by manufacturing.

To track the performance of agriculture, we must measure output per worker. This requires estimating agricultural production and dividing it by the number of farm workers. Determining agricultural output is difficult in the absence of agricultural censuses. The most successful method, at present, is to compute the volume of farm goods needed to clear agricultural markets and then to subtract imports and add exports in order to compute the volume of domestic production. Calculating the market-clearing volume of farm output requires specifying a demand curve for agricultural products (Crafts, 1976; Jackson, 1985; Clark, 1993; Allen, 1999). English agricultural production has also been estimated from

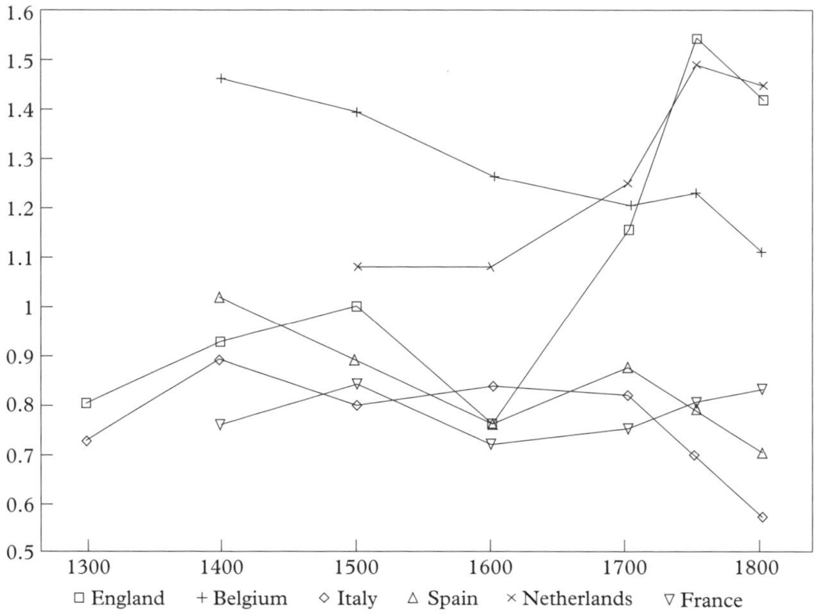

Figure 1.3 Output per worker in Agriculture 1300–1800

farmers' account books and from econometric models of farming and climate. These approaches point to substantially the same conclusion as the demand curve method for the period 1700–1850 (Brunt, 1997, 1999; Turner et al., 2001).

Output per worker in agriculture is obtained by dividing the estimates of farm production by the agricultural population figures presented earlier. Figure 1.3 shows the resulting figures for leading countries in Europe. Three different patterns are apparent.

The first is exemplified by present-day Belgium. Medieval Flemish agriculture was renowned for its efficiency, and the high labour productivity of the province meant that the farmers could support a large urban population. Pockets of high productivity were also found elsewhere in Europe – notably in north-eastern Norfolk (Campbell, 1983). Output per worker declined slowly in Belgium as the population grew and farms were subdivided during the early modern period. Nevertheless, Belgium continued to provide a high standard that took centuries for Europe's other farmers to meet.

The Dutch and the English exemplify the second pattern. Neither country exhibited impressive productivity in the Middle Ages. Between 1600 and 1750 each experienced an agricultural revolution in which output per worker reached and exceeded Belgian levels. Both countries are famous for their agricultural revolutions, and they show up dramatically in the graph of labour productivity.

The third group is all the rest. Italy, for whom the figures start in 1300, is a paradigm case. The Black Death cut the population in the middle of the fourteenth century. As a result, output per worker rose between 1300 and 1400. In the next hundred years, renewed population growth began to cut productivity back to pre-plague levels. The English series shows the same rise and fall, but the difference is that Italian labour productivity continued to decline throughout the early modern period. There was no agricultural revolution there. All the major continental countries showed a similar drop in productivity between 1400 and 1800 as the expansion of the farm population ran into diminishing returns.

Some insight into the nature of the Dutch and English agricultural revolutions can be obtained by factoring output per worker into components with the equation:

$$\frac{\text{Output}}{\text{Labour}} = \frac{\text{Output}}{\text{Improved area}} \times \frac{\text{Improved area}}{\text{Total area}} \times \frac{\text{total area}}{\text{Labour}} \quad (1)$$

This is revealing, since the components were determined by different factors.

'Improved area' includes the acreage of arable, meadow and pasture. Output per improved area rose in the early modern period, since the productivity of both crops and livestock rose. In most of England, the yield of wheat was about 10 bushels per acre *c.* 1500. While there is not unanimity among historians, several approaches suggest the yield of wheat doubled to 20 bushels *c.* 1700 and then only increased by a further 10 per cent over the course of the eighteenth century (Allen, 1992, 1999; Turner et al., 2001; Brunt, 1997, 1999; cf. Overton, 1996). Yields of other grains increased proportionally. The causes of this increase are several. First, a classic explanation is the increased application of animal manure (O'Brien, 1996). Probate inventories indicate that the number of livestock per cultivated acre did not rise, but their quality may have improved. Sheep produced more wool and meat in 1750 than they had in 1500 and cows gave more butter and cheese. The greater flow of product per animal required a greater consumption of feed, which, in turn, implies more manure to fertilise the land. Second, the quality of seed probably improved. There is evidence that farmers were more judicious in selecting seed, and there were also increased inter-regional sales of seed. The latter allows a better match between seed and environmental characteristics. Third, the cultivation of beans and peas was greatly expanded in the early modern period. Since these crops fix nitrogen, they may have increased soil fertility.

Labour productivity also increased because land was improved. This process was most dramatic in the Netherlands, where so much land was reclaimed from the sea. Reclamation was also undertaken in England, where Dutch engineers were employed to supervise the draining of the fens. In the eighteenth century, about eight million acres of 'waste' were converted to 'pasture' (Allen, 1994: 104).

The third reason that labour productivity increased was due to changes in the rural population, which translated directly into changes in total area/labour. Changes in that ratio can be analysed in terms of this reciprocal:

$$\frac{\text{Labour}}{\text{Total area}} = \frac{\text{Improved area}}{\text{Total area}} \times \frac{\text{Labour}}{\text{Improved area}} \qquad (2)$$

Land improvement raised the fraction of land that was improved, and this increased farm employment, since workers were required to cultivate the enlarged acreage. On the other hand, labour/improved area fell in England during the early modern period. Enclosure, which involved the conversion of arable to grass, cut farm employment. The shift from small-scale family farms to large-scale farms also reduced agricultural employment. The declines were particularly sharp for women and children, but the number of full-time male jobs per acre also fell (Allen, 1988, 1992). Agricultural employment expanded when the first effect predominated and declined when the second was the most important. The net effect rebounded onto labour productivity in accord with equation 1.[1]

The most long-standing explanation for the rise in efficiency in early modern English agriculture is the enclosure of the open fields. The shift from small-scale yeoman farms to large-scale tenant farms cultivated by wage labour has also been advanced as an explanation. Enclosed farms are supposed to have been more efficient than open farms since (1) common pasture, which was overgrazed, was converted to private property, which was more effectively managed, and (2) the need for group decision-making in the open fields was abolished. In the enclosures, enterprising individuals could adopt new practices without reference to the community, whereas in the open fields, backward villagers could block improvement. The large-scale tenant farmers are supposed to have been more innovative than yeomen farmers, since the former had to generate the

[1] Equations 1 and 2 treat output per acre and employment per acre as independent phenomena. This is different from the neoclassical view in which the real wage, in conjunction with a production function, determines employment per acre and output per acre simultaneously. In that perspective, a change in the real wage changes both output per worker and acres per worker. The view adopted here presumes that open and enclosed farms (and large and small farms) had different production functions and the shift between these functions had a greater impact on employment than shifts along any of the production functions in response to changes in the real wage.

cash to cover their wage bill and their rent, while the latter often owned their land and relied on family labour so they lacked the need for money that pushed the large-scale farmer forward.

The difficulty with all of these arguments is that there was little difference in efficiency between open fields and enclosures or between large-scale and small-scale farmers. All of these groups experienced similar rates of yield increase and output growth during the early modern period. International comparisons buttress the point, since the open-field farmers of north-eastern France, for instance, reaped about as much wheat per acre as enclosed farmers in England (O'Brien and Keyder, 1978; Allen and O'Grada, 1988). While tenurial differences affected employment, they did not greatly influence output. In view of these results, it is hard to see enclosure or large-scale farming as the causal factor pushing the English economy forward.

The growth of non-agricultural employment: rural industry

Not only did agriculture have to release labour, but manufacturing, trade and other activities had to absorb it. Jobs were created in both rural and urban areas.

Rural industry expanded north of the Alps and Pyrennees. It had a strongly regional character. The production of woollen cloth, for instance, which was eighteenth-century England's leading manufacturing industry, was not spread evenly across the country. Instead, it was concentrated in a few districts – East Anglia, the West Country and Yorkshire. The distribution was not static – the former two were declining regions while the latter was expanding – but it was regional blocks that rose and fell. Other industries across Europe showed the same regional concentration. Two factors explain this regionalism. The first was external economies of scale: the concentration of production in one area meant that specialised suppliers could emerge and guaranteed thick labour markets so that workers could always be found – even for esoteric tasks. The second was training: many proto-industrial jobs required great skill. Those skills were learned on the job rather than in school, so skill transmission was confined to established regions, and that reinforced their competitiveness.

Historians have examined the link between proto-industry and the agricultural economy. Mendels (1972), who coined the term, envisioned a process in which the subdivision of farms in Flanders increased the supply of off-farm labour, thus promoting rural manufacturing. The process became self-reinforcing since the expansion of industrial jobs meant that young adults did not have to wait to inherit the family farm in order to establish themselves economically. Consequently, the expansion of rural industry lowered the average age of marriage, and population growth accelerated. Eventually, farms got even smaller, and the supply of off-farm labour became even greater. Other historians have seen rural industry as the counterpart of seasonal declines in farm employment (Thirsk, 1961).

An alternative agrarian interpretation emphasised the link between enclosure and the growth of rural industry. This is the standard Marxist argument that enclosure eliminated small-scale farms and cut the demand for labour in agriculture. The result was an exodus of former agriculturalists, who became the industrial workforce. The argument can be traced back to seventeenth-century commentators like Samuel Fortrey (1663) who noted that enclosure led to the conversion of arable to pasture 'one hundred acres of which, will scarce maintain a shepherd and his dog, which now maintains many families, employed in tillage'. The 'people which lived in those towns they call depopulated' were not destroyed, however. Instead, 'they were onely removed to other places . . . and employed in the manufacture of the wooll that may arise out of one hundred acres of pasture'. Enclosure drove people from the land to jobs in the textile industry.

The expansion of rural industry in north-western Europe was associated with the emergence of new economic leaders, because it came at the expense of established producers. In the Middle Ages, Italian and Flemish cities produced woollen cloth that was exported across the continent. The English also produced and exported heavy broadcloths. By the sixteenth century, the English and the Dutch began to imitate the lighter Italian worsteds. These clothes were the 'new draperies'. They proved so popular that the Italians were driven out of the woollen business in the seventeenth century (Rapp, 1975; Harte, 1997). The new manufacturing industries flourished in East Anglia and the Low Countries. The Norwich industry was started in the middle of the sixteenth century by Flemish refugees, although it drew on an earlier craft tradition (Munro, 1997; Holderness, 1997; Martin, 1997). At the end of the seventeenth century, about 40 per cent of England's woollen cloth production was exported, and woollen fabrics amounted to 69 per cent of the country's exports of domestic manufactures (Deane, 1957: 209–10; Davis, 1954: 165).

The growth of non-agricultural employment: cities

The growth of cities was another way in which north-western Europe differed from the rest of the continent. Cities arose for at least three reasons.

One was physiocratic – the expenditure of the agricultural surplus. The state taxed some of the income generated in the countryside and spent it in the capital or the court – Versailles is the pre-eminent example – or in towns like Portsmouth, where arsenals and naval dockyards dominated the economy. The aristocracies of Europe also received income from the land and followed the monarch, spending their money on residences and lavish living in the capital and court. Cities like Bath were also supported by the agricultural income of landed society. Under these circumstances, increases in the productivity of agriculture that rebounded to the benefit of the state or the aristocracy could promote urbanisation by financing more conspicuous consumption and construction.

There were other sources of surplus, but their effects on urbanisation were more equivocal. Some of the income of merchants and capitalists was directed to urban construction, but there was also a tradition of investing these fortunes in landed estates, which reduced the importance of this income for urbanisation. A specific source of surplus that warrants mention is the vast treasure of gold and silver taken from Mexico and Peru by the Spanish crown and leading families. This financed the rapid growth of Madrid and, to that degree, accelerated urbanisation (Ringrose, 1983). However, the inflation of Spanish wages and prices reduced the competitiveness of Spanish manufacturing. This early case of Dutch disease led to the depopulation of traditional manufacturing cities and checked the growth of rural industry. The surplus derived from the New World did not lead to an overall increase in the share of non-agricultural employment in accord with table 1.1.

A second reason for urban growth was manufacturing. Dense populations created external economies and training opportunities that were greater than those found in rural manufacturing. Congestion, pollution, ill health and high rents offset these advantages, but cities were still suitable sites for some industries. The New Draperies were first established in the Low Countries in villages like Hondschoote. The manufacture of light cloth spread into other rural areas including the Ardennes, but, more significantly, was re-established in cities like Leyden, Delft, Gouda, Haarlem and Utrecht (Pounds, 1990: 235, 293). In England, the framework knitting of stockings was carried on both in Leicestershire villages and in Leicester itself during the eighteenth century. Other manufacturing industries were primarily urban. London, for instance, was the centre of English publishing and furniture making from an early date. Indeed, London was a major manufacturing city. Some of the production (like food and drink) was derivative in that it fed the workers of industries that sold goods beyond the city. Many manufacturers were of the latter sort and provided an 'export base' to London in the early modern period.

A third reason for urban growth was trade and commerce. This connection was particularly important in north-western Europe. In the seventeenth century, intra-European trade was the basis of London's expansion. There were close connections to rural manufacturing. The New Draperies that were woven in East Anglia and exported to the Mediterranean were shipped through London. They made a bigger contribution to the trade of the capital than they did to the country as a whole (Rapp, 1975: 502). Between 1500 and 1700, the population of London increased tenfold. The export of New Draperies played a significant role (Davis, 1978: 390; Wrigley, 1987: 148).

Intercontinental trade became more important in the seventeenth and eighteenth centuries. Portugal was the most successful European power in South Asia in the sixteenth century. It monopolised the spice trade and seized important colonies including the Moluccas, the 'Spice Islands', which were the source of cinnamon and nutmeg. The Netherlands, in turn, took these islands from Portugal in the early seventeenth century and established its Indonesian empire. This imperial success contributed to Amsterdam's becoming Europe's wholesaling centre for tropical produce. A vigorous colonial policy, the navigation acts and three wars with the Dutch helped London wrest that trade from Amsterdam. Trade with India and China added tea, cotton textiles and porcelain to the list of Asian imports. As the eighteenth century progressed, intercontinental trade loomed larger in England's international accounts, and the growth of that trade contributed to the growth of Britain's cities.

What caused what?

Change occurred in all three sectors of the European economy – farming, cities and rural manufacturing – but at different rates in different countries. It was only in the Dutch Republic and England that change occurred vigorously in all three areas. But what caused what?

The modernisation of agrarian institutions has often been suggested as the prime mover behind the economic success of north-western Europe. England is the classic case in these accounts. The enclosure of the open fields is usually treated as the key change since it is supposed to have created an efficient system of private property that rewarded successful innovators for their enterprise. In addition, the amalgamation of small-scale, peasant holdings into large-scale, tenant farms operated by hired labour is also seen as an institutional change that modernised agriculture and released labour for industry. Sometimes the shift to large farms is presented as the result of enclosure and sometimes as an independent development. In either interpretation, these changes are treated as autonomous, so they caused change elsewhere without being caused by it, in turn. In this view, agrarian change boosted the rest of the economy through the provision of food to feed the non-agricultural workers, wool and hides for them to process, and (in Marxist versions) the actual provision of the manufacturing work force itself.

A powerful historiography has developed around the agrarian explanation of the industrial revolution. It contends both that modern, 'capitalist' agriculture was responsible for England's economic success and that the persistence of traditional, peasant or 'feudal' institutions held back the rest of the continent. This historical monolith, however, is collapsing under hammer blows from both sides. As noted earlier, detailed comparisons of open and enclosed farms in England fail to find the great differences in efficiency that the agrarian hypothesis supposes. Indeed, both farming systems achieved considerable productivity growth over the early modern period. Moreover, investigations in other countries of institutional arrangements once thought to have held back agriculture – share cropping along the Mediterranean and the Mesta in Spain – have called these negative conclusions into question (Hayami and Otsuka, 1993; Hoffman, 1996; Nugent and Sanchez, 1989; Simpson, 1995). If 'bad' institutions have not held back agriculture when their effects can be measured and analysed, how could 'modern' institutions have propelled it forward?

If the impetus for change did not come from agriculture, it came from the proto-industrial and urban economies. Here we must be careful to distinguish between proto-industrialisation and urbanisation themselves, which were elements of the evolving system, and those changes which promoted these social processes in the first place. The key factors were the development of the New Draperies and the empires of the English and the Dutch. These were the prime movers that led to the growth of rural industries in the sixteenth century and the expansion of cities throughout the period.

Some of the growth of London, for instance, can be traced immediately to these developments: that portion of London's growth that was due to the growth of its export trade was a direct result of the growth of the East Anglian woollen industry. The rest of London's growth, however, had other immediate causes: a portion, for instance, was due to the expenditure of the agricultural surplus by the crown, the aristocracy and the gentry. The agrarian interpretation would attribute this surplus to changes like enclosure that are viewed as autonomous. As just noted, this interpretation founders on the finding that the open fields were as effective in raising productivity as the enclosures. To establish that

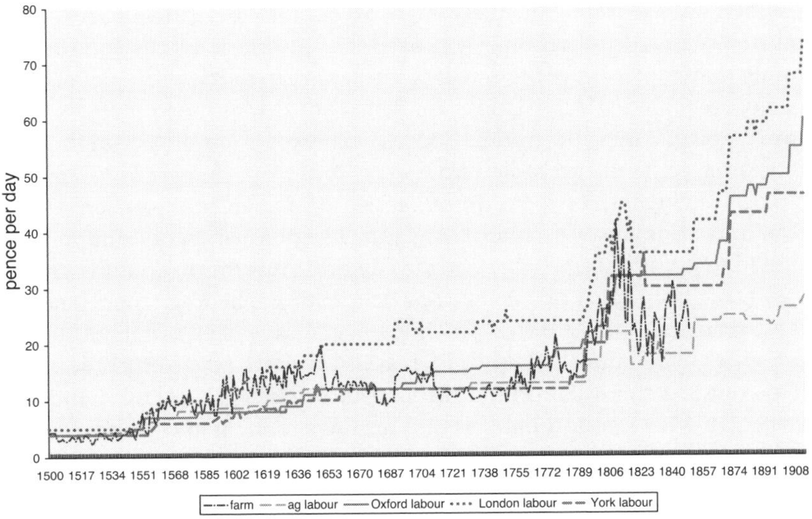

Figure 1.4 Farm and labourers' daily earnings

causation ran from city to country, however, more is required: productivity growth in agriculture must be traced back to the growth of cities and proto-industry.

Hints on causation come from the labour market: rising wages in one sector (relative to another) indicate that the former is expanding more rapidly than the latter. Read that way, the labour market is a thermometer that locates the hot spots – the engines of growth – in the economy.

Figure 1.4 shows readings of the wage thermometer. The graph plots the real wage of building and agricultural labourers in London, Oxford, the countryside around it and cities in northern England. An adjustment has been made to the data for differences in the rent of a labourer's house *c.* 1770, so the series show the relative standard of living between places as well as over time. In the fifteenth century, the differentials were relatively modest. In the sixteenth century, London wages begin to rise above those in the rest of England and remained high until the end of the seventeenth century at least. From 1500 to 1700, the population of London exploded. Death rates in London exceeded birth rates, so a huge immigration was necessary for rapid growth. The high wages in London were the incentive for people to move, but migration was not rapid enough to dampen the increase.

International comparisons help interpret the wage changes. The gap between London wages and rural wages could have emerged because

London wages were unusually high or because the rural wages were unusually low. International comparisons show that it was the former rather than the latter. In other words, the wage gap did not emerge because enclosures flooded rural labour markets with dispossessed farmers who drove down wages, but rather because the expansion of the metropolis increased demand and pulled up wages.

In the eighteenth century, the dynamism of England's expansion spilled over into the towns of southern England. The population of London continued to grow, but the cities outside London grew more rapidly between 1700 and 1800 (de Vries, 1984; Bairoch, 1988). The wage thermometer is a harbinger of these developments, for the wage of labourers in southern cities like Oxford began to increase in the late seventeenth century. This upward trend continued through the eighteenth century, and the wage gap with London narrowed. This linkage, it should be noted, did not extend to farm workers in the southern countryside, for their wage failed to rise throughout the period.

By the late eighteenth century, the wage thermometer indicates that economic dynamism extended to cities in the North of England. After 1750, the populations of the industrial cities began to grow rapidly as the cotton textile and engineering industries expanded in the first phase of industrialisation. This increase in wages indicates the industrial development of the region: wages were not rising in the north because labour markets were better integrated and workers were moving from Lancashire to London to find jobs. Instead, northern wages were rising because of the growth of labour demand in the north.

And what of agriculture? How was its development related to the ripples of growth spreading out from London? The wages of farm labourers are one indicator, but they are not the most pertinent one as it was farm operators – not their employees – who were making the decisions that cumulated to make the agricultural revolution. Figure 1.4 also plots the net income of a small-scale yeoman farm. The farm assumes 15 acres of arable land and typical numbers of animals, as indicated by probate inventories. The annual net income is converted to a daily basis assuming 350 working days per year to make the income comparable to the daily wages of labourers. A key feature of the calculation is that it assumes medieval crop and livestock yields. The farm income shown in figure 1.4, therefore, shows what the position of small farmers would be if they did not modernise their methods.

Figure 1.5 shows us why open-field farmers increased their productivity in the seventeenth century. During the price revolution – roughly 1550 to 1620 – agricultural prices inflated more rapidly than any others. In this period, yeomen farmers did well without modernising their

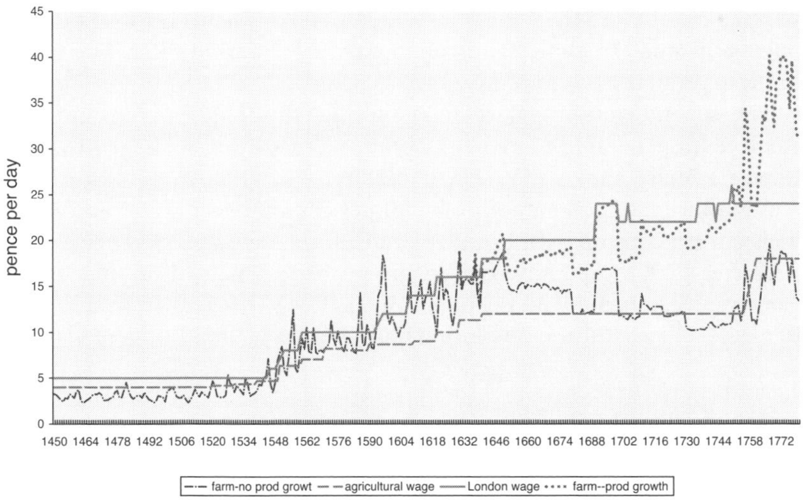

Figure 1.5 Alternative farm incomes with and without productivity growth

methods. This was the period when London was exploding, and the wages of London labourers leaped ahead of those elsewhere in the country. The rising farm prices meant that small farmers kept up with London living standards and moved ahead of labourers in the county towns. There was no great incentive to modernise in this period.

After 1620, the situation changed. Agricultural prices stopped rising, and farm incomes stagnated. As the ripples of growth spread to the small towns of southern England in the mid-seventeenth century, yeomen found themselves falling behind not only Londoners but also their neighbours in the towns. These gaps were particularly distressing due to the spread of the consumer revolution (McKendrick et al., 1982; Thirsk, 1978; Brewer and Porter, 1993; Berg and Clifford, 1999; Shammas, 1990; Weatherill, 1988; van der Woude and Schuurman, 1980; de Vries, 1975). The high real wages of the seventeenth century allowed artisans in the leading cities of north-western Europe to enlarge their consumption beyond the bread, beer and meat that marked affluence in the late Middle Ages. Well-off workers could consume the newly abundant products of the tropics – pepper and other spices from the Indies, coffee, tea and sugar. In addition, 'luxury' manufactures were also added to the normal standard of consumption. These luxuries included books, clocks, cutlery, crockery, better furniture and so forth.

Farmers wanted this standard of living, too. They had two options. One was to sell the farm, move to London and join the urban economy. Many yeomen did that. In the eighteenth century, great estates grew, in part, by buying up small freeholds and copyholds (Habakkuk, 1940). The sellers of these properties were the yeomen leaving agriculture.

The second option was to raise productivity. Higher crop and livestock yields generated more net income and made the small farms viable. Figure 1.5 also shows the net income that a small farm could realise if real output increased smoothly by 50 per cent between 1630 and 1730. This curve keeps up with London. Indeed, the renewed food price inflation after 1750 would have once again pushed farmers ahead of London workers. Keeping up with the high living in the Metropolis was the motive to create an agricultural revolution, and it was a viable course of action.

Conclusion

The view of development advanced here has much in common with Braudel's (1981–4) vision. International commerce was the key to growth, and the great commercial centres – first Venice, then Amsterdam, and finally London – were the growth poles. But what caused the cities to grow? On this question, we differ from Braudel, who saw the great merchants and bankers at the apex of the system as the leaders of change. Instead, two sets of actors are central to our view. The first were the humble artisans and the small-scale merchants who figured out how to make the new draperies, to market the cloth, and, indeed, to make the other new products of the consumer revolution. The yeomen farmers who responded to the demand for wool and food by finding ways to increase yields made similar and equally critical contributions. The second actor was the state. Establishing London's commercial pre-eminence required seizing a world empire, organising it to the benefit of British trade and industry, and the defeat of rival imperial powers including Spain, France and the Dutch Republic. The creation of a favourable geo-political environment allowed the enterprise of Britain's merchants, craftsmen and farmers to produce the most successful economy of early modern Europe.

2 Comparative patterns of colonial trade: Britain and its rivals

Javier Cuenca Esteban

> 'Le commerce des Anglais dans le Bengale est porté à un tel point que les autres nations ne peuvent rien faire. Ils achètent au moins 30 p. 100 meilleur marché que les autres nations et ils paient avec les revenus des provinces conquises.' (Quoted in Levasseur, 1911: 475)

The French administrator who thus wrote to the Compagnie des Indes in 1768 was pointing to one of several advantages of British merchants over their European rivals: they paid lower prices for Asian commodities because the English East India Company, in firm control over Bengal since the battle of Plassey (1757), could most effectively perform the familiar state functions of privatising gains and socialising costs and losses.

What the French administrator possibly ignored, and could not easily foresee, is that Britain's far stronger foothold in India was, had been and would remain one of the pillars of her trading system. Another distinctive pillar was the long-standing trade and common commercial practices with the thirteen colonies that would become the United States after 1776–83. A third British advantage arguably stemmed, despite a slow start and temporary losses in the late 1800s, from the profitable exports to rival Empires through the Free Ports that were successively opened in the British West Indies since 1766.

The significance of these and other British trades lay not so much in their comparative size as in the effective coordination that their number, their geographical spread, and their commodity composition made possible. The French, Dutch, Spanish and Portuguese empires also stretched to America, Asia and Africa, but their respective footholds were less firm and turned progressively weaker during the eighteenth century. Long before the Industrial Revolution began to have an impact on overseas

The author wishes to thank David Eltis for extensive commentary on the slave trade and for updated estimates of slave numbers and prices. Gregory Clark kindly provided his most recent series of English agricultural output. Lively discussion in the Economic History Seminar of the Universidad Carlos III (Madrid, March 2002) prompted further elaboration in section IV. All errors and omissions are the author's own.

markets in the 1790s, British interests as a whole could more easily replace declining with rising trades, expensive raw materials with cheaper sources of supply. They could more readily exclude competitors in strategic areas at lower unit costs of aggression and defence. They could draw on dynamic demand from prosperous trade partners with independent sources of wealth, and from outside of pre-existing networks of commodity flows and payments. Those who neglect comparative analysis of national commercial systems, or who focus on individual branches of external trade, too often ignore further 'inseparable connections' with fiscal States (O'Brien, 1993, 1998), and the cumulative advantages that small initial differences could eventually confer on the stronger or luckier nation.

This chapter will trace, in broad quantitative terms, the main differences between Britain's non-European trades and those of its closest rival through 1716–1820, with the balance sheet on the eve of the French Revolution as a point of reference. Section 1 outlines the main trades involved and contrasts real values by commodities and geographical areas in 1787–9, in 1797–1815, and in 1816–1820. Section 2 speculates on the relative contributions of the colonial and quasi-colonial world, the United States and Europe and Levant to the British balance of payments in selected periods. Section 3 suggests a contextual framework for real trends in British and French trade values through 1710–90 and beyond. The chapter concludes with some thoughts on the links between external involvement and Britain's rise to economic and military pre-eminence. It will be argued that Britain's most clearly distinctive, long-standing, and cumulative advantages in trade and Empire probably had the widest range of strategic and economic implications – when compared to those running from uncertain rates of local agricultural growth, from domestic markets not clearly larger than the French Five Farms alone, from widely shared economic institutions, or from questionable degrees of technological prowess.

1

On the eve of the French Revolution, Britain's colonial and quasi-colonial trade with three continents had acquired a seemingly decisive pre-eminence. Holland and Spain had long been left behind. Most of French Canada, and four West Indian islands, had joined Britain's exclusive mercantile system by the end of the Seven Years War (1756–63). Both British and French merchants smuggled manufactures into foreign American colonies through the West Indies; but Britain alone had successfully established free ports for this purpose in Jamaica and elsewhere since 1766 (Buron, 1931–2: 573–4; Armytage, 1953). French merchants had failed to develop firm commercial ties with the independent United States. Both nations were major participants in the slave trade from Africa; as will be noted, however, French slavers had had a late start, were dependent on key British supplies, and were not as well placed to profit from the trade. Several European countries including France had strongholds in the Far East, but Britain had strengthened her military forces in Bengal in the 1740s and decisively consolidated control over this important area after the battle of Plassey (1757).

Transoceanic trade was linked to European networks in a number of ways. In the north, Amsterdam and Hamburg had long been major markets for distribution of colonial goods. British subjects made large profits on Irish exports of linen and provisions to British America. Spain and the Indies were linked to France by intermittent dynastic alliance, and Portugal and Brazil to England since the treaty of Methuen (1703). Both British and French merchants imported colonial goods, and exported domestic manufactures for American consumption, in varying degrees through Spain, Gibraltar and Portugal.

With a number of qualifications spelled out in the Appendix, tables 2.1 to 2.4 specify the main trades involved and their relative importance. Judging from the top section of table 2.1, in 1787–9 Britain's rapidly expanding non-European imports would have been larger and far more diversified than those of France at their eighteenth-century peak. The bulk of British imports from outside of Europe was evenly shared by Asia and by the British West Indies; Britain's quasi-colonial imports from Ireland stood at well over one half those from Asia. By contrast the French West Indies alone, notably Saint-Domingue, probably supplied an overwhelming proportion of France's transoceanic imports. One important consequence of France's relatively narrow base was that her colonial imports were crippled by the slave revolts in Saint-Domingue since 1791; but France's gains during the 1780s were unlikely to be sustained (Tarrade, 1972: II, 776–84; Stein, 1983).

Subsequent trends during the French wars are best traced at constant prices. The deflated values of Britain's transoceanic imports more than double in the 1790s, fluctuate around the acquired gains through 1797–1815, and further increase in 1816–20. Significantly, Britain's largest gains during the wars were those in Asian goods; also important were increased supplies from Ireland, from the British West Indies, from British North America, from the conquered American islands (1794–1815), and from Brazil and Spanish America. By contrast, France's direct imports from outside of Europe and Levant do not appear in the French Tableaux for *c.* 1797–1809, barely revive under licensing agreements with

Table 2.1 *Great Britain and France: Imports CIF excluding bullion, 1787–1820*[1] *(period averages of annual values in £000 at constant prices of 1787–9)*

	1787–1789		1797–1812, 1814–1815		1816–1820	
	Britain	France	Britain	France	Britain	France
TOTAL IMPORTS	27,132	21,539	42,062	9,220	53,194	11,146
from own colonies, Africa, Asia	14,830	9,173	21,670	51	29,435	1,891
of which Ireland	3,358		4,396		5,138	
West Indies	5,582	8,000[2]	7,283		9,594	
Canada	268		1,136		1,813	
Asia	5,465	900[2]	8,620		12,526	
Africa	157	273[2]	234		363	
from Britain's conquered islands			2,788			
from foreign American colonies	1,096		2,469		2,774	
from all colonies, Africa, Asia	15,927	9,173	26,928	51	32,210	1,891
from the US	1,246	401	2,544	969	5,225	901
from Europe and Levant	9,958	11,964	12,589	8,199	15,759	8,353
IMPORTS OF NON-EUROPEAN GOODS[3]	18,278	10,496	36,172	4,139	45,779	4,162
from all colonies, Africa, Asia	15,927	9,173	26,928	51	32,209	1,891
of which Asia	5,465	900	8,620		12,526	
from or through the US	1,246	401	2,544	969	5,225	901
through Europe	1,104	922	6,699	3,119	8,343	1,369

Asian calicos, muslins, nankeens	2,115	1,023	2,391	1,160	1,717	20
from Asia	2,115	685	2,391	1	1,717	2
through the US	0		0	90	0	6
through Europe	0	339	0	1,069	0	12
Indigo	687	637	1,161	554	1,457	457
from all colonies, Africa, Asia	215	429	1,097	6	1,439	78
of which India	137		1,003		1,417	
from or through the US	327	3	30	29	3	29
through Europe	145	205	35	519	14	351
Silk from China and Bengal	761	5	703	0	1,277	15
Cotton[3]	2,068	961	6,243	648	13,589	1,694
from all colonies, Africa, Asia	1,307	844	3,263	4	7,010	202
of which India	0		506		3,679	
from or through the US	21		2,347	253	6,339	863
through Europe	740	116	632	391	240	630
Other raw materials	1,232	235	1,278	176	858	59
Other (sugar, coffee, etc.)	11,415	7,635	24,394	1,601	26,879	1,916
IMPORTS OF EUROPEAN GOODS[4]	8,853	11,042	5,889	5,080	7,415	6,983

[1]Provisional estimates of imports from the foreign American colonies through Spain, Gibraltar, Portugal, the British West Indies, Britain's conquered islands and the United States have been discounted from the relevant sub-totals and added to 'foreign American colonies'.

[2]Rough estimates. One problem here is that Tarrade gave no breakdowns for French colonial trade with Newfoundland.

[3]'Imports of non-European goods' include all Irish commodities and exclude cotton and raw silk from the Mediterranean.

[4]Irish goods excluded.

Sources and procedures: see Appendix.

Britain in 1810–13, and regain only one-third of the 1787–9 levels at the height of recovery in 1820. France made up for some of the war losses through European networks and through the United States (Crouzet, 1987, 1990b); but the combined real value of her direct and indirect imports of colonial goods seldom exceeds a quarter of the 1787–9 level.

Selected breakdowns by commodities in table 2.1 further highlight the importance of Britain's Indian connection and other British advantages over France. Asian commodities, most notably Indian textiles and Chinese nankeens until 1805, would have accounted for over 30 per cent of British transoceanic imports through much of the period 1772–1820. France's Asian trade was far smaller and some of the Asian textiles recorded in France as direct shipments in 1787–9 probably came from London and Lisbon (Levasseur, 1911: I, 479). Indigo came into Britain from several areas, notably the Carolinas, France, Flanders and Spain in the 1760s and 1770s; and from the United States and Spain in the 1780s. India became the overwhelming source of Britain's indigo from the mid-1790s onwards. The distribution of France's non-European supplies has not been ascertained, but indigo was, together with cotton, one of the two raw materials with significant import levels from French America (Tarrade, 1972: II, 747–9). Most of Britain's raw silk came from China and Bengal, whereas France relied on the Mediterranean for its external supplies. Even in cotton, where Whitney's invention of the mechanical gin in 1793 would soon establish the United States as the world's leading exporter, British imports from India rose to more than half the US share by 1816–20. Unlike France, Britain secured significant quantities of other raw materials from outside of Europe, notably textile dyes such as logwood and fustic from Central and South America; tobacco, turpentine and timber from the United States and Canada; superior saltpetre from India; and whale oil from the northern fisheries. In other non-European commodities, British imports appear to have taken the lead by 1787–9 and certainly covered a wider spectrum, with tea values already rivalling those of sugar.

The re-export trades only partially reflect differential import patterns. Asian commodities appear to have accounted for more than half the value of British re-exports of non-European goods throughout 1772–1820. Judging from table 2.2, in 1787–9 France enjoyed a clear edge over Britain in re-exports of American goods despite smaller import volumes. This paradox is explained, in part, by the larger share of raw materials for domestic consumption within British imports; in part by lower production costs of sugar and coffee in the French West Indies; and also by weaker demand in French domestic markets. During the Napoleonic wars, British re-exports of non-European commodities

Table 2.2 *Great Britain and France: re-exports FOB excluding bullion, 1787–1820*[1] *(period averages of annual values in £000 at constant prices of 1787–9)*

	1787–1789		1797–1812, 1814–1815		1816–1820	
	Britain	France	Britain	France	Britain	France
TOTAL RE-EXPORTS	4,852	6,960	11,764	537	11,770	323
to own colonies, Africa, Asia	1,719	33	3,504	0	3,437	52
of which Ireland	961		1,556		1,195	
West Indies	208		623		371	
Canada	240		562		1,125	
Asia	54		311		495	
Africa	257		451		249	
to Britain's conquered islands			300			
to foreign American colonies	2		231		148	
to all colonies, Africa, Asia	1,721	33	4,035	0	3,585	52
to the US	334	5	410	2	498	70
to Europe and Levant	2,797	6,921	7,318	534	7,687	201
RE-EXPORTS OF COLONIAL GOODS	3,605	5,868	10,776	155	11,113	17
Irish goods	453		508		705	
American goods	1,008	5,810	6,161	134	6,646	17
Asian goods	2,143	58	4,107	21	3,761	
of which Asian textiles	1,498		2,450		2,076	
RE-EXPORTS OF US GOODS	568	431	400	99	614	29
RE-EXPORTS OF EUROPEAN GOODS	679	662	588	282	44	277

[1]The French figures probably exclude some values wrongly classified as domestic exports.
Sources and procedures: see Appendix.

would have doubled and those of European goods nearly quadrupled. By contrast, French re-exports to Europe and Levant collapsed during the wars and kept falling in 1816–20.

Transoceanic sources of food and raw materials also were important markets for European home industries (see table 2.3). Here again, in 1787–9 British domestic exports to the non-European world were larger and more widely distributed than those of France, with a significant edge in favour of the United States and Asia; the Irish market was not far behind and rivalled those in the British West Indies. The merchants of both nations sold about one-third of their respective home wares outside

Table 2.3 *Great Britain and France: domestic exports FOB excluding bullion, 1787–1820*[1] *(period averages of annual values in £000 at constant prices of 1787–9)*

	1787–1789		1797–1812, 1814–1815		1816–1820	
	Britain	France	Britain	France	Britain	France
TOTAL DOMESTIC EXPORTS	17,846	10,617	34,297	12,487	50,746	13,851
to own colonies, Africa, Asia	6,919	3,610	12,277	41	14,854	790
of which Ireland	1,569		3,358		4,180	
West Indies	1,761		3,718		4,105	
Canada	781		1,671		1,946	
Asia	2,170		2,863		4,166	
Africa	636		665		456	
to Britain's conquered islands			1,174			
to foreign American colonies	617	200	3,923	275	7,554	251
to all colonies, Africa, Asia	7,537	3,810	17,375	316	22,409	1,040
to the US	2,567	56	7,232	704	8,706	1,176
to Europe and Levant	7,741	6,750	9,689	11,467	19,630	11,634
Cotton manufactures	1,629	837	7,135	424	32,162	875
to all colonies, Africa, Asia	502	666	7,593	17	12,894	34
to the US	365	3	3,289	5	4,023	1
to Europe and Levant	763	168	6,252	402	15,243	841
Linen manufactures[1]	991	1,221	1,122	1,557	1,667	1,332
to all colonies, Africa, Asia	707	598	875	80	987	232
to the US	237	2	187	52	462	103
to Europe and Levant	47	621	61	1,424	218	998
Woollen manufactures	6,318	768	9,165	1,406	8,487	2,089
to all colonies, Africa, Asia	1,934	166	3,928	26	3,467	126
to the US	978	2	3,070	20	2,434	60
to Europe and Levant	3,404	600	2,166	1,360	2,585	1,903

Silk manufactures		1,142		2,244		2,934
to all colonies, Africa, Asia		104		25		93
to the US		3		216		608
to Europe and Levant		1,034		2,003		2,233
Iron and steel manufactures	1,012	140	1,884	57	1,952	26
to all colonies, Africa, Asia	604	82	1,093	0	1,048	7
to the US	191	1	365	1	546	2
to Europe and Levant	217	58	427	56	358	18
'Industrie générale'		1,499		654		717
to all colonies, Africa, Asia		754		2		67
to the US		10		30		61
to Europe and Levant		735		622		588
French brandy		731		733		427
to all colonies, Africa, Asia		74		0		16
to the US		19		141		72
to Europe and Levant		637		591		340
French wines (Bordeaux and others)		1,265		2,281		2,587
to all colonies, Africa, Asia		288		7		202
to the US		3		102		132
to Europe and Levant		974		2,172		2,252
Other domestic exports	7,894	3,012	4,989	3,129	6,476	2,862
to all colonies, Africa, Asia	3,789	1,078	3,886	157	4,011	265
to the US	796	13	321	137	1,240	137
to Europe and Levant	3,309	1,921	783	2,835	1,225	2,460

[1] Some of the French figures, particularly those for linens, probably include some re-exports. Provisional estimates of domestic exports to the foreign American colonies through Spain, Gibraltar, Portugal, the British West Indies, Britain's conquered islands and the United States have been discounted from the relevant sub-totals and added to 'foreign American colonies'.

Sources and procedures: see Appendix.

of Europe and the United States; but Britain's hold over the latter market brought her transoceanic sales to half of the total in 1787–9 – and to 63 per cent on average in 1797–1815. Selected commodity breakdowns in table 2.3 add some precision to well-known patterns. In 1787–9, textiles alone accounted for half the value of British home exports, with a clear predominance of woollen manufactures that would soon be reversed in favour of cottons; wines, silks, and brandy stand out among France's major single commodities. The war period 1797–1815 witnessed phenomenal growth in all branches of British transoceanic exports, notably to the United States until Jefferson's embargo (December 1807) and to Brazil and to Spanish America after 1806. Many of the latter markets probably were loss-makers in 1806–10 (Crouzet, 1987: 182–9, 580–7), but they appear to have outgrown the British West Indies and Asia to rival the United States by 1816–20. Despite much progress in cotton manufacture and elsewhere, France barely made up for a near collapse in transoceanic exports during the wars, in part by imposing semi-colonial braces on European neighbours (Bergeron, 1981: 173–90; Ellis, 1981: 264–73). When peace returned, French total home exports settled well below pre-war levels while British goods flooded continental markets.

The British and French official records are silent on multilateral trades, most notably those involving slave shipments from Africa. There seems to be something special about a business where average cargo values doubled or even tripled upon arrival in American plantations. Historians have convincingly argued that the costs and risks involved were unusually large, to the point that the profits of British slavers could have averaged 8 per cent of total outlays in 1757–84 and possibly fell thereafter (Behrendt, 1993: chapter 2). The rough calculations in tables 2.4 and 2.5 take a novel tack by specifying the slave trade's contribution to the British balance of payments through 1772–1805. The 'net inflows from the slave trade' in table 2.4, line 10 are larger than available estimates of slavers' profits in the accounting sense, because many of the costs of procuring and shipping slaves did not involve payments to foreign residents. Thus, line 10 excludes payments to British manufactures and shippers by British exporters to Africa, and all other relevant settlements among British citizens.

Here as elsewhere, Britain's larger and better coordinated external involvement afforded distinctive advantages. By the early eighteenth century African slavers had developed a taste for coloured Indian calicos that would soon be supplied by English merchants at cut-throat prices. English slavers appear to have been more efficient than their French counterparts (Eltis and Richardson, 1995: 470–5), but Britain's privileged Indian connection may partly explain lower slave prices in the British islands. Long

Table 2.4 *Great Britain and France: slave trade 1716–1805 (period averages)*

	1716–1735	1736–1755	1766–1785	1786–1790	1791–1805
GREAT BRITAIN:					
1. Slaves embarked in Africa	26,570	23,015	32,146	31,290	35,244
2. average price (£/slave)	5.26	5.74	13.62	18.60	23.98
3. payments for slaves (£'000)[1]	142	134	448	585	858
4. other payments to Africans (£'000)				18	26
5. idem to other foreigners (£'000)				147	180
6. Total payments to foreigners (lines 3 + 4 + 5)				750	1,063
7. Slaves delivered in America	22,203	19,439	28,622	28,527	33,482
8. average price (£/slave)	18.64	23.94	32.61	38.35	52.72
9. Sales revenue in America (£'000)[1]	413	461	946	1,094	1,774
10. Net inflows from the slave trade (line 9 minus line 6)[2]				344	710
FRANCE:					
11. Slaves embarked in Africa	7,300	13,060	17,365	38,280	5,167

[1]The annual figures underlying the period averages in line 3 equal the products of the respective annual figures in lines 1 and 2; the same applies to line 9 (line 7 times line 8).
[2]Excluding settlements among British citizens. Estimates for other selected sub-periods are given in table 2.5. This is a balance of payments concept, not to be confused with profits in the accounting sense: see text.
Sources and notes: Line 1: 1716–79 in Richardson, 1991: 52–5; 1780–1805 in Behrendt, 1997: 194. Line 2: Richardson, 1991: 52–5. Line 4: 3 per cent of line 3 for African rice, maize, yams, services, etc. (compare allowance for total non-slave items in Eltis and Richardson, 1995: 469–70). Line 5: rough estimates for foreign goods re-exported to Africa plus foreign inputs embodied in domestic exports to Africa. Line 7: line 1 reduced with decadal mortality rates as given in Richardson, 1989: 186–95. Lines 8 and 11: personal communication by David Eltis.

before the Industrial Revolution began to have a major impact on overseas markets in the 1790s, British slavers could most readily assemble ad hoc cargoes of Indian and European merchandise to take full advantage of market information, scale economies and transaction cycles on three continents (Behrendt, 2001: 200–202).

French slavers had a late start and made comparatively little progress through the eighteenth century, but in the late 1780s they took the lead over their British rivals. One major determinant of trade volumes in a mercantilist world was access to captive markets: while British slavers relied on Britain's less prosperous West Indian islands and on volatile sales in foreign colonies, French merchants could profit from booming demand at rising prices in Saint-Domingue, Guadeloupe and Martinique until 1792 (Stein, 1979: 141).

In most important respects, however, Britain was best placed to profit from the trade and drew greater advantage than France over a much longer time span. By the 1730s the British cotton industry was reaching the limits of growth within a heavily protected domestic market. The rise of British cottons exports in the third quarter of the century is explained, to a considerable extent, by the sale of cotton and linen checks for the purchase and clothing of slaves. Competition with Indian calicos and with Flemish fabrics in West African free markets also provided the opportunity and the stimulus for technological innovation in the British cotton industry (Inikori, 1989: 354–8, 365). Prior to the Anglo-French Commercial Treaty of 1786, French slavers already supplemented Indian calicos, foreign textiles and other wares with duty-free imports of Manchester cotton goods (Boulle, 1975: 312; Tarrade, 1972: I, 125–7). In 1787–9, one-third of French imports of non-Asian textiles came from Britain. As noted in connection with table 2.1, some of the Asian textiles recorded in France as direct shipments in 1787–9 probably came from London and Lisbon. In any event the slave revolts of Saint-Domingue brought French business to an abrupt stop, while British slavers continued to profit from further price increases until the trade was abolished in 1807.

2

The uncertain balance of payments estimates in the top panel of table 2.5 probably underrate the contribution of the colonial and quasi-colonial world to Britain's international position. The 'net India transfers' and the 'Irish rents' are minimum estimates; non-merchandise inflows from the British West Indies are not included for lack of annual evidence. But this margin of confidence should be weighed against the inevitable errors in the residual totals for 'illegal imports' and in their regional allocation.

In any event the 'partial balances' with the colonial and quasi-colonial world might easily have covered Britain's massive payments to foreigners for war expenses in 1797–1815. Overall, Britain's involvement abroad since the consolidation of English control over Bengal in 1757 would have brought the national debt back from the Dutch and others by the late 1790s. It might have subsequently raised net claims on foreigners to some £46 million by 1820 (Davis, 1979: 55; Cuenca Esteban, 2001).

The most striking message of table 2.5 is the phenomenal growth of British carrying earnings on the colonial and quasi-colonial trades during the French wars. Since the routes in question were largely served by British shipping under the Navigation Acts, mounting carrying earnings per cargo unit are largely explained by soaring rates of freight and insurance; elsewhere in the trades with northern Europe and with the United States, neutral vessels took growing shares of British cargoes as British merchant ships and seamen were diverted to convoy duty or to war service.

The course of France's external fortunes is even less clear. It has been suggested that French net foreign investment was zero in 1815 (Cameron, 1961: 531). Speculation on prior trends can go either way. To be sure, French overall deficits on commodity account turn into large credits through 1808–16; France drew considerable sums from helpless or compliant neighbours (Manger, 1923: 110; Buist, 1974); and French predatory warfare probably was less onerous in foreign exchange than were British subsidies and land armies. But French mercantile profits and carrying earnings can hardly have been substantial – particularly as France's largest and most dynamic trades, those with the Hanse towns, Scandinavia and Russia, were handled by foreign merchant houses through their subsidiaries in French ports (Asselain, 1984: I, 61). The loss of Saint-Domingue alone involved considerable liquidation of French assets with consequent loss of earnings. In any event, French foreign claims and holdings after the post-war indemnities were a fraction of their British counterparts.

3

In 1787, British centres of power were well on their way to controlling the lion's share of non-European resources and markets. In 1716, their claims to pre-eminence had already been considerable. Britain's trading system encompassed some of the most promising areas of Asia and North America. The exclusive right to deliver African slaves and other commodities in Spanish America, once held by the Dutch and then by the French (1701), had turned into British hands (1713–50). The dice

Table 2.5 *Great Britain and France: balance of payments components by areas, 1772–1815 (period averages of annual values in £000 at current prices)*

	1772–1775	1776–1783	1787–1789		1797–1812, 1814–1815	
	Britain	Britain	Britain	France	Britain	France
COLONIAL WORLD (CW = own and foreign colonies + Ireland + Asia + Africa)[1]:						
Imports from CW	−10,719	−10,375%	−15,927%	−9,173	−32,085%	−98
Idem re-exported[2]	4,618	4,422	3,630	5,505	9,352	10
Domestic exports to CW	5,461	5,649	7,537	3,810	19,787	357
Illegal imports from CW	−680	−1,125	−450		−350	
Net merchandise exports	−1,319	−1,428	−5,209	142	−3,294	269
Freight and insurance earnings	1,337	2,421	1,768		8,095	
Mercantile profits[3]	752	837	1,182		1,467	
Net inflows from slave trade[4]	546	210	353		426	
Minimum net India transfers	403	499	1,074		195	
Minimum Irish rents[5]	366	490	614		903	
Partial balance with CW	2,085	3,028	−217		7,793	
UNITED STATES[1]:						
Imports from the US	−3,175	−245	−1,246	−401	−4,236	−1,523
Idem re-exported[2]	1,368	101	282	234	1,180	97
Domestic exports to the US	2,153	595	2,567	56	8,075	789
Net ship purchases	−110	−89	−55			
Illegal imports from the US	−170	−125	−90		−116	
Net merchandise exports	67	237	1,458	−111	4,903	−637
Freight and insurance earnings	516	155	311		378	
Mercantile profits	55	11	65		132	
Emigrants' funds	−79	−61	−46		−94	
Partial balance with the US	559	343	1,788		5,319	
EUROPE AND LEVANT, EXCLUDING IRELAND[1]:						
Imports from 'Europe'	−6,869	−8,431	−9,958	−11,964	−18,849	−13,614
Idem re-exported[2]	1,118	694	940	1,220	2,203	885
Domestic exports to 'Europe'	6,068	6,150	7,741	6,750	11,306	12,725
Illegal imports from 'Europe'	−850	−1,250	−360		−699	

Net merchandise exports	−533	−2,836	−1,636	−3,993	−6,038	−4
Freight and insurance earnings	661	1,442	724		1,543	
Mercantile profits	208	183	319		337	
Partial balance with 'Europe'	336	−1,211	−594		−4,157	
OTHER BALANCE OF PAYMENTS COMPONENTS:						
Foreign war subsidies		−646			−2,630	
Foreign war expenses					−4,333	
Balance of debt service	−301	−579	−553		1,348	
Current account balance	2,679	936	425		3,339	
Change in foreign reserves	2,900	206	2,217		354	
Capital outflows	−221	730	−1,792		2,984	
Accumulated balance of Britain's net credits (end years: 1775, 1783 . . .)	−13,000	−7,163	−16,896		30,000	
FRENCH NET BULLION INFLOWS				2,531		1,875
from Spain				2,158		776
from Holland				−1		345
from England				180		553

[1]Provisional estimates of imports and domestic exports from and to the foreign American colonies through Spain, Gibraltar, Portugal, the British West Indies, Britain's conquered islands and the United States have been discounted from the relevant sub-totals and added to, or retained within, the 'colonial world' figures.

[2]Total re-exports of non-European goods annually allocated to the 'colonial world', to the United States, and to 'Europe and Levant excluding Ireland' with the shares of direct imports of non-European goods from the respective areas out of total imports of such goods. Re-exports of 'imports from "Europe"' include both 'European' and non-European goods.

[3]Mercantile profits on the slave and Asian trades excluded.

[4]Inadvertently mislabelled as 'Mercantile profits in the slave trade' in Cuenca Esteban, 2001: 60, 65. Now recalculated as in table 2.4 above (line 10). Entered as 'zero' since 1808.

[5]One-half of Irish rents seemingly remitted to absentee landlords residing in Britain. Annual series of total remittances constructed with contemporary estimates for 1779, 1783, 1797 and 1804, as in George O'Brien, 1918: 62. The soundness of this procedure depends on whether or not such rental transfers remained stable over time; note that the bulk of Irish land appears to have been let by long-term leases: Mokyr, 1983: 83, 100.

Sources and procedures: British figures by geographical areas calculated with similar sources and procedures as in Cuenca Esteban (1997, 2001). A major error in the import total for 1811 has since been corrected; all import totals now incorporate additional evidence. The only other substantial changes or additions are those mentioned in table notes 4 and 5 above. Strong qualifications still apply. Irish rents as in table note 5 above. The French current trade values are those used to calculate the values at constant prices in tables 2.1–2.3: see Appendix.

had been thrown in a cluster of events whose long-term significance could hardly have been foreseen at the time. In the first half of the seventeenth century, Dutch commercial tactics in South-east Asia had driven English merchants from the spice trade to India (Irwin, 1991). In the 1640s, Dutch merchants had introduced sugar cultivation in the future English-colony of Barbados. The capture of Jamaica from Spain in 1655 had been a disappointing second prize to the coveted Hispaniola. A late arrival in North America had initially confined English settlements to Virginia. Subsequent expansion to the Hudson basin had come as a compromise in the second Anglo-Dutch war (1665–7). By 1677–88 Indian labour at a halfpenny a day, and rising demand at falling prices in European markets, had opened a broad re-export trade to Europe in Indian calicos, Bengal silks, sugar and tobacco (Davis, 1954: 150–3). In 1688, dynastic accident and political unrest at home had brought Dutch help against France and Spain in the Nine Years War (1689–97) and in the War of the Spanish Succession (1702–14). It has been argued that Indian goods alone had decisively contributed to England's successful war effort in Europe in 1702–8 (Jones, 1988: 27, 211–22). To be sure, in 1716 French competition in India and elsewhere remained a threat, and Dutch priorities in Asia had switched from pepper and finer spices to textiles and tea. But Britain's North American colonies, and the English East India Company's trading posts or 'factories' in Madras (1639), Bombay (1661) and Calcutta (1696), were to prove solid and distinctive assets. It is tempting to suggest that only a major redrawing of the colonial map could have redressed the balance.

As it was, subsequent warfare most often turned in Britain's favour. The uncertain comparisons of transoceanic trade in figures 2.1 and 2.2 must be regarded with extreme caution: the procedures involved are fraught with technical problems, and the long-run trends in French values are thought to incorporate unmeasurable upward bias. The short-term cycles in figure 2.1 most clearly underline the relative weakness of French colonial trade during the war of the Austrian Succession (1740–48) and during the Seven Years War (1756–63). Subsequent growth in French transoceanic imports was burdened with hesitant or contradictory policies and was confined to the tropical crops of Saint-Domingue – themselves dependent of the slave trade (Tarrade, 1972: I, 776–84; Stein, 1983). One of France's missed opportunities was failure to develop firm commercial ties with the United States after 1783. By contrast, since the late 1750s Britain's non-European trade, now strengthened by political control over Bengal and enlarged with four West Indian islands and with French Canada, would have soared on a wide geographical front well above French levels. In the quasi-colonial trade with Ireland, both

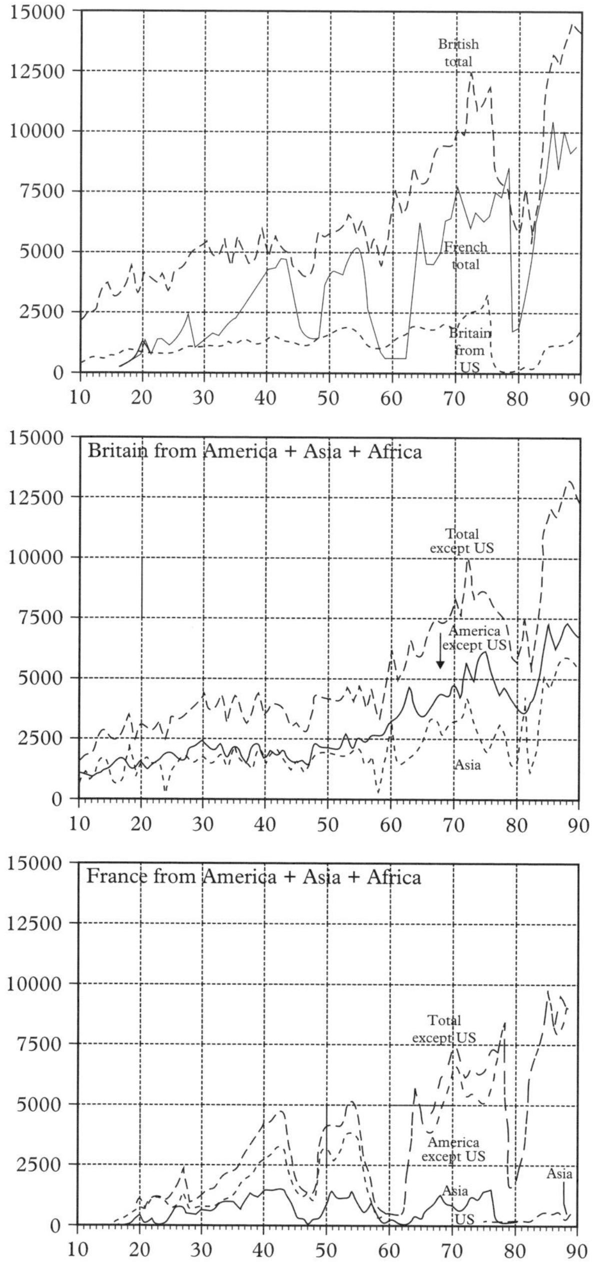

Figure 2.1 Imports CIF from the non-European world, 1710–90* (annual values in £000 at constant prices of 1788)

*British and French imports from Africa are negligible throughout.

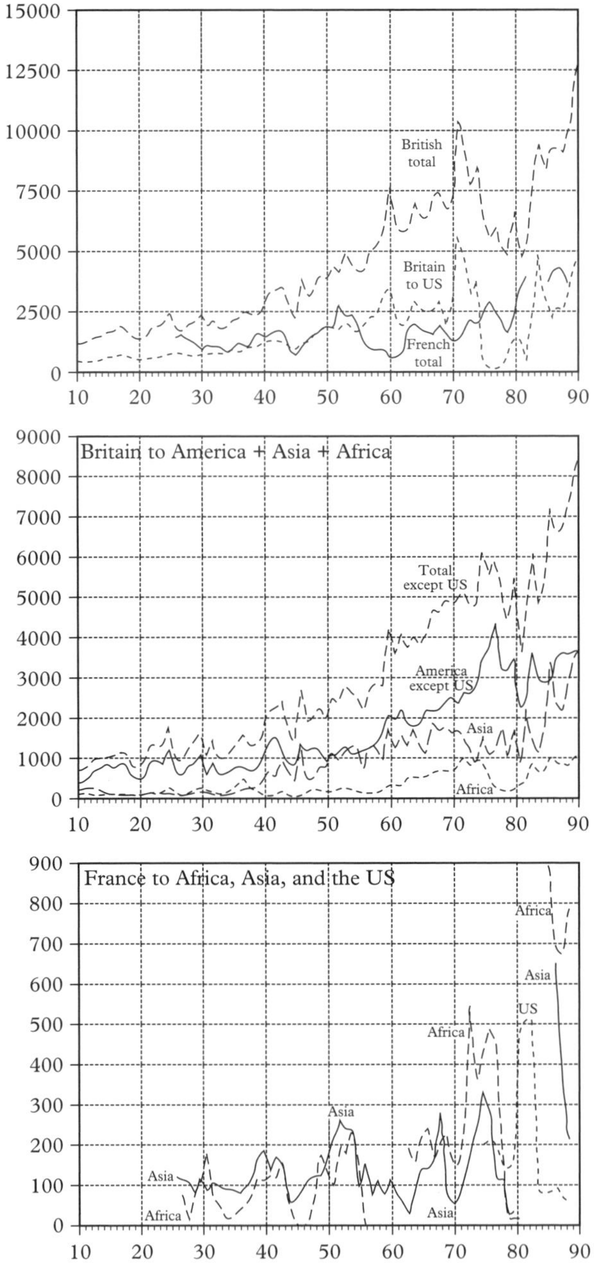

Figure 2.2 Total exports FOB to the non-European world, 1710–90 (annual values in £000 at constant prices of 1788)

*British and French imports from Africa are negligible throughout.

import and export volumes came close to those with the United States and grew at a similar pace up to 1775.

Ralph Davis portrayed long-term growth in British total exports as driven by 'a series of spurts, each touched off by some new factor which operated violently for a time and then lost its initial force'. Through 1700–70, the old wave on the wane would have been re-exports of Indian textiles, and the new dynamic factor was demand for domestic manufactures in captive markets of America, Ireland and India. Demand from these areas was reinforced, from mid-century onwards, by cottons exports to West Africa and by the growth to maturity of new re-export trades to Europe in Carolina rice, China tea and eventually West Indian coffee (Davis, 1962a: 293–6). As noted in section I, Indian commodities appear to have remained Britain's largest re-export trade in non-European goods through 1772–1820. But the most dynamic factor during the long boom of 1783–1801 and beyond was American demand for British domestic exports – notably in the United States through 1788–1801, but also in Britain's 'conquered islands' in 1794–1815 and in the Iberian empires through much of the period. The famous industries of the industrial revolution, cotton goods and iron manufactures did not play dynamic roles in the growth of British domestic exports until the 1790s and the 1810s respectively (Crouzet, 1980: 52–66, 69–72).

4

> 'It would not be worth my while to make [your engine] for three counties only, but I find it very well worth my while to make for all the world'
>
> (Matthew Boulton to James Watt, 1769, as quoted in Scherer, 1984: 13).

Did external involvement make a major contribution to Britain's rise to economic and military pre-eminence? Since Britain's overseas connections were far wider and more dynamic than those of her European rivals, external causal roles would seem most plausible if Britain's domestic economic performance had also been exceptional. But it has been speculated that British economic growth was slow, that British per capita income grew no faster than the French, and that any British technological lead was limited to a few famous industries. Less uncertain work has stressed that, by the end of the eighteenth century, parts of the European continent had attained similar industrial growth, albeit in different sectors, as parts of England. These findings highlight long-term pan-European development and downplay the role of extra-European factors, but their implications do not need to be entirely Eurocentric. Recent perspectives are shifting the focus from British-led technological growth to Europe's ability to overcome a Malthusian trap in the eighteenth century. By drawing attention to western Europe's food supply, and to income growth from all sources, such views explicitly leave an open door to major external contributions (Komlos, 2000; Clark, 2001: 65–69).

The external dimensions of European economic growth are best outlined in a global context. In Pomeranz's view, as late as 1750 parts of western Europe show remarkable similarities in living standards, in capital stock and in economic institutions, with parts of China or Japan. The key common constraint on self-sustained economic growth would have laid in land-intensive production. Western Europe's eventual lead would thus owe much to privileged access to forest-saving coal, and to overseas land, in a timely set of global conjunctures. By comparison to China, some of western Europe's vast coal resources were secure from Mongol raids and lay close to waterways, skilled labour and markets; as an added bonus, the flood-prone British coal mines stimulated the early development of widely understood principles in the application of steam power. Fortuitous circumstances favouring Europe's access to scarce land and energy also included China's withdrawal from overseas expansion in the fifteenth century, China's massive demand for silver, and the unanticipated impact of European diseases in America. Europe's overseas frontier was *distinctive* in a number of ways also involving chance. Land-intensive production required substantial workforces, but much European labour could be spared for industrial production with exceptional degrees of coercion over American silver miners, African slaves and Asian weavers. The African slave trade, and the plantation economies it helped to create, were sufficiently dependent on external food and on European manufactures so as not to pose 'small-market' constraints. And American silver also spared European inputs, as it could be exchanged in Asia for land-intensive products. Overall, Europe's *distinctive* overseas frontier provided vital land resources and a host of dynamic, non-quantifiable windfalls involving low-cost territorial expansion financed by trade and by overseas taxation, learning opportunities in land management and in military deployment, stronger and more stable states drawing on less unpopular modes of taxation, and a more intensive reorientation of 'industrious' labour effort towards market activity. Without privileged access to external resources, and to external demand, western Europe could have fallen back onto labour-intensive paths, and the spinning and weaving inventions of the late eighteenth century might have remained a footnote in technological history (Pomeranz, 2000).

Pomeranz's global view includes chance elements, permissive ecological considerations and dynamic European connections centred on coal and empire. On the matter of chance, we may expand on the obvious corollary that Britain was best placed to lead industrialisation and to avert what came to be perceived as an impending subsistence crisis. Britain's deck of cards included well-located coal mines requiring drainage, an optimal resource mix that had focused inventors' and craftmen's attention over two centuries (Harris, 1997: 557–8), a late American settlement in most promising areas, an insular location that held off foreign armies and fostered 'blue water' policies and a French coastal geography not suitable for harbouring fleets of large warships in the English Channel (Baugh, this volume, p. 237). Arguably, chance also was involved in bestowing Britain with a relatively docile working class, with mechanical skills brought by Huguenot refugees and with a strong state most responsive to commercial and industrial interests (O'Brien, 1993). As noted in section III, in the areas of warfare and transoceanic trade the dice had been thrown, seemingly in England's favour, in a cluster of fortuitous events prior to 1716.

On matters of ecology, Pomeranz has used physical coefficients to estimate the amount of average-yielding British land that would have been required to replace the energy supplied by coal and by several colonial commodities. One implication of Pomeranz's coefficients is that sugar and cotton imports alone, excluding cotton from the United States, effectively 'saved' 1.5 million domestic acres in 1772, 2.6 million in 1790, 6 million by 1815, and 8.1 million by 1820 – out of a total arable land of 17 million acres. To this must be added the direct contribution of the remaining colonial and quasi-colonial farm products, and such other benefits as the appetite-suppressing qualities of tea and sugar. Indirect land savings also resulted from the adoption of New World plants such as the potato – 'without which neither Ireland nor Prussia could have exported grain to England' (Pomeranz, 2000: 274–6). The alternative estimates at current prices in table 2.6 are not directly comparable but they suggest two additional points. Contrary to Pomeranz's calculations, the contribution of the colonial and quasi-colonial world to Britain's land savings possibly was more substantial than that of coal since the 1770s at least. And the major leap forward would have been made in the periods 1699–1701 and 1772–5.

Such timely contributions were not merely permissive. Long before Britain's naval pre-eminence and the Industrial Revolution consolidated privileged access to massive external resources, coal and empire helped to support Britain's differential population growth – the most distinctive feature of the Industrial Revolution period in one recent view (Clark, 2001). The domestic inputs freed by net agricultural imports helped to sustain further market expansion overseas and fostered structural change at home. Related urban growth has been linked to technological progress

Table 2.6 *Agricultural and coal consumption in Britain, 1699–1820*[1] *(annual averages by selected periods in £m at current prices)*

	1699–1701	1772–1775	1784–1789	1790–1797	1798–1808	1815–1820
1. Farm net output	32.3	44.8	46.7	52.2	54.7	70.7
2. Domestic coal consumption	0.9	3.3	4.6	6.0	10.7	15.9
3. percentage of line 1	3%	7%	10%	12%	19%	22%
4. Net imports of farm products[2]	1.0	9.6	14.5	19.5	32.1	40.9
5. percentage of line 1	3%	22%	31%	37%	59%	58%
Geographical origin of net imports of farm products (line 4):						
6. from the 'colonial world'[3]	0.3	4.8	9.4	10.5	15.0	21.2
7. from the US[1]		0.7	0	−0.7	0.6	3.8
8. from Europe excluding Ireland	0.7	4.1	5.2	9.7	16.4	15.9

[1] England and Wales in 1699–1701 only.
[2] Imports minus re-exports minus domestic exports. The latter include estimates of the raw-material content of textile exports.
[3] 'Colonial world' = British and foreign colonies + Ireland + Asia + Africa (as in tables 2.1–2.3 and 2.5 above).
[4] The US figures for 1699–1701 are included under 'colonial world'.

Sources and procedures: farm net output estimated from decadal figures for England, kindly supplied by Gregory Clark (times 1.2 since 1772 to account for Wales and Scotland). Net imports in 1699–1701 calculated from Davis, 1962: 300–303; for 1772–1820 estimated as in Cuenca Esteban, 1997, 2001. Raw material content of textile exports in 1699–1701 guessed as 30 per cent of textile export values; shares for 1772–1820 roughly as in Cuenca Esteban, 1994, Appendix. Domestic coal production linearly interpolated from relevant benchmarks in Flinn, 1984: 26. Coal exports in 1700 as in Davis, 1962: 302: 1699–1701; for other years calculated from quantities in PRO (Customs 5, 9, 11, 17) times prices in Beveridge, 1939: 193–6.

(Allen, this volume; Komlos, 2000: 316). The relative importance of colonial raw materials cannot be measured for lack of domestic output figures; but Britain's exceptionally large and often cheaper imports should have lowered local industrial costs to a greater extent than elsewhere.

The position taken here builds on the permissive and dynamic dimensions of Pomeranz's view by specifying further distinctive British connections centred on trade and empire. General reasons for this choice may be sought by way of controlled exclusion, with a primary focus on the eighteenth-century roots of Britain's subsequent economic pre-eminence. Industrial growth had regional dimensions, but the power that mediated such growth was exercised or delegated at national levels. The search for national environments most conducive to self-sustained industrial growth is narrowed down by political, economic and military considerations. Central Europe's polities and markets were fragmented and comparatively small. Spain and Portugal were reduced by poor domestic resources, by dynastic accident and by fortuitous patterns of early American settlement in densely populated areas, to subsidiary roles in providing bullion, slaves and markets. The fiscal implications of Holland's vulnerability to French territorial power seemingly override any other explanation of Dutch economic decline (O'Brien, 2000). By comparison to France, English coal helped to alleviate Britain's relative land scarcity and focused inventive effort on iron and steam technology. Aside from coal, Britain's most clearly distinctive advantages would seemingly have run from trade and empire to technological and industrial growth, to domestic income and investment, and to state finances and warfare. All such connections are inseparable from one another in the sense that none of them needs to be claimed as decisive or indispensable in a world of unique historical conjunctures. The central point is that Britain's most clearly distinctive, long-standing and cumulative external advantages probably had the widest range of strategic and economic implications – when compared to those running from uncertain rates of local agricultural growth, from domestic markets not clearly larger than the French Five Farms alone, from widely shared economic institutions, or from questionable degrees of technological prowess. The argument that follows is that long-standing hypotheses on the size and significance of external influences have been raised to the status of presumptions by unsuccessful efforts to refute their validity.

The first distinctive British connections highlighted here run from trade and empire to technological and industrial growth. One such connection would stem from Britain's privileged access to technology-intensive imports of Indian calicos and muslins. It has also been suggested that British commercial expansion fostered invention and innovation through its impact on urban growth (Allen, this volume, p. 000; Komlos, 2000: 316). Figure 2.3 further reminds us that the British domestic economy, unlike the French, was almost continuously exposed to rapidly expanding overseas demand through 1726–71 and since the early 1780s – long before the technological breakthroughs of the late eighteenth century began to play dynamic roles in the 1790s. British external markets were distinctive in the breadth of products involved, in the overall rate of growth and in the relative continuity of this growth through peace and warfare.

The argument does not need to be that British technological growth was import-driven or export-led; but that the weight of suggestive inference, in a comparative context, is sufficiently strong to place external influences on a par at least with indigenous creativity. The notion that British inventiveness was vastly superior is no longer tenable for the early eighteenth century at least (Inkster, 1990; O'Brien, 1997); Britain did not set the pace in silks, linens, needles, cutlery, glass, woollens, porcelain, paper, calico printing and tin-plate rolling (Komlos, 2000: 309–12). By 1815, however, the commodity composition of British domestic exports reveals comparative advantage in many of these products (Temin, 1997). It is now widely believed that Britain's main advantage here lay in the ability to apply and to refine foreign and domestic inventions. But such 'microinventive' activity is thought to be most responsive to demand shifts and to sustained demand stimuli. Other potentially dynamic effects of expanding markets pivot around inventive focusing, learning by doing, cumulative knowledge and external economies between firms and industries (Mokyr, 1999: 61–4). The fact that such dynamic effects cannot be measured does not grant the right to allocate the burden of proof; theoretical arguments on the primacy of supply or demand factors in this connection run both ways (Cuenca Esteban, 1997: 899–900). It is nevertheless worth noting that the fastest technological growth occurred in British cotton and in British iron products – the very European industries most directly exposed to technology-intensive imports of Asian fabrics and to dynamic American demand. And that recent work has documented further specific connections between export demand and product and process improvement in British industrial sectors (Burt, 1995; Bowen, 2002).

If Britain's external demand did have a dynamic impact, one would expect to see rising ratios of British industrial exports over industrial output in significant time periods. Several authors have adduced Crafts' small and erratic ratios to question the causal role of export markets; but the alleged statistical grounds were undermined, on their own contestable terms, by Crafts' subsequent downward revision of his industrial growth rates. More recent and still unchallenged calculations, from eleven-year

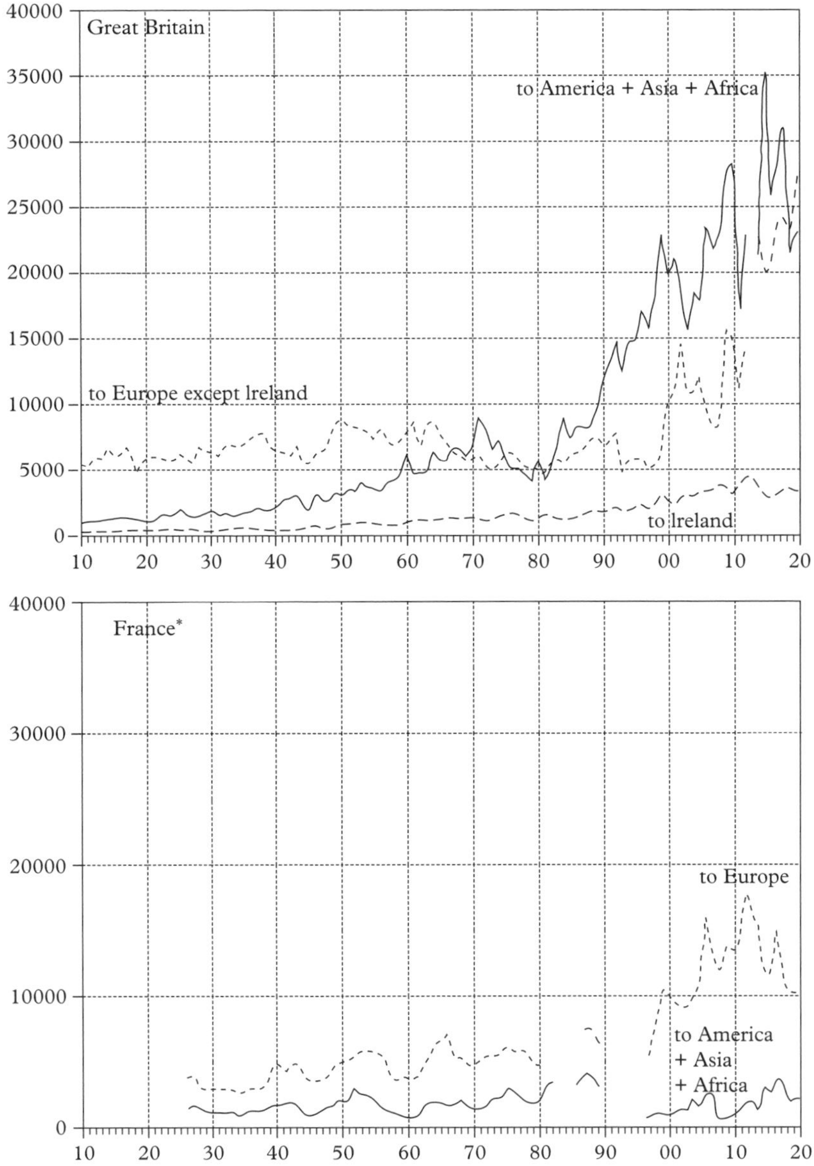

Figure 2.3 British and French domestic exports, 1710–1820 (annual values in £000 at constant prices of 1788)

*Conjectural trends for 1726–82 calculated as total exports by destination times the relevant ratios of domestic over total exports in 1787–9.

averages of domestic export values at constant prices yield almost continuously rising export ratios through 1723–1851 (Cuenca Esteban, 1997).

Mokyr has pointed to the modestly rising trend in 1760–83, at a time of 'feverish' technological progress, to suggest that 'the causality may be running from technology to exports and not the reverse' (Mokyr, 1999: 70). It should be noted that the upward trend in export ratios from 1760 to 1783 is substantially flattened by the use of eleven-year averages, because British industrial exports rose during the Seven Years War (1756–63) and fell during the American War (1776–83). Moreover, such figures are too blunt an instrument to distinguish between the potential impact of export demand on technological breakthroughs, on the gradual improvement of existing technology and on simple additions to factors of production.

Trends in export ratios are most suggestive if we regard technological growth as a *long-term process* involving gradual improvement of machines and skills. Considering that such 'microinventive' improvements are most clearly responsive to sustained demand stimuli, it is worth stressing that 47 to 72 per cent of Britain's *additional* industrial output appears to have been exported in 1700–70. The famous technological breakthroughs from the late 1760s to the early 1780s were no 'accident' but the likely culmination of long-term, possibly export-driven progress. The particularly steep upward trend in export ratios in the 1780s and 1790s went along with vital improvement in the early spinning machines and in related workers' skills. In any event, the only point that needs to be made here is that highly publicised efforts to downplay the dynamic role of British domestic exports have been found to lack statistical and theoretical foundation.

In a different key, few economists today are easily persuaded that such ratios and correlations necessarily imply causation from the demand to the supply side of the economy. Those who think in terms of neoclassical models regard purchasing power as an endogenous variable, ultimately originating in the volume and efficiency of production. Even when the economy is viewed as open to international trade the question can be raised, from theory alone, as to whether overseas demand was simply a function of home-generated income that was made available abroad via imports and factor flows.

Here again, empirical work has not been kind to such supply-side arguments. One test was aimed at Deane and Cole's perception of British export growth as a lagged response to import expansion within a closed colonial system of commodity flows and payments. Hatton and others identified non-British sources of colonial demand and found no support for the alleged line of causality under short-run conditions; if anything, the admittedly inconclusive results point in the opposite direction through 1746–1800 at least. Their restrained conclusion that 'exports cannot be regarded as a purely passive element in eighteenth-century trade' is supported by Smith's test on the American and African trades through 1701–70 (Hatton *et al.*, 1983; Smith, 1992: 7–8).

Theoretical argument also points to export-led growth during the eighteenth century. It has long been recognised that, under short-run conditions and with less than full employment, exogenous demand growth from overseas markets, from government spending and from autonomous domestic investment can provide significant Keynesian stimuli to industrial production. Judging from decadal estimates through 1740–80, Crafts speculated that exports were the largest of these categories of British expenditure in 1740–60; similar considerations might apply to peacetime years in 1700–60 and in 1780–1801 (Crafts, 1985: 134; Crafts, 1981: 14–15). In the more prevalent war periods, government spending, export demand, and their multiplier effects, most likely stimulated the iron and shipbuilding sectors; British loans and territorial acquisitions, themselves a source of new demand at the expense of foreigners, also contributed to domestic investment and possibly lowered the cost of capital (John, 1954–5: 332–3, 337–8, 342).

Further insight might be gained from intelligible and soundly specified models linking trade and industrialisation. One central requirement of such models is a series of export over import prices, generally referred to as the net barter terms of trade. But available calculations for the eighteenth century rest on small samples of commodity prices, and proxies from import and export volumes do not control for seemingly wide fluctuations in trade balances (Deane and Cole, 1962: 84–5; Smith, 1992: 18–20; Hatton *et al.*, 1983: 167–168). Judging from ongoing work, Britain's terms of trade with the colonial and quasi-colonial world were sufficiently favourable in 1784–1806 to offset an opposite trend with Europe. Another requirement of trade models is that domestic supply shifts due to technological progress be disentangled from those prompted by simple additions to factor endowments – a matter of guesswork in the present state of growth accounting. We can only speculate that, for relevant British trades in pertinent time periods, positive cyclical correlation between export volumes and export prices might lend support to the contention that shifts in demand, rather than in supply, largely explain the most significant short-term variations in exports.

Pending further empirical work on the eighteenth century, existing alternatives to the export-led hypothesis are not demonstrably sounder. Supply-side argument has focused on the last two decades of the century and beyond – a questionable choice because British industrialisation had acquired a dynamic of its own by the 1790s. The more extreme claims from economic historians rest, not always explicitly, on a choice of neoclassical reasoning where demand cannot play but a passive role. Critics of such claims have seemingly overlooked hasty calculations and undisclosed sources and procedures; they have questioned the relevance of such key assumptions as full employment and, less directly, the explanatory power of complex general equilibrium models (O'Brien and Engerman, 1991: 200–205; Mokyr, 1999: 71; O'Brien, 1998: 75; Temin, 2000). Findlay alone has made a transparent attempt at modelling, albeit with questionable data and with neoclassical assumptions. Significantly, he qualified his initial supply-side position with common-sense considerations and subsequently concluded that there can be 'little doubt that British growth in the eighteenth century was "export-led" ' (Findlay, 1982: 186–7; Findlay, 1990: 22).

A second set of distinctive British connections runs from trade and empire to domestic income and investment. These connections are not central to Pomeranz's view, in so far as capital was relatively abundant in both western Europe and parts of Asia; here the main external contribution would have laid in the land-intensive products that freed other European inputs for industrialisation. Still, Britain's financial returns from quasi-colonial trade and empire were distinctive within western Europe. Estimates of British colonial wealth grow by leaps and bounds with every dose of archival research (Burnard, 2001: 506–7). British profits on the slave trade, as calculated by Engerman, could have amounted to 39 per cent of British commercial and industrial investment around 1770 (Solow, 1985: 105–6).

It has been argued, from undisclosed calculations on Solow's terms, that similar investible sums were generated in banking, insurance, horse-breeding and other domestic activities (Eltis and Engerman, 2000: 135–6). On the matter of size, it may be countered that the reference calculations should extend to the entire external inflows from the colonial and quasi-colonial world into the British economy. Eltis and Engerman have focused on British profits from the slave trade and from the West Indian plantations; other potentially relevant items include carrying earnings, mercantile profits on British colonial trade in general, those on re-exports of Asian commodities in particular, net India transfers, and Irish rents remitted to absentee landlords in Britain. Judging from the provisional calculations in table 2.5, Britain's 'partial balance' with the colonial and quasi-colonial world would have stood at £2.64 million per year in 1772–5. In sharp contrast, Engerman's original argument rests on slave-trade profits alone – at £342,200 in 1770 (Engerman, 1972: 440; Solow, 1985).

On matters of significance, it is true that the accumulating evidence on the share of colonial funds invested in British industry and commerce remains inconclusive. The most recent account has placed this investment share at 30 to 50 per cent of 'triangular trade profits' (Blackburn, 1997: 541–552). But 10 per cent of Britain's 'partial balance' with the colonial and quasi-colonial world would still amount, in 1772–80, to 55 per cent of Feinstein's estimate of 'gross domestic fixed capital formation' in industry and commerce through 1771–80 (Feinstein, 1978: 41: £520,000 per year). This ratio falls substantially in subsequent decades, but Britain's external gains prior to the Industrial Revolution were arguably the most important. Such calculations by themselves prove nothing – nor do the opposite, often hidden judgements they are meant to expose; but the point is worth making because 'small ratios' arguments of various types have been claimed to *disprove* significance in this context, despite suggestive inference to the contrary (references in Cuenca Esteban, 1997: 881, note 7).

In any event, the argument does not need to be that any particular source of investible funds was decisively large, but that some historically unique *combinations* of such funds played more significant roles than others over longer time periods prior to the Industrial Revolution. Financial returns on several British domestic activities were not distinctive in a western European context – French horse-breeding was by far the larger industry; British banking and insurance probably drew larger returns from transoceanic trade than did their continental counterparts. Overall, as noted in section II, Britain's net financial inflows from trade and empire were far more substantial than those secured by France. It is not necessary to contend that such British inflows were larger than those generated within the domestic economy, or that they were vital or indispensable for industrialisation, to presume that the *total* sums involved, and the relative stability of these totals through peace and warfare, most likely played major and *distinctive* roles in key British sectors – not least through their multiplier and cumulative effects within the British income stream.

The significance of external inflows is further enhanced when we focus on state finances and warfare. Here the main line of causation runs from domestic economies to trade and empire, but opposite trends were distinctive in the British case. Until the 1790s, both British and French wars were financed largely with government borrowing, followed by stepped-up domestic taxation to service and to amortise the accumulated debt. But Britain's privileged Indian connection, and her larger and better coordinated transoceanic trade, more substantially helped to engross government funding through the eighteenth century and beyond. The initial upswing in Britain's war expenses, from 1689 to 1713, owed much to large loans from incorporated trade companies with non-British sources of wealth (O'Brien, 1998: 64–5). It has been argued that Indian goods alone decisively contributed to England's successful war effort in Europe in 1702–08 (Jones, 1988: 27, 211–22). After the British victory at Plassey in 1757 and the seizure of Indian territorial revenues in 1765, Indian wealth seemingly helped to pay down Britain's foreign debt and to finance expenses abroad during the French wars (Cuenca Esteban, 2001). On the fiscal side, only a fraction of the additional tax revenue required for British warfare can be attributed to domestic economic growth. In 1788–92, close to 20 per cent of British tax revenue came from customs and excise duties on colonial or quasi-colonial commodities excluding tobacco. This contribution was all the more significant because indirect taxation, Britain's largest source of revenue as compared to France, was less visible and less unpopular than were direct taxes and contributions. More generally, potential gains from trade and empire possibly encouraged direct beneficiaries to shoulder mounting rates of taxation during warfare (O'Brien, 1988: 6–7, 11). Actual gains certainly helped to retain bullion at home – the government's 'war chest' for the purchase of armaments, for subsidies to allies and for military deployment overseas (O'Brien, 1998: 55).

Trade and empire only partly explain Britain's growing financial strength while the French state came close to bankruptcy by the 1760s (Bordo and White, 1991). In the British case, however, chance and industry reinforced one another in a long-term process where small initial differences were most likely to turn into cumulative advantage. War was financed in part by the domestic economy, but successful warfare swelled the inflows of land-intensive inputs, the size of markets, the domestic income stream, and the home tax base; related economic growth further increased the likelihood of further military advantage. This positive feedback process was self-financing so long as a perception of military superiority enhanced the likely winner's credibility to repay war debts. It cannot be stressed sufficiently that the British economy drew differential returns from successful warfare, not least by encroaching upon foreign supplies and markets and by slowing down technological diffusion at critical junctures. Over the long run, any implication of British superiority would be robust only if one or more competing nations had enjoyed similar opportunities overseas and still had been left behind.

5

Accident plays a role in history but its vagaries provide no useful lessons; all we can hope is to encroach upon the domain of chance. This chapter has drawn on multi-level comparisons to specify a unique set of permissive and dynamic factors underlying Britain's rise to economic and military pre-eminence. On a world scale, western Europe's key advantage over the most prosperous parts of Asia would have laid in privileged access to external land resources and to optimally located coal. The argument does not need to be that a land-locked Europe would have suffered a crippling Malthusian crisis, but that timely inflows of land products most likely saved western Europe, and Britain in particular, from falling back onto labour-intensive paths (Pomeranz, 2000: 279–81). Nor is it denied that, in Britain and elsewhere, previously acquired endowments and arguably distinctive institutions possibly afforded significant advantages on a world scale. By comparison to such domestic factors, however, Britain's long-standing and cumulative *external* connections seemingly were most distinctive, most numerous, and most wide-ranging. The central question posed in this chapter is why a particular European country, with no clear superiority in the early eighteenth century and with unexceptional inventive prowess, eventually acquired a temporary but lasting lead within western Europe. It has been submitted that the *sum total* of Britain's fortuitous advantages, related patterns of *external* involvement, and inseparable feedback loops, predominantly accounts, more than any other set of domestic factors, for Britain's military pre-eminence and for permanent structural change in the British economy.

Appendix: sources for tables 2.1–2.3, table 2.5, and figures 2.1–2.3

The period coverage in tables 2.1–2.3 and 2.5 was imposed by the relatively poor quantity and quality of the French statistics. By 1787–9 the French official records had improved in accuracy and comprehensiveness; contraband trade had sharply declined in Britain and is likely to have shrunk in both countries as a result of the Anglo-French Commercial Treaty of 1786 (in force until 1791). Still, the British trade quantities have required uncertain valuation with incomplete price evidence, whereas the French official values were calculated at rates that often differed significantly from market prices. Resulting errors may be further compounded by the use of a single series of annual exchange rates to convert the given values in francs into pounds sterling.

As noted in the text, the uncertain comparisons of transoceanic trade in figures 2.1–2.3 must also be regarded with extreme caution. The British figures to 1771 are official values at constant prices, scaled to current values on the relevant ratios for 1788. Deflation of the French current values through 1716–86 rests on eleven price series with constant weights.

Most of the sources and procedures for the new breakdowns of British trade and balance of payments (1772–1820) are those specified in Cuenca Esteban (1997, 2001). A major error in the import total for 1811 has since been corrected. The import totals now incorporate additional evidence. See also notes to table 2.5. The key source for Britain's indirect trades with foreign America is Armytage (1953); also Crouzet (1990a) and Cuenca Esteban (1984) among others.

French trade values by areas and commodities for 1787–9, *c.* 1797–1806 and 1807–20 were compiled from Archives Nationales de Paris, F 12, Carton 251, 'Tableaux imprimés des importations et exportations'; note that Chabert's annual totals from this source inconsistently include or exclude sizeable bullion flows: Chabert (1945–9). Most of the French trade values for 1716–80 are Bruyard's area totals as rendered and supplemented in Romano (1957). French trade with the United States in 1775–86 as in Buron (1931–2). Other trade figures and perceptive analysis of French official valuation procedures in Tarrade (1972). French prices in Chabert (1945–9), Fourastie (1958), Hanauer (1876–8), Hauser (1936) and Labrousse (1933); partly dated methodological work in Cuenca Esteban (1987). Annual rates of exchange (London on Paris) were calculated from the first monthly quotations in the bi-weekly issues of the Course of the Exchange.

Part II

Agriculture and industrialisation

3 European farmers and the British 'agricultural revolution'

James Simpson

Indebted in great part to Arthur Young, the traditional view of European agriculture over the long eighteenth century sees rapid technological and institutional changes taking place in England, but stagnation on the continent. Both these views have been challenged over the past decade or two. Today the concept of an 'agricultural revolution' in England is rejected by some historians, and others have questioned the contribution to productivity growth of the well-known technical and institutional changes that took place. Likewise most French historians now reject the idea of a '*société immobile*' and argue that if change was slow, there were usually good economic reasons to continue using traditional farming systems and technology. Despite this change of emphasis, even the most revisionist historians have not challenged the idea that a significant productivity gap existed between Britain and other leading European economies in 1815.[1] This paper tries to suggest a few reasons why this gap existed. The first section examines briefly the recent literature on long-run agrarian change in several European countries. I argue that incentives for investment in British agriculture were considerably more favourable than in most other countries in the period 1650 and 1750. The rest of the paper considers a number of areas where British agriculture developed along different lines to that of two major European economies, namely France and Spain. Section 2 looks at livestock specialisation, section 3 at the opportunities for labour-intensive farming during this period of population growth, and section 4 the restrictions to changes in land use because of the nature of property ownership. I argue that population growth, urbanisation and falling transport prices encouraged farmers everywhere to increase output, but that the large, capital-intensive farms in England (and northern France) were more efficient in utilising factor inputs than either the small

Universidad Pablo de Olavide. Funding has been provided by the Spanish government (PB98-0033 and BEC 2003-06481).

[1] Clark, for example, believes that although productivity growth in Britain was minimal in the seventeenth and eighteenth centuries, it was still a third greater than its nearest competitor in 1850. Clark, 1999: table 4.2.

family farms which were widespread in continental Europe, or the large estates in the Mediterranean.

1 Demographic change, urbanisation and agricultural specialisation

English agriculture was both distinctive and more productive than that found in other European countries. In 1815 about two-thirds of the active population was still employed in agriculture in most countries, but in England the figure was only 55 per cent in 1700 and less than 25 per cent in 1851.[2] Between these two dates the numbers employed in farming remained stable at about 1.5 million, although total population grew from five to almost seventeen millions.[3] Farm labour was also more productive. Crafts has estimated that, whereas in England in 1840 there was no sectorial gap between agriculture and the rest of its economy, the European 'norm' at similar levels of per capita income was for farm labour productivity to be only half as productive as the rest of the economy.[4] Although wheat yields perhaps were not significantly higher in England than elsewhere in northern Europe (Allen, 1988: 117; Allen and Ó'Gráda, 1988), table 3.1 suggests that labour productivity was at least a third greater in the early nineteenth century. Recent estimates by Allen show labour productivity in English agriculture in 1600 as being similar to other countries but, with the exception of the Netherlands, the experience over the next couple of centuries was very different (Allen, 2000: figure 1). Therefore even if growth was slow over the period 1680–1815, English agriculture performed considerably better than most other European countries.

However it would be a mistake to believe that major changes in agricultural practices or productivity growth were totally absent elsewhere. According to Hoffman's calculations, although French agriculture stagnated between 1500 and 1789, there were considerable differences across regions and over time,[5] with labour productivity increasing during fifteen of the thirty-one periods, but declining in the rest.

[2] The 1700 figure is given in Wrigley, 1985: table 4 and refers to England. The 1851 figure is for Britain (Crafts, 1985: table 3.4). The Netherlands is the major exception, with 45 per cent in 1850 (de Vries and Van der Woude, 1997: 524).

[3] Allen, 1994: table 5.3. Clark (1999: 209) argues that there was a small increase from 0.9 to 1.1 million workers. For population, Wrigley and Schofield, 1981: 208–9.

[4] Crafts, 1984: table 2. Figures refer to male labour in agriculture and extractive industries.

[5] His upper bound figure for annual TFP is +0.12 per cent a year and the lower bound −0.08 per cent. In the eighteenth century the range was between +0.19 and +0.04 per cent (Hoffman, 1996: table 4.9).

Table 3.1 *Indicators of European agricultural performance, 1800–1910*

	Net output – calories per male worker (Britain[1] 1800 = 100)	Output per worker (Britain 1851 = 100)	Output per male worker (Britain[1] 1910 = 100)	Output per acre (Britain 1851 = 100)	Total productivity (Britain 1851 = 100)
Britain	100	100	100	100	100
Netherlands	51	54	69	94	76
Belgium	40	37		122	73
Ireland		47		78	67
France	37	44	62	82	66
Germany	37	42	89	56	56
Austria	28[2]	32		54	50
Sweden	24	37		45	49
Italy	28		34		
Spain	24		24		

[1]Figures for Britain have been obtained by multiplying the United Kingdom estimate by 1.33.
[2]Refers to Austria-Hungary.
Sources: Column 1: Bairoch, 1989: table 6; columns 2, 4 and 5: Clark, 1999: table 4.2; and column 3: O'Brien and Prados de la Escosura, 1992: table 6.

In pre-industrial Europe, demographic growth was a major stimulus to agricultural change (Boserup, 1965). Because a very high proportion of food consumption was produced domestically,[6] changing population densities altered the relative prices of land and labour. Changing relative prices in turn influenced farm organisation and product mix, and the demand for technological and institutional change. In the sixteenth century, growing population in Europe increased the demand for bread cereals and encouraged a greater specialisation in their production. As Boserup argues, population growth encouraged farmers to work their land more intensively, with natural pastures being turned to arable and cereal rotations shortened. In the sixteenth century the larger population needed an expansion of agricultural output but, because labour inputs increased faster than output, productivity fell.

After a slow growth or stagnation in the first half of our period, there was an unprecedented growth in population in the second half of the eighteenth century (table 3.2). However, even before this, contemporaries in various European countries already believed that English agriculture

[6] Most recently Allen, 2000: 13–18. The importance of Europe's 'Ghost acreage' increased over the period (Jones, 1981: chapter 4). Both Wrigley (1988) and Clark (1999: 233–4) stress the decline of domestic agriculture as a supply of raw materials and energy.

Table 3.2 *Population growth and urbanisation in select European countries*

	1600	1700	1750	1850
England and Wales	4.3	5.8	6.0	18.0
France	18.5	22.0	24.0	36.0
Netherlands	1.5	2.0	2.0	3.0
Germany	12.0	13.0	15.0	27.0
Italy	12.0	13.0	15.0	25.0
Spain	8.5	8.0	9.5	15.0
London	200	575	675	2685
Paris	220	510	576	1053
Naples	281	216	305	449
Madrid	49	110	109	281

Population of countries in millions and cities in thousands.
Sources: McEvedy and Jones, 1978: 41–119; de Vries, 1984: appendix 1; Mitchell, 1975: 76–8.

was significantly more advanced than their own. Space does not permit a detailed discussion of the changes that were taking place, but they are in any case well known. The planting of legumes increased the nitrogen content of the soil, produced more fodder for animals and reduced the area of unsown fallow. Root crops allowed more livestock to survive the winter months, leading to larger herds. Large numbers of animals produced greater quantities of manure which, with their better integration with the arable, increased crop yields.[7] Finally, by enclosing common land and the open fields, English landowners were able to establish large, compact farms.

The work of Eric Jones and Bob Allen, amongst others, suggest that English agriculture followed a very different trajectory to most European countries in the century between 1650 and 1750. As population pressures eased, a combination of low wheat prices and high real wages depressed agricultural investment, as many farmers found it difficult to switch into other crops or specialise in livestock. However, English farmers appear to have suffered less than their European neighbours for three reasons. First, wheat prices fell by less (table 3.3). Stronger wheat prices in England were the result of state intervention that protected farmers

[7] That some of these options had been known in previous periods is also not in dispute as 'new' crops and farming methods appear to have advanced and retreated over the centuries. See especially Ambrosoli, 1997 and Thirsk, 1997. Grantham (1999: 212) argues 'that by 1300 farmers in the more intensively cultivated districts of Europe were sowing up to 25 and perhaps even up to 40 per cent of arable in bean, peas and vetch'.

Table 3.3 *Trends in European wheat prices, 1620s–1820s; 1601–50 for each country is equal to 100*

	England	France	Italy	Belgium	Spain
1620s	104	113	127	107	102
1630s	106	112	92	120	91
1640s	119	105	89	121	100
1650s	101	107	61	105	111
1660s	100	94	54	91	100
1670s	104	73	66	98	75
1680s	81	65	48	77	73
1690s	120	92	53	116	55
1700s	89	77	57	93	68
1710s	96	66	50	74	45
1720s	89	60	39	59	42
1730s	80	64	54	63	57
1740s	72	54	58	67	40
1750s	93	62	57	61	52
1760s	106	68	59	70	88
1770s	110	79	73	73	84
1780s	115	84	79	83	87
1790s	153	96	97		110
1800s	202	105	110		
1810s	210	130	116		
1820s	143	97	72		
Decade when prices lowest	1740s	1740s	1720s	1720s	1740s
Number of decades lower than 76% of the 1601–50 price level	1	8	14	7	9
Average silver price 1661–1760 in grams/ 100 kilos	96.6	78.0	64.6	78.3	98.1
Index. England = 100	100	81	67	81	102

Prices have been calculated in grams of silver per 100 kilos.
Sources: Abel, 1966. For Spain (Castilla la Nueva) Hamilton, in Feliu, 1991: table III.6. See also Lindert, 1991: table 2.4.

rather than consumers, as was the case elsewhere in Europe (Lindert, 1991). In the 1740s, which was the worst decade for English farmers, prices were 72 per cent of the 1601–50 average, which was significantly above the lowest level found in Belgium (59 per cent in the 1720s), France (54 per cent in the 1740s), Spain (40 per cent in the 1740s), or Italy (39 per cent in the 1720s).[8] In only one decade, that of the 1740s did prices fall below 76 per cent of the 1601–50 average, compared to seven

[8] If Bowden's price index is used instead (1985: 812–31), the minimum for the 1740s is slightly higher at about 76 per cent.

decades in Belgium, eight in France, nine in Spain and fourteen in Italy. High grain prices encouraged investment in enclosures, farm buildings, livestock, fencing, drainage, etc., even if this might have had an adverse effect on industrial growth.[9] A second factor was the relative decline in the farm population from 60 per cent of the total in 1670 to 46 per cent in 1750, which increased the number of people dependent on markets for their food, and therefore encouraged specialisation. By contrast, in France the numbers occupied in agriculture fell from 69 per cent to 61 per cent over the longer period 1600–1750.[10] Finally this movement of labour out of agriculture in England was also accompanied by an 80 per cent increase in the urban population between 1670 and 1750 (calculated from Wrigley, 1985: table 3.4). Urban markets allowed farmers access to a concentration of consumers, which in turn reduced transport and transaction costs. Furthermore, the concentration of high-income consumers in the largest cities gave farmers a major incentive to specialise in commodities whose income elasticities of demand were higher than wheat.[11] Per capita meat consumption in capital cities, for example, was often two or three times the national average.[12] By contrast, demand conditions in France, for example, did not encourage significant livestock specialisation until the 1840s (Grantham, 1978: 331). As a result, Kussmaul has argued for a 'once and for all' increase in productivity in England brought about by regional specialisation, which she claims was largely 'won' by the end of the seventeenth century.[13] One feature of this specialisation was the appearance of 'new crops' in England, such as woad, madder, hemp, flax, rape seed, saffron or hops, which were intensive in the use of labour and provided farmers with greater employment throughout the year.[14]

[9] O'Brien (1985: 777–8) argues that terms of trade favoured industry between 1635 and 1705, were stable between 1705 and 1745, and then between 1750 and 1815 net barter terms of trade 'moved decisively against industry'.

[10] Wrigley, 1985: tables 4, 8 and 9. Over the period 1600–1750, England declined 24 percentage points (from 70 per cent to 46 per cent), three times more than France. By contrast, between 1650 and 1750 the figure in the Dutch Republic stagnated at about 43 per cent.

[11] Smith, (1776) 1976: book 3, chapter 4. Major studies include Fisher, 1935 and Wrigley, 1967, for London, Grantham, 1989 for Paris and Ringrose, 1983, for Madrid. Even so, the income elasticity for dairy products among the rural poor in 1787–96 was 0.97, meat 0.87 and grains only 0.34 (Clark *et al.*, 1995: table 3).

[12] In France in the 1840s national consumption was around 20 kilos per person compared to 60–75 kilos in Paris (Grantham, 1978: 334).

[13] Kussmaul, 1990: 111. See also Grantham, 1991. Hoffman (1996: 183) claims that falling transport costs explain 'much of early modern productivity growth, not just in France, but in Germany and England as well'.

[14] Thirsk, 1997: 36–8. Output remained relatively small, however. Gregory King in the 1690s estimated the contribution of industrial crops, fruit, vegetables and garden produce as about 9 per cent of total agricultural production (cited in Thirsk, 1997: 70).

In Europe, both the growth in urbanisation and the drift away from agriculture was slower than in England (or the Dutch Republic), thereby reducing the role of the market in allocating food supplies and farm specialisation. This, together with low farm prices for cereals, provides a noted contrast between the growing intensification and specialisation in England and *la grande malaise* in French agriculture during the period 1660–1740. Furthermore, and unlike the sixteenth century, growth in output was now achieved through higher levels of capital investment per acre and per worker (O'Brien, 1985: 779).

With the upturn in farm prices from the mid-eighteenth century there were incentives for farmers everywhere to invest heavily once more. This interest is reflected in the leading works on British agronomy being translated, and the ideas contained in many more being summarised and divulged in different languages, leading Voltaire to remark that although 'useful books were written about farming, everybody read them except farmers'.[15] Although demand-side changes are essential for understanding the diversity of change in European agriculture in this period, the supply elasticities of the sector also differed significantly between countries. We shall now consider a number of these differences, not in an attempt to highlight British 'superiority', but rather to understand better why demand-side changes were more likely to lead to increased productivity in that country compared with France or Spain.

2 Livestock specialisation

As Patrick O'Brien and others have stressed, English farmers had perhaps two-thirds as much animal power per worker as their French counterparts in 1800.[16] There are problems in these types of calculations, especially if they are to be pushed back into the eighteenth century. Not only is it difficult to determine herd size, but it is almost impossible to know when farm animals were kept primarily for farm work, rather than for their meat or dairy produce.[17] In traditional agriculture with weak market integration, animals were used for a variety of different functions, which made it difficult to improve breeds. However, by the eighteenth century animal specialisation in Britain had advanced significantly, allowing horse-breeders to concentrate on improving animals for work, and livestock

[15] Cited in Blum, 1978: 248. For the influence of English farming methods in France, see especially Bourde 1967 and 1953; for Spain, García Sanz, 1974.

[16] O'Brien and Keyder, 1978: 115–9, O'Brien, 1996: 221–2 and Wrigley, 1991: 326–30.

[17] Toutain (1992: 11, p. 224), for example, gives 2.8 million horses and 1.4 million oxen for French agriculture in 1892, compared to 1.3 and 1.4 million by O'Brien and Keyder (1978: table 5.5). This difference is sufficient to remove the supposed energy gap present on French farms.

Table 3.4 *Agricultural output by major products*

		Crops	Livestock	Total	% livestock products
England and Wales	1700	19	21	40	53%
	1750	25	34	59	58%
	1800	37	51	88	58%
	1850	56	79	135	59%
UK	1910				75%
Ireland	1850–4	19.3	14.1	33.4	42%
	1910–4	8.0	40.7	48.7	84%
France	1852	5779	2715	8494	32%
	1910				45%
Germany	1910				66%
Italy	1910				32%
Spain	1850				26%
	1910				32%
Portugal	1850				35%
Denmark	1850				46%
Sweden	1850				47%
Norway	1850				51%

Notes:
Unless otherwise stated, figures are in English £millions for *c.* 1850.
Figures for 1910, with the exception of Ireland, are final agricultural output. O'Brien and Prados de la Escosura, 1992: table 3.
England: Allen, 1994: table 5.1. Figures refer to 'principal commodities' and prices to 1815.
Ireland: final agricultural output. Turner, 1996: table 4.2.
France: Demonet, 1990: table 13, in millions of francs.
Denmark, Norway, Sweden, Portugal and Spain: Reis, 2000: table 2.3.

breeders for the production of milk or meat, and helps explain the greater importance of livestock in farm output compared to most other countries (table 3.4).

Important as the level of demand and market integration are in explaining different livestock densities in countries, they were not the only explanations. Animal husbandry might be profitable, but it was risky investment for those with little capital.[18] A farmer making the investment of about £3 for a young cow, the equivalent of two months' wages, could expect an annual gross income of about £5 in the 1730s.[19] However, there

[18] Bowden (1985: 102–17) calculates an annual return on investment of 23 per cent on his notional farm of 100 acres in south Devon in the 1730s and 1740s, with costs including £99 for rent and maintenance, £86.5 for purchasing twenty bullocks for fattening and £34 for labour.

[19] Bowden, 1985: 102–11. Land and labour were the major expenses to be subtracted from this figure.

were three problems facing small farmers who wanted to own livestock, namely the cost of farm animals, credit constraints and the high element of risk involved in losing animals through disease (Dercon, 1998). It is not surprising therefore that if some smallholders owned only one or two animals, many others had to depend on formal and informal rental markets for the use of draft animals for ploughing. The highly seasonal demand of farm work led to the overwork of animals and inferior-quality ploughing, making the poor-quality animals one of the more visible signs of backward agriculture for contemporaries. This was especially true of Europe south of Poitou, where the possibility of growing spring cereals was limited because of summer droughts, and where the obstacles to increasing farm animals were the shortages of summer, rather than winter, fodder as in the north.[20] In conclusion, one explanation for the high cereal yields in early nineteenth-century England was that the country's large, wealthier farmers were better able to substitute 'animals for manpower and fertiliser for land' (Young, 1929: 286; O'Brien, 1985: 779).

But large-scale livestock farming was also present in continental Europe. In central and southern Spain, for example, the very low population densities had for centuries been ideal for extensive sheep farming, and the low cereal prices until the 1750s encouraged a recovery in flocks from about 1.6 million sheep in the early 1630s to over 4 million in the 1740s (Phillips and Phillips, 1997: 293–4). From the mid-eighteenth century the combination of growing exports and rising population drove up both wool and grain prices, and led to a further increase in the number of sheep. There were important economies of scale in the organisation of livestock, which were achieved at different levels. First, as winter and summer pastures were separated by a distance of up to 500 miles, a legal authority and supervisory body (the Mesta) was required to organise the movement of sheep and the allocation of pastures (Nugent and Sanchez, 1989; García Sanz, 1994). Second, the movement of sheep and sale of wool over large distances in areas of very low population density created its own problems of organisation, which favoured large owners. The monasteries of El Paular and Guadalupe, for example, each owned 30,000 sheep in the mid-eighteenth century (Dillon, cited in Phillips and Phillips, 1997: 329). Finally, the optimal flock size appears to have been between 1,000 and 1,500 animals, which employed five shepherds (Phillips and Phillips, 1997: 103 and 125).

The Mesta, and some of the other transhumant organisations in the Mediterranean, are good examples of the benefits to be achieved from specialisation and scale in ranching activities (Carrier, 1932; Moriceau,

[20] This division is given in Bloch, 1966: 31. However, the lighter soils of southern Europe partly compensated the much lower densities of work animals.

1999: chapter 5). Although most of the sheep's manure was 'lost' because it fell on uncultivated land, Spain's low population densities allowed extensive crop rotations, thereby preserving crop yields.[21] Therefore, if the regions bordering the North Sea witnessed a growing intensity of cultivation and higher cereal yields in response to population growth, large areas of the Iberian Peninsula and southern Italy saw few changes in yields, but a significant increase in the area cultivated.[22] Was this difference important? On the one hand it clearly was not, as farmers responded to different sets of factor endowments. But productivity in Spanish sheep farming, whether measured by wool output per animal, or area of grazing required per animal, probably changed little over the period. Supply instead was adjusted by changing the number of animals and area used. Only from the mid-eighteenth century, when more land could not be easily brought under plough, did the Mesta and other institutions of the *ancien régime* begin to appear to contemporaries as a serious barrier to future growth. By contrast, conflicts between livestock and arable farmers in Britain were largely absent, and the relative importance of the former was maintained after 1750, in spite of the country's growing population (table 3.4). Not only was livestock better integrated with arable than in most other countries, but the rearing of young animals often took place in the less densely settled parts of Britain, where land was cheaper. Furthermore, while London and increasingly the northern industrial cities encouraged dairy farming and livestock specialisation, the growing imports of food and beverages discouraged the widespread conversion of pasture to arable.

3 Farm size and labour-intensive farming

Arthur Young believed that England's comparative advantage lay in the size of its farms and level of capital investment. Despite the absence of statistics before the late nineteenth century, there is little doubt that land ownership was much more heavily concentrated in England compared to most western European countries (Lindert, 1987), and a sizeable part of the land was rented in large farms and on long leases, supposedly encouraging capital accumulation. Yet in the eighteenth century there were limited economies of scale in agriculture, and the use of wage labour

[21] By the late eighteenth century the Mesta controlled five million animals (García Sanz, 1994). By contrast, the smaller transhumant flocks of southern Italy were more integrated with the arable (Marino, 1988), as were the local village flocks in Spain which numbered eight million sheep in the late eighteenth century.

[22] Elsewhere the addition to cultivated land was relatively small. In France, for example, the area of land in crops, forage and fallow increased from 23.1 to 23.9 million hectares between 1700/10 and 1781/90 (Blum, 1978: 253).

created potential problems of moral hazard and work incentives. In addition, under-employed family labour on small farms could be used to accumulate capital assets by collecting and spreading manure, digging drainage or irrigation ditches, improving fences, hedges or walls, constructing and mending farm buildings, planting olives, fruit trees and vines. The supposed advantages associated with large farms therefore need some explanations.

At the beginning of our period cereals were the major crop for most European farmers, and bread the basic element in most diets. For the small, family farmer, cereal cultivation had a major disadvantage in that labour requirements were relatively small, leading to under-employment. The growth in population, especially after 1750, encouraged an intensification of cultivation, and as Le Roy Ladurie (1976: 56–7) has noted, the 'classic response of Mediterranean agriculture' was to plant trees or vines on old or new assarts, thereby increasing the returns from agriculture by more intensive forms of land utilisation. In viticulture, entry costs for small growers were low, plough teams were not essential and the best wines were often produced on land that was marginal to cereals. The period 1688 and 1815 saw some major developments in wine-making techniques, with the leading Bordeaux châteaux establishing their reputations. The draining of the Médoc in the mid-seventeenth century greatly improved the possibilities for viticulture, and the use of cylindrical bottles and corks allowed the best wines to be matured in bottles (Pijassou, 1980). In Portugal, the 1703 Methuen treaty encouraged merchants to find a suitable wine for the British market, which was achieved by adding brandy during, rather than after, the fermentation (Francis, 1972: 205–6). Growers and wine-makers showed the same sort of ingenuity in adapting products to suit market conditions as British farmers.[23] Yet these are isolated examples. The poor keeping quality of most wines, high transport costs and high level of taxation everywhere limited the possibility for European farmers to utilise labour more intensively and obtain productivity gains through market specialisation in wine (Simpson, 1995).[24]

In fact, except in those areas especially blessed with good communications or close to urban areas, the presence of small, family-operated farms severely limited the incentives to specialisation. Weak factor and product markets encouraged small farmers to diversify output, rather than risk

[23] Indeed, many of the pioneers were of British origin, as 'many viticultural communities remained passively dependent on external initiatives for marketing and financing their wine trade' (Brennan, 1997: xii).

[24] Though viticulture contributed 24 per cent of final agricultural output in Aquitane in 1840, and 22 per cent in the Languedoc and 20 per cent in Poitou-Charentes, for France as a whole it was only 10 per cent of final agricultural output (Toutain, 1992: 11, table 2.35A).

crop failure. Even a small rise in the price of wheat created 'misery' for the 'lower classes',[25] forcing a reduction in their savings and on occasions the sale of animals and other capital items. As a result, French agronomists showed considerably more interest than their English counterparts in the potato, a crop especially suitable for small farmers in a poor economy with poor communications.[26] Elsewhere, risk was reduced using sharecropping contracts. For Arthur Young (1929: 298) it was the poverty of so many small farmers that explained the widespread use of sharecropping contracts (*métayage*) in France because, if the landlord did not stock the farm, it would not have been 'stocked at all'. Sharecropping therefore was a consequence, not a cause, of rural poverty.[27] But if sharecropping and potatoes were efficient for small producers during a period of strong population growth when formal capital and insurance markets were weak, they were unlikely to lead to productivity growth. Indeed, the poverty of many European farmers implied that large areas of land were cultivated under sub-optimal conditions.

Finally, labour market organisation suggests that the lower transaction costs associated with small family farms were in fact also enjoyed by English farmers. In 1700, the English agricultural workforce consisted of family labour 'supplemented by young adults in their late teens and early twenties hired on annual contracts as servants'.[28] The paternalistic nature of these labour contracts helped reduce problems of moral hazard, and provided incentives for good work. As labour was recruited on annual contracts, large farmers also used the slack periods of the year to create capital assets as small family farmers did. A major difference did exist, however, with the large farms or *latifundios* of southern Europe, where the highly seasonal demand for agricultural labour discouraged the use of annual contracts except for those working with livestock (Bernal, 1988). Instead, most workers were recruited by the day or the task, and labourers lived in the towns rather than on the farms, discouraging the use of off-peak labour for farm improvements.[29] Labour was not necessarily unemployed the rest of the year, as there were opportunities for employment in construction, transport, farm maintenance and rural industry. However, seasonal unemployment was much greater in southern Europe than in the north, and it was the inability of farmers to be able to devote more

[25] Young, 1929: 278. Fogel (1991: 46–7) estimates that 20 per cent of the French had insufficient energy to do more than three hours of light work daily. At the same time, they were often unable to benefit when prices were high (Persson, 1999: chapter 1).

[26] See, however, Hoffman and Mokyr, 1984.

[27] Hoffman (1996: 69) makes the same point.

[28] Allen, 1994: 106. See especially Kussmaul, 1981.

[29] By the late nineteenth century farm labour was only employed for about half the year in southern Spain (Carmona and Simpson, 2003: chapter 3).

of their resources to labour-intensive agriculture which helps explain a major cause of the productivity gap found in table 3.1.[30]

4 Land ownership and farm organisation

Changes in relative prices reduced the efficiency of traditional farming practices, and encouraged change. One area where this occurred, and which has been controversial for both contemporaries and economic historians, is the nature of land ownership in the *ancien régime*, and in particular the enclosure of open fields and common land.

Recent research has questioned the high level of profitability and the contribution to productivity growth of common fields in England, and instead has emphasised its impact on income distribution, with the large, enclosing landowners gaining at the expense of farmers who lost their land in the open fields and rights to common land (Allen, 1992; Humphries, 1990). An induced model of institutional change would suggest that land was only enclosed when it became sufficiently profitable to do so (Crafts, 1977a; McCloskey, 1975; Clark, 1998). Interest in enclosing appears to have grown with greater livestock specialisation, and hence the need to improve and control grazing, and during periods of high grain prices.[31] A recent estimate suggests that perhaps 45 per cent of England had been enclosed by 1550, and 75 per cent by 1760. A further 19 per cent was enclosed by Acts of Parliament over the period 1760 and 1914.[32] Although the area of unenclosed land in 1750 probably contained a greater share of the nation's arable and agricultural population than these figures suggest, most land had already been enclosed before the age of Parliamentary Enclosure.[33] An Act of Parliament reduced the high transaction costs involved in achieving voluntary agreements which had undoubtedly delayed enclosure in some areas. Resistance to enclosure by villagers was sometimes significant but, because enclosure stretched over several centuries, conflicts tended to be localised.[34] Indeed, *if* there

[30] Reis (2000: 26–7) also makes this point, by noting the greater importance of livestock farming in northern Europe.

[31] Overton, 1996: 147–67. See, for example, Wordie, 1983: 492, footnote 23 for the pre-1520 period, and Prince, 1989: 48–9 for the eighteenth century.

[32] Wordie, 1983: 501–2. Over 4,000 Acts were granted between 1750 and 1850, with nearly three-quarters occurring in the periods 1764–80 and 1875–15 (Chambers and Mingay, 1966: 77–9).

[33] Perhaps 21 per cent of the nation was enclosed by Act of Parliament between 1750 and 1820, covering 30 per cent of agricultural land (Neeson, 1993: 329).

[34] If prior to the 1620s there had been official resistance to enclosing, the period from the mid-seventeenth century to the 1790s saw the development of 'a public argument in favour of enclosure even when it *did* cause local distress' (Neeson, 1993: 19, emphasis in the original). See also Thirsk, 1967: 213–38.

had been widespread institutional 'inertia', caused, for example, by the opportunistic behaviour of a few farmers, then we would have expected that the subsequent enclosure of the land under an Act of Parliament to have produced significant profits. Instead, the considerable number of voluntary agreements before 1760, and the relatively low profitability from enclosing after 1760, suggests reasonably flexible institutions.

However, in most other countries there was a significant delay in enclosing land. One argument for the delay in France before the Revolution was the supposed higher transaction costs, caused by the combined opposition of the crown and the peasantry, together with a legal system that encouraged opportunistic behaviour by a few farmers (O'Brien and Heath, 1994: 48–58; Hoffman, 1988; Rosenthal, 1992: chapter 2). After the Revolution the seigniors lost their political power, so it 'was relatively easy to give all common property rights to villages' (Rosenthal, 1992: 18). This suggests much less institutional flexibility, and the significant profits which enclosure should have produced once they eventually took place perhaps were lost in the post-war depression. However, there are two other possibilities. First, given the much smaller size of farms in France, the insurance that the dispersion of holdings in the open fields provided remained important much later than in England. Another argument suggests that the stimulus given to livestock specialisation, a major element in the profitability of enclosures, remained weak in France until the 1830s (Grantham, 1980). Indeed, Young's observation in the 1780s that farming practices were no different on unenclosed land than on 'nine-tenths' of all enclosed land seems to suggest that it was the weakness of incentives to specialise which was a determining factor in the speed of French enclosures (Young, 1929: 291).

Another feature in agriculture in the late eighteenth century was that relatively low population densities in parts of Europe were accompanied by widespread complaints of 'land hunger' and restricted access to land for small farmers. By contrast, the larger populations found after 1820 were fed with apparent ease, and with no obvious improvements in technology. One explanation for this was the changes to property ownership that took place between the 1780s and 1820s. In addition to the large areas of land with common rights of various descriptions already mentioned, there was also a high concentration of property in the hands of the nobility and the Church. Violence was often required to change ownership, and with it incentives for small farmers to increase output. In Spain, for example, the political and military upheavals at the turn of the century during the Napoleonic Wars, encouraged a 'revolution from below' producing widespread invasions of common property, the ploughing-up of pastures and the refusal of many farmers to pay tithes to the Church

(Fontana 1985: 224; Llopis, 1983: 143–4; García Sanz, 1985: 24–7). These gains were then consolidated and extended by the legal changes associated with the 'Liberal Land Reforms' in the nineteenth century, which allowed farmers to shift resources more easily between crops in response to market signals, and thereby increase output without having to change traditional technologies. Similar changes took place elsewhere in continental Europe.

But why did the large landowners in the eighteenth century not convert pasture to cereals more quickly if wheat prices were increasing (table 3.3)? We can advance two reasons. First, because of common property, livestock ownership was often distinct from that of the land on which they grazed. In France, for example, 'seigniors had the right to claim as their own one-third and sometimes two-thirds of the commons, and even to seize all of it if the villagers' rights were based only on prescription and long usage instead of specific title'.[35] Rising livestock prices during the century encouraged large graziers to control the large areas of municipal 'common' pastures for their own animals.[36] Whatever the level of wheat prices, these graziers would still have had incentives to protect 'their pastures'. In Spain, the opposition of large flock owners was sufficient to limit cultivation by small farmers on the common land, despite the support that these had from the crown after 1766 (Sánchez Salazar, 1988).

If this helps explain why common land was not converted more often to cereal production, why did large landowners not take advantage of rising land values to rent *their own land* to small farmers to cultivate? In the first instance, the potentially higher rents which landowners might have received by renting to large numbers of small tenants ignores the greater transaction costs caused by the need for a more efficient administration (Llopis, 1989: 279–82). In addition, the highly volatile prices in this period significantly increased the risks of small farmers being unable to pay their rents in some years. Indeed, the rise in rents is itself a reflection of the attempts by landowners to protect their incomes in the face of default by some. In turn the high rents and major price fluctuations made it difficult for small farmers to accumulate resources, especially livestock, and explains over-cultivation and declining cereal yields in the late eighteenth century. An even more pessimistic interpretation is that small farmers made little attempt to increase output, believing that a greater surplus would simply be appropriated by the state or seigniors (Blum,

35 Blum, 1978: 148. Rosenthal (1992: 16) by contrast claims that common land 'was frequently in a state of well-defined use and poorly defined ownership'.

36 For Spain, and especially Extremadura, Llopis, 1989: 282–6. For France, Hoffman, 1996: chapter 2.

1978: 119). In general, market conditions before about 1820 encouraged Europe's landowners to look for large, prosperous tenants to farm their land, thereby reducing the risks of unpaid rents.

The growth in per capita food consumption in Europe in the early nineteenth century was partly caused by changes in land ownership. In particular the Church lost virtually all of its land, tithes were abolished and common land sold. More efficient commodity markets were produced by the decline in internal market regulations throughout Europe, and transport improvements. However, changes in relative prices perhaps also need to be considered. Landowners after 1820 faced lower commodity prices and higher real wages, conditions that favoured renting their land to small farmers, and thereby encouraging a more intensive cultivation. But while these conditions in many areas of Europe encouraged labourers to stay in farming because of improved access to land, in England farmers tried to cut labour costs by mechanisation (Hobsbawm and Rudé, 1985).

Conclusion

Although the advantages of the large capitalist farmers which had impressed Arthur Young and some of his English and European contemporaries were perhaps exaggerated, they probably were more efficient than small, family farms for reasons we have already noted. But three other features of English society also appear to have contributed to a more efficient agricultural sector.

First, agriculture was no longer the 'employer of last resort'. Landless labour flocked in numbers to the towns. In France, and in Europe more generally, access to land for those who lived in the countryside was greater and the urban demand for labour less. As O'Brien and Keyder have reminded us, 'in France underemployed or low-productivity labour tended to remain in peasant households in the countryside. In Britain, by contrast, the tenurial institutions of agriculture could not hold much "excess" population which crowded into towns as a "lumpen proletariat" or reserve army of labour' (O'Brien and Keyder, 1978: 73). From a much earlier date the situation in England appears to have changed from one of finding employment for surplus agricultural labour to that of farmers having to make contingency arrangements to have sufficient labour during the harvest (O'Brien, 1996).

Second, the relatively low physical and institutional barriers to trade *within* the country led to a much greater level of market integration. The fear of famines, which were widespread throughout the eighteenth century in continental Europe, was virtually absent in England. Average food prices may have been higher, reflecting a grain policy designed for farmers, but consumers could be much more certain of finding food available. In addition, the geographical shape and the relative abundance of navigable rivers presented farmers with more market opportunities than their counterparts in France or Spain. In fact, for wine producers in Jerez or Bordeaux for example, transport costs were cheaper to London than to Madrid or Paris.

Finally, and as Crafts (1989) has argued, Britain's comparative advantage was in industry and not agriculture. As manufacturing goods left the country, raw materials and food produce entered in vast quantities. Britain was not adverse to follow mercantilist policies when it was in its interest, but imported food occupied a large and growing share of the national market on a considerably greater scale than any other European country, with the exception of the Dutch Republic. Many of these products, such as sugar or tea, started as luxuries, but quickly became consumed by large sections of society. But it was not just tropical crops. British merchants also helped to create new markets for products such as wine, silk and timber, thereby encouraging greater farm specialisation within Europe itself.

4 Precocious British industrialisation: a general-equilibrium perspective

N. F. R. Crafts and C. Knick Harley

1 Introduction

The British Industrial Revolution created an industrial economy. While casual discourse conflates industrialisation and economic growth, Britain was remarkable primarily for the pronounced structural change that occurred rather than for rapid economic growth. Uniquely the British labour force became highly industrialised even prior to the move to free trade in the 1840s. On the eve of the abolition of the Corn Laws the share of agriculture in employment had already declined to levels that were not reached in France and Germany until the 1950s.

Table 4.1 reports levels of agricultural employment in other European countries at dates when, later on, they reached the British real income level of 1840. In every other case the share of agriculture was much larger. This reinforces the claim that precocious industrialisation was a key aspect of British economic development. It also means that, in Patrick O'Brien's words, Britain was 'something of a special and less of a paradigm case' (1986: 297). The aim of this paper is to explore how Britain became such an outlier.

An argument that has endured through the decades is that British industrialisation reflects the unusual ability of its agricultural sector to raise productivity. Looking at the period 1500–1800, Wrigley pointed out that

> In a closed economy . . . a substantial rise in the proportion of the population living in towns is strong presumptive evidence of a significant improvement in production per head in agriculture, and may provide an indication of the scale of the change. Sufficient information is now available to justify an initial application of this line of thought to early modern England. (1985, p. 684)

Although Wrigley's numbers have been refined by Allen (2000: tables 2 and 8), the estimates still show the pattern from which the inference was drawn. Whereas between 1500 and 1800 in France the agricultural population fell from 73 to 59 per cent of the total while agricultural labour productivity was unchanged, in England agricultural population fell from

Table 4.1 *Agricultural share in total employment at British 1840 real income level (%)*

	Agricultural Employment	Year
Austria	64.1	1890
Belgium	44.4	1860
Britain	22.2	1840
Denmark	44.8	1890
Finland	64.6	1930
France	44.1	1890
Germany	39.9	1890
Greece	53.7	1930
Hungary	53.0	1930
Italy	55.4	1910
Netherlands	37.4	1860
Norway	39.5	1910
Portugal	48.4	1950
Spain	56.1	1920
Sweden	53.5	1900
Switzerland	42.4	1870

Sources: labour force data from Bairoch, 1968, except for France from Dormois, 1997; income levels from Maddison, 2001.

74 to 35 per cent of the total and agricultural labour productivity rose by 43 per cent.

A variant on this stresses the role played by agrarian institutions. In particular, capitalist farming came to dominate in Britain while small-scale family farming prevailed in most continental European countries during nineteenth-century industrialisation. O'Brien restated the point thus: 'British families left the countryside . . . essentially because the institutions of capitalist agriculture will not retain as much redundant labour . . . the evolution of [Britain's] peasantry into a virtually wage-dependent labour force . . . can be contrasted with the tenurial systems not only of France, but of Italy, Germany, Spain, and other parts of Europe as well' (1996: 226).

These views would not surprise many earlier writers but fell out of favour in the 1950s and 1960s, when it was widely argued that the main impetus to industrialisation of the labour force came from demographic rather than agricultural change. Landes summarised this counter-claim as follows: 'the agricultural revolution associated with the enclosures increased the demand for farm labour . . . the rapid growth of population created a surplus of labour in the countryside much of which found its way into the new urban centres' (1969: 115–6). As it stands, this argument is not entirely persuasive. The substantial growth of the industrial labour force relied on increasing agricultural labour productivity such that each agricultural worker could feed more urban workers as time passed. By 1850 labour productivity in agriculture was almost three times the level of 1700 (Allen, 1994).

While population growth alone seems inadequate to explain Britain's precocious industrialisation, the suggestion that progress in agricultural technology was not central can be made more plausible by recognising that Britain was an economy open to international trade instead of adopting Wrigley's closed economy perspective. By the Industrial Revolution period, if not earlier, this seems appropriate. Thus, Williamson (1985), who developed a formal model of the nineteenth-century British economy, argued that the structural changes of the Industrial Revolution were a consequence of much faster technological advance in industry than in agriculture: 'Unbalanced productivity advance [was] the primary supply-side force driving industrialization and urbanization' (1985: 89).

His analysis implied that a faster rate of agricultural productivity improvement tended to slow down industrialisation because agriculture would have been more able to withstand import competition. Rapid agricultural advance could even have converted it to a sector exporting to the rest of the world. Williamson's model does, not, however, support the suggestion that population growth was responsible for rapid industrialisation. On the contrary, his model predicts the opposite. He sees population growth driving down unskilled wages and 'in response to an augmented labour supply, labour-intensive agriculture expands far more rapidly, which implies de-industrialization and a trade contraction' (1985: 142).

The effects of agricultural productivity performance need, however, to be analysed in the context of the whole economy. This was clearly understood by leading economists of the time, particularly David Ricardo, who discovered the concept of comparative advantage. He wrote in 1817 that

> a country possessing very considerable advantages in machinery and skill, and which may therefore be enabled to manufacture commodities with much less labour than her neighbours, may in return for such commodities, import a portion of the corn required for its consumption, even if its land were more fertile and corn could be grown with less labour than in the country from which it was imported. ([1817] 1971: 154)

This has resonance for mid-nineteenth-century Britain, which had a substantial lead over its European rivals in agricultural labour productivity yet imported over 20 per cent of its agricultural consumption. These trade flows were associated with Britain's dominant position in cotton textile exports based on a huge lead in labour productivity in that sector (Crafts, 1989).

This review of the literature has established some useful guidelines for the development of a satisfactory understanding of Britain's precocious industrialisation. It is clearly important to take account of the roles of increased population and technological advance in an open-economy, general-equilibrium perspective. Attention has to be given to interactions between agriculture and industry bearing in mind that international trade offered opportunities for importing consumption goods and exporting production that modified the relationship between domestic production and consumption. Repercussions of population growth, for example, will be felt on labour markets, product markets and the balance of external payments. Prices will rise and fall in response to excess demand and supply respectively. Labour allocation, production and trade will respond to incentives created by price movements to create a new balance between supply and demand.

The historiography clearly does not offer a consensus on the origins of Britain's unusually pronounced industrialisation. In this paper, we explore the issues with the aid of a computational general equilibrium (CGE) model that facilitates a quantitative analysis of the competing claims. The model is a slightly modified version of the one that we have used to address the question of whether the 'Crafts-Harley' view of the sectoral dispersion of productivity increase during the Industrial Revolution is consistent with the pattern of British trade in industrial products (Harley and Crafts, 2000). As such, we know that it is capable of broadly replicating the transformation of the economy between 1770 and 1841 in response to changes in factor endowments and productivity and is explicitly designed to examine adjustments in international trade. The model has two key features that we believe have not been adequately appreciated in previous work. First, British population grew rapidly but land resources did not. Second, Britain was large relative to world markets especially for its main exports so that expansion of exports tended to lower prices such that revenue grew much less quickly than export volume.

In this chapter, we address the following questions explicitly in order to analyse both the direction and the magnitude of their impact on the industrialisation of employment during the period of the industrial revolution.

What were the implications of population growth?

What was the effect of improvements in agricultural techniques?

How important was the lead that Britain established in industrial technology?

Would things have been different if peasant farming had persisted as in France?

As it turns out, our answers to these questions do not amount to an endorsement of any single position from the historiography. They do, however, provide considerable support for the emphasis placed on agrarian institutions by Patrick O'Brien.

2 A Primer on general equilibrium in an open economy

A general-equilibrium approach emphasises the fact that an economy allocates resources among a range of alternative uses to produce a particular mix of goods. The allocation of resources and the mix of production will change systematically as underlying technological and market conditions change. The value of adopting an open-economy, general-equilibrium perspective can be simply illustrated using diagrams based on the concept of the production possibility frontier, which will be familiar to many students from elementary economics. The exposition that follows will also help to establish intuitions that aid the interpretation of the detailed numerical results that we present later in the paper.

Figures 4.1 to 4.3 display permutations of a production possibility frontier (PPF) diagram where the two axes show the output of agricultural and industrial goods per person. If the economy is organised efficiently it will be on the PPF where more of one good can only be obtained by having less of the other. The slope of the PPF represents the marginal opportunity cost of one good in terms of the other, i.e., how much extra industrial output can be gained by giving up one unit of agricultural production. In equilibrium, this will be equal to the ratio of the prices of the two goods since at the margin when productive resources could be switched from one good to the other the revenue that would accrue must be the same, i.e., $\Delta A \times p_a = \Delta I \times p_i$ and $\Delta I/\Delta A = p_a/p_i$. This is shown at point C in figure 4.1. At this point prices would be represented by the line AB with slope p_a/p_i. Line AB is also just tangential to an indifference curve drawn for a representative consumer whose slope is the rate at which that consumer is willing to substitute one good for the other while maintaining a constant level of satisfaction.

Point C is the best outcome for an economy closed to international trade since it lies on the highest indifference curve that can be reached given the constraints of technology and resources represented by the PPF. Now suppose that the PPF in figure 4.1 relates to an economy which can trade with the rest of the world but is too small to have any influence on world prices. If prices on world markets are such that p_a/p_i is lower than would have prevailed in the closed situation, then the economy will

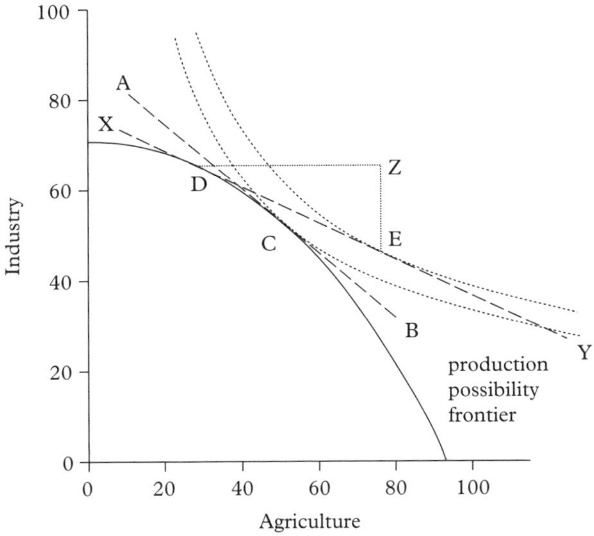

Figure 4.1 Production possibility and autarchy and trade equilibria

shift resources from producing agricultural goods to producing industrial goods. In the diagram this is illustrated by a move round the PPF to produce at D. D is tangential to the XY line whose slope is the world price ratio. This move represents an increased specialisation in the production of industrial output. International trade occurs at the prices embodied in the XY line. The economy sells industrial goods and purchases agricultural goods so the consumer can now reach a higher indifference curve at E. The differences between the amounts consumed and produced of each good are agricultural imports and industrial exports, DZ and EZ, respectively. The higher is p_i relative to p_a the more specialised the economy will become in industrial production and the greater will be the consumer's gains from trade.

Now suppose that population increase reduces the economy's land endowment per person. The maximum agricultural output per person the economy can produce falls, but maximum industrial output per person is unchanged. This case is shown in figure 4.2. The reduction in agricultural land per capita shifts the PPF per person inwards along the agricultural goods axis. In the absence of trade, per person consumption of both goods will fall to point F with a higher relative price of agricultural products. With trade at unchanged international prices XY, the economy will shift resources to produce more of the industrial good and less of the agricultural good at G. Per person consumption of both goods declines

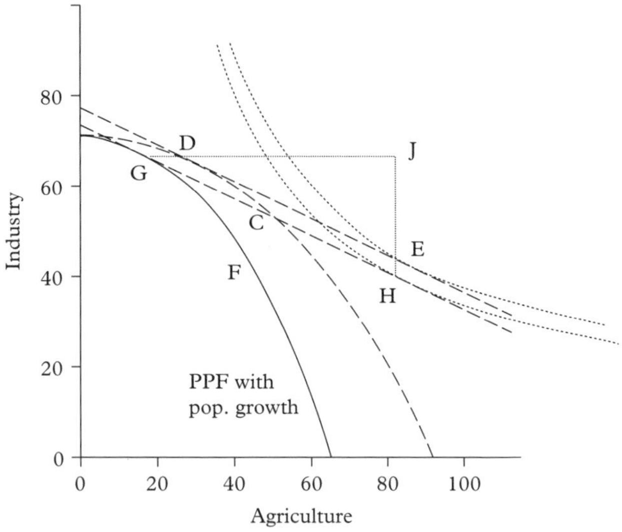

Figure 4.2 Population increase

(at H) but by much less than in the absence of trade. Industrial exports increase from EZ to HJ and agricultural imports from DZ to GJ.

Figure 4.3 represents a case where technological progress has raised the economy's industrial (but not agricultural) production capabilities. The PPF is extended along the industrial goods axis but not the agricultural goods axis. With unchanged world prices, the open economy moves to production at N with more industrial and less agricultural output while consumption is at M, where exports and imports are now higher at MP and NP, respectively.

Figure 4.4 summarises the key implications of the previous three figures. Williamson's (1985) arguments about the implications of unbalanced productivity advance, noted in section 1 above, fall directly within this context. However, the exposition from these figures is incomplete because it refers to a 'small open economy', i.e., where world prices are unaffected by anything that this economy does. We feel that this is inappropriate in the case of Britain during the Industrial Revolution.

To understand the importance of this point, return to figure 4.1. If we now consider a large economy entering international trade with supplies and demands that influence world prices, the analysis needs to be modified somewhat. We have seen that with unchanged prices the economy moves to point D. If the economy is large, increased demand for agricultural imports may raise international agricultural prices. This price change is represented by a rotation of the XY line to a less steep gradient.

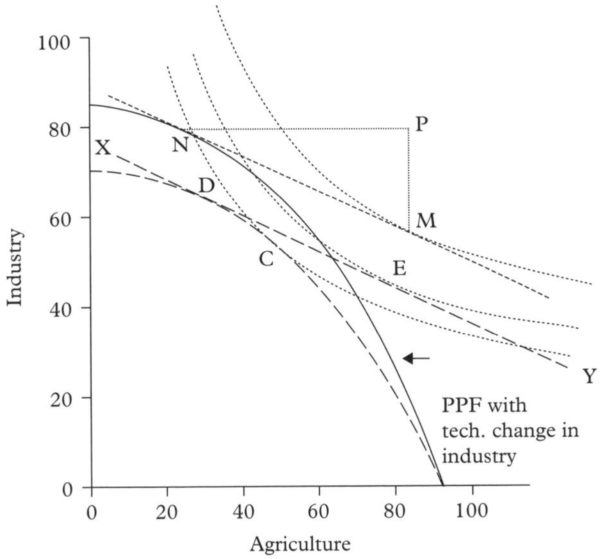

Figure 4.3 Technological advance in industry

Specialise More in Exportable	*Specialise Less in Exportable*
Relative price of exportable rises	Relative price of importable rises
Production possibility of importable falls	Production possibility of importable rises
Production possibility of exportable rises	Production possibility of exportable falls
Exports and imports rise	Exports and imports fall

Note: in rows 2 and 3 imports and exports rise by the same amount but not in row 1.

Figure 4.4 Specialisation in A Small Open Economy

The higher international agricultural price would lead to an equilibrium in which the move round the PPF does not go as far as D. The economy ends up at a point somewhere intermediate between C and D. Similar qualifications would be necessary for figures 4.2 and 4.3 if world prices are affected by changes in the PPF.

This exposition of an elementary general-equilibrium analysis for an open economy has worked through some simple 'five-finger exercises'. The objective has been to generate some heuristic insights that will be useful in considering the results of simulations of the CGE model in the following sections. A key message for the Industrial Revolution period that should now be readily comprehensible is as follows: 'When productivity grew very fast in Britain's exportable textiles, had productivity not increased at all in agriculture it would have been appropriate to specialize still more in textiles and import more food' (Crafts, 1985: 137).

3 An initial simulation of the CGE model

Figures 4.1 to 4.3 provide useful introductions to the general-equilibrium workings of an economy undergoing changes in openness, population and technology but they also have serious limitations. In particular, while the diagrams provide useful insights into the qualitative directions of change, they are poor guides to the quantitative magnitudes. Equally important, the diagrams cannot cope with economies with more than two goods. For some purposes, aggregating economic activity this drastically may be acceptable but it seems inappropriate for understanding the Industrial Revolution. Our interpretation of technological change in this period has stressed the diversity of technological histories among manufacturing industries and that rapid advance concentrated in textiles and metals was crucial to the British experience (Harley and Crafts, 2000). It is also important to recognise that by 1841 the service sector employed 35 per cent of the labour force and accounted for over 40 per cent of national income.

It is possible to represent more complex economies using computational general-equilibrium (CGE) models in which consumption and production relationships are embodied in mathematical equations. The equations are chosen to correspond to actual numerical values so that the model provides quantitative as well as qualitative results. This paper explores the British Industrial Revolution using a CGE model that is an extension of the one set out in Harley and Crafts, 2000. Minor modifications were necessary to adapt the model to address the issues now at hand. Most importantly, we replaced a single representative consumer with three classes (wealth-holders, urban labour and rural labour) and modelled much of the demand for services as dependent on the distribution of goods from producers to consumers.

The CGE model works out the impact of changes in factor endowments and technology on output and prices by calculating new equilibria that balance demand and supply for goods and factors of production and equalise the money value of imports and exports. The structure of the model is predicated on the standard assumptions of neoclassical economics and Britain in the Industrial Revolution is modelled as a large economy, i.e., one whose output decisions do affect world prices.

Table 4.2 reports some of the results of a first simulation of the model with a view both to providing some familiarity with its workings and also

Table 4.2 *CGE simulation of 1841 economy with volume of agricultural imports constrained to 1770 level*

	1841 Benchmark	Simulated Value (capital not adjusted)	Simulated Value (capital adjusted)
Agricultural Imports	100	15	15
Industrial Exports	100	58	63
Agricultural Output	100	108	110
Industrial Output	100	90	99
Value Added in Agriculture (%)	22	28	28
Value Added in Industry (%)	35	30	30
Agricultural Employment (%)	22	26	26
Industrial Employment (%)	41	37	37
Price of Agricultural Goods	100	116	121
Price of Industrial Goods	100	93	91
Real wages	100	94	99
Real land rents	100	151	167
Real return on capital	100	93	82
Capital Stock	100	100	118
GNP/person	100	102	108

to making clear that being open to international trade makes a substantial difference. The model was initially calibrated to replicate the British economy of 1841 in its key features. Most benchmark values are reported in column 1 as a base of 100 to facilitate comparisons. The sectoral shares in value added and employment, however, are reported as actual percentages.

The simulation provides insights into the difference between a closed and open British economy. During the Industrial Revolution the British economy responded to changes in technology, demography and capital accumulation by relying increasingly heavily on agricultural imports. To illustrate the effect of trade we solved a variant of the model in which the volume of agricultural imports was reduced to the level of 1770, about 15 per cent of the actual 1841 amount. Columns 2 and 3 of table 4.2 show what would have happened if the economy had not been able to increase agricultural imports by limiting foreign supply to only 3.6 per cent instead of 24 per cent of 1841 benchmark agricultural consumption. It will be useful to refer to figure 4.1 to get a feel for the responses that the model predicts while considering the detailed results in table 4.2.

The counterfactual proposed is equivalent to the imposition of an even higher level of protection for domestic agriculture than existed in the early nineteenth century. Since the simulation does not eliminate trade, it would represent a situation where the relative price line rotated to a position intermediate between XY and AB. In figure 4.1 this would move the equilibrium to a point on the PPF between D and C where agricultural prices would be higher relative to industrial prices than at D, while industrial output is smaller and agricultural output is greater than at D. While the simulations reported in table 4.2 are more complex than this, the flavour of these responses is clearly visible.

The simulation in column 2 of table 4.2 shows that if international trade had been severely restricted the economy would have been considerably less industrialised notwithstanding the technological progress of the Industrial Revolution period. The counterfactual industrial employment and value added shares are 37 per cent and 30 per cent, respectively, compared with 41 per cent and 35 per cent in the 1841 benchmark. The relative price of agricultural goods at 121/91 is about a third higher and agricultural output is 8 per cent greater and industrial output 10 per cent lower than in the benchmark. The economy is less able to exploit its comparative advantage in industrial production.

An interesting, and at first sight perhaps surprising, feature of this simulation is that this restriction of trade raises GNP per person by 2 per cent, although real wages fall by 6 per cent. The key to this result is that during the Industrial Revolution Britain was a big country in terms of world trade. Accordingly, Britain faced a downward sloping demand curve for its industrial exports. Restricting imports would reduce Britain's specialisation in industrial production and thus reduce the supply of exports to the world market. A higher price would be obtained for the remaining exports and this is equivalent to the exercise of market power. In other words, Britain could move the international terms of trade in its favour, i.e., British export prices would increase relative to the prices of goods produced in the rest of the world. In fact, because Britain was the major supplier of its main exports, the impact on prices could be very substantial.

It is well known that in such circumstances imposing what the economics literature calls an 'optimal tariff' will make the home country better off.[1] The economic history literature has long accepted that this argument applies to early nineteenth-century Britain and that in these

[1] Of course, there are several other potential effects of protecting domestic producers that might also be considered. These include the possibility that with reduced import competition home producers are less energetic in controlling production costs and that protection encourages a waste of resources in the pursuit of rewards from lobbying politicians, seeking favourable treatment in procuring imports, etc. It should not be assumed that a move from free trade to restricted trade generally raises economic welfare. Indeed we believe that in general the opposite is the case.

terms its adoption of free trade in the 1840s reduced real national income (McCloskey, 1980; Irwin, 1988). There is no suggestion that the restriction that is imposed in table 4.2 was 'optimal' in this sense, but it does have a similar income-increasing effect. In the simulated equilibrium of column 2 of table 4.2 the volume of Britain's exports falls by 42 per cent but, because their relative price rises by about a third, the volume of imports falls by a little under 30 per cent. British imports cost significantly less to purchase in terms of the home economy's resources.

Restricting trade raises agricultural prices and this pushes up the rent of agricultural land substantially. This raises the share of property incomes and lowers the share of wages in national income, a point that was not lost on the protagonists in the struggle over the abolition of the Corn Laws. This would naturally have implication for savings and capital accumulation in an economy where the saving rate from wage income was probably negligible and certainly much lower than those from rents and from profits (Horrell, 1996; von Tunzelmann, 1985). Economic theory suggests that the stock of assets accumulated by the propertied class would maintain a constant ratio with their income and the simulation of column 3 in table 4.2 adopts this assumption.

Allowing the capital stock to adjust in this way in response to the changed distribution of income raises the counterfactual capital stock relative to the 1841 benchmark by 18 per cent. Accordingly, production possibilities across all sectors of the economy expand and the PPF shifts out. The increased capital per person entails a further increase in GDP per person to 108 in this counterfactual. The higher level of capital and the shift of income to high-income consumers are responsible for the trivial ultimate decline in industrial output relative to the benchmark.

In the context of Industrial Revolution Britain we believe that taking account of the impact of changes in the distribution of income for savings and capital accumulation is appropriate. Indeed, this has been the traditional assumption in the literature. Therefore, in the tables that follow we only report simulations incorporating capital adjustment.[2]

Does this example have much historical relevance? The answer is surely yes for at least two reasons. First, the Industrial Revolution saw a sustained political struggle over the extent of agricultural protectionism, i.e., over how far the economy would be allowed to take advantage of the gains from international trade which only saw the landed interest finally defeated with the abolition of the Corn Laws in 1846 (Barnes, 1961).

[2] This way of modelling the 'capital adjustment' would not, however, be appropriate in many other circumstances. In particular, it would be inappropriate in a fully globalised world in which capital markets allow countries to have unlimited access to foreign savings.

Table 4.3 *Simulated 1841 economy with 1770 population*

	1841 Benchmark	Trade Adjusting	1770 Agricultural Imports
Agricultural Imports	100	62	15
Industrial Exports	100	42	29
Agricultural Output	100	70	82
Industrial Output	100	41	38
Agricultural Employment (%)	22	29	34
Industrial Employment (%)	41	34	30
Price of Agricultural Goods	100	77	86
Price of Industrial Goods	100	111	105

Note: 'trade adjusting' in this and the following tables means that volumes of both imports and exports are free to respond to market signals and the economy is fully open to international trade.

Second, as O'Brien (1989) has underlined, failure to defeat Napoleon would in all likelihood have curtailed British trade and thus have pushed the allocation of resources in the direction of the closed-economy case. Thus, in the simulations that follow, on each occasion, we report results with trade free to adjust fully and results where agricultural imports are constrained to the 1770 level.

4 Simulating the effects of population growth and technological progress

At this point we return to the claims of the historiography that relates to factors promoting the unusual degree of industrialisation in the British economy. Our approach will be to present the results of a series of simulations of the CGE model designed to illuminate these arguments. In this section we explore successively the impact of holding the population at its 1770 size (about 45 per cent of its 1841 level), of eliminating post-1770 total factor productivity growth in agriculture, and of restricting the advance in British industrial technology to the rate achieved in the rest of the world.

Table 4.3 reports the results of a simulation in which population is reduced to 45 per cent of its actual 1841 level. This is equivalent to there being no population growth between 1770 and 1841. Figure 4.2 is the reference point for these results but the counterfactual considered is the reverse of that discussed earlier.

In the case where trade adjusts fully, the counterfactual elimination of post-1770 population growth is significantly de-industrialising. Agricultural employment rises by nearly a third from 22 per cent of the labour force in the 1841 benchmark to 29 per cent while industrial employment falls by an equivalent amount from 41 to 34 per cent. This is somewhat similar to the move from G to D in figure 4.2 but here we are considering a large, not a small, economy and this occurs despite a rise in the relative price of industrial goods. This result mainly arises because our model has strongly diminishing returns to labour in agriculture. When population pressure is reduced, labour productivity increases, rents fall and the sector can afford to attract a bigger share of the labour force even though relative prices have moved against it. In addition, the lower agricultural goods price increases per capita agricultural consumption well above its 1841 level.

Column 3 of table 4.3 combines the eliminating of the population growth after 1770 and a constraint on agricultural imports (thus limiting exports of the manufacturing sectors where technological change had been most rapid) and illustrates the combined effect of population growth and trade. Constraining agricultural imports to the 1770 level (as in column 2 of table 4.2) with the much smaller population leads to more de-industrialisation than does just population change. The agricultural share rises from 29 per cent in column 2 to 34 per cent (and up from 26 per cent with limited trade but unchanged population in table 4.2, column 2). In terms of figure 4.2, with the economy closed to trade expansion, production has moved from F to C but with quite a marked rise in the relative price of industrial goods (steepening of the AB line) from 91/121 to 105/86. Allowing trade fully to adjust reduced this effect but the relative price of industrial goods still rises by 44 per cent. Again, however, the severity of the diminishing returns in the agricultural sector and the increase in agricultural consumption stimulated by lower food prices is such that, compared with F, the equilibrium point C has much greater agricultural output but relatively little increase in industrial output.

The simulations in table 4.3 show clearly that the population growth of the Industrial Revolution era stimulated industrialisation. In terms of our earlier literature review, this supports the position advanced by Landes (1969) but not that of Williamson (1985). Williamson's argument is undermined by the fact that agriculture is always an importable and by the strongly diminishing returns which ensue in the agricultural sector as demographic pressure intensifies in our model. Population growth also tends to shift the distribution of income in favour of capital and land especially in the less open-economy case, thereby leading to more savings and a higher capital to labour ratio in the economy as a whole.

Nevertheless, it hardly seems plausible that demography fully accounts for precocious British industrialisation of employment. Although population grew about twice as fast during the British Industrial Revolution

Table 4.4 *Simulated 1841 economy with 1770 agricultural technology*

	1841 Benchmark	Trade Adjusting	1770 Agricultural Imports
Agricultural Imports	100	142	15
Industrial Exports	100	132	66
Agricultural Output	100	59	73
Industrial Output	100	103	98
Agricultural Employment (%)	22	19	26
Industrial Employment (%)	41	45	38
Price of Agricultural Goods	100	109	151
Price of Industrial Goods	100	96	82

as in continental Europe (Tranter, 1994: 37–8), Table 4.3 indicates that this would account for only around 3 percentage points difference in the share of agriculture in the labour force in 1841.

Table 4.4 reports the results of simulations in which there are no advance in total factor productivity in agriculture after 1770. This is equivalent to raising each of the required factor inputs (land, labour and capital) per unit of output by 50 per cent in 1841. This case can also be considered with reference to figure 4.2. Suppressing post-1770 technological improvement in agriculture in this way corresponds to the maximum agricultural production point on the PPF moving in towards the origin.

Here the results of the simulations are rather different depending on whether trade adjusts. In the simulation in which trade is allowed to adjust (column 2 of table 4.4) we see that imports paid for by industrial exports replace some inefficient agriculture. Agricultural employment falls from 22 to 19 per cent of the labour force while industrial employment has risen by an equivalent amount from 41 to 45 per cent. National income and real labour income fall substantially (about 15 per cent) reducing demand for all goods. As a big country, Britain experiences a small change in relative prices with agricultural prices rising but the main effect of lower agricultural productivity is a large increase in agricultural imports. The outcome is reasonably similar to the move from D to G in figure 4.2. In this trade adjusting case, the distribution of income moves against property because land is significantly less productive. In response, the capital stock is 16 per cent lower than in the benchmark.

If agricultural imports, along with agricultural productivity, are kept constant at the 1770 level, there is a bigger impact on real labour income which falls by about 50 per cent. GNP, however, falls only about a third as much as when imports increase (about 5 per cent) because property incomes and, in consequence, the capital stock increase. The structure of employment changes only modestly. Agriculture employs 26 per cent of the labour force, up from the actual 22 per cent but the same as in column 2 of table 4.2 where trade is also constrained. Industrial employment at 38 per cent is somewhat below the 1841 level but slightly higher than in the trade constrained case of table 4.2. This is similar to the move from C to F in figure 4.2 and is accompanied by a rise in the relative price of agricultural goods from 121/91 to 151/82. In this case, income shifts a bit towards property and the capital stock is 6 per cent higher than in the benchmark.

Table 4.4 bears out Williamson's (1985) predictions. In the open economy of Industrial Revolution Britain, if productivity growth had been more unbalanced in favour of industry, industrialisation would have been enhanced. It would have been appropriate to specialise more in exportables like cotton textiles exports of which rise in the counterfactual by about 40 per cent. However, the overall impact is not dramatic; a substantial change in counterfactual agricultural productivity causes only a modest fall in the share of the labour force in agriculture.

Table 4.5 explores the effect of Britain's lead in industrial technology by simulating what the economy would have looked like if the rate of post-1770 technological progress in British industry were reduced to that in the rest of the world. This amounts to increasing the required primary inputs in cotton production by 50 per cent, in metal production by 20 per cent and in other textiles by 5 per cent. This can be understood in the context of figure 4.3 but with the reverse shift as the industrial goods end point of the PPF moves toward the origin.

As would be expected, in column 2 of table 4.5, we find that, relative to the benchmark case, with full trade adjustment the reduction in industrial technological advance is de-industrialising. Once again, however, the effects are quite modest. Agricultural employment rises from 22 to 24 per cent of the labour force. This is similar to a move from N to D in figure 4.3 but with some offset from the large country effect on relative prices which shift in favour of industrial goods. Lower profits from lower productivity reduce the capital stock by 8 per cent. Restricting agricultural imports (column 3) results in greater de-industrialisation but the structure of the economy is almost the same as occurs when restrictions of imports act alone (table 4.2, column 2).

Table 4.5, like table 4.4, supports the position put forward by Williamson (1985). With an economy that can take full advantage of international trade, a greater imbalance in productivity growth towards industry causes a more industrialised labour force. But since in Britain, while productivity growth was skewed towards exportable manufactures, notably textiles, there was also significant advance in agriculture, an

Table 4.5 *Simulated 1841 economy with no British lead in industrial technology*

	1841 Benchmark	Trade Adjusting	1770 Agricultural Imports
Agricultural Imports	100	62	15
Industrial Exports	100	60	47
Agricultural Output	100	103	109
Industrial Output	100	75	76
Agricultural Employment (%)	22	24	26
Industrial Employment (%)	41	40	38
Price of Agricultural Goods	100	101	113
Price of Industrial Goods	100	113	106

extreme degree of unbalanced technological progress does not seem adequately to explain precocious British industrialisation. Broadly speaking, most of northern Europe adopted improved crop rotations leading to substantial gains in arable yields such that the level of total factor productivity in French and Irish agriculture in 1841 was not far below that of Britain (Crafts, 1989: 422–3). So the unusual aspect of British technology was industrial rather than agricultural and table 4.5 suggests that this only explains about 2 percentage points of the 1841 industrialisation of employment.

5 Capitalist versus peasant farming

In 1841 the share of the labour force in agriculture in Britain was some 25 percentage points below the level that regression methods suggest was normal for a nineteenth-century European country at the same income level (Crafts, 1985: 62). The simulations above show that both unusually strong population pressure and unbalanced productivity growth can explain only a relatively small part of this gap between the British experience and the 'European Norm'.

Early modern British agriculture was remarkable less for its technological leadership than for the emergence of an agrarian structure based on capitalist farming. British agriculture, with its landlords, tenants and wage labourers on large holdings, contrasted with family or peasant farming elsewhere. As was noted earlier, this has been reasserted by O'Brien (1996) as a major reason for the much greater industrialisation of the British labour force. This section examines the plausibility of such an argument in terms of our CGE model.

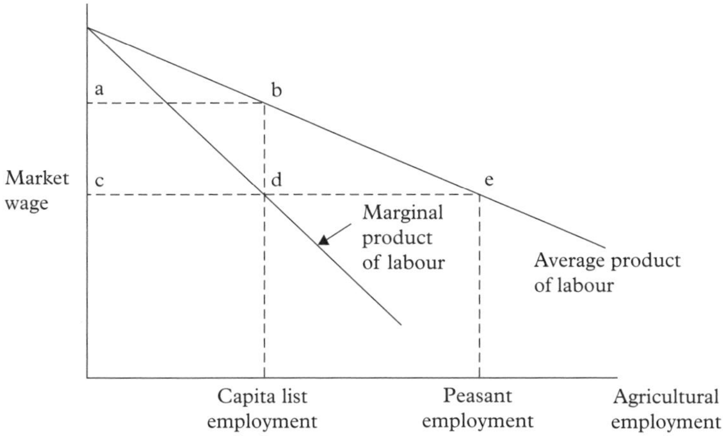

Figure 4.5 Peasant and capitalist agriculture

Cohen and Weitzman (1975) presented a simple theoretical model to justify predictions along these lines. The model relies on the assumption that peasant workers receive wages based on the average product of the household while in profit-maximising capitalist agriculture workers are paid wages equal to their marginal product. The difference that this makes for a given technology is shown in figure 4.5.

In the peasant case labour remains on the farm so long as the income of the farm allows the family to share total farm product and earn an income equal to that which could be earned in the labour market off the farm. Thus employment is at E, where the average product of labour equals the market wage rate. This implies that rent is dissipated among the peasants. In the capitalist case, farmers hire labour to the point where marginal product of labour equals the market wage and employment is at d. This results in rent equal to the rectangle abcd, which is made up of the difference at d between average product and the wage times the amount of employment. In comparison, the peasant family uses more labour, its members earn the equivalent to the market wage and it retains 'surplus labour', the average and marginal product of which are below that in capitalist farming. Replacement of peasant by capitalist farming would lead to a reduction in farm employment and a transfer of income towards rents.

Figure 4.5 does not consider the wider (general equilibrium) implications for the economy as a whole of a move from peasant to capitalist agriculture. Cohen and Weitzman did an analysis of this kind. They found that a switch from peasant to capitalist farming resulted in the use of less labour-intensive methods in agriculture, a rise in rents and a net outflow of labour from agriculture to the rest of the economy. GDP increased as labour was used more efficiently, but real wage rates declined as the displaced workers were absorbed by the labour market. Looked at the other way around, if peasant farming leads to the equalisation of average product wages in agriculture with marginal product wages prevailing elsewhere in the economy, it leads to a more agricultural labour force than would be observed in the neoclassical equilibrium.

The Cohen and Weitzman model has three important limitations, however. First, it does not allow for the accumulation of capital to respond to the increase in property income. Second, it is essentially a closed economy model. Third, it is abstract rather than quantitative and deals only in directions of change not magnitudes. We can address all these issues using our CGE model. Our simulations distribute labour between the capitalist and peasant sectors using the assumption that small family farmers equalise the average product of labour to the market wage.

Allen (1992) described a 'landlords' revolution' in eighteenth-century England that amounted to the 'disappearance of the yeoman', i.e., to the virtual elimination of small-scale family farming. Identifying peasant farms as those with less than 60 acres while capitalist farms had over 100 acres, he argued that, while in 1688 the peasantry occupied almost two-thirds of the land, by 1800 the proportion had fallen to only about 10 per cent (1992: 85). Moreover, his analysis of farm surveys clearly reveals the classic result that farms of under 50 acres used substantially more labour per acre and have higher output per acre than capitalist farms of 100 acres or more. Accordingly, the move to large farms lay behind the gains in agricultural labour productivity during the eighteenth century (1992: 211–25).

Continental countries such as France were much less affected by developments of this kind. In the mid-nineteenth century average farm size in France was about 30 acres compared with over 100 acres in Britain and farms of 100 acres or more accounted for only 29 per cent of French land at that time. In 1840, French agricultural labour productivity was 60 per cent, whereas total factor productivity was about 84 per cent of the British level. Rather more of the labour productivity gap came from lower French land and capital-to-labour ratios resulting from the persistence of small farms than from lower crop yields (Crafts, 1989).

In the light of this literature, it seems relevant to model the general equilibrium implications of a switch from peasant (average product wages) to capitalist (marginal product wages) farming. This provides insights into both the consequences of the 'landlords' revolution' in English agriculture and the basis of precocious British industrialisation. Table 4.6 presents

Table 4.6 *Simulated 1841 economy with two-thirds of the land in peasant farming*

	1841 Benchmark	Trade Adjusting	1770 Agricultural Imports
Agricultural Imports	100	101	15
Industrial Exports	100	80	41
Agricultural Output	100	105	111
Industrial Output	100	69	55
Agricultural Employment (%)	22	47	57
Industrial Employment (%)	41	28	21
Price of Agricultural Goods	100	94	113
Price of Industrial Goods	100	113	94

Note: TFP in peasant agriculture is assumed to be 0.8 the actual 1841 level as is the capital to land ratio.

the results of a simulation based on a switch from fully capitalist agriculture in the 1841 benchmark case to a situation with two-thirds of the land devoted to peasant farming. As in the earlier simulations, capitalists' assets (now reduced by land and agricultural capital in the hands of peasant families) are assumed to adjust to maintain a constant ratio to their incomes. Since there are suggestions in the literature that a move to capitalist agriculture with better property rights may have encouraged innovation, we assume somewhat lower total factor productivity in peasant agriculture at 80 per cent of the 1841 benchmark. This is in line with the discussion in Allen (1999) which suggests no more than a modest impact of this kind from the landlords' revolution. We have also assumed that capital in peasant agriculture was 20 per cent lower than on the same land in 1841; this is a land-to-capital ratio about halfway between the actual 1770 and 1841 levels.

The results in table 4.6 show that replacing capitalist with largely peasant farming has a big de-industrialising effect – much larger than that of any of the earlier counterfactuals that we have considered. The results are consistent with the predictions of Cohen and Weitzman (1975). The impact in the fully open-economy case is to more than double agriculture's share in the labour force to 47 per cent and to reduce industry's share by 13 percentage points. In this case there is also a noticeable effect on the services sector, where employment falls by 12 percentage points. This occurs primarily because there is a much-reduced need for distribution services to bring food to an urban population. Income moves from property owners to peasants and labourers. Real wages fall by less than 5 per cent despite a fall in property owners' real incomes, and consequently of the non-agricultural capital stock, by over 40 per cent. This case also involves a move in production space from the PPF to a point within it – in figure 4.1 this would be to the south-west of D – and GDP falls by 22 per cent.[3]

In the case where agricultural imports are restricted to the 1770 level, table 4.6 reports that agriculture's share in the labour force rises by 31 percentage points while industry's share falls by 16 percentage points compared with table 4.2, column 2. Increased dependence on inefficient peasant agriculture increases the reduction in GDP to 26 per cent and lowers workers' welfare by a similar 4 per cent. While agricultural output increases slightly, industrial output falls by 44 per cent. In this simulation, Britain has moved all the way to the 'European Norm'.

Comparison of tables 4.4 and 4.6 permits clarification of the relationship between productivity change in agriculture and industrialisation. In table 4.4 it emerged that, given that the British economy was based on capitalist farming, as it was by the mid-nineteenth century, improvements in agricultural technology that raise land and labour productivity slow down industrialisation. From table 4.6 we learn that a move from peasant to capitalist farming would raise labour productivity and at the same time would promote industrialisation very significantly. Since this latter change was a large part of the exceptional eighteenth-century British experience, it seems right to conclude that agriculture did release labour as Allen (1992) and Wrigley (1985) supposed. The reason for this was a move to relatively large-scale farming rather than enclosure per se but, even so, the emphasis placed by Landes (1969) on population growth rather than agrarian change as the main impetus to industrialisation of the labour force is clearly misleading.

In terms of our earlier work, these various simulations also make for more coherence. There was a transfer of labour to industry from the British agricultural sector which itself achieved comparatively high levels of productivity because it adopted large-scale capitalist farming (Crafts, 1989). Rapid technological change in exportable manufactures and diminishing returns in agriculture in the face of substantial population pressure were industrialising forces of unusual strength (Harley and Crafts, 2000). 'Both industrial technology and mobility out of agriculture were important' (Crafts and Harley, 1992: 705). But apropos of this

3 It is possible that other feedbacks from a move to peasant agriculture should be added in to the simulation. The most obvious would be to allow a move away from proletarianisation of the labour force to reduce population size through later marriage and lower fertility, as argued by Goldstone (1986). In further simulations (not reported here) we have explored this possibility and we do not believe it would make very much difference to the results on deindustrialisation reported in table 4.6.

last remark, the quantification that we have now achieved indicates that a distinctive agrarian structure mattered considerably more than we have previously recognised.

6 Conclusions

There are several important messages to take away from this analysis both methodological and substantive. With regard to the former, we believe that the paper has reinforced the point that CGE models can be valuable tools for economic historians. At the same time, it should also be clear that to understand structural change in the British industrial revolution requires an open-economy framework and explicit recognition that, in the terminology of international economics, Britain was a big country.

In terms of the historiography of British industrialisation, our simulations suggest that various familiar explanations for pronounced structural change do indeed have some validity. These include the suggestion by Williamson that unbalanced sectoral productivity growth played a part and the argument of Landes that population growth was conducive to industrialisation. But we have also demonstrated that it is crucial to distinguish between a release of labour associated with a switch from family to capitalist farming and agricultural productivity improvement in a fully capitalist economy.

Indeed, our most important substantive conclusion is that the key feature of the British economy was its (virtually) complete conversion to capitalist farming. Without taking this into account, it is not possible to explain British exceptionalism in its mid-nineteenth-century employment structure.

Part III

Technological change

5 The European origins of British technological predominance

Christine MacLeod

While western Europe as a whole had enjoyed an upsurge in inventive activity since the Middle Ages (Mokyr, 1990: 31–56), Britain assumed the technological leadership during the eighteenth and nineteenth centuries in specific, but economically important, industries and processes – primarily cotton textiles and the heavy industry network of coal, iron, and steam power. Why was it in Britain, a country previously on the periphery of European technical progress, that the technological changes characteristic of the Industrial Revolution were made? The questions of technological creativity and economic development are rife with nationalistic undertones, and as long as we imagine that Britain had become a peculiarly inventive society, this paradox cannot be resolved. For a more critical perspective on British exceptionalism this chapter approaches the debate through a recognition of the specificities of the sites of technological change during European and American industrialisation (Inkster, 1996: 41–9).

The flowering of technological change in the Industrial Revolution had deep roots which led back, through several centuries, to medieval sources that were only partly British. Indeed, two separate streams of technological progress were converging. One was a pan-European stream, of which different parts of Europe assumed the leadership at different times and in different industries. The other, based on the technologies of coal extraction and use, was more distinctly British – until, in the mid-nineteenth century, it was diverted to encompass continental Europe and North America.

This schema echoes E. A. Wrigley's interpretation of the British Industrial Revolution as a dual phenomenon, comprising two independent and overlapping phases. The first phase, during the eighteenth century, saw Britain replace Holland as the most advanced exponent of a traditional ('organic') type of development familiar, to varying degrees, throughout western Europe. Its principal features were: population increase and urbanisation, sustained by commercial agriculture, international trade and a proto-industrial (or domestic) system of textile production. But it was the second phase which was revolutionary, for it was this one which allowed Britain (and subsequently others) to escape the resource constraints of the 'organic' economy. It involved the transition to a 'mineral-based' economy, without which, Wrigley argues, the British economy would have followed that of Holland into stagnation. Dutch attempts to escape from the constraints of the traditional resource base of land, wood and water by burning peat had failed: their peat reserves quickly approached exhaustion and, in any case, lacked the high calorific value of coal. Britain's advantage lay in its huge and relatively accessible coal reserves. The intensifying competition for space on the surface could be resolved by digging beneath it: coal, steam engines fuelled with coal and iron made with coal could be substituted for wood, water and wind power, and timber structures and iron made with charcoal, respectively. Yet the transition to mineral resources, although by the early nineteenth century vital to continued economic growth, was so smooth that it has been scarcely recognised for the revolution it represented. For the technologies of coal-getting and coal-using had been developed piecemeal, in response to the emerging resource crisis, during three or more centuries before they became absolutely indispensable. When British economic growth finally pressed up against the 'organic' energy ceiling, it burst straight through to the new world of seemingly inexhaustible resources on the floor above (Wrigley, 1988: 8–33).

Wrigley's Industrial Revolution is essentially an *energy* revolution. Utilisation of a new type of energy, which was available cheaply and in relatively unlimited amounts, removed the brakes from a host of other technological changes which otherwise would have stalled. Some of these were directly coal-related, but many were the outgrowth of the traditional sectors of the European economy in such fields as textiles. The primary long-term gains here were in labour productivity, via mechanisation. They are emphasised by David Landes in his influential book *The Unbound Prometheus*.

> The heart of the industrial revolution was an interrelated succession of technological changes. The material advances took place in three areas: (1) there was a substitution of mechanical devices for human skills; (2) inanimate power – in particular, steam – took the place of human and animal strength; (3) there was a marked improvement in the getting and working of raw materials, especially in what are now known as the metallurgical and chemical industries. Concomitant with these changes in equipment and process went new forms of industrial organization. (Landes, 1969: 1–2)

Here Landes points to the factory in particular: more than just a larger unit, it was essentially a new system of production. A further set of defining technological and organisational changes comprised the development of machine tools (machines to make machines) and of a specialised machine-making industry dedicated to their production and use, which supplied equipment to manufacturers, farmers and the transport sector (Paulinyi, 1986b: 261–89).

This chapter will survey these developments in turn, looking first at the principal technological changes that constitute the 'Landes type' Industrial Revolution (which corresponds roughly with Wrigley's first phase), then at the stream of coal-related advances. In both cases, it explores the historical and geographical reasons why Britons, rather than other Europeans, prioritised these particular technologies. By contrast, the final part of the chapter assesses critically some of the factors often advanced to explain exceptional British inventiveness: in particular, the direct and indirect influences of 'the scientific revolution' on technical practice and attitudes to technological change; the stimuli to invention provided by the state through, for example, patents and privileges, the promotion of technical education, or protective tariffs; and wider socio-economic changes such as urbanisation, improved transport and communications, and receptiveness to immigrants.

Historically, British advances drew heavily on continental expertise. The government of Elizabeth I promoted the introduction of new techniques and products through immigration – German miners and metal workers, French and Italian glass makers, Dutch and Flemish cloth makers. Encouraging and protecting them from exclusive guild regulations provided the primary reason for granting letters patent, the beginnings of the English patent system (MacLeod, 1988: 10–12). During the seventeenth century, Dutch engineers were contracted to drain the East Anglian Fens, and Huguenot refugees from France boosted the standards of many trades, not least watch- and clockmaking, textile printing and papermaking; Italian glassmakers were closely involved in the invention of lead ('flint') glassware in London in the 1670s. Some Britons actively spied out continental techniques: John Lombe in 1716, for example, notoriously stole Italian machinery designs for his Derby silk factory – and was lucky to escape with his life (Harris, 1998: 535–43). Daniel Defoe was voicing a common perception when he wrote in 1728:

> it is a kind of proverb attending the character of Englishmen, that they are better to improve than to invent, better to advance upon the designs and plans which other people have laid down, than to form schemes and designs of their own and which is still more, the thing seems to be really true in fact, and the observation very just. (Defoe, 1728: 299)

Just at that time, however, this proverb was losing its plausibility. It had never been completely true – William Lee's invention of the stocking frame in the 1590s is a striking counter-example, but the first Act, in 1719, to prevent the emigration of British artisans to the continent indicated a new phase in the transfer of technology. Subsequent eighteenth-century legislation extended the ban to the export of certain machines and tools (Harris, 1998: 7–27).

It was notoriously in the field of textile production that, during the eighteenth century, Britain began to take the technical lead through a series of mechanical inventions: why it was in Britain is far from evident. We have been urged to relinquish the search for causes and to ascribe it to chance, as unpredictable as the outcome of a single football match (Crafts, 1977: 429–41). This would seem reasonable advice if we were dealing with only one or two inventions – a happy British brainwave which could as easily have been French or Dutch or Italian. Since it is a question, however, of numerous inventors producing a variety of prototype machines and devices, across all four sectors of the cotton industry – preparation, spinning, weaving and finishing – some sort of rational explanation seems to be called for.

Superficially at least, there was little to differentiate the British textile industry from its continental competitors at the start of the eighteenth century. Textile manufacturing throughout Europe was organised increasingly on a 'proto-industrial' (or domestic) basis, which linked decentralised households and small workshops into national and international markets. In itself this was a form of innovative organisation, which was liberating the textile industries from the limitations of household production, which had previously prevailed throughout Europe. The principal productivity-raising inventions of the eighteenth-century textile trades originated in the domestic industry (Berg, 1994: 236–42). Kay's flying shuttle, Hargreaves' spinning jenny, Crompton's mule, even Arkwright's water frame were first designed to raise the productivity of decentralised workers. (Since the demand for cotton yarn and cloth was outstripping supply, it seems probable that expanding output by re-equipping workers was more urgent than reducing the cost of labour.) Only once the mechanised factory had been introduced did its particular requirements start to shape invention. Organisational innovations then became a powerful impetus to complementary technological change; in combination with mechanisation, they strongly boosted productivity.

Patrick O'Brien suggests the British domestic textile industry was distinguished by the fortunate combination of two factors: the suitability of raw cotton for mechanical spinning and weaving *relative* to other fibres, and the exceptional size of the British cotton industry *relative* to the rest of Europe's in the mid-eighteenth century (O'Brien *et al.*, 1991: 394–423). Several English patents issued since the late seventeenth century attest to inventive interest in mechanising the spinning of other fibres, such as wool and flax, but technical success escaped them all until the 1730s when Lewis Paul (the son of a French Huguenot) and John Wyatt turned to cotton. It was also with (mixed) cotton fabrics that, simultaneously, John Kay's flying shuttle first succeeded in speeding up weaving (Paulinyi, 1986a: 149–66). The mechanisation of woollen and linen processes was always to follow that of cotton by several years or more.

In other ways, however, cotton was not the most obvious candidate for mechanisation, because protective legislation, secured by the woollen and silk industries against Asian imports, restricted its use to mixed fabrics, mostly 'fustians' (linen warps, cotton wefts). Between 1721 and 1774 pure cotton cloth was banned from British domestic markets. Despite this, the twists and turns of British protective legislation fostered a much larger 'cotton' industry than either Dutch free-trade policies or, at the other extreme, the complete ban on printed cottons and linens favoured by the French and most other European governments. If textile-spinning machinery were going to be invented in eighteenth-century Europe it was likely, for technical reasons, to be for *cotton*, and if it were cotton-spinning machinery, then it was unlikely to be anywhere but England – specifically Lancashire and Derbyshire – because nowhere else had a cotton industry of any size. We might also note the geographical proximity of the west Pennine fustian industry to the two cases of successful textile mechanisation already extant in early eighteenth-century England, which by their demonstration of the feasibility of similar inventions may have inspired prospective inventors. It was at Derby in the 1720s that John and Thomas Lombe established a highly visible factory to contain their silk winding and throwing machinery of Italian design. And it was to Derbyshire, Leicestershire and Nottinghamshire that the London hosiery industry was simultaneously removing its mechanically sophisticated stocking-knitting frames (of William Lee's invention) – an industry which both Hargreaves and Arkwright recognised as a customer for machine-spun cotton yarn.

The cotton industry's mechanisation in Britain was an offshoot of western European technological development in the way that a biological species stranded on an island evolves differently from its relatives on the mainland. But the coal-related industries were *sui generis*. Britain's relative shortage of wood and abundance of coal were responsible for its early, though protracted, transition to coal-burning technologies. Medieval England had a substantial open-cast coal-mining industry, which supplied mainly domestic hearths: London's residents were served by the coastal trade from Tyneside, and already suffered from smoke pollution. Fifteenth-century Leicestershire's coal mines were 100 feet deep and were worked by the pillar and stall method. This method of underground working gradually spread through British coalfields, until its replacement by the productivity-raising 'longwall' technique during the eighteenth century. By then gunpowder (introduced by German metal miners) was in use for sinking shafts, if not for extraction, and more effective means were being devised to line the shaft and combat the drainage and ventilation problems which arose as miners worked deeper and further underground (Flinn, 1984: 74–99, 442–3). But it remained a labour-intensive industry: male face-workers hewed the coal with picks and shovels; in many pits women and children hauled and carried it hundreds of feet to the surface, until winding engines began to release them from this drudgery in the mid-eighteenth century. By 1700 British miners were producing 3 million tons of coal per annum; by 1800, over 15 million tons – an estimated 80 per cent of world production (Flinn, 1984: 26).

Debate has raged over the existence of an early modern 'timber famine'. The most recent research restores the case for a serious shortfall in supplies of wood fuel and building timber (especially for the expanding Royal, and Merchant, Navies) during the seventeenth century, and again in the second half of the eighteenth. In both periods charcoal prices climbed steeply; importers of Scandinavian iron and timber responded on a large scale to undercut domestic producers (Thomas, 1988: 129–41; Harris, 1988: 19–29). So did inventors.

Experiments with burning coal began where the raw material could easily be separated from noxious coal fumes: soap, salt and sugar boilers, dyers and bleachers were using it widely by the late sixteenth century, if not earlier. By the early seventeenth century, makers of cheaper types of glass found they could burn coal if they redesigned their kilns and covered their melting pots – techniques sufficiently developed by the 1670s for use in the production of best lead crystal. Maltsters discovered that coal was viable if they decarburised it first, to make coke. During the second half of the seventeenth century, smelters of non-ferrous metals adopted the (Italian glassmakers') reverberatory furnace and adapted it to burn coal (Wrigley, 1988: 77–8). Repeated attempts to smelt iron with coal met with little success, however, until about 1709, when Abraham Darby, following the maltsters' practice, experimented with coke in a blast furnace. But Darby operated in the small, cast-iron sector, where coke pig iron offered distinct advantages. To produce wrought iron, coke pig required more processing; this only became economical as the difference between coke and charcoal prices widened after 1750. Further delay resulted from the necessity of training sufficient workmen in the new techniques. In the refining sector, Henry Cort's puddling and rolling process, patented in 1783–4, effectively completed the transition to mineral fuel. It allowed both the complete replacement of charcoal in wrought-iron production and massive economies of scale, which, through dramatic cuts in prices, promoted rapid expansion (Harris, 1988: 30–40). By 1800 Britain was approaching self-sufficiency in iron, despite magnified wartime demand. Its ironworks produced about 220,000 tons per annum, eleven times more than a century before (Harris, 1988: 50).

The substitution of iron for timber as a structural material proceeded rapidly during the second half of the eighteenth century. It was already employed for industrial and agricultural tools, cooking pots, nails, hardware, cannon and shot; by 1800 its uses had extended to bridges, buildings (especially iron-framed factories), rails, machinery parts, steam-engine cylinders, water pipes (soon gas pipes too) and boats. Iron founders extended their skills to produce ever larger and more complex castings. However, the era of iron's most rapid expansion was in the mid-nineteenth century, and was principally in wrought, not cast, iron. New demand came primarily from the railways, while advances in both blast-furnace and puddling technologies further increased outputs and reduced costs (Harris, 1988: 57–63, 79). Steel remained virtually a precious metal until Bessemer introduced his converter in the 1850s and made cheap bulk steel the successor to wrought iron. The 'crucible' method, however, invented by Benjamin Huntsman (of German parentage) in the 1740s, which used coal to remelt 'shear steel', produced a more uniform material, suitable for the exacting demands of toolmakers; with experience it also permitted the controlled production of differing grades of steel (Harris, 1988: 41–7).

The availability of cheap fuel kept costs down across a range of heat-using industries, not least in the production of chemicals used by the textile industries (sulphuric acid, soda, chlorine bleaching powder and dyes). It spawned the gas industry, pioneered in the 1790s by William Murdoch, of the steam-engineering firm of Boulton & Watt, who recognised the potential of coal gas for lighting factories – which could now operate twenty-four hours a day. Gas was soon lighting urban streets and upper-class houses. The downside of this was half a century's worth of the waste product tar, before William Perkin discovered he could distill it to produce synthetic dyes (first, mauve).

Beyond permitting the expansion of important staple industries, the growth of coal mining also had important 'spin-offs' through its need for improved drainage and transportation. One of these was the steam engine; a second was canals; a third was the railways (Wrigley, 1988: 73–87). Adequate drainage was the most pressing obstacle to the deepening of mines. This is attested by the large number of inventors it attracted. In the period 1660–1750 over 100 patents covered water-raising devices or power sources which claimed water-raising as their main function: twenty-five of these cited mines-drainage as their exclusive or principal application and a further forty mentioned it as one of several (MacLeod, 1988: 175–7). Thomas Savery in 1698 advertised his steam engine as 'the miners' friend'. It was Thomas Newcomen's atmospheric engine, however, introduced in 1712, which proved to be the true miners' friend: it provided both a means of effective drainage and an important source of demand for coal. Approximately 100 Newcomen engines had been erected when the patent expired in 1733; nearly 2,500 by 1800 (Kanefsky and Robey, 1980: 169). Watt's invention of the separate condenser in the late 1760s made the steam engine more fuel-efficient – a godsend to the tin and copper miners of coal-starved Cornwall, though less appreciated among coal owners. Cornish engineers, such as Jonathan Hornblower, Richard Trevithick and Arthur Woolf, took the search for fuel efficiency further in high-pressure and compound steam engines. Watt's adaptation of steam power to rotative motion made it available to the textile industry from the 1780s. Although it was slow to replace water power at first, except in Manchester and other towns on the Lancashire plain which lacked good water courses, by 1840 over 80 per cent of British cotton mills were steam-powered (Von Tunzelmann, 1978: 30–7). By then steam power was also well established in the transport sector, for locomotive and marine engines.

The coal industry's need for improved means to transport its heavy produce was a major stimulus to innovation. A short canal had been built to Exeter in the 1560s, but for the next two centuries the English concentrated on improving river navigation, leaving the French to solve many of the engineering problems posed by building canals in hilly terrain. Canal construction resumed with a vengeance in England after 1760 to service the requirements of the expanding coal industry, beginning with the Duke of Bridgewater's canal to link his pits at Worsley with Manchester. The Duke had been impressed by the French Canal du Midi – one of the sights of the Grand Tour. His engineer, James Brindley, took the Bridgewater Canal, underground, almost to the coalface – such were the advantages of water transport (Flinn, 1984: 181–9). By 1800 Britain had an inland-waterways system of canals and rivers exceeding 3,000 miles in length. It was available for the carriage of passengers as well as manufactures, food and raw materials, but without the impetus from the coal industry it is doubtful whether more than a few of the canals would have been built, or operated at a profit.

Many of the engineering techniques developed on the canals – cutting, embanking, tunnelling and bridge-building – were transferred to the construction of the railways which began to supersede them from the

1820s. The concept of a railway originated in the metal mines of central Europe in the sixteenth century, where small wagons were pushed manually along wooden rails laid underground, and it may have been transferred to Britain by immigrant miners. From the early seventeenth century, British coal owners began to build these 'wagonways' both above and below the surface, using gravity where topography allowed and horsepower where it did not. In the 1790s rails made entirely of cast iron began to replace wooden ones in the coalfields, and it was largely there, during the next two decades, that the steam locomotive was first developed (Flinn, 1984: 146–63). It was the colliery engineer George Stephenson who famously pioneered the steam locomotive on public railways, beginning with the Stockton & Darlington in 1825.

While textile technologies were transferred almost immediately to north-western Europe, it was the mid-nineteenth century before coal-based technologies began seriously to penetrate continental Europe. It was only with the rising demand for iron in railway construction that ironmasters switched over *en masse* from charcoal to coke fuel: in north-western Europe the output of both coal and pig iron quadrupled between 1830 and 1860, and kept rising (Mitchell, 1978: 184–5, 215–6). This delay was the result, partly of a different resource situation, and partly of difficulties inherent in transferring technologies which were heavily dependent on tacit knowledge and on skills learned through experience. The attempts of spies sent by the *ancien regime* to master British coal-using techniques repeatedly ended in failure: they lacked the depth of experience necessary to grasp the essentials (Harris, 1998: 238–61). Unlike Britain, much of continental Europe was still well forested, and until the discovery of new coalfields in the Pas de Calais and the Ruhr in the mid-nineteenth century, neither France nor Germany had access to good coal deposits in proximity to iron ore; thereafter rail transport further improved this situation. The Scandinavian countries and Italy were even less well endowed with coal. If there was anything fortuitous about the British Industrial Revolution, it was, as Wrigley has suggested, its natural resources. Ample deposits of coal, many of them located conveniently close to the coast, were nature's best gift to Britain and the greatest 'chance factor' in its early industrialisation (Wrigley, 1988: 28–9, 113–15). Moreover, there were good deposits of iron, non-ferrous metals, clays and rock salt.

We have so far concentrated on the twin pillars of British industrialisation – the mechanisation of cotton textiles and the development of coal-related technologies – not because these were the sole areas of British industry to be modified by technological change, but because they constituted the definitive industries of the British Industrial Revolution. Cotton and steam power occupy the stage, whether as the glory of Britain celebrated by the early Victorians, or as the dark satanic mills condemned by the first generation of professional economic historians, or as 'the wave of gadgets' notoriously conceived of by T. S. Ashton's schoolchild (Coleman, 1992: 1–42). It is these particular inventions that generations of historians have been called on to 'explain'. It must be emphasised, however, that Britain had not suddenly become a peculiarly inventive society, and it is therefore a forlorn quest to search for explanations couched in those terms. We are dealing with a phenomenon common to western Europe as a whole, one several centuries old – though, more recently, also extending to European settlers in North America. Britain *appears* to be unusually inventive because Britons were the major protagonists in developing the two technologies which together first revolutionised industrial production: the mechanisation of cotton textiles and the expansion of energy resources needed to sustain it. But there were sound historical and geographical reasons why Britons, rather than other Europeans, should have focused on these particular problems. Only the British 'enjoyed' – for several centuries – the stimulus of a timber shortage in the context of a wealth of coal. Only the British had a thriving cotton industry in the eighteenth century. To reach solutions to the challenges they faced in these two fields, Britons were able to draw on a reservoir of techniques accumulated across the whole of Europe. For example, neither the blast furnace nor the reverberatory furnace, used in coal-fired metallurgical processes, were of British origin; nor were the wagonways used in coal mines, nor the pound locks deployed in canals (Harris, 1988: 14–18). *Pace* nineteenth-century nationalistic writers, the steam engine was not a purely British invention (Harris, 1998: 288). When we turn to textiles, British inventors had before them the examples of Italian silk-winding machinery and the Dutch loom for weaving half a dozen ribbons simultaneously, as well as the native example of Lee's stocking frame.

Perhaps there are sufficient examples here of continental inventiveness, but to bolster the case, one could point to a host of inventions in other industries which were better established elsewhere in Europe. It is irrelevant that these did not lead to the First Industrial Revolution, because the issue here is relative *inventiveness*, not entrepreneurial success. France, for example, was strongly inventive in the chemical industries (including revolutionary new methods of making soda and bleach), in the silk industry (the looms of Vaucanson and later Jacquard, with their precursors of punch-card computer technology), in the paper industry (Robert's papermaking machine – 'the Fourdrinier'), and, as a spin-off from papermaking, the era's most astounding invention, the Montgolfier hot-air balloon. In response to wartime shortages, Frenchmen pioneered the interchangeability of parts in musket production (Adler, 1997: 273–311), and discovered how to refine sugar from beet and preserve food by bottling. French engineering skills in building canals, roads and fortifications were universally admired and imitated; a famous 'British' engineer, M. I. Brunel (father of Isambard) was in fact French. The first steam-driven car was probably made by a Frenchman (Harris, 1998: 540–3; McNeil, 1990: 434, 441, 482–9, 982–3). More generally, the number of applications for French *privilèges* follows a very similar pattern to that for English patents during the eighteenth century – including a sharp rise from the 1760s (Hilaire-Pérez, 2000: 55).

All inventions are the creatures of a particular society, selected and shaped by its dominant values and priorities. This is even more apparent when we look across the Atlantic. To some extent the United States borrowed European technologies, including early textile machinery and iron made with coal. But Yankee ingenuity emerged early and not only began adapting that textile machinery to specific American conditions, but also led the way in certain fields suggested by its own resource situation. Advances in woodworking technology, epitomised by Blanchard's lathe, offer a clear example, as does the cotton gin, which played a major part in reducing the cost of cotton cloth by mechanically cleaning the raw material. Steamboats may or may not have been an American invention, but they were developed more quickly on the Mississippi than elsewhere. Oliver Evans' automated flour mill, Jacob Perkins' nail-making machine and the US government's pursuit of interchangeable rifle parts all attest to success in technologies that Europe did not prioritise (Cochran, 1981: 50–72).

It follows that we should identify those factors that made Europeans (and European emigrés) in general, rather than Britons in particular, invention-oriented. Indeed it has proved extremely difficult to isolate factors which might account for exclusively British inventiveness, leading many commentators, from Hume onwards, to resort to an ultimately ideological celebration of free speech or God's providential care for his chosen race (McCloskey, 1995: 114–32). A widening of the question in this way is likely to invite the objection that it becomes too broad to allow for meaningful comparisons or falsification. There is some justice in this objection, but some speculation remains both possible and valuable, not least because it is perhaps hard for us, in the era of the 'technical fix', to remember that this creative response, let alone its success, was neither automatic nor guaranteed. Societies may tolerate, or adapt to, difficulties *without* recourse to technological change. A timber shortage might be eased by planting more trees (as advocated in *Sylva*, John Evelyn's great work for the Royal Society published in 1664), or by importing wood, or by using it less wastefully (Thomas, 1988: 141–3). A labour shortage might be met by employing new sections of the population (perhaps more married women and younger children), or by extracting more effort from existing workers. Tried and tested ways might actually be preferred in the face of uncertainty. What made Europeans at this time both willing and able to invent and to assume the risks of innovation? How did Britain compare with its continental competitors?

A much debated causal factor is the advance in experimental science associated with the 'scientific revolution' of the seventeenth century; the chronology offers a temptingly neat fit. This was certainly a Europe-wide phenomenon. Most historians, however, downplay the role of science in the British Industrial Revolution, limiting its impact to an indirect promotion of experimentation and precise measurement (Mathias, 1979: 72–87). Neither the mechanisation of the textile industries nor the new coal-using technologies required new scientific knowledge. With the exceptions of Watt's separate condenser and industrial chemistry, pioneered chiefly in France, it was the mid-nineteenth century before inventors began regularly to draw on the discoveries of the laboratory. The pace of discovery had quickened from the seventeenth century, as the community of investigators and the resources available to them expanded. Consequently, the inventor's intellectual resources also broadened. In the longer term this was immensely important, but it offers limited help with explaining eighteenth-century inventiveness.

Of greater significance in this respect is the cultural change of which the scientific revolution was itself symptomatic. An interest in science became a major component of both polite and artisanal culture, particularly in Britain (Jacob, 1997: 2–11, 105–15; Inkster, 1991: 33–45; Stewart, 1992: passim). Gentlemen met in clubs and state-sponsored academies, in coffee houses and country houses, to explore scientific discoveries, natural history and new inventions. Itinerant lecturers and provincial societies fostered an interest in all things scientific and promoted the idea that problems could be solved via invention. 'By 1750 British engineers and entrepreneurs could talk the same mechanical talk' (Jacob, 1997: 115). The Society of Arts, formed in London in 1754, offered premiums and prizes for inventions, which it published. It was imitated – with less success – in Paris in 1776. French provincial academies and informal British societies (such as the Lunar Society of Birmingham and the Manchester Lit and Phil) provided new opportunities for contact between creative people of disparate backgrounds and mutual encouragement to investigate, experiment, invent (Hilaire-Pérez, 2000: 189–220; Musson and Robinson, 1969: 87–189).

The stimulus to invention offered by the state was widespread in Europe but quite varied in form. It is hard to credit the British government with the most enlightened or effective policy. Many continental governments actively sponsored scientific discovery and technical education. Again, the French example is instructive. In 1666 Colbert founded the Académie des Sciences, which, unlike the contemporary Royal Society of London, received state funding and government commissions to investigate practical problems. French government schools of naval design and of military and civil engineering followed in the mid-eighteenth century. The Revolution spawned the Ecole Polytechnique in 1794, which offered a rigorous course in mathematics, scientific theory and engineering, and was emulated in several European capitals – but not London (Inkster, 1991: 42–5; Jacob, 1997: 131–64).

The concept of protecting and promoting inventions by patents of monopoly spread from fifteenth-century Italy throughout western Europe, potentially providing a major new impetus to technological change, by capturing for inventors the material rewards of their ingenuity. The British state offered a positive, if hesitant, approval, preserving patents for invention despite massive opposition to monopolies in general during the seventeenth century, and increasingly withdrawing support from workers whose livelihoods were menaced by technological change (MacLeod, 1988: 14–19, 164–7). However, although England's patent system was probably better than nothing, it was far from ideal. To the multiplying band of professional inventors, who were dependent on selling or licensing their inventions, patents provided the sole available protection – an imperfect, but perhaps necessary, encouragement that often disappointed in practice. Patents were very expensive to obtain and hard to enforce. The system's very existence enjoined its use, partly by inspiring a defensive anxiety that an inventor who failed to patent might be pre-empted by an industrial spy, partly by bestowing kudos on a product – an implied but specious, royal guarantee of quality (MacLeod, 1988: 75–96). Again one is forced to wonder whether the French system of *privilèges* might not have offered greater encouragement. Provided the application survived a much more rigorous investigation than in England (and a large majority of them did), the *privilège* was awarded without payment, enforcement was backed by the state, and the inventor often enjoyed further financial benefits. Alternatively, he could elect to relinquish all claims over the invention in return for a state pension (Hilaire-Pérez, 2000: 69–142). The main contributions of the British state to inventive activity were more indirect and unintended, one being the peculiar combination of tariffs and prohibitions on the cotton industry, at the behest of rival textile manufacturers, which allowed the fustian industry to thrive (O'Brien *et al.*, 1991: 394–423). The massive expansion of the Royal Navy in the seventeenth and eighteenth centuries produced technical spin-offs: not only did it exacerbate Britain's long-term deforestation, thereby helping to narrow the price differentials between wood and coal fuel and between charcoal-iron and coke-iron (Thomas, 1988: 135–6); more positively, it stimulated invention in ship design and a wide range of auxiliary and provisioning industries (O'Brien, 1991: 19–21).

When we look to the wider social context, there were many changes underway which may have promoted inventiveness, but any assessment of their role remains unavoidably speculative. In many of them Britain was more advanced than most parts of Europe – except Holland. All channels of information were running more freely by the eighteenth century. Expanding transport networks, regular newspapers and postal services, complemented by a high level of literacy (especially in towns), speeded up and widened the flow of information through the country at large. Britain was the second most urbanised country in Europe by 1750: 20 per cent of its population lived in towns of over 5,000 inhabitants (Wrigley, 1988: 13). Urbanisation was especially conducive to innovation: concentrated populations circulate information more quickly, and townspeople appear to be more open to novelty. Proximity stimulated competition among manufacturers and facilitated the exchange of ideas by stealth or consent. Patentees were overwhelmingly urban – regularly over half from London alone before 1800 (MacLeod, 1988: 119). This is a phenomenon that has also been identified in France and North America (Hilaire-Pérez, 2000: 58; Sokoloff and Khan, 1990: 7–8).

Inventors of mechanical devices, especially perhaps in Britain, also enjoyed increased access to professional technical assistance. By the late eighteenth century, particularly in London, Birmingham and the northern textile regions, 'engineers' and 'machine makers' started to specialise in supplying the expanding manufacturing sector with equipment. Competing on performance as well as price, they became conduits for innovation, disseminating the improvements embodied in their products (MacLeod, 1992: 285–7). Moreover, they advanced the standard of machine tools, which often proved crucial to the feasibility of an invention reliant on accurate metalworking skills: Watt's steam-engine cylinders, for example, were dependent on Wilkinson's cannon-boring machinery. According to Mokyr, Britain's comparative advantage lay in its wealth of machine-making skills (Mokyr, 1990: 103–5, 240–1). It is certainly a more precise speculation than McCloskey's emphasis on 'freedom of speech', but it remains an unproven one relative to the continent (McCloskey, 1995: 124). Such skills may indeed have arisen *in response* to the demands of Britain's mechanising industry: Arkwright notoriously advertised for clockmakers, watchmakers and similar tradesmen to fill his factory with machinery. British watch- and clockmaking skills had been boosted only a century before by the influx of Huguenot refugees.

Striking innovations in technique and organisation invigorated all sectors of Britain's industrialising economy. In a largely commercialised economy with rapidly widening markets, both at home and overseas, and increasingly unfettered competition, the returns to innovation were growing. A slight reduction in costs or an eye-catching variation in design could beat off a manufacturer's competitors. The material gains from technological change helped to prompt scientific enquiry, setting up a 'virtuous circle' of knowledge creation, and perhaps made entrepreneurs more receptive to innovation. Inventiveness was widespread, but as constraints, resources, and tastes varied across Europe, so did technological strengths and preferences. In Britain, particular opportunities and constraints on expansion had directed inventors into exceptionally fruitful channels. Neither the design skills nor the high degree of craftmanship and experience required to make new insights practicable should be underrated. Through years of practising their trade and honing their skills, working men and women discovered how best to manipulate their tools and materials; they adjusted their methods and adapted their instruments in the light of experience. Herein, most evidently, lay the advantage of Britain's early shift to coal-using technologies, where complex techniques took time to acquire and to finesse (Harris, 1998: 555–6).

Britain's other great strength was its receptiveness to new ideas and immigrants, although it was certainly not unique in this. Foreign inventions continued to be naturalised: new products, processes and ideas were successfully adapted and improved, boosting Britain's reputation for technical innovativeness (Harris, 1998: 540–3). A relatively mobile, tolerant, and flexible society facilitated this eclecticism, as did a reservoir of appropriate skills, partly imported, partly built up among artisans, the domestic industries, and the coal-using technologies. From the late seventeenth century, a hard-won ethos of religious toleration (at least for Protestants of various hues) and a general openness to new ideas, evinced by the ferment, especially in London, of pamphlets, lectures and demonstrations of scientific phenomena, marked out Britain as a society where inventors might expect a hearing – increasingly even approbation (McCloskey, 1995: 123; MacLeod, 1988: 216–22). Inventors and inventions were attracted from Europe and sometimes back from America, although many British inventors still sought their fortunes abroad. The direction of technological transfer did not suddenly turn 180 degrees in the eighteenth century: while becoming increasingly conspicuous exporters of particular technologies, the British continued to be astute importers of technology and technicians (Inkster, 1991: 51).

It was fortuitous that Britain had excellent coal reserves and a peculiar set of protective legislation which had stimulated the growth of Europe's largest cotton industry during the eighteenth century, but, given these circumstances, it was less fortuitous that important inventions in these fields were made in Britain rather than elsewhere. The needs and opportunities arising in these fields acted as 'focusing devices' to attract the attention of British inventors. To meet these technical challenges, however, British inventors drew on a reservoir of technical knowledge and skills which did not stop at national boundaries; it had been filling for several centuries, fed by streams from across the European continent and beyond. The British Industrial Revolution was ultimately a European achievement.

6 Invention in the Industrial Revolution: the case of cotton

James Thomson

Patrick O'Brien's research in the area of concern of this festschrift volume has been so wide-ranging that it seems likely that all its chapters will be making some reference to his work. In the case of the subject which has fallen to my lot, however, his contribution has been so substantial that when I set to work I wondered whether there remained anything for me to do beyond reporting on his achievements. To do this, I concluded, certainly represented part of my brief, and would be helpful for diffusing his ideas on the issue as they have been developed over a period of some ten years and are scattered among journals and essay collections.[1] But following my rereading of what he and his collaborators, Trevor Griffiths and David Hunt, had written, I perceived that there might also be room for a personal contribution on my part in the form of some reflection on the *process* of invention within the cotton industry. In the chapter in which O'Brien and his team come closest to such reflecting – entitled 'Technological change during the First Industrial Revolution: the paradigm case of textiles, 1688–1851' – they do so with respect to the textile sector as a whole – focusing purely on cotton, I had gained the impression, had the potential of yielding some value added.[2]

Concerning the choice of a methodology for such an exercise, O'Brien, with his rare ability to build bridges between econometric and 'traditional' approaches within economic history, and his openness to the approaches of other disciplines, has been as eclectic as he has been in the range of subjects which he has studied: the only prescription which could come from him would be to be imaginative and receptive, but not exclusively so, to new research techniques. That on which I finally settled is one described by him as 'dealing in narrative form with one innovation after another'. The description comes in the chapter just referred to in the context of a rejection of the use of the method in view of the breadth

The researching and writing of this chapter were made possible by a grant from The Economic and Social Research Council (award reference R000238515).

[1] The publication which first marked his interest was O'Brien *et al.*, 1991.

[2] O'Brien *et al.*, 1996a.

of the subject: he does not, on the other hand, dismiss it out of hand, stating that: 'that kind of tightly focused research is a precondition for the interplay of fact and concept required to theorize about technological change'.[3] In the more restricted context of interpreting inventions relating to a single fibre I felt that it might be helpful. Support for such a 'hunch' can be gleaned too from O'Brien. In one of his first publications on the subject he claimed that 'the discontinuity signalled by these two major inventions [Hargreaves' and Arkwright's]. . . is more effectively caught by traditional, narrative methods of analysis than by simple number counts'.[4]

The consequence of this thought process is that my chapter consists of three sections, a first in which I summarise O'Brien's views on the subject, a second providing a narrative of invention in cotton, based on standard sources, up to the invention of roller spinning by Arkwright, and a conclusion in which I tease out what additional conclusions to those already reached by O'Brien are suggested by this narrative.

1 Patrick O'Brien's interpretation

For my summary I shall use the article 'The paradigm case of textiles' as a framework, for it itself represents something of a synthesis of the range of his work on the cotton industry as well as developing his argument further. I shall also make specific reference to his other publications on the subject, in particular his study, with Trevor Griffiths and David Hunt, 'Political components of the Industrial Revolution: Parliament and the English cotton industry, 1660–1774' which is a masterpiece of research and interpretation.[5]

In 'paradigm case' O'Brien declares scepticism concerning the advantages of the use of demand and supply-side models of technological change drawn from economics or sociology in accounting for the exceptional British record for technological change in textiles during the eighteenth century. He provides both a priori and empirical grounds for doing so. The former take the line that profitable inventions were always in demand, so to argue for their causal role is taxonomic, and that supply side stimuli (in terms of shortages of raw materials or labour) were (similarly) 'neither sufficient nor necessary to prompt merchants and businessmen actively to seek . . . or encourage the search for innovation'. The data which he cites as inconsistent with such explanations include the impossibility of identifying a specificity in the British demand situation, or 'material culture' (in the context of an international analysis of progress in the industry) to account for the monopolisation of the inventive

[3] O'Brien *et al.*, 1996a: 159. [4] Griffiths *et al.*, 1992: 896. [5] O'Brien *et al.*, 1991.

process in textiles. Pursuing the comparative approach within a single set of frontiers, he claims that it is likewise difficult to identify distinct, and thus potentially causal, demand or supply conditions pertaining during the critical twenty years for textile inventions between 1764 (Hargreaves' jenny) and 1779 (Crompton's spinning mule).

He then delivers a specific attack on what are the two preferred, text-book interpretations of the inventive upsurge: of its being a consequence of labour shortage and of its having benefited from an exceptional degree of stimulus in view of the character of division of labour in textile production – invention, and thus productivity gains, in one process forcing invention in another. The former argument he discounts on the grounds of the evidence for labour shortage being far from conclusive in view of the rising population levels at the time of the inventions and the contemporaneous 'industrious revolution' which was leading to an increase in the supply of women's and child labour.[6] The key consideration, besides, he speculates, may have been that of labour skills rather than price. The latter argument he questions in view of the lack of evidence for clusters of inventions around stages of production 'under pressure' following technological change in one process. He puts particular emphasis here on the failure of the paradigm case for the argument, that of the flying shuttle, to conform to the theory either in its origins (there was no prior progress in preparatory – carding and spinning – processes) or in its consequences (there was more than a thirty-year gap between its invention by John Kay in 1733 and Hargreaves' development of the jenny).[7]

Having exposed the 'fault lines' in what he describes as 'the imported theoretical assumptions behind text-book accounts of the pace and pattern of technological change during the industrial revolution', O'Brien was concerned not purely to revert to a dense, chronological narrative of the inventive process. He makes his case on the basis of two databases which he and his collaborators have been compiling over a period of eight or nine years, one of inventive activity over the period 1675 to 1850, drawn from patent evidence as well as other sources, and the other of the origins of some 2,500 inventors. They are not complete sources and, besides, the legitimacy of using the patent lists as a method of assessing inventive activity has long been debated by economic historians, O'Brien among them,[8] but he argues that, if both quantitative and qualitative evidence is drawn from the databases, they permit the identification of trends in the level of inventive activity and of changes in the types of inventor and of

[6] De Vries, 1994.

[7] O'Brien *et al.*, 1996: 158–64. O'Brien's discussion on the imbalance thesis is taken further in Griffiths *et al.*, 1998.

[8] See Griffiths *et al.*, 1992: pp. 885–9.

inventions achieved. This then permits the construction of 'some acceptable middle-range generalizations about technological change in textiles as a whole'.

The first of the two databases serves to confirm emphatically a sharp upturn in inventive activity from the mid-eighteenth century, and a yet more decisive discontinuity from 1775, showing technological change becoming 'a pervasive component behind British economic growth'. Qualitative information drawn from it also reveals significant changes in the characteristics of inventors over the time period with which we are concerned, with a growing proportion of inventions being the work of 'professional inventors', with two or more inventions to their credit.

Disaggregating from the macro figures which are for all areas of technological change, the data confirm the importance of textiles to the transformation of the economy: it is the sector accounting for by far the largest number of inventions for any industry. Within textiles the same process of professionalisation of invention is observable and in addition a geographical shift in the locus of invention from the old manufacturing centres of East Anglia, the West Country and London towards the new ones of the Midlands, Lancashire and Yorkshire. Relatively autonomous subcultures of technological progress are shown to have been emerging in 'well defined manufacturing regions', consistent with Sidney Pollard's characterisation of Britain's industrialising economy as a range of distinct but interacting regional economies with their own technological traditions.[9] Finally, and centrally, the data permit the making of a distinction between 'an age of discovery', in which major inventions (termed 'prototype' or 'macro' inventions by O'Brien) were made first in spinning, then in the preparatory and finishing processes and finally in weaving, and a more prosaic period after 1815 characterised by improvements to, and diffusion of, the innovations of the heroic age by inventors who were drawn now mainly from within the textile industry. The evidence for the existence of this crucial, 'heroic' phase of invention, one which conditions the inventive process from the turn of the nineteenth century, is O'Brien's grounds for affirming that the 'most interesting and difficult problem to explain is why so many of the prototype innovations happened to be British in their origin and early development'.[10]

Responding to the challenge which he thus sets himself, he argues that a permissive factor for the changes was the well-developed character of the entire textile sector by the early eighteenth century, such that it 'could emulate most varieties of foreign cloth and yarn, absorb new technology, and even generate a flow of indigenous innovations'. He distinguishes, though, between 'traditional', 'product innovations', which can

[9] Pollard, 1981: 12–21. [10] O'Brien *et al.*, 1996: 165–9.

be accounted for in this way, and these 'macro' inventions in cotton, and the fact of their concentration in a 'truncated period', which, he maintains, cannot. Insofar that these macro inventions, as is well known, were concentrated particularly in cotton, the critical questions thus become 'Why cotton?' and 'Why cottons in Britain?'

The first of these questions has been the more effectively answered. O'Brien summarises the conclusions which have been reached. The 'tensile properties of cotton fibres' make them 'peculiarly amenable to mechanized spinning' and in addition cotton holds the advantages of taking a better dye than other fibres and enjoying a more elastic supply situation in view of the production possibilities provided by its extensive cultivation on colonial plantations.

In tackling the second question, O'Brien follows the argument developed in 'Political components of the Industrial Revolution'. Pride of place there he attributes to 'political economy'.[11] The governmental response in England to the threat posed to its staple industries by the calico mania of the late seventeenth century was uniquely favourable to the development of an import-substituting cotton industry insofar that its restriction of the Indian trade came late, allowing a taste for the new fibre to be diffused, and took a form – the restriction of Indian wares but a permissiveness towards their imitation within the British Isles – which stimulated first calico printing, then linens and finally cottons, in the forms of checks, stripes and fustians. Linens, he emphasises, received additional support, export bounties and an unusual degree (in '*laissez-faire*' Britain) of technical assistance from the Linen Boards of Ireland and Scotland (founded 1711 and 1727). Their nurturing in Ireland (as a *quid pro quo* for restrictions on the wool industry there) and in Scotland (as a sweetener to acceptance of the 1707 Act of Union) were irreversible governmental compromises in view of the political insecurity of the monarchy between 1689 and 1750. The consequence of such support was the growth of substantial, and increasingly competitive, linen industries within the British Isles and, above all, the development of the largest cotton concentration in Europe. Between them the two industries provided the basis, too, for extensive experience in manufacturing mixed cloths, composed of linen and cotton. The existence of such an industrial build-up provided a springboard for invention, 'given that technological innovation . . . become[s] more probable once industries attain critical scales of production and experience'.[12]

[11] O'Brien *et al.*, 1991. O'Brien's other publications on the issue include the joint articles Griffiths *et al.*, 1992, 1996a, 1996b and O'Brien, 1997b.

[12] O'Brien *et al.*, 1991: 412 for this last quote. For the summary O'Brien *et al.*, 1996a: 170. For the Celtic dimension see O'Brien *et al.*, 1991: 408 and O'Brien *et al.*, 1996b: 548.

Timing? The trigger, O'Brien argues, was a growing shortage of linen warp yarn from the 1740s for the mixed cotton cloths being produced (adequate cotton warp was not achievable) as linen itself became an exporting industry, absorbing its own yarn production, and supplies of continental yarn were restricted by warfare. This prompted 'fustian producers to seek technical solutions to mitigate the impact of the rising price of linen yarn'. But what determined the length of the delay before the trigger was pulled? The accounting for the timing of the inventions still 'eludes explanation', O'Brien continues.

The resolution of this final riddle O'Brien seeks in a prosopographical survey of the 'collectivity of inventors, improvers, craftsmen, and promoters of technological innovation in the industry [textiles as a whole]' from 1688 to 1851, one which runs to 2,500 names. The data from this – particularly those formed by records of the aims of inventors – enable him to identify differences in the attributes of pre- and post-1800 inventors to match that contrast in type of inventions established earlier: 'the subset . . . in this earlier period', he notes, are more 'Schumpeterian and interesting to contemplate than their nineteenth-century successors, who adapted their ideas in response to familiar market forces and pressures'. More specifically their aims 'tend to be pitched at a level of generality and optimism that suggests a rather widespread, somewhat "pre-professional" interest in techniques'. The establishment that there was a specificity in the character of inventors during the eighteenth century then becomes his basis for arguing that the proto- or macro-inventions have their source on the supply side – in other words, the quality and quantity of inventors in eighteenth-century Britain. Samuel Johnson's well-known comment, 'the age is running after improvement. All the business of the world is to be done in a new way', which O'Brien cites, crystallises his conclusion.[13]

2 Narrative of invention in cotton

This begins with Thomas Lombe's founding of a silk winding factory on the River Derwent in Derbyshire in 1717. The five-storey, water-powered mill, a few miles downstream from where Arkwright was to establish his pilot Cromford enterprise, provided precedents for the design, hydraulic power sources and organisation of production of the later cotton mills. 'Its size and complexity excited admiration,' Christine MacLeod writes.[14] Stanley Chapman's conclusion is similar: 'It was the first successful power factory in England and the model for industrial units set up in the last decades of the century.' What is more, the mill had emulators and silk

[13] O'Brien *et al.*, 1996a: 155, 168, 169, 171, 172–5.

[14] MacLeod, 1988: 219.

became the staple industry of the Derby area during the eighteenth century. Some of the influences on the later cotton industry are mentioned by Chapman. The buildings and organisation of the Derby silk mill were copied in six mills in Stockport between 1732 and 1768. Jedediah Strutt, later to be one of Arkwright's partners, had a silk mill in Derby by 1771, possibly before his mill building in conjunction with Arkwright, and it is certainly to the Lombe mill traditions that he referred when establishing the work regime in his cotton mills. The twelve-hour day which he introduced for the labour force, and the arrangements for food breaks, respected, Strutt himself stated, 'the invariable practice at the original silk mill in Derby, (and) in this neighbourhood for more than a hundred years'.[15] Of more specific relevance was the impact on machine-making in the Derby/Nottingham area in which, it will be recalled, both Hargreaves and Arkwright were to choose to develop their prototypes. The construction and maintenance of a varied range of machinery – Italian winding engines on the top three storeys, and spinning and twisting mills on the bottom two – stimulated local skills in machine-making.[16]

Until 1750 developments in machinery, and in equipment relevant later to cotton manufacturing, were confined principally to weaving and knitting. William Lee's stocking frame, invented in 1589, was in use in Leicestershire by 1640; the ribbon loom, developed in Germany and Holland at the end of the sixteenth century, reached London by 1616 and Lancashire by 1680; the draw-boy system for patterned weaving was being diffused in cotton producing areas by the 1730s; John Kay invented his flying shuttle in 1733; calico-printing was diffused from London to Lancashire during the 1750s; and Strutt's ribbing machine for attachment to the stocking frame dates from 1756.[17]

Kay's case repays a little more consideration, as he is probably the best example of a 'vocational inventor' which Lancashire possesses[18] and the response to his flying shuttle provides insights into attitudes to invention in the Lancashire region. In addition to the shuttle, Kay's inventive output included a machine for twisting thread (1730), one for opening and dressing wool which was produced in conjunction with his shuttle, the devising of major changes to the shuttle between 1733 and 1735, including the substitution of a fixed bobbin for the customary revolving one, a windmill for raising water, an invention for working Dutch looms by water power, a machine for making salt 'without much fire',

[15] Chapman, 1966: 53–7. See also Chapman, 1987: 14–15.
[16] Hills, 1970: 29–30.
[17] Hills, 1970: 25–8, and Chapman and Chassagne, 1981: 25.
[18] The other claimant would be Samuel Crompton, who, as well as being author of the spinning mule, developed a new type of carding machine and loom for fancy cloths as well as a form of domestic mangle (Rose, 1965–6: 17).

a card-making machine (1752) and finally an 'invention for spinning of cotton by water', conceived in the 1750s. Kay chose to develop the shuttle away from Lancashire, in the bay industry of Colchester. It was introduced to Lancashire shortly afterwards. Opposition to the shuttle was occasioned not by the fact of the invention per se but because of the patent which Kay obtained for it which hampered its diffusion. Particularly controversial were the improvements to the shuttle which Kay made between 1733 and 1735. Weavers justified their ignoring of the patent in terms of the prior existence in the area, drawn from other sources, of the improvements for which Kay claimed originality. Near-simultaneous invention, rapid diffusion of invention and a hatred of patents were to be characteristics of Lancashire and their occurrence reflects the breadth already of the process of technological advance in the region. Extensive pirating of his patent led to Kay's suing seventeen Lancashire weavers in the course of 1737. Litigation continued into the 1740s and the crippling cost and the worry occasioned by this caused him to try his fortunes in the service of the French crown from 1748.[19]

The solitary exception to the lack of early spinning initiatives is provided by the 1738 patented machine of Lewis Paul and John Wyatt, which included an element of roller spinning. The former, whose idea it was, had a French, probably Huguenot, father who had been Lord Shaftesbury's physician.[20] Wyatt was a Midlander, from Lichfield, of humbler social extraction but highly literate, a carpenter/machine-maker within the Birmingham metal trades. Both men were professional inventors/exploiters of patents but with slightly distinct pedigrees. Paul in 1732 had devised a pinking machine for making the edges of shrouds and had had an earlier connection with Wyatt for the exploitation of a file-making machine. Wyatt, who rivalled Kay as a 'vocational inventor', was also responsible for gun barrel boring and weighing machines. The spinning machine, however, was an invention of such significance that it absorbed most of the two men's efforts from the moment it was first planned, about 1735.

Wyatt moved to London to develop the machine and a patent was then requested for it in August 1736. It took him nearly two years to complete the working model which was necessary for securing the patent. There were technical, organisational and financial problems. Collaboration between Wyatt and Paul was difficult as Paul was now living in Birmingham, technical discussions taking place by letter. Both men were

[19] Wadsworth and Mann, 1931: 449–65; Hills, 1970: 22–4. On the Lancashire aversion to patents see Griffiths *et al.*, 1992: 889.

[20] Day and McNeil, 1996: 545.

distracted by some continued involvement in other enterprises and they were dogged by shortage of capital throughout. Paul appears to have also spent time in Nottingham at this stage experimenting with yarn production for the hosiery industry, which had recently moved there. The machine itself was seized for debt in June 1738 and Wyatt spent time in a debtors' prison in 1743. One of the reasons for Paul's presence in Birmingham was to get funding and in 1738 the backing of the bookseller Thomas Warren was secured.

It had been intended to use the machine for wool spinning but, though offered to wool manufacturers, once patented it was used only for cotton. Apart from the eluded-to matter of cotton's qualities for mechanisation, it was the expansion in the production of checked and striped cottons and cotton-linens, for export to the African market, during the 1730s, and a sudden crisis in the supply of imported spun yarn at the time of patenting which explains this choice. It was within London's industry, centred in Spitalfields, that the machine was first used; a manufacturer James Johnson, who had had shroud dealings with Paul and had worked the African market since 1735, agreed in January 1740 to buy a licence for ten spindles. These were put to work in a silk throwster's shop.

The transition from model to working machine revealed further technical problems. The preparation of adequate rovings for spinning was the principal of these. Devising a carding machine to resolve the difficulty occupied Wyatt and Paul for most of 1740. Use of this machine was then granted in the indentures between Wyatt and Paul and their spinning licensees in 1741 and 1742. In addition to Johnson, these included Warren, Wyatt himself, Edward Cave, editor of *The Gentleman's Magazine*, and Samuel Johnson's publisher and Paul's attorney, Dobbins. In most cases this represented granting of licences to pay off debts. Licensing itself was the resort of patentees lacking funds to develop an invention in their own right.[21] Paul also tried marketing his machine in Manchester in early 1740: he informed Wyatt that 'I have spun here without any ill accident, nay I have spun a sample of yarn to fine company at the rate of a penny p. skein at their own measure . . . people well pleased with the operation.'

The first 'Paul mill' was set up by Paul and Wyatt themselves in Birmingham in the summer of 1741. Two years later it was reported to be in a 'pitiful state'. More sustained were the efforts of Edward Cave, initially in London then in Northampton, where he founded England's first water-powered cotton mill. To manage it he recruited a millwright, Thomas Yeoman, another inventive craftsman, who duly enrolled himself in the

[21] MacLeod, 1988: 90.

Northampton Philosophical Society, of which he was soon president, and seems to have devoted as much time to his scientific and other interests as to the mill, carrying out experiments with electricity, building machines (including ventilators, weighing machines and other 'engines'), surveying rivers, surveying estates, acting as agent for the sale of mills and for Paul's shrouds and lecturing throughout the Midlands. It was a sub-manager, Harrison, assisted by his wife and two women overseers, who must have borne the brunt of the considerable day-to-day duties to which a labour force of fifty carders, spinners and girl assistants working on five machines with fifty spindles each must have given rise.

It was the establishment of another mill in Leominster, with some Lancashire capital, which represented the principal success of the Paul machine. 'If the interest of the men actually engaged in the trade should be considered a passport to success Paul had chances almost as favourable as those which Arkwright later enjoyed,' Julia Mann writes. Daniel Bourn, its founder, appears to have been a Birmingham man – a relation of his was in business with Warren and Paul in 1738. In 1743 we find him in Birmingham, meeting up with Wyatt, and involved in discussions with one Henry Morris, a Lancashire dealer representing other Lancashire investors, who had bought a spindle licence from Paul. Bourn's possessing Lancastrian and Birmingham links may have caused his agency in the Leominster mill. This was probably running by 1744. That it was doing so in 1748 and, more, had become the principal hope for the new technology, is evident from Bourn's patent application then for a carding machine. Paul also, apparently prompted by Bourn's initiative, patented his carding mechanisms in 1748 and then negotiated with Bourn, using Wyatt as intermediary, the buying back of the spindle licence of the Leominster concern. It looks as though the achieving of a monopoly in the use of the machine was being attempted, probably as a preliminary to a parliamentary extension of the patent. The Leominster mill lasted till 1754 when it was burnt down.

This disappearance left Cave's Northampton mill as the only relay for the new technology. It was not a promising one. Cave had died in 1754 and by 1756 his brother and legatee, William Cave, would appear to have let the mill to Paul but to have received no rent. Litigation was only avoided by the mediation of Samuel Johnson, who was close to most of those involved in Paul's enterprise, from Wyatt, whose family were Lichfield neighbours, to Paul and Edward Cave. Only four of its five spinning machines were in use in 1756. Paul's illusions for the machine, however, were to last until the end, a second patent for it being obtained in 1758, a year before his death. From this point there is some confusion about the fate of the machines. Wadsworth and Mann accept the evidence left by

Charles Wyatt, John Wyatt's son, that they were sold in 1764. On the other hand Stanley Chapman argues for some continuity for the Lewis/Paul spinning efforts in the form of 'thread-making' in Birmingham (a dozen mills), the initiation of 'an era of experiments in mechanised spinning in Nottingham' from which Arkwright and Hargreaves later benefit and the Northampton factory itself which he claims did not stop spinning until 1806. He concludes that 'The evidence is not sufficiently strong to demonstrate a continuity of development between his experiments and Arkwright's success, but it is not too much to suppose that roller spinning was an idea that had been well circulated.'

The failure is attributed by Julia Mann to managerial deficiencies – she cites Matthew Boulton's view that the Birmingham mill 'would have got money had it been in good hands' – and to the machine's excessive complexity and resultant delicacy. Hills purely blames the technical limitations. Despite the confusion which has arisen from a very broad patent description designed to hamper rivals, it turns out that the machine did not make proper use of rollers for drawing out the sliver of fibre before spinning and consisted essentially in a mechanisation of the Saxony wheel or 'bobbin-flyer' spinning method. (This involved a spindle, flyer and bobbin, spindle and bobbin both being driven by the flywheel, and twisting and winding on being combined in a 'continuous' process. It was the obvious process to mechanise rather than the 'intermittent' Jersey or 'Great Wheel' method, in which the drawing out/putting in twist and winding-on were distinct processes). The problem was that this form of spinning was seriously deficient for producing yarn of any quality as the winding of the bobbin communicated significant tension, via the flyer, to the sliver of cotton intended for spinning, thus preventing it being fully drawn out as twist was put in. This was to prove a barrier to Arkwright's machine's producing fine yarn and where no adequate method of attenuating the rovings via rollers had been developed the problem was all the greater and apparently only remedied by prior manual preparation of rovings of the right thickness. The machine was based on a 'wrong basic principle for spinning and drawing', Hills writes, though he credits Paul and Wyatt with an ingenuity 'which was quite remarkable . . . in their writings it is possible to discover a great many ideas which were incorporated into later textile machines'.[22]

If the Saxony flax wheel was the model for spinning for Paul's machines, Thomas Lombe's mill appears to have been that for the manner in which power was delivered to them, for their curious, circular form, with a

[22] Wadsworth and Mann, 1931: 411–48, 472–6; Hills, 1970: chapter 3; Chapman, 1966: 58–62.

central, vertical power shaft driving a large drive wheel, followed the design of the silk twisting and spinning machines, representing a contrast to the later, linear lay-out for belt-driven spindles. English attributes the machine's difficulties to this drive's system's requirement of the same degree of precision as that of the delicate spindle, one which, in view of the size of the wheel and drive, was beyond the capacities of the contemporary metal industry.[23]

Paul's failure 'dampened what enthusiasm existed for spinning machinery'. It is true that shortly after his death the Society of Arts offered a reward for improvements in the common spinning wheel and for 'a wheel or machine that would spin six threads of wool, cotton, flax or silk at the same time; and require only one person to attend it', but while several awards were made in the first category and a claim for one made in 1763 for the second, the rewards were soon dropped, in the belief, the society's historian recorded, 'that they would never come to anything' and that Paul's unsuccessful machine had 'carried this application of mechanics to the greatest extent it is perhaps capable of'. That such views were widely held is suggested by Arkwright's claimed initial response to the proposal to attempt a machine for roller spinning which was made to him by the Warrington clockmaker John Kay: 'that will never be brought to bear . . . several gentlemen have almost broke themselves by it' was his response. Gravenor Henson, author of an 1831 study on framework knitters, also documents such a reaction: 'the repeated failures of the Nottingham mechanics, made cotton spinning be regarded in nearly the same light as projects for discovering perpetual motion', he wrote.[24]

The fact of the blind alley which Paul's machine had turned out to be does not, on the other hand, mean that progress in spinning was at a standstill. The industry in Lancashire was in full expansion during the years of his efforts, with progress being logged in two spheres in particular, that of checks and cottons for Africa, whose exports multiplied by six between 1752 and 1763, and that of fustians, in which a steady process of product innovation in patterns, finishes and fibre mixtures had been occurring. Milestones here were the introduction of the draw-boy loom, facilitating complex weaving patterns and the development of pure cotton thicksets, introduced before 1740, cotton velvets, introduced soon after this, veleverets, 1763, and velveteens, 'incomparably the most important development in the middle of the century' (Mann), patented in 1776. The tendency has been to give prominence to the meteoric

[23] English, 1973: pp. 68–83.

[24] Wadsworth and Mann, 1931: 448, 475–6; Hills, 1970: 52, 55; Bates, 1998: 237–52. Henson is cited by Chapman, 1966: 62. Arkwright's remark shows his guile but would reflect, too, the general view.

expansion in cotton stripes and checks among these developments but this may be mistaken, firstly insofar as their growth led to few technical improvements in spinning – more of the same was demanded, the selling point coming from dye and pattern – and secondly in that this growth was reversed from 1763. The developments in fustians, in contrast, were a purely English achievement, a first first for its cotton industry; they spawned a new export trade in this case in competitive European markets, and they did depend on significant technical improvements, in spinning as well as weaving.

The stimulus to the former came from the need for yarn spun in a special way for the pile of the finer velvets and thicksets whose production, initially for the domestic market, was expanding. There was consequent specialisation in spinning methods, different techniques being used for the spinning of cotton warps for fustians and weft for velvets, which had to be spun in the opposite direction from ordinary weft. There was also a division of labour developed between roving and spinning, specialised rovers being used to serve several spinners. The various developments were described as 'English practice' when an attempt was made to introduce them in the Rouen area by the Lancastrian Jacobite refugee John Holker in the mid-1750s. Superiority of English to French spinning, in a range of linked practices, was being recognised.[25]

In explaining the 'macro-inventions', then, the growing technical sophistication of Lancashire's manual cotton working and the evident increase in the availability of different sorts of raw cotton and in the understanding of their qualities for different uses must be considered *in conjunction* with the great increase in the demand for labour. The diffusion of the flying shuttle also played a part. Its adoption for cotton did not take place until the 1750s but its adaptation then to the requirements of cotton serves as a further illustration of the breadth of this front of technological advance. The shuttle was adapted in cotton's case to the narrow loom, thus rather than releasing a weaver its importance lay in the acceleration in weaving speed, and the ease of loom operation, which it enabled. These changes had consequences for quality. Shuttle automation freed the weaver to focus his attention on other parts of the weaving process, in particular figuring work for patterned cloth and the thorough beating up of the weft to ensure a tight weave. Further advantages were the larger quantities of weft which could be carried on the spool of the shuttle (five times), saving time on spooling and swapping shuttles, and the more economic use of the weft in the weaving process, causing a lowering of costs and further tidying of the weave.

[25] Wadsworth and Mann, 1931: 145–69, 173–83.

There is no question that these technical changes, the development of new cloth types and the parallel progress in hosiery in the Midlands, with the diffusion of Strutt's ribbing frame, were generating an unprecedented demand for yarn only met with difficulty by hand spinning: 'it was this way that the cotton industry came to feel acutely the shortage of weft', Mann writes of the rapid take-up in the shuttle. The Society of Arts' promotion of spinning inventions reflects the consciousness of this imbalance between supply and demand for cotton yarn in the country.[26]

Returning to the attempts to resolve this bottleneck mechanically, between Paul's invention and that of Hargreaves three other attempts were made – that of Kay, already mentioned and that of one Lawrence Earnshaw of Mottram in 1753, who, though, destroyed the machine to 'spin and reel cotton in one operation' which he had succeeded in making when he perceived the danger that it presented to employment. A third machine, not apparently put into use either, was patented in 1755 by James Taylor, a clockmaker from Ashton-under-Lyne. The successful invention came finally, as is well known, from an unexpected source following an industrial accident. A great Jersey spinning wheel, belonging to the carpenter/hand-loom weaver James Hargreaves, toppled over while in use and continued spinning on its side. The event was the source of Hargreaves' intuition that cotton could be spun with vertical spindles and a horizontally slung wheel (the position in which the spinning wheel had carried on spinning), facilitating duplication in the number of spindles.[27]

What is of interest is the phenomenon of near-simultaneous invention, and then the rapidity of take-up, of the jenny. Hargreaves' primacy in invention was challenged by Thomas Highs, who made a similar machine driven by a vertical wheel between 1764–6 followed by a prototype in which the spindles were set circularly, as with Paul's machine, and driven by a drum. Haley of Houghton Towers, a third near-co-inventor, replaced Hargreaves' awkward horizontal wheel with a vertical one and introduced a cylindrical, tin, drive-shaft along the breadth of the machine, allowing individual gearing of spindles and thus an increase in their number.

Diffusion was nearly immediate, Hargreaves made jennies for his friends soon after developing his prototype and his early commitment to diffusion is shown by his establishing of a machine-making business to turn out jennies. It was riots which this occasioned that forced his move to Nottingham. Use of the jenny was such by 1770 that its patent, issued then, was unenforceable. Highs' claims to priority are not sustainable but his, and Haley's, examples illustrate the extent of machine-making ability in Lancashire and speed of deployment of the machinery illustrates

[26] Wadsworth and Mann, 1931: 470–1. [27] Hunter, 1951–3: 143–5.

the extent of development of the spinning sector before the inventions, the necessary skills in the preparation of rovings, for example, existing already. Treating the spinning inventions as part of a general process of technical change in the industry, rather than one of once-off inventions, is further justified by the evidence of prior progress in carding in the county. Robert Peel, the introducer of calico-printing, had been working on carding machinery since 1762 with James Hargreaves' assistance. The machine developed was a cylindrical one like that developed at Leominster, on which it was possibly modelled. It was not successful, but a simpler device of Hargreaves' own invention, consisting in an enlarged hand card suspended from a rope which passed over a pulley to a counter-balance weight, doubled output.[28]

Aspects of Richard Arkwright's pioneering of roller spinning and continuous carding support too this argument for the spinning inventions forming part of a broad process of technical advance. Arkwright, barber, wigmaker and, later, publican by trade, lived himself in the heart of those areas of Lancashire undergoing rapid change. He was born in Preston, apprenticed in Kirkham, to Preston's west, and then worked for eighteen years in Bolton, where his two marriages drew him into contact with key participants in the developing industry. The first, in 1755, into a Bolton family, made him brother-in-law to Thomas Wood, a fustian-weaver and himself patenter of a carding machine in 1776. The second, in 1761, provided him with an entrée into a centre for the machine-making which was to transform the industry. His bride was from a village close to Leigh, where Thomas Highs was at work on his range of machinery, amongst which, from approximately 1763, was a new roller-spinning device. Arkwright must have heard of Highs' efforts, made in conjunction with the Warrington inventor John Kay. They were discontinued on two occasions, the second one definitively, and Arkwright, having met Highs in 1764/5, and Kay in March 1767, took advantage of the second hiatus to co-opt the inventive process, visiting Kay in Warrington, to which he had returned, and persuading him to make models of the machine he had been helping with. The two men then sought assistance from one Peter Atherton (probably then of Warrington) to locate a smith and a watch-tool-maker to make the heavier parts of the machine. Kay himself contributed the more delicate clockmaking skills as well as coordinating the initiative.

From this point the story is well known. Arkwright transferred the machine that had been constructed (whose true purpose was being concealed under the pretence that it was designed to measure longitude)

[28] Hills, 1970: 75–7.

firstly to Manchester and later to Preston. There it was nearly perfected. The 1768 transfer to Nottingham was probably undertaken in consequence of the treatment inflicted on Hargreaves' machine-making enterprise that year though Chapman argues that an additional inducement was the good chances for obtaining financial backing there in view of the shortage of cotton yarn from which local hosiers were suffering. Arkwright's earlier involvement in the area as an itinerant hair-dealer had acquainted him with this situation.[29]

In Nottingham, Arkwright was joined by some distant Lancastrian relatives with whom he formed an association to exploit the invention in May 1768. He submitted a request for a patent in June and this was granted in the course of 1769. It was at this stage that the inadequacy of his and his partners' financial resources to take the invention through the development phase became apparent and that he turned to local businessmen for support. A partnership was brokered with Samuel Need, Nottingham's wealthiest hosier, and Jedediah Strutt, the leader of the Derby stocking industry. In addition to his wealth, and an outlet for the machine yarn that would be produced, Strutt brought his experience with the 'Derby' rib machine into the partnership. He would have been aware of the requirements of perfecting a machine of the type which Arkwright had developed and could contribute his experience in the administration of patents.[30]

It was the success in continuous spinning which forced giving attention to carding. Arkwright concentrated on this process from 1772. As with roller-spinning there were precedents for what Arkwright claimed to have 'invented'. A witness at the 1785 Arkwright patent trials, John Lees, stated that he began work on a better cotton feeder for carding three years before Arkwright obtained his 1775 carding patent, having established a small, specialised carding concern in Manchester. Lees' cotton feeder was developed in conjunction with a mechanised cotton opening device whose output took the form of a continuous broad strip of cotton which could be fed directly into the carding machine. Arkwright's system, in contrast, involved rolling up carded cotton in a blanket which unwound as the machine drew out the cotton. In the doffing process – disengaging the carded cotton from the carding cylinder – there were, too, multiple inventions, though Arkwright's crank and comb for achieving this is judged superior to other methods.[31]

[29] Chapman, 1966: 87–8: they were suffering reverses at the hands of Tewkesbury hosiers, who could benefit from a labour force previously employed in spinning short stapled wool for fine cloth and hence excellent cotton spinners.

[30] Fitton, 1989: 1–27; Chapman, 1966: 88.

[31] Hills, 1970: 77–81.

3 Conclusion

This narrative account of invention in cotton could easily be extended, and should by rights include the development of Samuel Crompton's spinning-mule but space does not permit this.[32] Sufficient detail, however, has been put together, to provide some scope for further reflection on the questions concerning the causes of invention in cotton which are raised by O'Brien's work.

A problem is that there are two quite distinct 'macro-inventions' to be explained, Hargreaves' and Arkwright's. The former's, it has emerged, in view of the fact of near-simultaneous invention and rapid diffusion, is quite reasonably interpretable in O'Brien's terms of the Lancashire cotton industry's having achieved 'a critical scale of production and experience'. A simple machine, in fact hardly a machine, rather a duplication of manual processes, requiring considerable skill in its use, its consequences were great but its causes appear to have been simple. The latter was far more difficult to develop; indeed it could be argued that it took some forty years to be sorted out, if Paul's initial inspiration is taken as the starting point and the ability to sell warp yarn in Lancashire as the end one, and the explanation for it is more complex. Here, the culture of invention was significant, Paul and his côterie being archetypal in this respect, and Arkwright, reputedly fascinated by mechanics, and an inventive wigmaker, illustrating how far down the social scale such a culture had spread.[33] However, the invention did not survive the developmental process until it met with that favourable environment – in terms of a cotton culture and machine-making skills – which had been generated in Lancashire and needed too the additional assistance which the Midlands could provide in terms of *savoir-faire* with patenting, skills in making more complex machinery than that used in Lancashire and, importantly, a very large capital injection.[34] Even with all this it took time for complete success to be achieved – five years elapsed between patent application and full commercial operation.

32 It can be noted, though, that what has been said about the Hargreaves and Arkwright machines can also be said of Crompton's: his spinning machine was born within an expanding industry in which he worked as a weaver. Technologically it could not have been more explicitly a product of a general process of technological advance in that it was the fruit of a marriage between the operating principles of the two earlier technologies (hence 'mule'), and although his invention itself was indisputably a solo effort, its perfection involved a range of other skilled machine-makers (Rose, 1965–6: 13–17).

33 Fitton, 1989: 9: he is held to have had 'a valuable method of dyeing hair which wig makers held to be superior to any in Lancashire'.

34 On the growth of patenting in the Midlands, east and west, see MacLeod, 1988. For the enormous capital investment made into a 'macro-invention', see O'Brien, 1997b.

The narrative thus suggests that of the various explanations offered by O'Brien, it is his dual argument of a specific British political response to cotton leading to an exceptional growth in the industry, and of technical change coming as a consequence of this scale, that is the most satisfactory, as it serves to account for all of one invention (probably the more important of the two) and at least half of the other. Such an interpretation would be consistent with Julia Mann's characterisation of the inventive process in cotton some seventy years ago:

> Looking back on the obscure ten or fifteen years before Arkwright's monopoly finally ended and Crompton's mule came into use, one receives the impression of a period in which nothing was permanent. The idea of mechanical production had seized the industry. Scores of men were making machines, and were equipping small factories; scores of inventive minds were at work, contributing a modification here, and adaptation there, which passed into the common stock. There was no machine without its history of trial and error, and the men whose names have become household words were surrounded by a whole society of inventors to whom the progress of cotton machinery owes hardly less than it does to them.[35]

[35] Wadsworth and Mann, 1931: 503.

7 Continental responses to British innovations in the iron industry during the eighteenth and early nineteenth centuries

Rainer Fremdling

1 Introduction

Apart from the question of whether spectacular inventions were more important than continuous improvements for the Industrial Revolution, it seems pretty clear that an integral part of that path-breaking event in the history of mankind was the transition from techniques using vegetable fuel (wood or charcoal made from wood) to techniques using mineral fuel (coal). For this transition the primary iron industry can serve as a foremost example; also, in the long run, innovations in this sector were highly important.

In the following, I want to give a summary account of this transition process in Great Britain and its transfer to some continental countries during the second half of the eighteenth century and the first decades of the nineteenth century.[1] The period is thus mainly confined to the time before the crucial demand of railway construction made the iron industries in most continental countries completely switch to the economically successful British model. Both for Britain and most countries on the continent following later, the transition from an organic/wood economy towards a mineral-fuel/coal economy (Wrigley, 1988) raises the question of 'Why the delay?'(Landes, 1969: 126). Landes asked this question when comparing the continental achievements in industrial performance with those of Britain around the Crystal Palace World Exhibition in 1851. At bottom, the question can even be turned against Britain, though. Going beyond Landes' linear retrospective view on British accomplishments, one might see Britain's transition to a coal-based technology as a rather long-drawn-out desperate attempt to overcome the scarce endowment with the most important natural resource of the organic economy, namely wood.

[1] For a detailed treatment, including the railway age, see Fremdling, 1986 and the summary account in Fremdling, 2000.

Stage of Production	Process		Product
	traditional	modern	
First Stage	Smelting in the blast furnace		pig iron
	with charcoal	with coke	
Second Stage	Refining		wrought iron
	in a hearth with charcoal	in a puddling furnace with coal	
	Shaping		bar iron (rails)
	by the hammer	by a rolling mill	

Figure 7.1 Primary wrought-iron industry

In this view, Great Britain was the first country to resort to an Industrial Revolution in order to overcome the bottleneck of running short of wood. This limit to growth had hit Britain earlier than most parts of the continent. Within a sketch of a broader framework at the end of my essay, I will try to explain why the differences between the British and continental technologies persisted for such a long time.

In order to present evidence for the existence of various ways, in which the other countries did not follow Britain, typical cases are here described and explained in their historical and national context. But before that, a brief introduction into the primary iron industry is given with a simplified model of the production stages and processes. Figure 7.1 distinguishes between traditional and modern methods in the production and in the processing of wrought iron.

In the pre-industrial or traditional method, the iron was smelted in the blast furnace by using charcoal as a fuel. Charcoal (which is derived from wood) was then replaced by mineral fuel (mainly coke derived from coal). The output, 'pig iron', contained a lot of impurities and a high content of carbon. Therefore it was brittle and could not be shaped in a cold or warm state. The only way to use it directly for final products was to cast it in a molten state into forms for cast-iron products. To some extent, this was done directly with the molten pig iron flowing out from the blast furnace. For the second stage of the primary iron production, the pig iron had to be refined, which in essence meant a reduction of carbon. By refining, wrought iron was obtained, which could be shaped into the desired bars or rails. These were elastic enough, not brittle any more, and could endure mechanical shocks without breaking easily. Distinguishing between the two stages of production is essential,

Table 7.1 *English imports of bar iron, 1700–1799, yearly averages in thousands of metric tonnes and percentages*

Decade	From Sweden tonnes	Per cent	From Russia tonnes	Per cent	From other countries tonnes	Per cent	Total tonnes
1700–09	14.3	88	0.0	0.0	2.0	12.0	16.3
1710–19	10.7	65	0.0	0.0	5.5	35.0	16.5
1720–29	15.2	76	0.4	2.0	4.3	22.0	20.0
1730–39	19.3	74	3.4	13.0	3.3	13.0	26.0
1740–49	17.1	75	3.7	16.0	2.1	9.0	22.9
1750–59	19.0	64	8.2	27.5	2.6	8.5	29.8
1760–69	19.9	49	17.7	44.0	2.7	7.0	40.3
1770–79	17.0	38	25.7	57.0	2.1	5.0	44.8
1780–89	15.5	34.5	28.2	63.0	1.1	2.5	44.9
1790–99	18.5	40	26.7	58.0	1.0	2.0	46.2

Source: Hildebrand, 1958: 10. Less than 10 per cent was re-exported.

because smelting on the one hand and refining/shaping on the other were not necessarily integrated in one production unit or even at the same location. This rough outline of the production process in the primary iron industry is necessary to comprehend the specific transition from an iron industry based on wood fuel to an iron industry based on mineral fuel. On the continent, some traditional and some modern methods were combined in the two stages of production, which were often performed in different, independent locations. Within the history of technology, such interplay of 'old' and 'new' is still too neglected an issue.

2 The innovations of the coke blast furnace, of puddling and rolling in Great Britain[2]

At the beginning of the eighteenth century, the primary iron industry in Great Britain was rather small and not able to meet the demand of indigenous users of iron products. Furthermore, the costs of production were comparatively high. This was due to expensive fuel; i.e., charcoal made from wood. The gap between demand and indigenous supply of iron was met by imports from Sweden and, increasingly in the second half of the eighteenth century, also from Russia (see table 7.1). Still around 1750,

[2] There are numerous books and articles on the development of the British iron industry. I mainly draw on the standard work by Hyde (1977). Furthermore, on output see Riden (1977), the summary account by Harris (1988) and the classical articles edited by Church (1994).

Table 7.2 *Share of imports of bar iron in the supply (production plus imports) in Britain, 1750–1815, thousands imperial tons and percentages*

Year	Estimated British production (tons)	Imports tons	Share per cent
1750	18.8	35.0	65.1
1788	32.0	47.0	59.5
1794	50.0	37.0	42.5
1805	100.0	23.1	18.8
1810	130.0	8.8	6.3
1815	150.0	7.4	4.7

Sources: Hyde, 1977: 92 ff.; Hildebrand, 1958: 9.

more than 65 per cent of the British bar-iron supply was imported (see table 7.2 and the chapter in Hildebrand, 1992: 25–42). In combination with import duties, the gap induced high incentives to increase the indigenous production. The traditional processes based on the charcoal technology, however, could not achieve this. The price of charcoal increased and thus made indigenous charcoal iron less competitive than imported iron or iron produced by a new technology.

The transition from charcoal to mineral fuel techniques and consequently the import substitution, took quite a long time, i.e., the whole of the eighteenth century. There had been numerous attempts even before that time to substitute coal for charcoal in the smelting of pig iron in the blast furnace. These attempts to develop a coal-using technology were greatly enhanced because iron ore and coal could frequently be dug at the same location. That gave British ironmasters in the long run an important locational advantage over their continental counterparts, who later tried to implement the coal-using technology in their countries. In essence, the physical and chemical properties of pig iron smelted with coal made it more costly to produce a commercially viable product. Furthermore, for a long time, iron smelted with coal was of inferior quality compared with charcoal iron. Hence it was extremely difficult for coal pig iron to compete against charcoal pig iron and subsequently against wrought iron, the refined product of pig iron. This is indicated by charcoal wrought iron imported from Sweden and Russia at significantly higher prices than British iron (see table 7.3).

Abraham Darby was the first to successfully operate blast furnaces using coke (made from coal) from 1709 onwards. Before 1750, the Darbys were the only ironmasters who applied this technique. Until the

Table 7.3 *Prices of bar iron and import duties in Britain, 1790–1815, £ per imperial ton*

Year	Import Duty	Price differences between British bar iron in London (including the duty) and Swedish	Russian
1790	2.81	6.00	1.48
1795	2.81	6.75	1.75
1800	3.78	10.00	4.50
1805	5.05	12.90	4.75
1810	5.49	13.75	6.75
1815	6.49	14.10	5.50

Source: Hyde, 1977: 105.

middle of the eighteenth century, it was still cheaper in Britain to produce wrought iron in the traditional way. The Darbys, however, were commercially successful because they used their 'inferior' pig iron for thin casting products. For this purpose, the pig iron with a high content of silicon was even better than traditionally smelted pig iron. And the expansion and diffusion of coke pig iron after 1750 was mainly due to the increasing use of the product for castings.

There were, however, numerous attempts to find a suitable technique for refining coke pig iron in order to produce wrought iron. Before Henry Cort got a patent in 1784 on his famous puddling and rolling process for refining pig iron with coal, the best-known alternative technique was the process of stamping and potting. In the 1780s, when puddling was introduced, roughly half of the wrought iron was produced by potting, using coal for refining. Very soon, however, puddling in combination with rolling prevailed in the production of wrought or bar iron made from coke pig iron (see figure 7.2). As import duties increased,[3] this mineral fuel iron was substituted for imported wrought iron from Sweden and Russia. And at the beginning of the nineteenth century, Britain had even become a net exporter of iron products, whereas she had formerly been one of the foremost importers of bar iron (tables 7.3 and 7.4). But until far into the

[3] Within the mercantile framework, import duties formed a major source for the state budget rather than a device of protection. Thus the increase of these duties has to be viewed mainly as a means of raising additional revenues to finance the wars against France. For a more general treatment of the underlying causes for the establishment of British hegemony internationally by warfare financed through a superior fiscal system see O'Brien, 2000.

Stage of Production	Process		Product
	traditional	modern	
First Stage	Smelting in the blast furnace		pig iron
		with coke	
Second Stage	Refining		wrought iron
		in a puddling furnace with coal	
	Shaping		bar iron (rails)
		by a rolling mill	

Figure 7.2 The British model (wrought iron)

nineteenth century, Swedish and Russian bar iron still met the demand for high-quality users, e.g., as input for cutlery.

Within one century, the British iron industry thus transformed itself from a small producer at high cost to the leading supplier of iron products for the world market. With the new technology, her disadvantage turned to a competitive advantage in a long-drawn-out process of innovation, diffusion and improvement.

As already touched upon in the introduction, the British iron industry by this means got over what Sombart (1928: 1137) labelled the 'wood brake' (*Holzbremse*). In a more recent interpretation, Wrigley (1988) put forward that the limits to growth of the 'advanced organic economy' (based on wood) could only have been overcome by a 'mineral-based energy economy' (based on coal). The iron industry is a foremost example of this:

> An iron industry whose scope for expansion must take account of the scale of present and possible future supplies of wood for charcoal is an iron industry certain to count its output in hundreds, or at best thousands of tons. Cheap mineral fuel allowed ore to be dug and converted into iron or steel on a scale that caused output to be measured by millions rather than thousands of tons. (Wrigley, 1988: 81)

After the end of the Napoleonic Wars, the British iron industry was not only free from any real competition in her domestic market, but was increasingly able to export much of her output abroad. From 1815 to 1830, 'exports usually amounted to between one-quarter and one-third of total output' (Hyde, 1977: 144, 172). From 1830 to 1870, exports jumped from one-quarter to roughly 60 per cent of total pig-iron

Table 7.4 *British foreign trade in bar iron, 1805–1818, in thousands of metric tonnes and percentages*

	Imports				
Year	Total tonnes	From Sweden per cent	From Russia per cent	Re-exports Tonnes	Exports Tonnes
1805	27.7	62.3	36.8	4.3	6.7
1806	32.6	37.2	62.2	4.8	8.3
1807	24.1	55.3	43.6	6.6	11.0
1808	21.3	78.6	16.1	6.7	16.5
1809	24.9	67.6	29.2	8.7	n.a.
1810	20.5	59.7	36.5	11.6	n.a.
1811	28.4	67.2	30.5	8.2	n.a.
1812	17.7	39.3	56.2	10.1	24.2
1813	n.a.	n.a.	n.a.	n.a.	n.a.
1814	22.3	55.4	44.0	10.4	23.0
1815	21.7	70.3	27.0	14.2	26.7
1816	8.6	71.1	28.2	8.8	26.7
1817	10.3	83.2	16.1	4.1	44.1
1818	16.9	72.8	26.2	5.1	52.3

n.a.: the original material was burnt.

Sources: Parliamentary Papers, 1814/15, vol. X, pp. 430 ff., 434 ff., 440 ff.; 1819, vol XVI, pp. 172, 186, 188, 192, 194.

production. From a British point of view, on the basis of available aggregate figures, it seems quite appropriate to conclude that British ironmasters 'maintained and perhaps strengthened the strong international competitive position they had established in the early part of the century' (Hyde, 1977: 173). This conclusion is supported by rather crude evidence, using aggregate export figures in relation to aggregate output figures. They inevitably conceal the considerable structural changes affecting Britain's competitive position in foreign markets, which took place from the 1820s onwards.

The bulk of British iron exports were made up of pig iron, bar iron and rails. Unfortunately, British export statistics subsumed rails under the category of bar iron until 1855. In subsequent years, when railway iron was registered separately, it constituted more than 50 per cent of bar iron. The growth of these exports between 1821 and 1870 is shown in table 7.5. To analyse the pace of this growth, I calculated average yearly growth rates. Whereas pig-iron exports grew by a remarkable 11 per cent, bar iron, including rails, still achieved the impressive growth rate of nearly 7.5 per cent. Both figures are well above the average yearly growth rate of

Table 7.5 *British iron exports, 1821–1870, thousands of metric tonnes, percentages and ratios, annual averages*

Years	Pig iron total tonnes	Germany/ Holland[a] per cent	France per cent	USA per cent	Bar iron (including rails) total tonnes	Germany/ Holland[a] per cent	France per cent	US per cent	Ratio total tonnes[b]
1821/25	4.5	4.6	56.3	28.4	30.5	7.2	12.6	11.4	8.5
1826/30	8.5	14.3	43.5	23.4	49.3	11.7	4.4	14.9	7.3
1831/35	21.6	13.0	22.5	44.9	76.4	12.1	2.0	27.8	4.4
1836/40	44.5	23.2	26.5	24.8	112.8	13.3	1.3	37.6	3.2
1841/45	103.7	43.7	17.7	17.4	183.0	28.6	1.8	22.8	2.2
1846/50	165.0	26.5	13.4	38.0	304.3	11.9	0.5	49.9	2.3
1851/55	276.4	26.1	12.9	37.8	575.7	7.1	2.4	56.8	2.6
1856/60	366.1	37.2	20.6	18.0	266.2[c] (475.9)[d]	10.2[c] (7.7)[d]	3.8[c] (3.9)[d]	28.5[c] (26.3)[d]	2.5
1861/65	470.0	33.4	29.9	10.2	256.7[c] (370.8)[d]	9.0[c] (6.9)[d]	5.4[c] (3.6)[d]	16.2[c] (15.1)[d]	1.7
1866/70	626.5	30.0	17.0	17.8	269.2[c] (605.4)[d]	6.3[c] (5.0)[d]	2.0[c] (–)[d]	16.5[c] (41.5)[d]	1.7

Notes: a) Holland is included because exports to Dutch ports were very often transit trade to Germany.
b) For bar iron a multiplier of 1.25 was used to obtain pig iron equivalents. Bar iron divided through pig iron.
c) Without railway iron.
d) Railway iron.

Source: See Fremdling, 2000: 221 ff.

British pig-iron production, which amounted to 5.6 per cent (Riden, 1977). They demonstrate quite patently the increasing dependency of the British iron industry on export markets. Not only did the product mix of British iron exports shift towards the lower stages of production (from bar iron to pig iron, as shown by the ratio in table 7.5), but, above all, Britain could only enlarge her export markets, especially after 1850, by diverting her incremental deliveries from her closest continental competitors, namely Belgium, France and Germany – constituting the European core – to the periphery and to the developing world.

3 Transfer patterns to the continent: coke smelting and castings

In Britain, the diffusion of coke smelting did not gather momentum before the 1750s, or even the 1760s, although in Coalbrookedale it had been a viable commercial process of producing cast-iron products directly from the molten coke pig iron from 1709 onwards. The now classical explanation for the rather belated diffusion of coke smelting comes from Hyde (1977), who maintains that charcoal prices had not increased sharply before the 1750s/60s. At a conference in Stjärnsund, Sweden, in 2000, Evans, however, challenged this view by pointing out that Hyde had not presented any convincing quantitative evidence. According to Hyde's own data, variable costs of charcoal smelting during the 1720s were even as high as in 1750s/60s. For Evans himself it remains rather a mystery, what had convinced ironmasters to increasingly apply coke smelting from then on. Without yet being able to substantiate his supposition, Evans states that there must have been a major technological breakthrough. The only example of such a breakthrough he mentions is that of the cast-iron-blowing cylinders for the blast furnace. Isaac Wilkinson received a patent on this innovation in 1757. I basically concur with Evans' supposition, but rather believe in the power of various minor innovations than in *the* major technological breakthrough. My hypothetical explanation is based on the fact that the technology of producing cast-iron products improved considerably. Whereas in the time from the 1750s to the 1780s the production of pig iron increased threefold, bar-iron production just doubled (Fremdling, 1986: 30 ff.). New casting techniques had been developed with the coke pig iron being molten again in a reverberatory or cupola furnace fired by coal. The rather homogeneous molten pig iron could be cast into complicated forms and high-quality cast-iron products resulted.[4] The best-known example is the still-existing iron bridge crossing the

[4] For technical details see Beck, 1897: 380–5; 753–6.

Severn near Coalbrookdale, built between 1777 and 1781. Moreover, much of the machinery of the industrial revolution including the cylinders of steam engines was made from cast iron. Cast-iron products served various purposes. As they were cheap they even replaced goods hitherto made from wrought iron (details in Hyde, 1977: 128; Beck, 1897: 755 ff.). And last but not least: 'The cannon and shot, as well as the small arms used against Napoleon, were cast in British foundries' (Hyde, 1977: 128). In order to produce accurate cylinders for steam engines or cannons, new drilling techniques had been developed. Best known for this achievement is John Wilkinson, Isaac's son.

There is a lot of evidence that foreign metallurgists visiting British iron works during the second half of the eighteenth century were highly interested in precisely these casting techniques, which allowed the production of superior and cheaper cast-iron goods for civil and above all military purposes (cannons).[5] I agree, however, with Broadberry's (1997: 78) principal notion, that all countries or entrepreneurs have access to a common pool of knowledge. Thus concepts of 'industrial espionage' (Harris, 1988), which are very common with technical historians, divert from the principal economic problem of technology transfer or diffusion.

On his travels through Europe during the 1760s, the French metallurgist Jars also visited British iron works. However, he neither got acquainted with the then modern processes of stamping and potting for making wrought iron from coke pig iron, nor did he even believe that this type of pig iron would be a useful input for wrought iron at all. Jars' description of the new British *casting* techniques, however, attracted the curiosity of several experts from the continent. As well as other Frenchmen, such as De la Houlière, Swedish metallurgists, who throughout the eighteenth century knew and described the state of the art minutely, regularly visited Britain. Furthermore, Prussian civil servants, such as Heynitz and von Reden, made their technological fact-finding visits to this country (Weber, 1976). Although these visitors did get acquainted with the new British methods of producing wrought iron with coal (stamping and potting and even Cort's puddling), they were not impressed by the outcome of these processes. They obviously considered the coal-based products as inferior to bar iron produced by means of charcoal pig iron. The new *casting* techniques with coke pig iron taken as input, however, convinced the French and Prussian governments to introduce these techniques into their countries. Together with the Frenchman Wendel, John Wilkinson's brother William got a contract in 1776 for establishing these

[5] In the following, I mainly draw on Harris, 1988.

techniques at the coalfields of Creuzot (Woronoff, 1984). This enterprise failed both economically and technically, finally collapsing in 1814. For instance, the cannons produced between 1788 and 1793 were too brittle. In my opinion, it is short-sighted to blame the quality of the inputs for this failure (Harris, 1988: 258 ff.); for from 1836 onwards, based on the same local raw materials as at the end of the eighteenth century (Roy, 1962), the brothers Schneider set out to make Le Creusot one of the most successful engineering and iron works of France.

The Prussian government tried to introduce the coke blast furnace early in Upper Silesia and eventually they planned the adoption of British cast-iron techniques for producing cylinders and cannons from this input. In 1788, William Wilkinson spent four months as a Prussian adviser (Weber, 1976: 227). In contrast to Le Creusot, the Prussian civil servants von Reden and Heynitz opted for a gradual introduction of the coal techniques. And at a very early date indeed, iron works in Upper Silesia did succeed in smelting iron ore in a coke blast furnace. The state-owned iron works of Malapane, Gleiwitz and Königshütte (Krołewska Huta) were the very first on the continent to continuously use coke for smelting pig iron. Starting as early as the 1790s, this transfer of technology was, rather uncritically, widely esteemed a striking success, making Upper Silesia the leading iron-producing region at the time of early industrialisation. Such an estimation, derived from a retrospective viewpoint, falsely suggests a fundamental advantage over other iron-producing regions on the continent. For in spite of coke smelting in the above-mentioned iron works the sector remained rather backward for quite a long time. In its backwardness the Upper Silesian wrought-iron industry neither applied the then available modern techniques employing coal (namely potting and puddling), nor did it resort to more efficient methods of charcoal technology, as did the Swedes. The technical problems of coke smelting were indeed solved, but these iron works did not make profits from this production. Prussian technocrats had been mistaken in imagining a programme for industrial development on a large scale would be capable of putting the British model quickly into practice; that is, applying coal techniques in various sectors. The Prussian technocrats had jumped to the conclusion that technical feasibility meant economic success. It did not, and thus coke smelting in Upper Silesia remained a heterogeneous element until the 1830s, having neither any serious consequences on the rest of the iron industry there, nor on the position Upper Silesia had in relation to other regions (Weber, 1976; Pierenkemper, 1992, 1994; Fremdling, 1986, 2000).

The erstwhile prevailing view (including my earlier writings on the subject), namely the reproach that Prussian technocrats modernised only an enclave of the iron industry, has to be modified considerably, however. Although von Reden in 1789/90 and other experts clearly got acquainted with Cort's innovations, for example, they obviously did not intend to introduce British methods of producing wrought iron wholesale. Why should they, if their region was not yet suffering from a serious shortage of wood and continental observers during the second half of the eighteenth century generally regarded both coke pig iron as an inferior input for wrought iron and the refining methods of stamping/potting (and later puddling) as inferior to continental forge practices? The term 'inferior' refers both to prices and quality.

It was otherwise with *cast* iron: continental observers readily conceded the superiority of (British) coke pig iron in combination with new *casting* techniques over continental practices (or at least saw it as a viable alternative or complement). Hence the endeavour to transfer casting techniques alone to the continent during the second half of the eighteenth century.

As a provisional result, the attitude of contemporary observers might be summed up as follows: in most respects, the British iron industry of the eighteenth century was regarded as different, unique and in parts even as backward, at least in comparison with Swedish best practices.

4 Transfer patterns to the continent: coke smelting and puddling/rolling

What consequences did the process innovations of the coke-using blast furnace, the puddling furnace and the rolling mill entail in the iron industries in continental Europe during the nineteenth century? According to David Landes' statement that these innovations were highly superior to the traditional procedures both technically and economically, the new techniques ought to have spread over continental Europe rapidly.[6] This implies that the old-fashioned iron industry based on charcoal should have perished fast and instead of, as formerly, being spread all over the country, the modern iron industry should have clustered round the coalfields. This did not occur for quite a long time, though. So David Landes' statement does not prove to be correct. He mixed up technical with economic superiority and thus – unjustly – blamed continental entrepreneurs for not quickly adopting the seemingly 'superior' technology.[7] In Great Britain, the new techniques had indeed surpassed

[6] 'Why the delay? Surely, the hardest task would seem to have been the original creative acts that produced coke smelting, the mule, and the steam engine. In view of the enormous economic superiority of these innovations, one would expect the rest to have followed automatically' (Landes, 1972: 126).

[7] On this very common fallacy, see Rosenberg, 1976: 189–210.

the old ones economically as well by the end of the eighteenth century, but this does not hold in most regions on the continent. Here, traditional or partly modernised procedures could endure very well within their native districts and with their markets of old. Moreover, when spreading over continental Europe the new techniques did not follow the British model strictly. Great Britain as the cheapest supplier worldwide (on the world market and on regional markets) created conditions to which continental regions reacted in different ways.[8]

4.1 *Indirect, embodied transfer*

A process innovation may provoke adaptations in other economic regions by being transmitted there directly and also by any trade in the new products that embody the new technology. At the beginning of the nineteenth century, British producers were undoubtedly the cheapest suppliers of iron internationally, but foreign ironmasters were protected from imports, firstly by tariff barriers, secondly by transportation costs and thirdly by differences in the quality of the iron, which meant a price threshold. Continental iron industries based on charcoal, which despite increasing productivity were finally doomed to extinction, could thus survive and even expand well into the second half of the nineteenth century. In the long run, however, these artificial, natural and quality barriers were reduced or disappeared completely, and British iron became competitive on the continental market for a long time. On the other hand, protection allowed the emergence of iron industries based on mineral fuel even where the natural resource endowment was less favourable than in Britain. This became evident when railway construction in countries such as Germany led to a sharp increase in demand for mass-produced iron and a modern iron industry emerged within a relatively short period. Britain herself helped her foreign competitors to accelerate the catching-up process by delivering vast amounts of cheap coke pig iron, which was worked up in foundries and rolling mills abroad.

Growing British iron exports showed fluctuating market shares for different customers.

Even the long-term development of demand for British iron was uneven, both in relation to the prominence of individual importing countries and the balance between pig iron and bar iron. The main clue to the fluctuations and shifts in the composition of British iron exports must therefore be found outside Britain, as her position as lowest-cost producer

[8] For detailed data, see Fremdling, 1986 or the article published in English, Fremdling, 1991a.

was already established at the beginning of this period. It is the internal development of the importing countries that has to be scrutinised for an appropriate explanation of these changes. Here I concentrate on France and the German states.

The French example during the first years of peace in the nineteenth century illustrates how powerfully British exports of bar iron produced with coal threatened the indigenous iron industry. The protective tariff France levied on bar iron had been adjusted according to Swedish prices in 1814. That was founded on the fact that Sweden had become the price leader and the most important exporter of bar iron after Russia during the eighteenth century. For bar-iron imports from Sweden this protective tariff might have indeed sufficed. Apparently unexpectedly, however, a new competitor gained against French ironmasters in their indigenous market, namely rolled iron, produced with coal, from Great Britain. In spite of the tariffs of 1814 it had a marked price advantage in several regional markets, in particular in places accessible by waterway such as Paris. (The ratio of imports to production accounted for around 16 per cent in 1821). Urged by their ironmasters, the French government raised the tariffs to fight off this perceptible competition. Doubling the price of British bar iron in the Channel ports, this new tariff was practically prohibitive. In table 7.5 the decline of British bar iron exports to France after 1822 is clearly seen.[9] Only in the 1850s was the tariff reduced for good. Thus the tariff of 1822 annalled the advantage of geographical proximity between Great Britain and France. The defence against an import of the new technology as it was embodied in the new iron products suppressed any import competition that would have forced the French iron-making regions into adaptations. The tariff policy indeed succeeded in shielding the new products from France, but the process innovations still made their way into the country.

Germany took a different path. Scattered all over the country, the German iron industry was hardly affected by British iron exports at the beginning of the nineteenth century. During the 1820s, British iron reached littoral places such as Hamburg, where it infringed less on the sale of German producers than on that of Swedish or Russian ironmasters.[10] The weakness of the British competition in inland Germany cannot be

[9] British pig iron kept a considerable market share in France, because of the demand from foundries. For an extended discussion, see my English publication on the French case (Fremdling, 1998).

[10] In this respect the correspondence of the Dowlais Iron Company with their agent in Hamburg, Uhthoff, is revealing. Uhthoff always compared the prices and quality of British bar iron from Dowlais with Swedish supplies. Two quotations from the incoming letters of Dowlais may suffice. Uhthoff wrote in 1822: 'I further noticed your high prices which in my opinion ought not to be so closely related to Swedish prices . . .' D/DG

attributed to prohibitive duties as in France, however. For Prussia and the Customs Union (Zollverein) levied merely a moderate duty on bar iron and even admitted pig iron duty free. And the geographical distance did not form an economically unsurmountable obstacle either, with the Rhine offering a way in to western Germany. The transportation costs to Cologne inclusive of the tariff (85 shillings) were far below the French tariff (200 shillings).

On the supply side, ironmasters such as those in the Siegerland or in the area around the Rivers Lahn and Dill could, in general, hold out very well against the British competition regarding both price and quality. For most customers still preferred the bar iron made with charcoal, which was then still of better quality. That is to say, bar iron made in Great Britain with the new technique had not yet entirely replaced the traditionally produced iron, which could only compete by means of substantial price differences. Competition was felt, however, in the traditional sales market on the lower Rhine and in Belgium and the Netherlands (Banken, 2000: 358 ff.). In the 1820s and 1830s, the Germans were hardly integrated into the world market, which was dominated by the British. This is clearly indicated by the fact that the relatively stable prices for German iron did not follow the violently fluctuating British prices.[11] Not until the 1840s did Germany become part of the international price connections. Before the 1840s, during extreme turns in the business cycles, the relative price inflexibility towards British suppliers nevertheless made British export flows to Germany swell rhythmically. When in Great Britain the iron price had dropped drastically in the early 1830s, much more iron had been exported to western Germany. That had threatened the traditional German iron districts for the first time. As the British prices recovered quickly and sales were consequently reduced, the preceding influx was considered a mere episode. A radical break occurred in the 1840s with falling prices in Great Britain raising the export flows to Germany. In vain did the Germans then try to protect their traditional iron industry by raising the tariff on bar iron and levying a duty on pig iron in 1844. For since the early 1840s at the latest, British iron produced by modern techniques had forced German ironmasters either to switch over to the new methods or to retire from production at least in part. This pressure from abroad was intensified through the erection of modern puddling

D.H. 1822 (4) F 540; furthermore, he complained of the quality, describing one cargo sent to him 'little more than a heap of rusting rubbish . . .' D/DG D.H. 1823 (5) F 251. Similar statements concerning British wrought iron can be quoted for the entire period from around 1820 to 1865.

11 See for example, British prices of merchant bar in Liverpool, quoted by Griffiths (1873: 288 ff.).

Stage of Production	Process		Product
	traditional	modern	
First Stage	Smelting in the blast furnace		pig iron imports
Second Stage	Refining		wrought iron
		in a puddling furnace with coal	
	Shaping		bar iron (rails)
		by a rolling mill	

Figure 7.3 The Ruhr model

and rolling mills in the very midst of German coalfields, from the late 1830s onwards.[12] These foundations were mainly due to the construction of railways. A brand-new iron industry centre emerged in the Aachen and Düren area, which thrived upon the still-existing traditional iron industry.

Typical of the German development is the link of indigenous economic regions with regions in Belgium or Scotland. The structure of German tariffs produced two effects: it made Belgium and British bar iron and rails more expensive. This however did not apply to pig-iron imports. Only from 1844 onward had pig iron to bear a duty worth mentioning. This tariff discrimination between bar iron and pig iron incited German ironmasters to turn to the second stage of iron production, where they owned a comparative advantage anyway. Thus in building puddling and rolling mills they quickly imported the modern technology directly. The first stage of iron production was modernised in a different way, though: here the modern technology came along rather slowly with the import of pig iron. Especially in the 1840s and 1850s, there was a pronounced partition in iron production between domestic and foreign regions, with the Germans producing bar iron and rails and the Belgians and Scots delivering the pig iron as input (see figure 7.3).

The competitive position of the three continental countries is revealed in tables 7.6 to 7.8. Exports and imports are compared by using the Balassa Index. It ranges from +1 to −1, where a positive value reveals

[12] This analysis is based on original research in archives and contemporary literature, which is documented in my Habilitations thesis (Fremdling, 1986: 59, 117).

Table 7.6 *French iron production, imports and exports, 1825–1870, thousands of metric tonnes and ratios, annual averages*

Years	Pig iron production (P)	Imports (M)	Exports (X)	$\frac{X-M}{X+M}$	$\frac{M-X}{P}$
1824/30	220.9	8.8	0.9	−0.81	0.04
1831/40	293.6	13.4	0.4	−0.94	0.04
1841/50	447.2	49.9	0.4	−0.98	0.11
1851/60	780.0	70.7		−0.98	0.09
		(+19.4)[a]	0.8	(−0.98)[a]	(0.11)[a]
1861/70	1191.5	79.1		−0.98	0.07
		(+73.1)[a]	0.7	(−0.99)[a]	(0.13)[a]
Years	**Bar iron[1] production (P)**	**Imports (M)**	**Exports (X)**	$\frac{X-M}{X+M}$	$\frac{M-X}{P}$
1825/30	148.6	6.9	0.5	−0.86	0.04
1831/40	195.2	5.6	0.5	−0.84	0.03
1841/50	301.7	6.7	0.8	−0.80	0.02
1851/60	480.0	18.1	2.1	−0.79	0.03
		(+1.9)[a]	(+5.1)[a]	(−0.47)[a]	(0.03)[a]
		12.2	2.5	−0.66	0.01
1861/70	767.0	(+16.4)[a]	(+28.9)[a]	(0.05)[a]	(−0.004)[a]

Notes: [1] Including rails. [a] The '*commerce spécial*' is a category in which imports allowed under the system of '*admission temporaire*' are not included. It can be corrected by means of the following formula: S = *commerce spécial*; G = *commerce général* $(M_G - M_S) - (X_G - X_S)$.
Source: Fremdling, 2000: 222.

a comparative advantage and a negative one the opposite. Furthermore, net foreign trade in pig and bar iron is expressed in relation to domestic production (see the last two columns of the respective tables).

French ironmasters clearly had a comparative disadvantage in foreign trade for the entire time span from the 1820s to the 1850s. With the system of '*admission temporaire*' during the 1850s and moderate free trade in the 1860s this improved to some extent for bar iron. In general, however, foreign trade never gained very high proportions compared with production.

In Germany, the ironmasters had an increasing comparative disadvantage in pig iron from the 1820s to the 1850s. Extremely high shares of net imports accompanied this in the 1840s and 1850s. Concerning bar iron and rails, this dependence on imports was even more pronounced during the same decades. The last two columns of table 7.7, however, also show the process of import substitution in the 1850s and 1860s. In

Table 7.7 *German*[1] *iron production, imports and exports, 1825–1870, thousands of metric tonnes and ratios, annual averages*

Years	Pig iron production (P)	Imports (M)	Exports (X)	$\frac{X-M}{X+M}$	$\frac{M-X}{P}$
1825/30	56.8	3.8	3.5	−0.03	0.004
1831/33	71.0	5.0	1.9	−0.45	0.04
1834/40	149.0	14.2	1.8	−0.77	0.08
1841/50	196.4	75.2	1.8	−0.95	0.37
1851/60	411.5	150.5	5.3	−0.93	0.35
1861/70	1,022.5	154.0	41.5	−0.58	0.11
Years	Bar iron[2] production (P)	Imports (M)	Exports (X)	$\frac{X-M}{X+M}$	$\frac{M-X}{P}$
1825/30	34.1	3.7	1.8	−0.35	0.06
1831/33	40.7	5.3	3.4	−0.22	0.05
1834/40	66.0	13.1	2.3	−0.71	0.16
1841/50	128.4	35.2	2.2	−0.88	0.26
1851/60	257.6	20.1	6.1	−0.53	0.05
1861/70	528.5	13.9	28.8	0.35	−0.03

[1]Until 1833 Prussia; from then on the Zollverein.
[2]Including rails.
Source: Fremdling, 2000: 222.

the last decade, Germany even became a net exporter of bar iron and rails.

4.2 *Direct transfer*

So far, I have concentrated on the British innovations as they were embodied in products, the import of which changed the regional economic pattern in France and Germany. Before railway construction on the continent demanded huge quantities of wrought iron mainly for rails, for which low-quality iron sufficed, Wallonia was the only continental region to follow the British model successfully (Reuss *et al.*, 1960). From the mid-1820s onwards, numerous works comprising coke blast furnaces as well as puddling and rolling mills were built in the coal-mining areas around Liège and Charleroi. Excelling the others, John Cockerill's factory at Seraing integrated all stages of production, from engineering to the supply of raw materials, as early as 1825. The natural locational factors of Wallonia were similar to those in British iron-producing regions with ore and coal situated closely together. Transportation costs and moderate protective duties screened Wallonia from the British competition while an ambitious government programme for industrial development was established on the British model (Fremdling and Gales, 1994). All these advantages did not in themselves distinguish the successful Wallonia from the still rather unsuccessful Upper Silesia. There were two main additional factors that favoured the Walloon iron industry: firstly, its vicinity to its customers, and secondly, the relatively high cost level of the traditional iron industry. In such an economic environment the technology transplanted from Britain could prosper. In the long tradition of processing wrought iron (for nails and engineering) Wallonia still had to import bar iron, for instance from the Rhineland, in the 1820s. Thus the establishment of the new technology there was not confined from the first by sales problems, as was the case with Upper Silesia or with most of the modern iron works in France. In Wallonia as well it took the modern iron industry more than twenty years to push aside the traditional competition. While the old-fashioned way of smelting iron with charcoal in the 1840s still dominated in Germany and France, it had already retreated into niches of the market in Wallonia. During the 1840s, roughly 90 per cent of pig iron was smelted by the use of coke (Fremdling, 2000: 212). Moreover, the Walloons even at that time had entered into serious competition with Britain in export markets (see the high export shares in table 7.8). Belgian ironmasters revealed a comparative advantage in foreign trade throughout from the 1840s to the 1860s. Concerning pig iron this changed from the late 1850s to the 1860s. The export quotas showed high values for pig iron mainly in the 1840s and early 1850s, which were due to preferential tariff rates to France and Germany in that period. The significant growth of the export quotas for bar and railway iron in the 1850s and 1860s reveals the increasing comparative advantage in this segment internationally.

In France, the conditions after 1822 seemed to favour establishing British-type iron works (see figure 7.2). By then, imports from Britain had shown that there was a demand for coal iron. With the customs policy guaranteeing a high price level, a big profit seemed to be in prospect. In expectation of this, iron works shot up in the coal districts of the Loire valley and the Massif Central from 1822 onwards. Following the British model, they were originally built as big iron works comprising several stages of production. These new establishments, however, had no economic success until well into the 1830s. Technical problems at the outset were solved little by little, but the new locations presented serious shortcomings. Unlike in Britain, iron ore had to be transported from a long way away, which raised the costs of production enormously. Moreover, the sites of the new iron industry were located far away from the centres of consumption, which made the sale dearer. To make matters worse, in

Table 7.8 *Belgian iron production, imports and exports, 1841–1870, thousands of metric tonnes and ratios, annual averages*

Years	Pig iron production (P)	Imports (M)	Exports (X)	$\frac{X-M}{X+M}$	$\frac{M-X}{P}$
1841/45	105.3[a]	1.4	37.4	0.93	−0.34
1846/50	178.5	0.3	74.9	0.99	−0.42
1851/55	231.1	0.1	78.6	1.00	−0.34
1856/60	317.4	2.8	53.4	0.90	−0.16
1861/65	396.2	10.4	28.2	0.46	−0.04
1866/70	488.7	55.1	17.5	−0.52	0.08

Years	Wrought iron production (P)	Imports of bar iron (M) and rails	Exports and rails (X)	$\frac{X-M}{X+M}$	$\frac{M-X}{P}$
1841/45	62.3[b]	0.4	3.5	0.79	−0.10[b]
1846/50	69.1	0.2	3.1	0.88	−0.04
1851/55	104.2	0.2	12.3	0.97	−0.12
1856/60	182.1	0.6	35.5	0.97	−0.19
1861/65	294.2	1.0[c]	68.5[c]	0.97[c]	−0.24[c]
1866/70	423.4	3.0	162.9	0.96	−0.38

Notes: [a]1841–4 estimated by Fremdling (1986: 78). [b]1845 only. [c]1861–4.
Source: See Fremdling, 2000: 222.

these centres the new products had to compete with those the traditional or partly modernised iron industry offered in a superior quality. The newcomers could not undercut the prices of the old-established firms enough for them to enter the markets. Thus for a long time, the changing economic structure of the coal-mining areas did not entail the decline of the traditional iron-producing regions (Roy, 1962; Vial, 1967; Gille, 1968; Belhoste *et al.*, 1994). The same holds true for German regions.

4.3 *Adaptations of the traditional sector*

Whereas Sweden succeeded in developing a completely alternative model, German and French regions could compete with the British iron industry only for a transitional period, albeit one covering several decades. In the following, I concentrate on adaptations of the traditional charcoal industry in Germany, France and Sweden which formed their particular response to the British challenge in iron producing.

Beyond imitation, the British model obtruded various strategies of adaptation onto the traditional iron industry. Hence, this sector did not remain passive at all, but underwent a development known from other sectors of industry as well, for instance from sailing ships: a technique becoming obsolete reaches its highest technical and productive level shortly before it disappears. Accordingly, calculations made for the Siegerland and Württemberg show that smelting iron with charcoal increased its productivity considerably in the decades from the 1820s to the 1850s, which is exactly the crucial period here.[13] This was achieved through extraordinary retrenchments on charcoal having the highest shares in the costs of smelting iron. In some traditional iron producing areas, even the output grew enormously during the crucial period. Only in the 1850s did this growth reveal itself as a short-lived success. And even then, several contemporary experts did not see it as certain at all, whether or not the traditional iron-producing areas that used nothing but wood and iron ore would more or less sink into insignificance by the side of the large-scale technology coming from Britain.[14]

The traditional iron industry struggled for survival by both increasing the productivity of smelting iron with charcoal and elaborately integrating parts of the new technique. The small forges could, for instance, substitute the new puddling furnace for the old refining furnace without changing the rest of the operation (see figure 7.4). Detached from the other modern techniques from Britain, the craft of puddling began spreading over many regions of the traditional iron industry, as early as the 1820s. As puddling furnaces were fuelled with coal, the charcoal was left only for the blast furnaces and the rise in charcoal prices was slowed down. These partial modernisations were widely spread over the most important regions with a traditional iron industry in Germany and France, namely the Siegerland and the Champagne. The bar iron produced by mixing old and new techniques was of as good a quality as the traditional iron but much cheaper. At the beginning, the iron made by use of coal through and through had been of inferior quality and thus had to compete hard against both the traditional iron and the new products of the technique combination (Fremdling, 1991b).

The hot blast was a further means to render the coexistence of the traditional and the new technology possible for a long time. It was the

13 See the calculations in Fremdling, 1986: 155–160. This statement is confirmed by using detailed Swedish data on the development of input and output prices: whereas prices for charcoal, iron ore and labour increased between 1820 and 1855, the price for pig iron remained constant or increased only slightly. See Jörberg, 1972: vol. I, 197, 697 ff., 702 ff., 721 ff.

14 On this see the results of an *enquête* which was conducted in connection with the Cobden-Chevalier treaty between France and the United Kingdom: 'Rapport sur les droits spécifiques à établir sur les produits de manufactures Anglaises, en vertu du traité de commerce avec la Grande-Bretagne', Archives Nationales F. 12 2483 (see Gille, 1986: 211–32). See furthermore the failure of the charcoal iron-producing 'Société des Hauts Fourneaux et Forges de la Côte-d'Or' in Jobert, 1979.

Stage of Production	Process		Product
	traditional	modern	
First Stage	Smelting in the blast furnace		pig iron
	with charcoal		
Second Stage	Refining		wrought iron
		in a puddling furnace with coal	
	Shaping		bar iron (rails)
	by the hammer		

Figure 7.4 The Champagne model

most efficient single innovation at that time, increasing the productivity of smelting both with charcoal and with coke. Instead of cold air, heated air was blown into the blast furnace. In 1828, the Scot James Beaumont Neilson got a patent for this invention. The hot blast raised the temperature in the blast furnace, which thus made better use of the fuel. It soon turned out that Neilson's innovation was of greatest advantage in regions with the highest fuel prices. Within Great Britain this holds for Scotland, which speedily proceeded to install the hot blast. During the short period from 1829 to 1833, Scotland took the place of South Wales in being the cheapest supplier of pig iron. Concerning Britain's ability to compete against the continental iron industry, however, Neilson's innovation soon proved to be a disadvantage. With the high fuel prices on the continent it was logical that Neilson's hot blast spread very fast there. As early as the middle of the 1830s, numerous blast furnaces in Belgium, France and Germany worked with the hot blast. And in France this innovation spread even faster than in Britain (Fremdling, 2000: 216). It could also be applied to charcoal blast furnaces with advantage, thereby extending their survival. In addition, a highly important supplementary innovation was introduced there. For a long time, the gases generated with smelting had been uselessly burnt off. In the 1830s, devices were installed to utilise the blast-furnace gases for heating the air of the blower. The small iron industry of Württemberg based on charcoal was on top of this development (Plumpe, 1982). Soon the modern coke blast furnace proceeded to utilise the blast furnace gases as well. This is a clear case of cross-fertilisation between traditional and modern methods. Economising on fuel like this both protected the traditional iron sector from the rising coal iron industry and also shielded the more cost-intensive coal districts from the less expensive. Nevertheless, during the 1860s, charcoal-using iron works retreated into niches and barely covered 10 per cent of the production of pig iron both in Germany and France (Fremdling, 2000: 212).

Sweden boasted of abundant iron ore, wood and sufficient waterpower for driving rolling mills. It did not dispose of coal resources, though. And the large Swedish iron industry based on charcoal was located too far from the coast or navigable rivers to allow the import of coal. Given these conditions, Sweden found her particular way of responding to the challenge of the new British iron production. Under the title of 'Responses to coal technology without any coal resources', Rydén presented a paper at a workshop on the iron industry at Stjärnsund in 2000. The following draws on his important findings (Rydén, 2002):

As early as 1789, Rinman had described Cort's innovation of puddling/rolling in Swedish. But not before 1830 was the process of puddling successfully applied for refining charcoal pig iron by the use of fire wood. The iron was shaped by rolling. During the 1850s, a number of ironworks applied this method; their production just reached a mere fraction of the total, though. Puddled iron was considered of an inferior quality compared with the product of the hitherto usual Walloon method. This traditional iron was the famous 'Oregrund' bar, which was still in demand even on the British market itself. In Sweden, too, as within the traditional iron industry in France and Germany, the hot blast was applied as early as during the 1830s.

The remarkable step in improving the production of bar iron by use of charcoal was the introduction of the Lancashire method in Sweden. Around 1830, the Swede Ekman had found a forge still applying charcoal for refining in the English county of Lancashire. The technique was very similar to the new puddling done with coal. From the 1830s onwards, Ekman tried to adapt the Lancashire method to local Swedish conditions, and in the mid-1840s, the Lancashire method became the dominant process of Swedish iron making. Sweden thus did not proceed to a coal-based method, but succeeded in following the path of a technology that was based on wood (charcoal). Rydén concludes 'that we should perhaps give more weight to a more developed machine-making technology and industrial organisation than to the actual use of mineral coal. A charcoal response to coal technology implicates that industrial production was possible even when no coal was available.'

The persistent differences of technology between Britain and the continent in iron making – either permanently (as in Sweden and similarly in Austria [Paulinyi, 1974]) or for a long transitional period (in France and Germany) – demonstrate that Britain was not merely the first but

Stage of Production	Process		Product
	traditional	modern	
First Stage	Smelting in the blast furnace		pig iron
	with charcoal		
Second Stage	Refining		wrought iron
	in a hearth with charcoal		
	Shaping		bar iron (rails)
		by a rolling mill	

Figure 7.5 The Swedish model

furthermore (nearly) the only country that completely proceeded to coal-based techniques. She thus took her own, unique path to the Industrial Revolution. At least for the eighteenth century and for long periods before the coming of the new liquid-steel processes in the second half of the nineteenth century (Bessemer, Thomas/Gilchrist and the open-hearth method [Siemens-Martin]), her exceptionalism holds true.

5 A sketch of an explanatory framework

Placing the case of the iron industry in a somewhat broader theoretical framework makes the British uniqueness even more palpable.

The iron industry – and probably other technological breakthroughs in Britain as well – could be seen as examples of leapfrogging, which has gained prominence in the recent literature on growth processes (Brezis *et al.*, 1993). The rather slow transfer of the modern iron techniques to continental Europe certainly fits this theoretical concept of comparing countries catching up and forging ahead. But the competitors did not have the same 'buck-horses', nor were these placed in one row and in one direction. For we witness the persistence of technological differences with an alternative sequence or path of productivity development in certain regions of the continent. For these deviating paths of development Broadberry's approach to technological differences between the United States of America and Great Britain in the twentieth century could probably be used analogously. Broadberry (1997: chapter 6) explains the productivity gap between the US and the UK by applying an evolutionary model of technical change, which integrates David's concept of path dependency with Mokyr's distinction between macro- and micro-inventions.

To illuminate the British-continental dichotomy (thereby neglecting differences between the continental countries), I 'translated' a part of Broadberry's text (1997: 77 ff.) to the case of the former iron production by merely replacing a few words: 'Great Britain' is substituted for 'New World', 'coal' for 'land/resource abundance', and 'wood' for 'skilled labour'. The substitutes are written in italics, followed by the originals in brackets.

The starting point is the Rothbarth-Habbakuk thesis, which traces the origin of *trans-channel* (transatlantic) technological differences to *coal abundance* (land and resource abundance) in *Britain* (the New World) . . . *British* (American) manufacturing substituted *coal* (resource-using machinery) for *wood* (skilled labour), which was in short supply in *Britain* (the New World). *In some continental countries* (Europe), however, *wood* (skilled labour) was abundant and *coal* (resources) scarce, so the *continental* (European) technology remained *wood-intensive* (skilled labour-intensive) . . . However, whereas *Landes* (Chandler) sees a unique best technology and assesses *continental* (British and German) industry according to how quickly they adopted *British* (American) methods, I follow the . . . literature in noting that competitive advantage requires developing distinctive capabilities rather than slavishly copying. Technical change within each country is therefore best seen as a path dependent process, with all countries able to draw on a common pool of knowledge but developing distinctive capabilities and adapting innovations to local circumstances. Finally, some common trends in the development of technology in all countries are noted.

Most of Broadberry's argumentation and even figures on the further pages in chapter 6 can be applied to the case study on the iron industry, similarly modified. In analogy to Broadberry's figures (on pp. 85 ff.), the point 'A' in figure 6.3 was reached in Belgium, France and Germany at least around 1860. Hence, the wood-intensive technology had by then become obsolete there, but definitely not in Sweden.

Touching upon the implicit comparison between the iron industry then and other technological transfers in another space and time places the persistence of technological differences between Great Britain and successful continental countries until well into the nineteenth century theoretically into the tradition of the Rothbarth-Habbakuk thesis. This provides an explanation of why there were different paths leading to modern economic growth into the twentieth century.

Part IV

Institutions and growth

8 The monetary, financial and political architecture of Europe, 1648–1815

Larry Neal

Among Patrick O'Brien's enduring contributions to the economic history of Britain is his work documenting the steady rise of central government taxation in the eighteenth century, even though Britain was already one of the highest-taxed economies in the world by 1688.[1] While the successive rises in taxation, either by widening the tax base to include more sources of taxation or by increasing the rates of existing taxes, were clearly driven by the wars of the eighteenth century, the puzzle he put to the profession was, 'How was the British government able to do this?' The puzzle arose from the constraints placed upon the monarchy by an elected parliament that had complete control over tax policy and was loath to tax its members, comprised of landed gentry and wealthy burgers. Moreover, given the splendid isolation of Britain from the land mass of Europe and the professional armies that ranged over it from the fifteenth century on, it was never clear that Britain had to be committed to participation in any of the dynastic wars continually erupting on the continent. Provisionally, O'Brien and Mathias in an earlier article had suggested that the answer lay in Britain's increasing reliance upon indirect taxes, at least until the imposition of the income tax by Pitt the Younger in 1799.[2] Until the threat of French domination of the continent motivated the British ruling classes to tax themselves, they argued, excise taxes were the tax of choice, rather than customs revenues. In 1988, O'Brien amplified this argument, pointing out that excises could be levied on goods, the demand for which enjoyed the twin virtues (from the perspective of tax collectors) of being both price-inelastic and income-elastic. As incomes rose over the eighteenth century, therefore, the tax base consisting of excise duties on spirits, sugar, tobacco, tea, coffee, leather, candles, malt, beer and soap rose as well, and as more of these goods became dependencies rather than luxuries, the tax rates could be increased as well without diminishing the total of tax collected. In passing, O'Brien noted that the collection of the excise became increasingly professional and effective over the eighteenth

[1] O'Brien, 1988. [2] Mathias and O'Brien, 1976.

century, an *aperçu* that was expanded into the major work of John Brewer on *The Sinews of Power*.

Central to the emphasis of both O'Brien and Brewer on the quantity and quality of British taxes in the eighteenth century was the argument that the excise taxes were necessary for the continued existence and growth of the British national debt. Without such a reliable source of tax revenue that could be credibly committed for the foreseeable future to the service of British government's long-term debt, they argued, the British government could not have raised funds so easily for financing its successive wars. As important as this point is, economists are still puzzled why the government was able to raise the stock of national debt substantially with each successive war, and then raise taxes permanently to continue to service that debt. Republics with representative parliaments in other countries at other times with a similar record of debt and excise taxes have chosen to levy some taxes temporarily to reduce that debt – the United States in the 1830s and France in the 1920s, to mention just two examples. At the end of the Napoleonic Wars, in the case of Great Britain, the choice was clearly understood whether to continue the income tax to pay down the accumulated debt or to eliminate the income tax and continue to service the debt. The choice made then was to eliminate the income tax and cope with servicing the debt by refinancing it with lower-interest bonds. The nineteenth-century regime of gold deflation and stable taxes then replaced the eighteenth-century regime of mild inflation and rising taxes.

An important role in facilitating the continued rise of taxes in the eighteenth-century British economy was played by the very existence of the national debt, at least in the particular form it took in the British case. By providing everyone in the British economy an easily accessible and highly liquid financial asset, the British national debt served a valuable pecuniary function for all members of the ruling class. Because the financial return to national debt holders was typically inverse to the rate of return on investments in the private economy,[3] the British national debt served as an insurance fund available to all participants in the economy, either directly or indirectly through their creditors. So, debt holders were able to prosper economically regardless of the military outcomes in the wars being financed by the issue of new debt, or the outcomes of their own risk-taking ventures. As impressive and important as the clerks of the Exchequer became for the success of the British government and its war-making ability, the financial functions served by the huge and ever-growing stock of national debt and those charged with the responsibility

[3] Neal, 1994.

of recording, marketing and servicing the government's debt were also necessary for the rise of British hegemony.

I develop this argument by comparing the British with the French and Dutch, as O'Brien and Mathias did explicitly in their 1976 article, but in terms of their respective monetary and financial architectures, rather than in terms of their tax size and structures. The key point is that the British financial sector was, thanks to the existence of the national debt, able to withstand the subsequent shocks inflicted upon it by the ever-increasing demands of war finance over the eighteenth century in a way that eluded the rest of Europe.[4] In so doing, the British financial sector enabled the British government to play a peripheral, but increasingly important, role in shaping the political architecture of Europe that emerged in the nineteenth century.

From 1648 to 1688

The Treaty of Westphalia (1648) created the modern nation state system that has characterised the European political scene ever since. It broke up the Holy Roman Empire into 300 sovereign political entities, recognised both Switzerland and the Netherlands as sovereign states, and placed France and Sweden as the dominant political powers in northern Europe. The resulting political environment set the stage as well for the long-term success of financial capitalism. The numerous political units that emerged in Europe after the Münster treaty experimented with a variety of monetary regimes as they attempted to establish their legitimacy and consolidate their territory. During the wars that followed over the next 160 years, they extended and perfected the financial innovations that had emerged during the preceding Thirty Years War under the pressures of war finance. By the time the Treaty of Vienna was signed in 1815, a new system of public finance was firmly established as each country tried, as best it could within its political framework, to imitate the success of the British in establishing a funded national debt. The monetary regime of Great Britain, then based on the fiat currency of the paper pound, was not imitated, however. All Europe reverted to some form of precious metal standard – either silver and gold, silver, or gold.

The diverse legal and monetary regimes of Europe that emerged after 1648 were struck by a series of financial shocks as governments waged repeated wars upon each other, both on the continent and overseas. Especially interesting are the contrasting monetary regimes and

[4] Much of this is covered in Neal, 2000, but without explicit reference to the political architecture of Europe that concerns O'Brien in later work.

financial systems developed in the three leading mercantile powers – the Netherlands, Britain and France – over the period of intermittent warfare from 1651 to 1726. Other countries – Austria-Hungary, Portugal, Prussia, Russia or Spain – all imitated some variant, usually the French, of the financial systems developed by the three leading mercantile states. After 1726, each power then maintained a stable financial system with only minor modifications through the following decades that included the War of the Austrian Succession (1739–48), the Seven Years War (1756–63) and the War of American Independence (1776–84). The accumulated fiscal pressures on the French government finally led to a catastrophic breakdown of each country's regime and replacement by a new system of war finance from 1789 to 1815. First revolutionary France, then a conquered Netherlands, and ultimately an isolated Britain had to devise new systems under threat of military defeat during the French Revolution and the Napoleonic Wars. The Treaty of Vienna in 1815 eased the political uncertainties of this period for a generation or so, allowing the continental powers time to adapt elements of the British system of finance to their particular situations.

The Dutch system

The Dutch province of Holland, led by the international merchants of Amsterdam, emerged from the travails of the Thirty Years War unrivaled in wealth and the potential for increasing its commercial supremacy in the long-distance trade of Europe. From the Dutch viewpoint, the Thirty Years War was simply an intensification of its ongoing Eighty Years War with Spain begun in 1568, but with a wider range of allies and enemies. In the middle of the Eighty Years War, the desperate finances of the individual provinces led each of the fourteen mints in the Netherlands (eight provincial and six municipal) to follow its own policy in the timing and extent of successive debasements. Mints in the adjacent areas of the Spanish Netherlands and Westphalia took advantage of the resulting confusion in circulating coins to produce their own variants. Foreign coins were introduced in profusion as well by merchants from abroad. By 1610, it has been estimated that money-changers in Amsterdam had to keep track of nearly a thousand different gold and silver coins.[5] As would be the pattern throughout the period until 1795, the province of Holland took the initiative in clarifying the situation. In 1638, the city of Amsterdam determined that its silver currency should have slightly less than 10 grams of pure silver – a standard that remained unchanged until the 1930s. This measure also set the relative value of the current coin to the guilder of

[5] Dehing and Hart, 1997: 40. They cite H. Enno van Gelder (1978/9), p. 62.

account used to value deposits in the Amsterdamse Wisselbank, a guilder still based on the silver guilder established by Charles V in 1544. In 1659, the States General of the Netherlands followed the Amsterdam example.

More important than the stability in the intrinsic value of the newly minted coins was the ease of payment that merchants and citizens found in the always reliable bank guilder. This was the unit of account established for deposits in the Wisselbank, established in 1609 at the initiative of foreign, non-Catholic merchants coming to Amsterdam after being expelled from Antwerp by the Spanish. The central role of the Wisselbank was established by outlawing all existing money-changers and cashiers as well as their notes issued as receipts for coins placed with them for safe-keeping. The *kassiers* were allowed to resume business in 1621, but only as licensed officials and under the restriction that they could not hold specie for longer than twenty-four hours before depositing in their account at the Bank of Amsterdam.[6] In this way, the Bank of Amsterdam maintained a unified system of payments that was denominated in a single currency, the bank guilder, and that was centralised in a single institution. The receipts issued by the Bank of Amsterdam then became the preferred medium of exchange for the market place. A merchant dealing with scores of customers on the Amsterdam markets could more quickly credit his account at the Bank of Amsterdam by depositing their bank receipts rather than their coins, whatever their provenance. Coins would have to be assayed for their precious metal content and evaluated at bank guilder rates before being credited; bank receipts, by contrast, could be credited to the merchant's account immediately.

The centralisation of the payments system in the Bank of Amsterdam had two great benefits for the financial future of the Netherlands. First, it allowed an efficient giro system of net clearing to function that minimised the need for cash by merchants. This was more efficient, the greater the number of accounts. These rose to nearly 3,000 in the frenetic year of 1720, but numbered 1,350 already in 1625, far more than in any other exchange bank in northern Europe.[7] Merchants from all over Europe were content to leave their specie and precious metals in the vaults of the bank, creating the second benefit for the Dutch – management of Europe's treasure chest. This mass of silver and gold in the *Speciekammer* was then available for the outbound ships of the Dutch East India Company as well as for the English, French, Austrian and Danish East India Companies. It was also available for the defence of Amsterdam if the city was threatened by enemy occupation, an event that only happened once a century in this period. The availability of actual trade coins in the vaults of the Bank of Amsterdam also meant that bills of exchange drawn

[6] Dehing and Hart, 1997: 40–4. [7] Dehing and Hart, 1997: 46–7.

on Amsterdam were both reliable and prompt in payment. It became the entrepôt for commercial credit throughout Europe, credit extended on the basis of the bill of exchange payable in Amsterdam at the Bank of Amsterdam. The advantages of centralisation for the efficiency of the Dutch payments system were not allowed, however, to extend into the financial realm.

The political jealousies of the separate provinces and the individual trading cities towards the eminence of Amsterdam meant that shares in the United East India Company (VOC, for Vereenigde Oost-Indische Compagnie) were divided up among the seven participating cities. Amsterdam, by far the dominant city, had to agree to keep its share of the company's capital stock just below half. The remaining shares that were split up among the other six cities never provided a large enough body of tradable securities to allow an active stock market to emerge outside of Amsterdam. Even there, only the capital stock of the Amsterdam chamber of the VOC provided enough volume of trading activity to sustain the livelihood of a small group of stockbrokers. Public debt instruments were issued in prolific quantities, but they were all backed by specific taxes dedicated to a specific debt issued by a particular province or, most typically, the general taxes of an individual municipality.[8]

In short, the Netherlands, due to the fragmented character of its political structure, never issued a truly national debt backed by a national taxing authority in this period. This, despite the constant pressures placed on Dutch financial resources by the repeated assaults of the French or English. Consequently, the Netherlands missed out on the financial revolution that arose later in England, even though its constituent cities and provinces had developed the basic elements of funded, fungible and assignable debt backed by perpetual taxing authority that comprised the financial revolution of England.[9] What the Dutch citizens and bankers lacked was a liquid, transparent, secondary market for the securities issued by their various public authorities. Their financial system failed to match the effectiveness of their monetary system. From 1694 on, however, they were able to take advantage of the market in financial assets created in England by their countryman, William III, and his advisers.

The English system

William III, Stadholder of the Netherlands and military commander of the Protestant forces of northern Europe, seeking to limit the expansion

[8] See de Korte, 1983. [9] See Tracy, 1985.

of France under Louis XIV, became King of England and Wales in the course of the Glorious Revolution of 1688. When the expenses of his military efforts in the following years in Ireland, Scotland and northern Europe overwhelmed the tax resources allowed him by the English parliament, he was forced to try out on his British subjects some of the financial innovations that had been found successful on the continent.

In 1694, the English parliament issued three types of securities, all of which were intended to 'fund' the various forms of short-term debt arising from the expenses of the War of the League of Augsburg into long-term funded debt, on which only interest would be paid for the duration of the war. These were lottery tickets, tontine annuities and special bonds.[10] The first two, sold to the general public, failed to find a suitable market. The lottery tickets were too easily and too profitably imitated by the private sector for the government to wish to rely upon them for additional finance. While the full one million pounds worth of the tickets was sold, their implicit interest rate was 14 per cent and the lottery was expensive to operate. The tontine annuities, actually authorised in 1693, appeared too complicated and too foreign for the English public to respond enthusiastically, and barely one-tenth of the intended million pounds was raised, even with an implicit interest rate of 10 per cent. The rest of the million pounds had to be raised with later issues of simpler life or long-term annuities bearing an interest of 14 per cent. In the third attempt at creating funded debt, £1.2 million of bonds carrying a guaranteed eight per cent rate of interest, funded from specific taxes assigned to that purpose by the parliament of England, were sold only to subscribers in the proposed new Bank of England. If the subscribers bought up one-half of the issue by 1 August 1694, they were to be incorporated as the Bank of England. The Bank, in turn, issued easily transferable shares in its joint stock, promising purchasers at least a pass-through of the interest it was being paid by the government and a potential capital gain if the bank succeeded in turning a profit on its monopoly of the banking business of the government. The full £1.2 million of these bonds were taken up immediately and their success established the basis for a remarkable rise in further issues of debt.

The new public bank of the government was not given the monopoly of the payments system, however, so it was not a mere imitation of the successful Bank of Amsterdam. Unlike the Wisselbank in Holland, the Bank of England was not the creation of the merchant guild of the capital city. Rather, it was chartered by the national parliament of England at the urging of the king. Even so, parliamentary approval required acknowledging

[10] See table 2, 'Government long-term borrowing, 1693–8', in Dickson, 1967: 48–9.

the vested interests of the goldsmiths guild and their most important members, the goldsmith bankers. When the Bank of England was chartered in 1694, their interests were protected by allowing them to continue issuing their individual bank notes as the favoured medium of exchange within the City of London, at least until the Bank of England was given the monopoly of note issue in 1706. Then, the most fruitful reaction of the goldsmith bankers to the new public bank was to move into new forms of activity. They were able to manage portfolios for wealthy clients and, increasingly, to deal themselves in the emerging capital market of London, whether as brokers or dealers.[11]

After the South Sea Bubble was mopped up, the further issues of government debt were all made on the same principles as those first issues to the Bank of England. The debt was always redeemable by the government, but the government would not wish to do that unless the market value of the debt had risen above par and even then it would be better off by continuing to pay interest than to redeem the full amount. The original purchasers of the government debt could freely sell part or all of their holdings in the secondary market for securities. Readily accessible transfer facilities, low transfer fees and transparent pricing on the spot market for these securities facilitated the growth of active trading. At first, this kind of trading in government debt was limited to the shares of the Bank of England. Other forms of government debt were available to investors, but were not actively traded. But then the shares of the New East India Company (1698), the United East India Company (1708) and the South Sea Company (1710) continued the process of debt-equity conversion. This process eventually culminated after the collapse of the South Sea Bubble in the creation of the 3 per cent perpetual annuities of the South Sea Company (1723). These in turn led ineluctably to the creation of the Consols of 1758. Their inherent marketability was enhanced by the regular purchases on the market by the Commissioners for the Reduction of the National Debt.[12]

The national debt of Great Britain grew dramatically with each successive war of the eighteenth century. The wartime shocks produced the anticipated effect of a price reduction, given that a large addition was made suddenly to the stock of outstanding debt, so the market value of the debt might decline, but never the nominal value of the debt, or the taxes required to pay the semi-annual interest payments. After the joys of debt financing had been discovered, debt service became the most important item in the annual budgets of the British government. Only once did debt charges dip as low as one-third of tax revenues after the

[11] This is described in Quinn, 1994. [12] Neal, 1990: chapter 3.

creation of the South Sea Company in 1710. At the end of the American War of Independence debt service briefly touched two-thirds of the gross revenues available to the central government. The pressure of debt service that occurred after each war was a powerful force impelling the government to develop a larger tax base and to extract taxes more efficiently. The two processes – rising taxes and growing debt – obviously reinforced each other for the entire eighteenth century, but the direction of causation appears to be from war finance to increased debt to higher debt service/total revenue ratios to higher taxes.[13]

Why were Members of Parliament content to raise taxes permanently to service the perpetual debt rather than raise some taxes temporarily to retire the debt? Part of the answer, provided by O'Brien, is that the new taxes, or hikes in existing taxes, were perceived to be paid mostly by the rising middle classes, while the interest paid on the funded debt went into the pockets of the already rich and powerful represented in parliament. But another part of the answer must be that the rising stock of national debt was beneficial to the British economy, encouraging the entrepreneurial risk-taking and innovation that created the rising middle class.

For example, the truly extraordinary increase in the ratio of the stock of national debt to domestic product over the course of the eighteenth century does not seem to have had any retarding effect on the gradual rise in the share of investment expenditures in output that took place in the last quarter of the century.[14] Despite the alarms raised by economists throughout the eighteenth and nineteenth centuries about the burden created by raising and then increasing the national debt, the British economy continued to prosper and expand even as the ratio of the stock of national debt to the annual flow of gross domestic product rose sharply with each successive war.

How did it do this? The answer lies in the opportunities for risk sharing that arose within the English financial system. Unlike their continental counterparts, English firms were bound together in a secondary market for financial assets, rather than through a clearing house as in the Netherlands or an information network as in France. Small partnerships of specialised intermediaries characterised banking, foreign exchange and stock broking. Specialised brokers appeared in the London stock exchange by the end of the War of the Spanish Succession. By 1713, ample shares in not only the Bank of England but also the United East India Company and the South Sea Company were available and had been subscribed to initially by quite distinct groups of investors. The consequent reduction

[13] O'Brien, 1988. [14] A large literature has dealt with this issue: see Williamson, 1987.

of transaction costs for purchasers of the government funds obviously increased the value of government debt as a form of insurance against the risks incurred when dealing in the less liquid markets for real assets or private financial assets. A large part of the theoretical advantages to be obtained from creation of national debt depends upon it being created on a large enough scale and spread among enough asset holders with different tastes that transaction costs in its secondary market can be reduced. These advantages could be captured by holders of English government debt at least by the end of the War of Spanish Succession and most likely before it began in 1702.

The Bubble Act of 1720 eliminated dealing in a welter of bubble companies that had sprung up in the previous speculative boom, but it does not seem to have eliminated continued use of the joint-stock company for financing the continued expansion of British infrastructure – turnpikes, canals, docks and waterworks.[15] In short, the basic outlines of the British structure of finance were set by 1723 – a complementary set of private commercial and merchant banks all enjoying continuous access to an active, liquid secondary market for financial assets, especially government debt. The South Sea Bubble proved to be the 'big bang' for financial capitalism in England. Unfortunately for France, the collapse of the Mississippi Bubble there in 1720 proved to be the end of secondary markets for financial assets in that country.

The French system

The years following the Treaty of Westphalia saw the rise to power of the fabled Sun King, Louis XIV (1638–1715). Louis first defeated the rebellions of the traditional nobility, rebellions caused in large part by the continued fiscal demands placed upon them by the expenses of the Thirty Years War. He then created a new aristocracy under the leadership of his Comptroller of Finances, Colbert. Finally, in his old age and after Colbert's death, he dissipated the economic and financial resources of his kingdom in a series of increasingly expensive and indecisive wars. By the end of the War of Spanish Succession (1702–14), coming upon the heels of the War of the League of Augsburg (1689–97), the French government was bankrupt. The last years of the war required repeated borrowing and the creation of new offices to be sold to wealthy citizens. Sale of new bonds raised less and less money as they had to be sold at increasing rates of discount, amounting to 50 per cent by the war's end.[16]

[15] Harris, 2000. [16] Murphy, 1997: 128.

None of the traditional means that Louis had used to deal with the aftermath of war finance seemed to work after his death in 1715. These included simply repudiating all of the debt, repudiating it in part by means of a *Visa* that would acknowledge some debts and disavow others, or using a *Chambre de Justice* to impose a capital levy on the financiers who had profited most. All required a strong monarch in power to be effective. Under the circumstances existing in France after the death of Louis XIV, with the legitimate successor a sickly five-year-old great-grandson of the Sun King, and the regent under a cloud of suspicion, new expedients had to be proposed and attempted. The first series of innovations consisted of a series of devaluations and revaluations of the coin of the realm and the introduction of new means of payment – a paper currency bearing interest known as *billets d'état*. The repeated alterations of the currency disrupted drastically the payments mechanism of France, while the introduction of a new form of government debt only depreciated further the value of the existing debt. Into this dire situation stepped the financial wizard of the eighteenth century, John Law.

John Law proposed to combine the best features of the Dutch and English financial systems into an entirely new 'System' for French money and finance. This would combine a secondary market for government securities with a central clearing house for payments. The essence of Law's scheme was to displace the use of gold and silver as means of payment and store of value in the domestic economy with paper money backed by the tax power of the state. The attraction to the government was that this would allow it to amass in its treasury the gold and silver needed to mobilise and maintain the large armies and navies required for success in modern warfare.

To accomplish this, Law first expanded the powers of his Banque Générale by rechartering it as the Banque Royale, and making it a supposedly superior combination of the Amsterdam and London banks. Not only did it obtain a monopoly on foreign payments and tax remittances from the provinces as in Amsterdam, it also became a fractional reserve bank as in London, so it could expand the money supply at will. Then the Compagnie d'Occident was expanded to become the monopoly company for all foreign trade of France, as well as collector of all royal taxes within France, and was renamed the Compagnie des Indes. By combining the essential features of the Dutch and English financial systems and enlarging on each, Law felt sure that France could surpass both countries. Alas for the success of Law's system and the future of the French financial sector, the regent was equally entranced by the independence from the political constraints of the Paris Parlement that the Banque Royale provided him.

To meet the regent's desires for additional finance to consolidate his political situation both at home and abroad, Law put to use the new powers of his Banque Royale to begin the machinations on the stock of the Compagnie d'Occident that were to create the Mississippi Bubble in Paris. His machinations have been well described many times[17] and analysed brilliantly most recently by Antoin Murphy,[18] so the details will not be repeated here. Briefly put, Law used the money-making powers of the Banque Royale to finance a rise in the market price of shares in the Compagnie d'Occident. When the shares had risen sufficiently to provide a reference rate of interest of 2 per cent for the French economy, Law tried to stabilise his system, first by merging the two companies into one, thereby freezing out the financiers who had helped finance Louis XIV's wars from controlling the operation of the new system. Second, he tried to maintain convertibility at a fixed rate between the inflated shares of the company and the bank notes issued by the bank, by enforcing a reduction in the rate of interest on all alternative financial assets. Law's one-two punch of first inflation in the money of account, the *livre tournois*, and then an interest cap on new loans effectively demolished the existing credit structure in France.[19] His third effort to save his system required mopping up the excess liquidity he had created during the Mississippi Bubble. But the deflationary process that ensued ran afoul of the interests of the nobility backing the political fortunes of the regent. With the previous monied classes already against him, Law was forced first to resign, and then to flee France.

John Law's experiment in consolidating and then monetising France's national debt ended by a protracted *Visa*, which started in 1721 and lasted until 1723. The *Visa* was a classic French financial innovation, essentially a 'segmented default'. It divided holders of the French national debt into six categories, with each successive category getting less credit for their holdings, depending on how they had acquired them. Distinctions were made among payments made by exchanging previous debt of the crown, by specie, by city of Paris debt, by private debt, by foreign bill of exchange, by *billets de banque* and so on. Creating the documentation required for debt holders to claim as much as possible from the authorities gave an enormous boost to the information base at the disposal of the Paris *notaires*. These were the 113 officials appointed by the city of Paris to draw up and attest to the validity of legal instruments. Moreover, private French debts were always legally enforceable only in nominal terms of the official unit of account – the *livre tournois*. When this depreciated rapidly during the brief inflation set off by Law's issuance of paper money, debtors forced

[17] Faure, 1977. [18] Murphy, 1997. [19] Hoffman and Rosenthal, 1995.

their creditors to receive devalued *livres* for repayment, again through the notaries. The shock of inflation, arbitrary default by the crown and protracted scrutiny of citizens' affairs by the *Visa* officials combined to ruin the official credit market in France for at least a century.[20]

A unique private credit market, however, emerged from the ruins of public credit in 1723, or so claim recent studies of the private credit activities by the notaries of Paris.[21] The closely knit corporation of notaries was empowered to pass on their accumulated legal records, known as *études*, to designated successors. They used these to match up private lenders with private borrowers, sharing information with one another to make the matches as mutually congenial as possible in terms of amount and duration. Hoffman and Norberg (1994) claim that the concentration of notaries on brokering long-term lending among private individuals thereafter was an effective 'third way' for financial intermediation. The French, under duress, had spontaneously discovered an alternative to banks and capital markets as means of financial intermediation – an information network managed by information brokers entrusted with the responsibility of placing either funds or loans among their clients.

Thanks to the information network created by the notaries, the Paris credit market was thriving from 1726 to 1789. The quantity of private loans brokered by the notaries grew sharply to the eve of the French Revolution, equaling the size of the French national debt. These were private loans, usually secured by some form of property, whether real or personal. French national debt, largely in the form of life annuities, was not a major part of the placement services provided by the notaries. The large part of French *rentes* held by foreigners appear to have been bought by them through their foreign bankers and their agents in Paris. The French government apparently could not tap into the active private market for loans, save with very specific securities at much higher rates of interest than ruled in the private market. The only way the government exploited the information network of the notaries, apparently, was to use it to verify the continued life of the nominee named by each annuitant.

The private credit market continued to flourish, even while the French government's credit standing steadily worsened, especially after the expenses incurred while supporting the Americans in their War of Independence against the British. Hoffman and Norberg (1994) argue that the growth in volume of the private credit market brokered by the notaries demonstrates the efficacy of information networks as an alternative form of financial intermediation. Alternatively, its growth may have been a

[20] Kindleberger, 1993: chapter 6.

[21] Hoffman and Rosenthal, 1995.

manifestation of a 'flight to quality' by French domestic savers alarmed by the increasingly tenuous nature of French public finances. At any rate, even the shock of financing the expense of the Seven Years War could not transform the information network of the French notaries into a viable banking system.

There is no comparable study to date of the activities of Dutch notaries, possibly because the quantity of material available there is utterly overwhelming. But it is obvious that they provided as much, if not more, private credit facilities for their more commercially inclined clientele in the Netherlands than did the *notaires* in Paris and the French provinces. Moreover, their clientele were active investors in foreign long-term securities, especially the various forms of English national debt after 1720, as documented many years ago by Charles Wilson.[22] Much of the risk-averting activity of the wealthy Dutch was focused on British Consols as well as the original South Sea annuities issued in 1723. As yields on these forms of British debt fell, Dutch speculators showed more interest in English East India Company stock.

The English response to the shocks of the bubble years contrasted with that of both Amsterdam and Paris. The Bank of England was learning, reluctantly, to be a lender of last resort and in the process helping to strengthen the ties of the London private bankers with Amsterdam. Since 1717, Isaac Newton's overvaluation of gold had effectively put England on a gold standard while the Netherlands and France were on a silver standard. Even though all three countries were nominally on a bimetallic standard, defining their units of account in terms of both silver and gold, the differing mint ratios among the three put the Netherlands typically on a silver standard, England on a gold standard, and France moving between the two metals. The resulting scarcity of silver in England and consequently of small coins led to a variety of private innovations in developing alternative means of payment. During the Seven Years War, the spread of so-called country banks began, a development that gradually led to a dense network of local banks centred upon their correspondent banks in London. The financial links of the agricultural and industrial districts of England to the commercial and political centre of London provided Great Britain with the most varied and complex financial system in Europe. Subjected to the same shocks as the other mercantile powers in the wars of the eighteenth century, moreover, it proved flexible enough not only to survive, but to emerge from each war stronger relative to both France and the Netherlands.

[22] Wilson, 1941 (reprinted 1966).

The final shocks: Revolution and war, 1789–1815

The accumulated strains upon the French public finances following the conclusion of the American War of Independence caused the entire monetary and financial structure of the country to collapse as the French Revolution of 1789 unfolded. In sequence over the next four years from 1789 to 1794, free banking was allowed to emerge as the feudal system of privileges and tax exemptions were abolished; price controls and restrictions on banking practices were then imposed as the revolutionary governments attempted to legitimise their regimes in place of the deposed monarchy; and, finally, the issuance of *assignats* ran well beyond either the value of the Church and *emigré* lands put up for sale as backing for them or the value of the stock of circulating specie in France that they had displaced. The hyperinflation that followed destroyed once again the private credit structure of France just as during the Law episode in 1720. It also destroyed the credit of the state with no legitimate government in sight to re-establish political credibility à la Louis XV in 1723. Consequently, the Directory tried to implant in France the financial and monetary practices that had proved successful in England and the Netherlands.[23]

First, the debt was defaulted to the extent of two-thirds, to assure creditors that interest could be paid on at least the remaining one-third. Then a major currency reform was undertaken, replacing the now thoroughly discredited *livre tournois* with a new unit of account, the *franc germinal*, defined like the Dutch guilder in terms of both gold and silver with a fixed mint ratio. Finally, a public bank was established, the Banque de France. While required to maintain the value of the *franc germinal*, the bank was also expected to help the government avoid fresh deficits by improving the efficiency of its payments system. In the event, French public finances maintained their solidity by virtue of Napoleon's military victories. The satellite kingdoms, subjected to the new tax regime of the French revolutionaries and required to accept the *franc germinal* at fixed prices for military supplies, were able to support the continued war effort of France in a throwback to Roman-style war finance. Chief among the satellite kingdoms was Holland.

The political fragmentation of the Netherlands and the already high tax burdens imposed on the most commercialised provinces made it impossible to organise effective resistance against the French revolutionary armies. Indeed, the goals of national unification and elimination of feudal institutions espoused by the Revolution appealed to the Patriots, who welcomed the chance to put the Orangists and their claims

[23] White, 1995, and Sargent and Velde, 1995.

to hereditary privilege out of power once and for all.[24] The collapse of the French government debt had certainly harmed the Dutch financiers, who had been withdrawing from the British funds since 1784. The French troops had to win decisive victories in the Austrian Netherlands before annexing them over the resistance of the largely Catholic populations in 1794. By contrast, they only had to appear at the outskirts of Utrecht and Amsterdam to encourage the Patriot revolutionaries to seize power and welcome them.

The gratitude of the Dutch Patriots, however, had to be expressed financially to be meaningful to the French government. The specie reserves of the Wisselbank had been completely withdrawn by the time the French troops entered Amsterdam, despite the plunge of the agio into negative depths never seen before. Repeated payments to support the French forces forced the Batavian Republic and then the Kingdom of Holland to create more and more annuities, now issued by the national government. In 1814, the restored Kingdom of the Netherlands consolidated them into $2\frac{1}{2}$ per cent perpetual annuities, modelled on the successful British example. Amounting to over four times the national income of the kingdom, however, only a small part of the annuities, the activated portion, could actually be paid by the government.

At the start of French occupation of Holland, William V fled to Britain and the senior partners of Hope & Company, Henry Hope and John Williams Hope, moved from Amsterdam to London. William V signed over all Dutch colonial ports and fleets to Britain, whose naval forces quickly took possession of most, finally occupying Java in 1811. Although France now controlled the home ports and cities of the Netherlands, Britain acquired the global commercial and intelligence network of the seaborne Dutch empire. The course of subsequent events proves they exploited it fully, both militarily and, especially, financially.

First, the British government increased greatly the annual tribute (reimbursement) levied upon the East India Company to £10 million annually. Second, as the French monetary reforms threatened to encourage a speculative return of funds to France at the end of 1796, the Bank of England was allowed to suspend convertibility of its banknotes into specie. The resulting 'paper pound' lasted from February 1797 to May 1821, when the gold standard was formally resumed. Third, the government of William Pitt moved to competitive bidding among underwriting syndicates for placement of new issues of Three Percent Consols, with interest payments guaranteed against the increased revenues of the

[24] Israel, 1989: chapter 43.

income tax. The income tax allowed the government to tap into the profits of European merchants now directing all their affairs from London rather than dividing them between London, Paris, Amsterdam and Hamburg. The existing liquid market for British debt allowed huge sums to be raised on the capital markets. As most of the money raised for war finance was used after 1803 for paying and supplying British forces directly, rather than laying out subsidies to continental allies or hiring mercenary armies from Germany, domestic expenditures rose greatly. Entrepreneurs from all over Europe flocked to Britain to take advantage, either with direct or portfolio investment, of the profit opportunities that emerged in textiles, iron and steel, dockyards, waterworks, gas works and agriculture.[25] The flight to quality by the mercantile classes of French-occupied Europe, certain to be taxed heavily and dispossessed of privilege by Napoleon's forces, alit in large part in Great Britain.

The cosmopolitan bourgeoisie of Europe, indeed from much of the world, stayed and prospered, in large part due to the financial markets existing in London. These provided transparent information, security of title and ease of entry and exit as alternative opportunities appeared. The only capital controls that could be enforced were on foreign holdings of national debt as recorded in the ledgers of the Bank of England, the East India Company and the South Sea Company.[26] But with the floating pound, capital controls were not really needed. If foreign capital was withdrawn suddenly in sufficient quantity to cause concern to the authorities, the pound would fall and the remaining assets would be locked in, more securely the further the pound fell. In sum, the flexible shock absorbers of Britain's various financial markets – government securities, private debt, joint-stock company shares, bills of exchange – enabled investors from all over the world to deal effectively with the sundry shocks of war finance until 1815.

In close contact and frequent competition with each other, the Dutch, British and French developed alternative structures for money and finance – merchant banks, money markets, information networks for private credit and federated, parliamentary and monarchical authorities for public finance. Each European power was agreeable to the creation of large-scale enterprises engaged in long-distance trade as well as to the needs of a powerful nation state obsessed with the military demands placed upon it by frequent wars. Each system managed, under quite different legal and political regimes, to provide the intermediation between savers and investors necessary to keep each country in the forefront

[25] Neal, 1990: chapter 9, and Neal, 1991.

[26] Neal, 1990: chapter 10.

of economic progress from 1648 to 1815. International capital flows occurred frequently and occasionally on a large scale among the three nations. When subjected to shocks, however, the three systems reacted differently. Regardless of the source or severity of the shock, the British system with its rich mixture of varied financial institutions and its complex of interrelated financial markets managed to absorb the shock most easily and rebound most strongly.

9 Towards the comparative fiscal history of Britain and France during the 'long' eighteenth century

Richard Bonney

In his recent, globally expansive mode at Oslo, Patrick O'Brien comments that 'during an "imperial meridian" (1783–1815), European naval and military superiority over the states and societies of other continents emerged as virtually irresistible'. 'Europeans emerged from that conjuncture in their history', he states, 'with massive additions to the populations, territories and natural resources of other continents under their direct or informal control.' In this account of global history, the word 'fiscal', let alone the term 'fiscal history', does not occur.[1] Yet if the great work on war and public finance in Britain between 1793 and 1815 has never appeared in book form,[2] Patrick O'Brien has devoted much of his career to such issues, and the term 'fiscal crisis' appears elsewhere in his writings. Of Britain's experience in the eighteenth century, he writes (with Philip Hunt), that 'although politicians worried about it, the national debt went up and up without leading to fiscal crises of the kind that led to changes of regime in France and elsewhere on the Continent'. Historians, he adds, 'have recognized the obvious relationship between the power of states and the fiscal means at their disposal but they are also aware that the connections were never unitary or simple'.[3]

For Patrick O'Brien, two basic trends in British fiscal history stand out with clarity. The first is that between 1665 and 1790, 'a period when the kingdom's population and economic base potentially available for taxation remained relatively small compared to France, Russia, the Habsburg Empire and Spain, the amount of taxes which poured into the Exchequer in London multiplied sevenfold in real terms and increased as a share of national income nearly four times'.[4] Thus, 'with the possible exception of Holland, the revenue expropriated by the British government (measured on a per capita basis in both absolute and relative terms) was probably

[1] O'Brien, 2000c: 7. Though the word 'taxation' appears (p. 15).
[2] Announced as forthcoming in O'Brien, 1989: 273, note 31. However, consult O'Brien, 1989a. There remains a need for a publication of O'Brien, 1967.
[3] O'Brien and Hunt, 1999: 53, 63. [4] O'Brien, 1988. O'Brien and Hunt, 1993.

far higher than the financial resources that "despotisms" on the continent managed to expropriate for their dynastic and military ambitions'.[5] Britain's fiscal base 'expanded and diversified at a higher rate than the potential base for taxation available to rival states', but in O'Brien's view 'it would be misleading to suggest that faster economic growth or industrialisation provided the government with really decisive strategic advantages'. Other countries experienced rapid economic growth. Instead,

> what may turn out to be distinctive about the British state was a more radical and sustained improvement in its political and administrative capacity to appropriate and to retain an increasing share of a steadily growing and diversifying national product. That critical proportion grew from 3–4 per cent in the reign of Charles II, to 11–12 per cent of national income during the Seven Years' War and the American War of Independence.[6]

Is it possible to compare the fiscal position of Britain and France in the 'long' eighteenth century? Patrick O'Brien clearly thought so in 1976, when he published with Peter Mathias a seminal article on taxation in England and France between 1715 and 1810.[7] Subsequently, others have entered into the fray, notably Wantje Fritschy[8] and François Crouzet[9] for the eighteenth century and Michael Bordo and Eugene White for the period between 1789 and 1815.[10] In 1993, albeit with reservations, Margaret and Richard Bonney published a graph comparing revenues in England and France between 1660 and 1775 converted into pounds sterling.[11]

Nevertheless, some commentators, such as Joël Félix, doubt whether the extant figures for Britain and France (and the figures for France are in any case far from complete) are strictly comparable.[12] There are basically four types of evidence which, in an ideal situation, would be subject to comparison: a) revenue (and expenditure) comparisons over time, with the ability to distinguish between gross and net tax revenues and between these and other sources of government income; b) comparisons

[5] O'Brien, 1989: 166. Mathias and O'Brien, 1976. For a truly magisterial study of the fiscal structures of three of the Dutch provinces (Holland, Groningen and Overijssel), see van der Ent *et al.*, 1999.

[6] O'Brien, 1989b: 167. But then for no other country has an historian dared to produce O'Brien's proxies for national income: O'Brien, 1991.

[7] Above, note 5.

[8] Cf. Fritschy, 1990. Fritschy criticises the conclusions of Mathias and O'Brien in their seminal article, and argues that the fiscal burden was lighter in Britain than France; in the judgement of François Crouzet, 'cette proposition n'est pas tenable': Crouzet, 1993: 63.

[9] Crouzet, 1993. Brezis and Crouzet, 1995. For an appraisal of this and the other relevant literature: Bonney, 1998.

[10] Bordo and White, 1991, 1994.

[11] Bonney and Bonney, 1993: 96, figure 30.

[12] J. Félix, 1999. The view was expressed in a private communication to the author.

of the relative size of the public debt over time; c) comparisons of both a) and b) as percentages of gross domestic product; and d) comparisons of both a) and b) on a per capita basis. For reasons which arise from the patchy survival of evidence, a) and b) are difficult to achieve, although some suggestions for comparisons at fixed moments in time will be made in this chapter. The remaining two types of comparison are conjectural, since there is no firm evidence for the comparative gross domestic product or comparative population levels. The question of the exchange rate is also problematic for much of the period,[13] and particularly during the period of the 'paper pound' between 1797 and 1821.

Contemporaries did, however, make inspired or informed guesses, which is probably the best that can be achieved. Let us start with these inspired or informed guesses first, which provide an initial basis for comparison. Writing shortly after the Peace of Ryswick (1697), Charles Davenant concluded that the French debt was much higher than had been imagined (he placed the debts of England at £17.5 million, those of Holland at £25 million and those of France at £100 million).[14] In *Discourses on the Public Revenues and on the Trade of England . . .* (1698), Davenant compared the tax burden of the three states.[15] Correctly or incorrectly, Davenant considered that during the War of the League of Augsburg, the Dutch had contributed a third of their national income in taxation (an excessive fiscal burden made possible only by 'the equal manner used in taxing the subjects of their dominion')[16] and about a quarter in time of peace.[17] France had paid a fifth, and England an eighth, of its national income during the war. In other words, as a proportion of its national income, England paid little more in time of war than France had paid in time of peace.[18] Hence the importance of the fiscal burden as a proportion of the 'annual income' or what we would call the relationship of the tax base to the gross national product: '. . . where it bears too large a proportion with the whole, as in France, the common people must be miserable and burthened with heavy taxes'.[19] Political arithmetic had, in Davenant's view, revealed the reasons for the ending of the War of the League of Augsburg in 1697: 'time has now brought to light, that England had some millions more of money than was believed, and that France is indebted many more millions than was imagined . . . Though our taxes

[13] McCusker, 1978: table 5.1. [14] Davenant, 1967: I, 250.
[15] O'Brien, 2000b: 15. These figures were later edited by Forbonnais with conversions from the pound sterling to the *livre tournois* at a rate of 13 to the pound, which was the level in 1693 but not in 1698. A more realistic conversion would have been 15 to the pound: Forbonnais, 1758: II, 296.
[16] Davenant, 1967: I, 268. [17] Davenant, 1967: I, 253.
[18] Davenant, 1967: I, 142, 253. [19] Davenant, 1967: I, 251–2.

were heavy, our national stock was great, and not exhausted as was that of France, by former impositions'.[20]

The intractability of the fiscal problems of the French monarchy, and the large legacy of debt resulting from the wars of Louis XIV, encouraged solutions of an adventurous kind. John Law, in a letter to Desmaretz, the French finance minister, dated 26 July 1715, estimated French national revenue at 1,200 million *livres*, the same capital evaluation as Vauban's,[21] although he seems to have based his calculations on a comparison with England.[22] He seems to have derived his French estimate by multiplying the English estimated national wealth by three. On an English estimate of 'between 500 and 600 million French *livres*', the French national revenues 'ought to amount to 1,500 or 1,800 million'; he settled on the figure of 1,200 million. But he argued that his proposed bank 'might increase French [national] revenue from 1,200 million to 1,800'. Modern estimates have tended to place the national product higher, for example at 2,700 million,[23] but these should be moderated by Forbonnais' comment on the fall in national output during the War of the Spanish Succession.[24] Law presented Louis XIV and Desmaretz with a proposal for the redemption of public debt in May 1715 and a memorandum for the establishment of a bank (not dissimilar to the later System) in July 1715. State competition for resources was transmuted by Law into state competition for credit instruments.[25] Law maintained that the effect of establishing his bank would be comparable to a substantial increase in the money supply. It would act as a general stimulus to economic recovery. Law's System was thus intended to deal simultaneously with a chronic financial problem, namely the burden of debt carried over from the War of the Spanish Succession; with a lack of confidence resulting from the emission of worthless paper during the war; and with the need to stimulate the economy during a short-term commercial crisis in 1715–16.

A fiscal enquiry into the revenues of other European states was ordered by the French government shortly after the Seven Years War. In terms of fiscal resources alone (that is, excluding credit), France still dominated in 1764, with a revenue of 321 million *livres*. Next came England with 224 million. The United Provinces came third, with a revenue of 120 million (although this represented the total fiscal burden); disposable state revenue may have been as low as 85 million.[26] Of greater reliability was a second French enquiry, this time of comparative military expenditure and public debt of England and France during the course of the War of

[20] Davenant, 1967: I, 265–6. [21] Vauban, 1988: 66. [22] Law, 1934: II, 50–2.
[23] Riley, 1986: 22. [24] Forbonnais, 1758: II, 221–2. [25] Forbonnais, 1758: II, 45–6.
[26] Bonney, 1995: chapter 15, 74–5. Hartmann, 1979. Hartmann's excellent edition concerns only part of the enquiry.

American Independence. The report, which was produced by the French government in 1782, used an exchange rate of 23.17 *livres* to the pound sterling. The French government calculated that the British armed forces in the seven years after 1776 had cost 2,834 million *livres*; subtracting ordinary peacetime expenditure, war costs were reduced to 2,270.5 million. During the same period, the French armed forces had cost 1,732.5 million *livres*; again, subtracting the ordinary peacetime expenditure, war costs were reduced to 928.9 million. The cost of the British war effort was therefore over double that of the French, who had not been fighting a land as well as a sea war. The effect on the public debt showed a similar pattern. The British debt, including Exchequer notes, notes issued by the armed forces, and arrears, stood at 5,532 million *livres* bearing an annual interest charge of 220 million (the figures for the consolidated debt alone were respectively 4,538 million and 170 million). In contrast, the French debt (including the loans for 1782) was 3,315.1 million, bearing an annual interest charge of 165.4 million.[27]

The 1782 report is of interest because its findings have been echoed in the recent analysis by Velde and Weir. The French debt was smaller than the British in terms of value, and considerably so in terms of its ratio to gross national product (56 per cent as against 182 per cent) and to income per capita. However, debt becomes significant when it cannot easily be serviced. When expressed as a proportion of the debt, debt charges in France were much more significant than in Britain (7.5 per cent as against 3.8 per cent), while the proportion of debt service costs to tax revenues was also higher (62 per cent to 56 per cent). France maintained a consistently lower burden of debt interest on its tax revenues, but gained no benefit from its policy, since Britain paid for its national debt by raising taxes, whereas France was forced to contain its debt by partial defaults such as in 1770. One consequence of this tradition of partial default before 1774 was that the rate of interest was higher in France than Britain: the market lacked confidence in the French crown as a borrower. 'Default risk' thus added a persistent premium to the cost of the French debt in comparison to the British debt.[28]

A final comparison was made by Talleyrand, who justified what he called the French 'financial system', that is to say the budget of 1814, on the grounds that it would 'establish the prosperity of France on the

[27] Harris, 1976.

[28] Velde and Weir, 1992: 5, 18–19, 30, 35–7; Bordo and White, 1991: 309; Bordo and White, 1994: 250; Schwarz, in Bordo and Capie, 1994: 379, questions the argument of Bordo and White that the British government had greater 'credibility as a borrower' than did the French because of 'its long record of fiscal probity'. However, the research of Velde and Weir appears conclusive on this point.

basis of a public credit proportionate to the extent of its resources'.[29] He argued that Frenchmen were somewhat less taxed than Americans and were considerably less taxed than the British: the figures he cited were of a respective per capita fiscal burden of 23, 25 and 120 francs.[30] According to recent calculations, between 1803 and 1812, the British paid three times more taxes than the French on a per capita basis in terms of wheat equivalent. By 1818, the British public revenue was the equivalent of 1,184 million francs, the French 732 million. The repudiation of the public debt in France in 1797, and Napoleon's unwillingness and inability to borrow, tended to increase the disparity between the relative debt burden: the per capita public debt burden in Britain in 1818 was the equivalent of 1,210 francs, while in France it was a mere 80 francs.[31]

Talleyrand's calculations may have suffered from the vagaries of the exchange rate at a particular moment in time. Even so, the contrast between Britain and France is palpable. In France, in the course of the eighteenth century, and even into the 1790s, tax revenues constantly failed to increase sufficiently in real terms. The state was at a standstill, or actually becoming more akin to the post-modern concept of the 'minimal' state: 'Frenchmen paid insufficient taxes', at least for the needs of the state.[32] François Crouzet subscribes to the argument originally propounded by Mathias and O'Brien, and to a considerable extent confirmed by the researches of James C. Riley,[33] that there was little or no peacetime *real* increase in French taxation between 1725 and 1785. Tax revenue certainly declined, when expressed as a proportion of commodity output, between the last years of the *ancien régime* and the first years of the Revolution, perhaps to as low as 2 or 3 per cent in 1790 and 5 per cent in 1791.[34] The weakness of the *ancien régime* was not too much, but too little taxation, except and in so far that had war expenditure and debt servicing costs been reduced, there would have been less need for extra revenues.

[29] Bruguière, 1969: 131.

[30] Bruguière, 1969: 131, note 2. In the case of Britain, £60 million in tax revenue was taken to be the equivalent of 1,440 million francs; tax revenue for France was placed at 600 million. The population was taken to be 12 million for Britain and 28 million for France. O'Brien estimates direct taxes in Britain in 1814 at 21.2 million and indirect taxes at 42.1 million, that is 63.3 million in total.

[31] References cited by Bonney, 1995: 372, note 399.

[32] Crouzet, 1993: 60 (summarising the tables of Mathias and O'Brien, but with the index numbers recalculated on the basis of 1725 = index 100), 62–5, 96, 367, 461–2.

[33] For the money supply: Riley and McCusker, 1983.

[34] Bordo and White, 1991: 308, figure 5; Crouzet, 1993: 122.

It is appropriate to study the data of one period of warfare in greater detail. The period of the Seven Years' War has been chosen, since there is general agreement that this marked a fundamental turning-point in the eighteenth-century balance of power. It was the first conflict to start in America and the first in which a significant part of the conflict took place there; it led to a decisive defeat of one belligerent (France) and a dramatic rearrangement of the balance of power in Europe and North America; and there were important continuities between the war and the post-war conflicts.[35]

The extant French fiscal data for the period of the Seven Years War, summarised in the accompanying table 9.1, remains difficult to interpret and much depends on the criteria for making the distinction between total revenues and total tax revenues. According to Joël Félix's figures, total war revenues (taxation plus loan income) averaged 552.9 million *livres* per annum during the Seven Years War, substantially above the peacetime figures (the average of the figures in column a in the table); we may thus agree with Joël Félix's comment on Mathias and O'Brien's use of peacetime figures for calculating per capita tax burdens that this can give a misleading impression ('[cela] peut-être un exercice trompeur'). Yet the proportion of this increase brought about by taxation itself was relatively small (the average annual tax revenue was 311.5 million: that is, the average of the figures in column b in the table). If we take 269.7 million as the base for the pre-war or peacetime figure (the figure is that used by Tim Le Goff, based on the peacetime tax average for 1749–54; the actual figure for 1755 was 253 million), then the average increase in taxation was only 41.8 million a year, lower than Le Goff suggests (his estimate was 77.6 million), which in turn paid for only 26 per cent of the estimated cost of the war (1,150 million: column f in the table).[36] Félix suggests that the real difference in the cost of the Seven Years War as compared with the War of the Austrian Succession was 21 million a year, or approximately the levy of the *vingtième* after 1749; but, in the War of the Austrian Succession, increased taxation had paid 72 per cent of the cost of the war.[37] Because of the delay in establishing new tax measures, it was not until 1760 (the fifth year of the Seven Years War) that the government

[35] Greene, 2000: 8–9.

[36] Le Goff, 1999. Riley had estimated the tax contribution to the cost of the war at 40 per cent.

[37] Félix, 1999: 47. Here his estimates are radically divergent from those of Le Goff, who considers that the mode of financing of the two wars was similar and that increased taxation played a similar part as a proportion of the total cost of each war.

Table 9.1 *Summary of extant fiscal data concerning the finances of the French monarchy during the Seven Years War*

	a Félix taxes and loan revenues	b Félix taxes only	c Le Goff non-tax revenues 1755–62 average	d Félix net revenues	e Félix ordinary expenses	f Total cost of war excluding debt	g Félix total debt	h Le Goff total debt	i Le Goff liability of 1764 sinking fund	j Le Goff liability of 1764 sinking fund by 1769
1756	540,5	273,1	109							
1757	576,5	294,1	109							
1758	591,5	294,1	109	317,2	320,4					
1759	619,5	294,1	109	372,8						
1760	610,1	341,7	109	267,9	286,2					
1761	532,1	341,7	109	302,1	290,3					
1762	[400,1]	[341,7]	109	282,8	287,7					
1763					200,3					
1764									1,120,00	
Total	3,870,30	2,180,5 1762 incl. on basis of 1761	[763,3]			1,150	2, 210,2	2,460,00		731,321

All figures in millions of *livres tournois*.

Sources: a and b: Félix, 1999: 42, table 9.3; c: Le Goff, 1999: 387, table 14.4; d and e: Félix, 1999: 53, table 5; f: Ibid.: 47, table 9.4. The estimate is that of Morineau (1980); g: Ibid.: 140, table 7 (based on Mathon de la Cour, 1788, 59–62); h, i, j: Le Goff, 1999: 404–5, table 14.5.

found itself in as advantageous a position as at the beginning of the War of the Austrian Succession. Hence the financial crisis of 1759.[38]

Silhouette, the then finance minister, observed that for the following year (1760) only 140 million of revenues were guaranteed to pay total expenses predicted for 357 million. His successor, Bertin, later revised the calculations: the net revenues did not even amount to 116 million; in order to discharge expenses of 318 million, 640 million would need to be levied in revenues as a consequence of delays in collection and the general discredit of paper representing loan capital. Only 6 or 7 million out of an expected 15 million might be collected in advance on revenues worth 40 million even at rates of interest of 17 per cent.[39]

Clearly, if effective fiscal management rests in the ability to levy taxation and loan revenue, then France displayed effective management during the later stages of the Seven Years War, though not at the outset, when the recourse to wartime measures was too slow: this delay in generating increased resources for the war effort may have had a deleterious effect on the conduct of the war in the later years of the conflict. Even so, French tax revenues during the Seven Years War were insufficient to pay for the cost of the war. Félix suggests that to pay for the cost of the war (nearly 1,200 million over seven years) by means of tax revenues, there would have needed to be an average increase in taxes of 171 million per annum. This would have been equivalent to eight *vingtièmes* or 50 per cent of the landowners' net revenues: to increase direct taxation on this scale was politically impossible.[40] There was, therefore, no choice but to borrow money to pay for the war. Even so, while the levying of increased taxes is the *sine qua non*, effective fiscal management requires much more than this. There has to be an effective yield of taxation. *Vingtième* fraud was a serious issue, while the obstacles to the reform of direct taxes were immense.[41] Moreover, important constitutional issues imperilled any effort at reform.

The most coherent account of the debt redemption policy of the government between 1759 and 1770 is provided by Tim Le Goff. It was the failure of the larger economy that triggered the financial crisis of 1770,[42]

[38] Félix, 1999: 38, table 2, and 41, 49–51. Le Goff, 1999: 383, table 14.2, and 385, table 14.3. Le Goff takes the average annual short-term tax cost of the war = actual tax revenue 1759–62 minus projected 'peace' tax revenue 1756–62 (Le Goff takes this figure to be 1,899.4 million) divided by seven years. Félix points out that if the exercise is to demonstrate (as Le Goff seeks to do) the difference in costs between the War of the Austrian Succession and the Seven Years War, then there should be a common starting basis.

[39] Félix, 1999: 55. [40] Félix, 1999: 264.

[41] Félix, 1999: 208, 304. Kwass, 2000.

[42] Bosher, 1972. More recently, Félix, 1999: 413–45.

Table 9.2 *Post-war/pre-war revenues and expenses of the French monarchy, 1767–1776*

	Controller-general	a Gross revenues (taxation)	b Net to the Treasury	c Expenses	d Deficit
1767	L'Averdy	303,5	152	198	−46
1768	L'Averdy		166	201	−35
1769	Maynon		169,5	245	−76
1772	Terray	348,3	205	200	5
1775	Terray	367	210	220	−10
1776	Turgot	377	214,5	238	−24

All figures are in millions of *livres tournois*.
Source: Félix, 1999: 480, table 14.

but the way in which the crisis unfolded had been heavily determined in advance by a long period of financial instability resulting from the unsuccessful winding-down of the war. Le Goff argues that Terray's measures in 1770–1 were

> the concluding phase in a long 'bankruptcy on the instalment' plan, which the government started when it suspended payment on its notes in the autumn of 1759, continued by proclaiming all its term loans reimbursable at 5 per cent in 1763, and made concrete by converting 270 million *livres tournois* of outstanding wartime debt into perpetual annuities in 1767–8. In 1770, Terray was only continuing a policy on which there had been a tacit consensus between the *contrôle général* and the Paris *Parlement* ever since 1764 . . . The targets of these debt-reduction measures were the various borrowings devised, over the previous generation, to absorb, directly or indirectly, the government's short-term paper: in his view, and that of the *Parlement*, they were government junk-bonds; those who bought them had to be ready to take the bad times with the good.[43]

However, Tim Le Goff and Joël Félix disagree on the longer-term consequences of the debt rescheduling operation brought about by Terray in 1770–1. The argument needs to be reviewed in the light of the data summarised in table 9.2. For Le Goff, 'Terray virtually balanced receipts and expenditures' but his work was undone after his dismissal by Louis XVI. However, 'it is important to remember that France began the [American] war on a reasonably good financial footing, one which allowed Necker and his successors to finance that conflict almost exclusively on a combination of life and term loans. It was a fresh start to a new cycle of war finance.'[44] For Joël Félix, in contrast, the Terray bankruptcy had only an

[43] Le Goff, 1999: 409–10. [44] Le Goff, 1999: 411.

Table 9.3 *'Tax smoothing' during three wars: reliance on loan income in Britain and France*

	a France	b Britain
War of Austrian Succession	28	85
Seven Years War	74	81
American War	91	119

Source: Crouzet, 1993: 66 (modified for France in the Seven Years War). Crouzet notes that the British figure for the American war implies that some of the loan income was utilised for ordinary expenditure, notably debt servicing costs. The figures are percentages of the supplementary expenses in each war which were covered by loan income.

immediate effect, a short-term balancing of the budget; it did not bring about any durable financial amelioration. The rise in gross revenues from 303.5 million in 1767 to 367 million in 1775 was an increase of 21 per cent (column a); but the rise in net Treasury receipts was proportionately higher (from 152 to 210 million, or 38 per cent: column b). This defied the previous pattern of French fiscal efficiency, which required a proportionately higher increase in gross revenues to yield an increase in Treasury receipts: Félix contends that the explanation lies not in superior fiscal efficiency but in Terray's short-term cuts ordered in 1770;[45] once these had yielded their benefit, there was once more a return to annual deficits. Thus for Joël Félix, by the time that Turgot replaced Terray as controller-general of finance in 1776 'absolutely nothing had changed' in the situation of the finances of the French monarchy.[46]

To return to the Mathias–O'Brien model of the contrasting fiscal development of Britain and France in the eighteenth century, tables 9.3 and 9.4 require comment. Table 9.3 suggests that France never succeeded in mobilising such a high proportion of loan finance as Britain during

[45] Félix, 1999: 37: 'Or, en 1770, après la banqueroute partielle de l'abbé Terray, il est évident que les ressources ordinaires s'étaient trouvées libérées de multiples charges affectées à des dépenses qui n'avaient plus lieu. En sorte que si le total des revenus n'avaient pas bougé, les recettes de l'Etat rapportées au dépenses s'étaient accrues.' Terray was quite explicit: 'Je me trouvois au moment de cesser toute paiement, ce qui auroit entraîné une déroute générale, d'autant plus funeste, qu'elle se seroit faite d'une manière imprévue, & que tous les services auroient manqué à la fois, les uns parce qu'ils n'étoient pas assurés, les autres, parce que ceux qui les avoient assurés n'auroient pu faire aucune négociation. Le seul parti à prendre étoit donc de faire rentre le Roi dans ses revenus' (Terray, 1788: 64).

[46] Félix, 1999: 481.

Table 9.4 *Revision of the Mathias–O'Brien model proposed by Crouzet (1993)*

	Index of fiscal revenues at constant prices 1721–1745				Percentage of physical output (land + commerce) appropriated by taxation (constant prices)			
	Index numbers Total revenues		Per capita		Total output		Total per capita	
	a France	b Britain	c France	d Britain	e France	f Britain	g France	h Britain
1715	80	100	81	99	11	17	12	16
1725	100	100	100	100	13	16	14	16
1750	102	127	92	121	11	18	12	18
1770	110	149	85	125	9	18	9	17
1775	131	143	100	116	10	18	10	19
1780	135	170	117	134	12	21	12	21
1785	146	190	106	143	10	22	11	23
1790–1	167	227	120	164	11	24	12	24

Source: Crouzet, 1993: 60, table 2.2. Tax figures for 1785 are the mean for 1785–9. The per capita figure for France suggested by Félix for 1750 was 2 *livres* higher than that of Mathias and O'Brien, 1976. This has not been included in these calculations.

the last three wars of the *ancien régime*, though the modification of the figure for the Seven Years War (based on Felix's detailed arguments) suggests that it was beginning to catch up and was perhaps only 7 percentage points behind Britain in that war, a much more considerable achievement than has perhaps been recognised to date. Table 9.4 contains a modification of the Mathias–O'Brien model by François Crouzet, who has taken a different base for the calculations. The figures exclude the period of the Seven Years War, considered by Riley and Félix to be the high point of eighteenth-century taxation (that is, of taxation after 1715: the question of the all-time high being the great crisis of 1709–10 remains open).[47] In 1761, French revenues were equivalent to perhaps 12 to 13 per cent of national wealth.[48] At no stage in the eighteenth century, however, did France achieve the figures for Britain after 1745, that is, a figure above 20 per cent of national wealth appropriated by taxation. By this reckoning, Britain was able to extract at least 7 per cent more of national wealth per annum than France in years of peace, though whether it could do so in years of war remains an open question. According to Crouzet's reworking of the figures, the French proportion of national wealth extracted in taxation did not decline (as the original Mathias–O'Brien data had suggested) but it did remain inelastic: crucially, it failed to increase.

This leads us quite close to the Philip T. Hoffman–Kathryn Norberg thesis. By the eighteenth century, they argue, 'representative institutions, not absolute monarchy, proved superior in revenue extraction. Where representative bodies held the ultimate authority, as in the Netherlands or eighteenth-century England, they facilitated taxing.'[49] 'Absolutist regimes, despite their pretensions, were not able to borrow or tax at will', they continue. 'Only government with strong representative institutions could extract huge revenues and borrow large sums. Taxation and despotism were in the end incompatible. Liberty and the institutions which protected it proved much more able to monopolize resources and extract revenue.'[50] One of the issues addressed by Hoffman and Norberg is whether these difficulties were peculiar to one particular country, or whether certain types of state – or what have been called elsewhere different types of 'fiscal constitution'[51] – were more appropriate than others in meeting the fiscal challenges of the eighteenth century.

Contemporaries were aware of the argument. According to Gray, the first biographer of Law in 1721, the projector first 'offer'd his paper credit scheme to the Lord Godolphin [Lord Treasurer of England] before he

47 Bonney, 2001: 146, note 109. 48 Riley, 1986; Félix, 1999: 39.
49 Hoffman and Norberg, 1994: 306. 50 Hoffman and Norberg, 1994: 310.
51 Bonney, 1995: 431–8.

carry'd it down to the Parliament of Scotland' in 1705.[52] Godolphin did not lightly dismiss the 'fine and nice calculation' but argued that it 'could never be put into execution under a limited Government; that it would want the authority of an absolute prince to carry it through . . .' And yet, in 1715, Law met the opposite argument in France with regard to his later, more developed, proposals, namely that they could not be implemented under an absolute but only a limited monarchy.[53] It is clear that Law had to adopt more authoritarian strategies to ensure the enforcement of the System at its apogee;[54] but he had always contended (and argued as much in his proposals for a bank at Turin, which he made to the Duke of Savoy in 1711–2), that 'the arbitrary [*sic* = absolute] government of France was not the reason that [the earlier French experiment in] paper money had failed'.[55] Against the criticisms of Samuel Bernard and other financiers he made a similar comparative constitutional point:

> the reason generally received why credit has been lacking in France is the nature or form of its government. It is believed that credit will only succeed in republics or limited monarchies, as in England; but this is not the sole and principal reason which has led to the absence of credit in France, because [banks] have been established and will succeed in monarchies just as well as in republics . . . Once credit has been well established and managed, the king will not wish to put such credit in danger by helping himself to the treasury (*caisse*) which maintains it . . .[56]

The way in which Law addressed the issue of establishing his bank, touting it round Europe irrespective of whether the state was 'absolutist' or 'constitutionalist' in structure, suggests that the issues are sufficiently complex as to defy the easy generalisation of the Hoffman–Norberg model. A number of considerations suggest themselves, though the precise relationship between the factors might be a matter of debate. These are: a) the extent of publicity of information about government financial and fiscal policy; b) the reliability of government contracts, particularly relating to the political stability of government, its reputation for prudence and the realism of its commitment to a long-term policy; c) the sophistication of the domestic credit market and the government commitment to the survival and prosperity of that market; d) whether or not foreign loan capital was a significant participant in the domestic credit market; e) government monetary policy with regard to the bi-metallic ratio, and its awareness of the relationship between the foreign exchanges and the domestic money supply; f) government 'tax-smoothing' policy and the relationship between loan income and tax income, particularly

[52] Murphy, 1997: 21. [53] Lévy, 1969–80: II, 155, note 108.
[54] Kaiser, 1991. [55] Murphy, 1991: 3–29, at 24. Bonney, 2001.
[56] Law, 1934: II, 48; Bonney and Bonney, 1993: 85–6.

in wartime; g) the relative efficiency of the fiscal system, in particular the precise choices of types of loan and types of taxes levied; h) the degree of tax compliance within the state, which raises constitutional issues such as the degree of consent and public order issues such as the degree of tax resistance; and i) whether or not the state was in 'crisis', particularly the crisis of foreign warfare: thus was there a public perception that there was a short-term, manageable, period of wartime change which would later be reversed in peacetime? Taken together, consideration of these various factors may allow for greater precision in the comparative fiscal history of Britain and France over the 'long' eighteenth century.

On factor a), the publicity of information about government financial and fiscal policy, the relative weakness of France compared to Britain has been stressed by historians. Not until Necker's publication of his *Compte-rendu* in 1781 was real public debate on the royal finances possible in France. The information remained contested and was a source of vigorous debate in the last decade of the *ancien régime*. Bordo and White contend that 'the French monarchy was able to deceive the public because government finance was not open to parliamentary inspection as in Britain'.[57] Yet the evidence advanced by Crouzet suggests that the French credit market was more sophisticated in its understanding of the detailed operation of the crown's life rent contracts than the king's own financial advisers.[58] Deception, therefore, may have worked more the other way round than is commonly assumed and in any case, as observed below, there were mechanisms within the credit market allowing 'shared knowledge about the availability of a lender's funds . . . or about the soundness of a borrower's collateral'.

With regard to factor b), the reliability of government contracts, particularly relating to the political stability of government, its reputation for prudence and the realism of its commitment to a long-term policy, the evidence for French instability seems firm. Firstly, whereas in England there had been no 'stop' on the Exchequer since 1672 (that is, no default), in France before the Revolution numerous defaults were of recent memory (1715, 1721, 1726, 1759, 1764 and 1771). For some historians, the crown should have attempted to resolve its problems by a further debt repudiation in 1787, but was prevented from doing so by the political campaign led by Brissot, probably inspired by vested interests among the bankers, that there should be no further bankruptcy (his pamphlet, *Point de banqueroute*, was published in London in 1787).[59] Paradoxically, the crown paid a 'default premium' on its borrowing in comparison with

[57] Bordo and White, 1994: 250. [58] Crouzet, 1993: 67–9.
[59] Crouzet, 1993: 72, 79.

Britain, yet by the 1780s was not strong enough politically to adhere to the traditional policy of partial default.

The lack of continuity in royal financial policy in eighteenth-century France is further highlighted by the chronic instability affecting the central direction of financial affairs. Whereas Colbert died in office in 1683 after nearly eighteen years' service, only one controller-general of finance in the eighteenth century died in office (Clugny in 1776, and he had held office only for a few months). Nine ministers were appointed between 1746 and the death of Louis XV in 1774, averaging just over three years per ministry. Such instability was not conducive to reform, or indeed to the formulation of any consistent viewpoint; instead, as Necker observed, ministers were the sacrificial victims of intrigues laid by powerful vested interests. The cabals of prominent office-holders and the tension between the rival views of *la finance* and *la banque* precluded the emergence of a stable, long-term view, or public confidence in the government's political stability.[60] There was no comparable large-scale investment in venal office-holding in Britain which could act as a constraint on the adoption of a straightforward 'commercial' and banking viewpoint, nor were there comparable political pressures on the central direction of financial policy.

In Necker's (so-called 'English and Genevan') view,[61] the crown could not finance its wars without loan income and the exploitation of venality could not yield sufficient revenues. He published his *Compte-rendu* in 1781 to try to rebut an orchestrated campaign to blacken his reputation; but 'too many vested interests had been damaged and affronted by Necker's economies' and the financial office-holders in the end brought him down.[62] With his fall, the 'old [that is, French] principles of finance' came back with his successor, Joly de Fleury, including the receivers-general of finance, whom Necker had abolished. Could the venal structure have served the monarchy's interests better in peacetime than in war? There were three possibilities. One was to follow Necker's policy, which was to borrow even in peacetime in order gradually to buy out the holders of venal office. The second policy was to try to exploit the system financially without a confrontation between the crown and its office-holders. The third was to bring the whole structure under review, and thus threaten the world of *la finance* so that it provided the level of funding required. The French crown was unable to make any coherent choice or follow any

[60] Price, 1995: 90–1, takes Bourgade's memorandum denouncing Necker's abolition of the receivers-general as the 'classic definition of the differences between *la banque* and *la finance* in political terms'. For more detail: Price, 1997.

[61] Price, 1995: 55. Vergennes described Necker's political principles as incompatible with French monarchical tradition.

[62] Doyle, 1996: 142.

consistent policy in the last decade of the *ancien régime*. Only with the Revolution and its rejection of venality (though not without compensation for those who had purchased offices) was the French system able to compete with the British and operate a more consistent (and arguably, more 'modern' banking policy) as well as a longer-term financial and fiscal policy. But by then France was at war and in a completely different political situation.

On factor c), the sophistication of the domestic credit market and the government commitment to the survival and prosperity of that market, recent evidence suggests that the French credit market was more advanced than has usually been allowed for by historians. Rather than royal borrowing 'crowding out' private borrowers in the reign of Louis XIV, Hoffman, Postel-Vinay and Rosenthal argue that the effect was positive: financiers borrowed money from private individuals in order to re-lend to the crown. Since there was a spectacular growth in the private credit market in the eighteenth century, any version of the 'crowding out' thesis is rejected by these three historians. Economic recovery and a long period of currency stability played their part; but the rest of the growth in the private market in the eighteenth century was explained by the spread of the *obligation* and the capacity of the Parisian notaries to respond to new market opportunities.[63] Had Law succeeded, notaries would have been forced out of marketing the public debt in the 1720s. Instead, successive government defaults 'gave them unparalleled access to information about investors'.[64] Whereas in other historical accounts, the failure of Law's system in 1720 is held to have 'blocked financial growth in France by ruling out the sort of banking system that existed in England', Hoffman, Postel-Vinay and Rosenthal argue instead that it 'ushered in a long period of expansion and financial innovation in the Parisian credit market', allowing the notaries to take on the role of credit brokers.[65] Debt transactions were based on 'shared knowledge about the availability of a lender's funds, for example, or about the soundness of a borrower's collateral. Allocation therefore depended on information flows between the lenders and borrowers'.[66] The subordinate French credit structure therefore seems much more viable in this new account than in earlier depictions, and British exceptionalism less evident.

With regard to factor d), whether or not foreign loan capital was a significant participant in the French domestic credit market, the answer is in the affirmative, a rapid increase having occurred after *c.* 1770. Precise figures are difficult to establish, but it is thought that, between

[63] Hoffman *et al.*, 2000: 113. [64] Hoffman *et al.*, 2000: 297.
[65] Hoffman *et al.*, 2000: 95. [66] Hoffman *et al.*, 2000: 9.

them, the Genevans and the Dutch invested at least 380 million *livres* in France between 1776 and 1788, and perhaps 500 million; this represented between 24 and 41 per cent of the total value of new loans established by the French crown in this period.[67] Clearly the French money market was not perceived by foreign investors as an essentially unsafe investment in the last years of the *ancien régime*: it was the political uncertainty and declining exchange rates in the first years of the Revolution which led to the flight of capital abroad.[68]

Measured in real terms, the public debt in France had reached unprecedented per capita levels by the end of the reign of Louis XIV, and levels that would not be attained again until the Revolution. The collapse of Law's System in 1720 brought in its wake 'the harshest default that France would witness until 1797, amounting to 1.5 billion *livres*'.[69] Thereafter, measured in livres of constant silver value, the state's total debt fell some 10 per cent between 1715 and 1789; but while this was taking place, long-term debt rose at the expense of borrowing via short-term loans and the sale of offices.[70] In 1788, Louis XVI could have balanced the budget by repudiating the foreign debt completely and reducing interest rates on the domestic debt to 6 per cent. Nine years later, in 1797, the state defaulted on two-thirds of its debt, a loss of 2.6 billion *livres* to the government's creditors.[71]

Regarding principle e), the government's monetary policy with regard to the bi-metallic ratio, and its awareness of the relationship between the foreign exchanges and the domestic money supply, the most damaging actions for the private credit market in France before 1726 'were the monarchy's currency manipulations . . . [for] parties to long-term private credit contracts had no way to escape the effects of currency manipulation'.[72] Yet, surprisingly, after more than a generation of currency manipulation in France, the *livre tournois* was stable from 1726 until 1785. And, after the era of paper money and hyperinflation in the 1790s, the return to monetary rectitude with the *franc de germinal* of 1803 was at the same bi-metallic ratio as in 1785.[73] Bordo and White suggest that it was 'the nation's [that, is France's] weakness as a borrower, not its strength, that kept it on a specie standard'[74] except for the aberration of the 1790s. Just 'as France was returning to specie convertibility, the Bank of England

[67] Crouzet, 1993: 76. Riley, 1980. [68] Crouzet, 1993: 160–8.
[69] Hoffman *et al.*, 2000: 69, 87. [70] Hoffman *et al.*, 2000: 98, 105.
[71] Hoffman *et al.*, 2000: 197, 200. [72] Hoffman *et al.*, 2000: 57.
[73] Thuillier (1983: 32) considers the choice of bi-metallic ratio in 1785 'fort judicieux'. See p. 62 on the long continuity of the proportion of 15.5, established by Calonne in 1785, through the law of 7 germinal an XI, until 1928.
[74] Bordo and White, 1994: 242.

was forced to suspend convertibility in February 1797. The suspension, initially supposed to end in June 1797, lasted until 1821.'[75]

By 1790, on the eve of Britain's twenty-two year military struggle with France, it held a debt of £244 million, nearly fifteen times the annual revenue for that year.[76] Yet the banknote circulation rose from only £4.3 million in 1750 to £10.7 million in 1790. The face value of the national debt continued to rise in the war years against France, from £290 million on the eve of the war to £862 million by 1815. The increased borrowing of the British government resulted in interest payments to creditors totalling some £236 million between 1793 and 1815, almost the value of the debt itself in 1790. Yet the increase in the circulation of banknotes in Britain remained modest. The six-monthly average of banknotes in circulation rose from a low point of £9.2 million in the second half of 1796, before the Suspension Act of February 1797, to a peak of £29.5 million in the second half of 1817, an expansion of more than three times the money supply in nominal terms.[77]

Some commentators have suggested that on factor f), government 'tax-smoothing' policy and the relationship between loan income and tax income, particularly in wartime, the differences between France and Britain were less marked since both countries followed a broadly similar policy. For François Crouzet, commenting on the data which are reproduced in this chapter as table 9.3, 'the two governments . . . financed their wars in the same way'. The three main wars under Louis XV and Louis XVI cost Britain more than France, while its population was only a third of that of its rival and its gross national product no more than a half.[78] For Britain, Patrick O'Brien emphasises that 'taxes and not loans were the foundation of the kingdom's finances . . . interest on its perpetual debt or the redemption of that debt could likewise only originate in tax revenue. Taxes and taxes alone sustained the creation of public debt and the recourse to loans to fund mobilisation for war represented nothing more than deferred taxation.'[79]

Here the contrast with France was significant, because the additional revenues accorded in the eighteenth century tended to have time limits fixed on them. After 1715, the Parlements, especially the Parlement of Paris, gained something in the eighteenth century that had always been denied them by Louis XIV and his predecessors: they could impose a time limit on the key new direct tax of the eighteenth century, the 'tenth' (*dixième*), and above all on its successor, the 'twentieth' (*vingtième*), and

[75] Bordo and White, 1994: 242. [76] Weingast, 1997: 234–7.
[77] Mitchell, 1981: 706. Bonney, 1995: 380–1. O'Brien, 1989a, 1989b.
[78] Crouzet, 1993: 66. [79] O'Brien, 1989b: 172–3.

on the number of 'twentieths' accorded. In 1749, for the first time, Machault imposed a 'twentieth' in peacetime. But the idea of a second 'twentieth' was opposed without a firm commitment to limit the duration of the first. At the opening of hostilities in the Seven Years War, the Parlement of Paris opposed a second 'twentieth' because of the 'crushing burden of taxation',[80] and yet a third had to be imposed in 1759; with the return of peace in 1763 the third 'twentieth' was abolished, but the second extended to 1770.[81] Julian Swann comments that it was no 'coincidence that the years 1756, 1759, 1761, 1763 and 1770', when 'twentieths' were renewed, 'all saw serious clashes between the crown and the sovereign courts'. Direct taxation 'was the principal cause of dissent' in fiscal matters; 'the vast majority' of the judges were hostile to increases in direct taxes and only in the decade after the Maupeou Revolution of 1771 were they temporarily quiescent.[82]

On factor g), the relative efficiency of the fiscal system, in particular the precise choices of types of loan and types of taxes levied, it is true that, on the whole, the English landed classes accepted the fiscal demands of war (but less so of peace, when they expected reduced taxes rather than the reduction of the public debt) with greater equanimity than their counterparts in France. This was probably a consequence of greater fiscal equity and greater consensus about the crown's choice of taxes. In France, the management of the royal revenue farms of indirect taxes was severely criticised and, in 1794, twenty-eight of the last group of revenue farmers were guillotined. The tradition which Colbert started (and it was a point on which he had criticised Foucquet) was that the rent payable by the farmers of the indirect taxes should be increased at each renewal of the lease. This was the case at each renewal from 1726 to the end of the *ancien régime* but successive ministers are open to the criticism that too often the revenue farmers, rather than they, had the whip hand in the negotiations: Silhouette fell from power in 1759 because of the opposition of the farmers to sharing half their profits with the crown. Thus when profit sharing came in, under Terray, it was on a relatively modest scale (Necker estimated that the king received 13.5 million of the total profit of 55.5 million during the lease of Laurent David, 1774–80). The government is open to the accusation of doing too little too late to share in the profits of the farmers general, while the auditing and inspection procedures for their accounts remained very weak until the 1780s.[83]

Eugene White's review of the secondary literature on the royal general farms leads him to conclude that condemnation of the system should be

[80] Swann, 1995: 183. [81] Swann, 1995: 220.
[82] Swann, 1995: 286–7, 290, 367. [83] White, 1997.

tempered by a recognition of the problems facing the crown: revenue-sharing contracts might have led to salaried officials in the longer term, but 'the process was slow and halting, reflecting the political inertia of the *ancien régime*'. One reason why reform was so slow, which was endemic to the revenue-farming system, was a fatal confusion between government reliance on the revenue farmers to administer the indirect tax system and on them as providers of short-term credit. Munro Price argues that d'Ormesson intended, in his abortive reform of 1783, to abolish the revenue farms while simultaneously restructuring the government's reliance on short-term credit. The revenue farmers resorted to their usual pressure, including an inteview with Vergennes and a deputation to the king. Louis XVI became anxious at the threat to credit, Vergennes switched allegiance and by this pressure the revenue farmers secured the dismissal of d'Ormesson and his replacement by Calonne: 'it was thus the inability of the crown to liberate itself from dependence on *la finance* that accounts for the failure of its reform project in 1783.'[84]

Factor h), the degree of tax compliance within the state, which raises constitutional issues (such as the degree of consent) and public order issues (such as the degree of tax resistance), appears a less clear-cut divergence between Britain and France than is sometimes argued. The specificially 'parliamentary' aspect of consent in England can be exaggerated, since once parliament had secured an unchallenged right to refuse 'supply' it never did so and a strong form of 'ministerial absolutism', particularly a firm control of fiscal affairs by the Treasury, filled the political void. Patrick O'Brien notes that the parliamentary debates on supply were usually brief and uncontentious: 'members of the House of Commons paid so little attention to the details of tax administration or the management of the national debt that the Prime Minister's authority was virtually unchallenged'.[85]

Nor did the arrival of greater parliamentary intervention in the realm of taxation in France after the Revolution facilitate the raising of increased taxes. As Timothy Le Goff and Donald Sutherland argue, despite 'the hopes of the Constituent Assembly for a greater tax yield after the abolition of the tithe, direct taxes effectively collected in the Revolutionary years stayed well below *ancien régime* levels until about 1797, then rose to a level about one-third above. It took the crisis of the Empire after 1810 to bring direct taxes up to the level legislators had hoped for in 1791'.[86] The new regime of consent to taxation was a regime of lighter, rather than heavier, taxes as Necker had expected.[87] For all its rapid depreciation, the

[84] Price, 1995: 108–9. [85] O'Brien, 1989b: 173.
[86] Le Goff and Sutherland, 1991: 69. [87] Necker, 1791: 130–1.

assignat scheme provided the revolutionary governments with resources on a much larger scale (three times more, in real terms, according to Ramel) than under the *ancien régime*. Ramel contended that Frenchmen under the Revolution had paid only 300 million a year in taxes, when they should have paid 500 million, 'the rest being a net gain (*bénéfice*) for them'.[88] His figures may not have been entirely correct, but they take us to the heart of the under-taxation argument, another distinctive feature of French fiscal history. When a national assembly with fiscal powers emerged in France after 1789, popular pressure not only prevented the imposition of heavier taxes, it actually led to the dismantling of the indirect tax structure and an almost exclusive reliance on direct taxes.[89]

The final factor, factor i), is whether or not the state was in 'crisis', particularly the crisis of foreign warfare: thus was there a public perception that there was a short-term, manageable period of wartime change which would later be reversed in peacetime? This was the justification for Robert Walpole's original Sinking Fund of 1716, which was probably the inspiration for the various French *caisses d'amortissement* from 1721 to 1787: the intention of these various schemes was that the wartime increase in the public debt would be made manageable in years of peace.[90] O'Brien calls Pitt's Sinking Fund of 1786 'radical and imaginative', an attempt in the fullness of time to 'rid the government and the country of the incubus of debt'.[91] But it required the compliance of taxpayers, fiscal restraint on the part of government and a more peaceful world in which war expenditure was not the main driving force in the accumulation of an ever-increasing public debt. Necker noted that the Sinking Fund had frequently been raided, and for this reason did not regard it as an example of good practice.[92]

Britain avoided the disaster of an 'inflation tax' such as was paid by the French in the period of the 1790s. It is difficult to see the *assignat* period as a temporary, manageable period of wartime change. Inflation was the great enemy, not least because of the failure of the decentralised credit market in Paris to aggregate information under rapid inflation:[93] between 1789 and 1795, inflation wiped out over 99 per cent of the value of the French currency, costing lenders in the private market 1.67 billion *livres*, as the stock of private debt dropped to nearly zero.[94] The currency was stabilised in 1796. Outright repayment of loans was the wisest course of action for those who waited until 1795 to do so. For borrowers, properly

[88] Crouzet, 1993: 562. [89] Crouzet, 1993: 96, 120–3. [90] Le Goff, 1997a.
[91] O'Brien, 1989b: 176. [92] Necker, 1791: 145.
[93] Hoffman *et al.*, 2000: 206. [94] Hoffman *et al.*, 2000: 200.

anticipating the stabilisation was critical. Thereafter, borrowers preferred long-term loans, while lenders wanted the opposite.

The first experiments in fiat money emanating from the French experience suggest that most European governments had little or no ability to prevent an inflation tax from being added to the burdens paid by their taxpayers, not least because the yield from direct and indirect taxation was insufficient for the needs of government in wartime. Conversely, in Britain, where the per capita tax burden was extremely heavy, parliament acted as the custodian of the rights of property owners to prevent simultaneously a repudiation of the debt and an additional wartime inflation tax caused by any excessive issues of the 'paper pound'.

Kersaint had assured the Convention in 1793 that the credit of England rested on 'fictitious wealth'; Napoleon, too, was convinced of the 'gnawing worm' (*ver rongeur*) of the British public debt, which might lead to the overthrow of its economy. On the British side, even before the outbreak of war Lord Grenville had written that 'the bubble of French finance must . . . inevitably burst'. As late as the first months of 1811, 'French finances appeared victorious', write Bordo and White. 'Britain was encumbered by a growing debt, and the pound sterling stood at a substantial discount. France maintained the value of the franc, the Banque de France redeemed its notes at par, and the budget of the previous year was balanced. What destroyed the empire was the enormous expense and failure of the Russian campaign' and the 'crushing burden' of reparations after Napoleon's Hundred Days.[95]

The assumption that war would be of limited duration because of the financial problems of states proved to be an illusion during the revolutionary and Napoleonic period. It is tempting to conclude that Britain finally won the conflict against France in 1815, and permanently eliminated the Napoleonic threat to its hegemony, because of a preceding 'financial revolution' that made it adapt earlier than other states to meet the costs of war on a global scale.[96] It might even be argued that the experience of total war confirmed an economic lead in the Industrial Revolution because of the 'catalytic influence of military impulses on economic growth', that is military requirements as 'the principal determinant of the structure of production'.[97] In the course of European history there have been many technical innovations which might amount to a 'financial revolution'; to single out the English version of 'Dutch finance'[98] as the sole factor in

[95] Bordo and White, 1991: 315. Except where indicated otherwise, the references for this section are contained in Bonney, 'The struggle for great power status' (Bonney, 1995: 386–90).

[96] Dickson, 1967. [97] Sen, 1984: 93.

[98] Tracy, 1985; M. 't Hart, 1993.

success is clearly an oversimplification, though the English public debt alone avoided the excesses of 'hyperinflation' in the 1790s and thereafter.

To succeed, credit structures have to adapt constantly in order to command confidence among successive generations of investors. The English public debt had to be consolidated first into permanent, non-redeemable, stock; later, a prospect of redemption had to be offered; and in the period of the revolutionary and Napoleonic wars, both tax increases on an unprecedented scale and the abandonment of a metallic standard for the conversion of currency were needed in order to bolster the financial system in an era of total war. A sensible British strategy still had to be adopted in order to guarantee success. And, perhaps crucially, economic growth had to be maintained to generate a taxable increase in the gross domestic product. None of this could be guaranteed or was even foreseeable. The peaceful consumption of cotton was more important than military requirements as the source of foreign earnings and there is an argument, which has not been entirely laid to rest, that 'peaceful' investment in British economic growth was 'crowded out' by the financing of war – in other words, that the British economy might have done better had first the Convention, and then Napoleon, not been confronted in an almost permanent war between 1793 and 1815.

The change in the balance of power caused by French expansion was such that isolation was never a serious political option. There would have been a longer-term economic cost in the potential closure of European markets to British goods. The converse position to the 'crowding-out' hypothesis is that the prosecution of war raised overall levels of demand and absorbed manpower and resources which might otherwise have been unemployed or under-utilised. Taxes and loans for the military effort arose from increases in national income which might not have materialised but for the rise in government expenditure as a result of the war. Britain needed its population rise of between 3.7 and 4.3 million persons between 1791 and 1811; without it, the economic cost of the war effort would have been much more difficult to sustain. Britain also needed its colonial seizures and windfalls in terms of increased colonial penetration after the events of 1807–10, though here there is also a counter-argument which suggests that no more than 15 per cent of investment in the Industrial Revolution arose from British overseas trade with the 'periphery', that is, Latin America, the Caribbean, Africa and Asia.

If this last argument is true, were the benefits of the British 'blue water' policy worth the costs? Again, as with the continental war, the answer is likely to be found in the counter-proposition that economic losses might have resulted from other states penetrating colonial markets in advance of Britain and closing them off to British exports: for example, in 1808 the British Cabinet thought that 'the interval may be short between the seizure by France of the Spanish government at home, and the occupation by the same power of its colonies abroad . . .' What might have happened to Britain's share of world trade had she been forced to sue for peace with Napoleon, who sought to turn his military ascendancy in continental Europe to economic advantage? It is likely on balance that there was some net reduction in investment at home attributable to a 'crowding-out' effect in wartime, but the economic benefits accruing from the elimination of the threat posed by the most powerful state of the *ancien régime* in continental Europe clearly outweighed such losses: the total value of French exports in 1788 was not achieved again until about 1826. Without a vigorous debt repudiation policy, France could no longer afford her status as a great European power in 1789. The revolutionary upheaval and the wars of 1792–1815 brought about the loss of her relative position as a powerful threat to British economic superiority.

10 Money and economic development in eighteenth-century England

Forrest Capie

Introduction

In the course of the eighteenth century Britain emerged as the leading industrial and financial power. Over that same period the state grew enormously and taxed and borrowed on a large and growing scale. Across the 127-year period from 1688 to 1815 tax rose sixteen-fold and borrowing 240-fold (O'Brien, 1994).

Clearly something remarkable happened that allowed government to tax and borrow on these unprecedented scales. Some of the answer must lie in the transformation that was taking place in the behaviour of markets generally and in finance particularly. The likelihood is that a big part of the explanation can be found in fiscal affairs and in the establishment of reliable bond markets using improved financial instruments, backed by the credibility of parliament (see Neal, 1990). Wars were financed by the issue of short-term debt (army bills, navy bills, etc.). Long-term securities were used to retire the short-term debt. Long-term debt was less expensive and was improving in quality over the century, notably with the introduction of irredeemable 3 per cent Consols in the middle of the century. This kind of funding was carried out after the wars.

But within this explanation, is there a greater role for the contribution of money than has usually been granted? This chapter begins with a short recitation of some of the general considerations that provide the foundation that was either necessary for, or complemented, monetary developments. It is difficult to be precise about any direct contribution money could have made given the scarcity of hard data, but there are some leads that can be pursued, and some theory that indicates the direction that might be taken.

The story that might be imagined could be told runs along the following lines. Money is clearly important in economic development. Its introduction and increasing use lowers costs and so increases trade. The

I should like to thank the participants at the Festschrift conference in Madrid for comments, and Leslie Pressnell for reading and commenting on the manuscript.

emergence of stable money brings efficiencies and allows the maximum gains from financial intermediation to proceed. An important positive externality is that the greater the circulation the greater is the promotion of efficient tax collection. Sound money and a monetary economy did emerge in England at an early point. Nascent fractional reserve banking appeared in England in the late seventeenth century (Quinn, 2000). There was, too, the development of trust backed by legal institutions. The monetary economy was on its way to being established before industrialisation. Did it pave the way, or allow, or promote economic development? In the end there remain some puzzles over the contribution of money. The chapter takes these issues in turn. Section 1 notes some general considerations that might be useful in discussing monetary developments, and considers money more generally. Section 2 sets out a framework for exploring the money stock and brings together some highly tentative estimates of monetary variables for benchmark years. It also raises some of the questions the estimates prompt. Finally, some measures of financial deepening are presented.

It is not possible to make comparisons with other European countries since this approach has not as yet been used for these economies. However, it is possible to note some developments in France and the Netherlands that bear on the subject.

1 Money

There may have been something different about the English/British that allowed economic development to proceed at an earlier date and faster pace than elsewhere. Indeed, this is sometimes simply asserted and not only by those of an extreme patriotic or nationalist inclination (Grossman, 2001). Needless to say this is treacherous territory and not readily susceptible to investigation, never mind demonstration. But the idea that individual freedom and democracy matter has been taken up by leading economists in the last decade or so (see, for example, Barro, 2001). The idea is not exactly new. It lay behind Smith's *Wealth of Nations*, and was also part of Toynbee's explanation for British success in the eighteenth century, as told in his *Lectures* (1883). Toynbee wrote, 'On the moral side, our political institutions, being favorable to liberty, have developed individual energy and industry in a degree unknown in any other country' (Toynbee, [1883] 1969: 121).

The role played by religion has been introduced with greater confidence too, recently, and one line of research stresses the part that trust plays. Property rights also have a role to play. They have of course always been around, certainly for millennia. The question is at what time did they become sufficiently well defined and enforceable and extensive to allow and promote economic growth. Clearly, there were still some areas at risk in England, such as that exposed by the 'Stop of the Exchequer' in 1672.

The introduction of money in an economy improves economic efficiency. It is a clear improvement over barter, reducing the time spent in search of coincident wants, and so on. The use of money as a medium of exchange lowers the cost of gathering information by shifting attention to the properties of the asset and away from the personal attributes of the buyer, such as creditworthiness or income. The buyer gains because it is less costly to make purchases; and similarly the seller gains. Information costs are lower and so trade expands. The use of money as a unit of account also reduces information costs for transactions. Without the unit of account a transactor needs to know innumerable bi-lateral exchange values. This further reduction in costs should also encourage the expansion of trade. Thus the development of a commodity as money brings large gains. The emergence of paper money, so long as there is no over-issue causing inflation, brings a further resource saving if it substitutes in whole or in part for the commodity which had served as money. There are costs since the anonymity which it conveys means it is susceptible to loss or theft. The emergence of inside money (bank money) substitutes further for paper but anonymity is lost. The ever-wider spread in the use of money and ultimately, ideally, the complete monetisation of the economy therefore brings maximum efficiency from this source. A positive externality is that the monetary economy also allows for the efficient collection of tax and so promotes economic development by that means.

All that said, money should not be confused with credit. Trade and associated credits are simply means of postponing settlement in money. The scale of that kind of credit is of interest for a number of reasons but does not impinge directly on this discussion of the role of money. And trade credit needs to be distinguished from bank credit, which is of course money – inside money. (For a fascinating discussion of trade credit and social relations in this period see Muldrew, 1998.)

A monetary system and economy cannot simply be adopted once it is recognised that it is superior to whatever is extant at any particular time. It has to evolve and needs to adapt to the different circumstances in which it finds itself. The fundamental requirements of a monetary economy are a unit of account and a means of payment. Together these provide a payments system. The emergence of payment systems is hindered primarily by the lack of confidence in the stability of the value of money. That is, the means by which obligations are discharged must be seen to be stable and to hold for the future before a system will emerge. Thus a payments system will develop only when there are institutions (though these can be proxied in conventions or mores that are deeply held and are implicitly expected to continue) that guarantee, implicitly or explicitly, the future value of money.

What does it mean to say that such a system depends upon a degree of trust? The period under consideration here is one in which the distinction between inside and outside money was emerging. That is, it is at this time that the modern origins of the move from commodity money to supplementary paper money are found – fractional reserve banking. (Ultimately, commodity money disappeared altogether.) This is an important distinction. Commodity money is an asset for those who hold it. It has no offsetting liability. For all other forms of money the holder of the asset is holding someone else's liability. It is for this reason that 'in the end modern money – in contrast to gold and silver money – ultimately rests *on the trust of agents* in their own economies' (Burda and Wyplosz, 1997: 196–7, italics added). Does such trust derive from the prevailing religious culture, Judaeo/Christian at this time, as Sacks argues, or does it derive from, or is it affected by, the prevailing institutional arrangements the most important of which is the rule of law. It may be that the rule of law and the capacity to enforce it, and the extent of respect that there is for it, are all that matter. For example, with convertible money in the form of either metal-backed banknotes or deposit accounts, the holder of these has a claim to a specified good on specified terms at a certain time. But this kind of money needs to be stable in value and therefore depends on the enforceability of the claim. For this to obtain there must be clear, well-defined, and enforceable rights.

Trust and the rule of law

In England the financial sector in London was relatively small and one where, in the early days, most of the participants were well known to each other. This had to be the case for the system of private paper to become established. Either that or there had to be a powerful legal apparatus that could enforce the system. Bills of exchange (which at some points constituted money) needed 'good names', and these required trust or firm rule of law.

In fact as might be expected, there seems to have been some of both. There was considerable trust but if there were any serious risk of that not delivering then there was resort to law. Trust could often be found among members of religious sects and they were quite often important in the transmission of, and promotion of, paper credit. Thus, apart from the Jews, the Quakers were important in seventeenth-century England. But trade extended beyond the limits of these groups and trust might on occasions have to be supplemented.

From an early date in its history Bank of England notes were protected, so important were they regarded in relation to public credit. It was a capital offence to forge these notes. But over the next century or so there were scores of other pieces of legislation on forging: so much so that in the debates in the 1820s on the repeal of these measures the view was expressed that the early measures reflected too much emphasis on the value of property and too little on the value of human life. With the great expansion of commercial paper in the early eighteenth century new laws were devised to cope with the changing nature of this property. However, the scale of the legislation, while showing a concern for property, does bring out the need for some support for trust on its own.

Private paper was beginning to grow rapidly at the same time as government paper and some attention needed to be given to that. And while those in the financial sector were well known to each other, an increasing amount of business was being carried out by anonymous agents. They may still have been carrying and exchanging the paper of respected and well-known names but anonymity was increasing.

A particular case of the 1720s highlights the nature of the system and the dangers its abuse carried. William Hales, a man from an eminent family and himself a former goldsmith, had got into difficulties and debt. He devised, with the assistance of others, an elaborate fraud which brought out the nature of the system of credit that was developing at the time – where commercial paper circulated on the strength of a good name or names either as its source or as an endorsement. Hales abused the names and friendship of people to create the necessary bills and then exploited the anonymity in the system by using an agent to discount the bills or raise funds on the strength of them.

Hales was caught, convicted, and sentenced in 1728. However, at that time the penalty for forgery was pillory and in extreme cases imprisonment. Hales was in fact sent to prison and died there a short time later. Yet the seriousness of this particular crime – the size of the sums and the status of the people involved – meant a great debate ensued over the danger to the nationwide system of credit and to the national economy if such vulnerability persisted (see McGowen, 1999).

So new legislation was passed. A particular concern was to define carefully the types of paper that were to receive protection. It covered bonds, bills of exchange, promissory notes for the payment of money and the endorsement of any of these. The drafters tried to cover all the possible types of paper then in use. But the real challenge was to cope with a market that was in constant state of change. Ambiguity surrounded the definition of money then as now, with defendants claiming that their crime related not to money but merely to paper. Legal comment on the forgery was of the kind, 'It is a very great offence, a misdemeanour of the highest nature, not only as it affects particular persons, and charges the person whose name is made use of with the payment, but as it is destructive to all commerce' (quoted McGowen, 1999: 130) . . . 'Forgery is what concerns every Englishman: As paper credit is come to that height it is now, the utmost care ought to be taken to preserve that credit' (quoted McGowen, 1999: 130).

Thus it might be claimed that all the conditions for the emergence of inside money and the provision of stable money existed at the beginning of this period. There was also a desire for honesty and certainty in trade credit. More than that the law was empowered to back enforcement to ensure reliability. Trust and general good behaviour are highly desirable. David Hume among others pointed out that most disagreements were settled without going to law because the parties valued a good reputation. But that may have to be set against a background of a firm rule of law.

2 A framework for monetary estimates

How, then, did money develop and the money stock in its inside and outside forms grow over the course of the eighteenth century? We consider first the aggregate money stock and then the monetary base. In order to address the question of the money stock some simple theory is required that directs attention to the variables that can be of use and allows some speculation on their magnitude. The framework is the quantity theory, available at least in rudimentary form at the time. John Locke has been given credit for using the quantity theory to put England on sound money in the late seventeenth century (Eltis 1995). The theory dates back at least to Bodin in the fifteenth century and was certainly well known in the middle of the eighteenth century when it was set out so clearly by David Hume.

The well-known identity is:

$$MV = PQ$$

where M is a measure of the monetary stock; V is the velocity of circulation; P is the level of prices; and Q is output.

The attraction of this equation, even if it does not imply causality, is that a certain amount is known about the variables and the relationship between the variables can be used to make estimates, however crude, of

Table 10.1 *Some tentative estimates of monetary variables*

	1700			1750		1790		1870
M £m	12	*15*	20	22.5	30	63	*76*	540
V	5	*4*	3	4	*3*	3	*2.5*	1.75
P		100			92		116	
PQ £m		60			90		190	950

Source: See text.

the money stock. Some features from developing countries can supplement such speculation.

The starting point is to take estimates of income at the beginning of the century and at the end of the period in 1790 – to avoid the upheavals of the Revolutionary War period. These are shown as PQ or nominal income for 1700 and 1790 in table 10.1. Income at the beginning of the eighteenth century was about £60 million. Stopping short of the common estimate for the end of that century gives a figure of around £190 million (based on Mitchell, 1988). The price index is recorded here too. It is because there is little movement in that index that we can in effect ignore it and think in terms of nominal income. The price index is the Schumpeter-Gilboy one that runs from a base of 100 at the beginning of the eighteenth century to 92 in the middle and about 116 at 1790 (averaging roughly the consumer goods and producer goods). This is the very gentlest deflation followed by a gentle inflation across almost a century and can for practical purposes be ignored altogether.

Next, velocity can be introduced, though any such discussion is perforce highly speculative. Velocity was understood in the period. For example Locke wrote: 'This shows the necessity of some proportion of money to trade; but what proportion that is is hard to determine; because it depends not barely on the quantity of money, but on the quickness of its circulation. The very same shilling may, at one time, pay twenty men in twenty days' (quoted in Morgan, 1965: 182).

There is little on which to work empirically, though there is some evidence that can be drawn on from both later and earlier periods. For example, for the period after ours Bordo and Jonung (1987) examined velocity for several countries in the process of their economic development. They found values for the US, Canada and Sweden around 1870 of the order of 5 or 6. For the United Kingdom at that time there was a value of 2. But the United Kingdom was at that stage very advanced in terms of its monetary and financial system. Bordo and Jonung show that velocity starts high in the early stages of development and then falls as the use of money spreads through bank deposits – the 'monetisation' process. That is followed by some rise in velocity as the use of money declines with the availability of alternative financial instruments. Their data, however, did not go back far enough to verify the British case. But following their argument, and the value for Britain in 1870 (Capie and Webber (1983) estimate it to be 1.75) it could be postulated that since there was a long period of monetisation from 1820 to 1870 velocity might have been around 3 at the beginning of the nineteenth century. And given that, perhaps it would not be out of line to give it a value of 4 or even 5 for the beginning of our period, at 1700. In fact we take values of 5, 4 and 3 as the starting points and see where they lead. These surely cover the realistic range. On the assumption that the income figure is reliable these would give values for the money stock at that point of approximately £12 million, £15 million or £20 million.

Moving to the end of the period, 1790, where the growth of nominal output had reached £190 million, and accepting that velocity had at that point fallen to around 3 or 2.5, then the money stock must have been approximately £63 million or £76 million. The figures arrived at are surely not very far out. In fact, the velocity figures that seem most acceptable would be: 4 in 1700, 3 in 1750, and 2.5 in 1790. Obviously, some refinements to these could be attempted, but it would be dangerous and may introduce a spurious sense of precision.

Interestingly, Mayhew (1995) approached this subject of velocity in a similar fashion for an earlier period – 1300 to 1700. He constructed his own estimates of income and money stock and arrived at a velocity figure of 3.5 for 1700. We judge this slightly too high. His money stock figure is very close, but lower than ours, at £14.5 million. Mayhew, in fact, showed a sharp decline in velocity in the first half of the seventeenth century and then remarkable stability for the next fifty years. Perhaps the difference lies there. But his figures are clearly useful and not in serious conflict with our estimates.

Some interpolation of an income figure for mid-century would, in light of information on the pace of development in the century, produce a figure of around £90 million. Using the velocity figure of 3 would produce a money stock of £30 million. It so happens that David Hume spoke of a money stock of £30 million in 1750, which lends support to our speculation. These, then, are the rough-and-ready orders of magnitude for the money stock to be held in view.

The next logical step is to attempt some construction of the monetary base, estimates of which are useful for both elaboration of the money-supply process and to show the extent of bank or other credit. If such

Table 10.2 *Some estimates for monetary base*

	1700 £m	1750 £m	1790 £m	1870 £m
Coin	7	18	44	95
B of E notes	1.5	4	8	35
Other notes	0	1	4	4.9
Banks balances at the Bank of England	–	–	–	6.5
TOTAL	8.5	23	56	141.4

Source: See text.

estimates are based on completely separate information, they also allow some further check on the money stock estimates. The base in a period such as this with a metallic standard is made up in the main of gold and silver coin and bullion. Table 10.2 shows coin and bank notes with the latter regarded as a proxy for bullion. It was not until the second half of the nineteenth century that bankers' balances at the Bank of England had become a dominant feature.

In an economy with a metallic standard and fixed exchange rate the base is determined through the balance of payments. Although there is evidence on this, it turns out not to be helpful for our purposes. The few estimates there are are highly contentious. Brezis recently provided new estimates that showed there were continuous current account deficits across the century and concluded that there were steady capital inflows. These flows were modest to begin with but rose to close to £1.7 million per annum by the 1770s. Nash rejects these estimates and suggests that something closer to a quarter of that figure would be more appropriate. Cuenca Esteban (2001) too is critical and is more in line with Nash. Whatever the outcome of this research the direction of the flows might at least be agreed upon. We might be tempted to conclude that there was a steady if small increase in the money base from this source. However, there are three points to make here. The first is that strictly speaking there was not a fixed exchange-rate regime – with two other major economies on different systems. The second is that deficits in trade could always be covered by bills of exchange, and hence there may have been no specie movement at all. And the third is that since the metallic standard was not clearly defined, the monetary base could have other parts to it than specie.

But regardless of what these flows were, our approach is to examine the net effect by considering the output of the mint. That output would include all metal coming from all sources. There are some means by which rough orders of magnitude might be established for the amount of cash – notes and coin – in the country. That is, there is a reasonable prospect of saying what size the monetary base would have been.

Components of the money base

(a) *Coin* One starting point for guestimates of coin in circulation is to take a figure for somewhere in the middle of the nineteenth century, for which there are good estimates, and use that in relation to the proportion that coin was in the whole money stock. Of course, there are difficulties, but some indication can be useful and some upper and lower bounds can be indicated. The figure for 1870 is £95 million. Given the growth of the economy and arguments on the changing use of coin (Capie and Webber, 1983), that figure might be roughly twice that for 1790. This would give us a figure to hold in view for 1790 of around £45–£50 million.

For the eighteenth century there are data, gathered by others, on the silver and gold coin production of the mints (Pressnell, 1956 and slightly modified by Challis, 1992). These can be used as a guide to official coinage and, again following Capie and Webber on the nineteenth century, some application of wastage rates can allow estimates of the total value of such coins in circulation. There are records of all the gold and silver coins minted at the Royal mint from as early as 1688 or at least there are good estimates of annual averages (see Pressnell, 1956: 511). If annual averages were multiplied through for each decade and some other assumptions made about the size of the stock at the starting point, the figures in table 10.2 can be deduced. That is, £7 million at the start, £25 million for 1750 and a figure of £65 million would be obtained for 1790.

Although not wildly out of line with what might be expected in an economy of its kind the figures must be reduced for the following reasons. First is the survival rate, for coins did not always have a long life. There was also the possibility of melting down. And finally there was the flow of coins abroad. On the basis of some work by Capie and Webber (1983) each of these would have reduced supply and figures in the region of £18 million for 1750, and £44 million for 1790 would be arrived at. Again there is some confirmation to be found in Hume, who claimed that of the total money stock in 1750, £18 million was coin – our figure precisely. (This, though, does leave out of account the fact that there were other coins – privately issued tokens were at times in quite widespread use.) The figure for 1790 falls precisely in the range predicted.

(b) *Banknotes* It is possible to introduce some idea of the size of banknote circulation in the eighteenth century by virtue, in the first

instance, of the Bank of England's extensive publication of its balance sheets, from which can be derived the new notes issued in each period. There were other banks issuing and they were increasing in the latter part of the century.

The Bank of England's ledgers are almost complete from its inception onwards. The Bank of England Quarterly Bulletin (June 1967) reproduced in convenient form the Bank's balance sheets every five years from 1694 onwards. These show that at the beginning of the period notes in circulation were around £1.5 million. They did fluctuate across the century but had grown to £4 million in 1750 and around £8 million in 1790. Thereafter, they grew much more rapidly when the Bank was no longer under the constraint of convertibility into gold during the Napoleonic Wars. Something to bear in mind is that Bank notes did not circulate widely outside London – generally thought of as about a 30-mile radius from the Bank (Pressnell, 1956: 138). Against that, country banknotes, when they were issued, were payable locally and in London. With all notes it is important to remember that until 1793 they were in large denominations, of £10. (Notes under £1 were made illegal in 1775. In 1793, £5 notes were legalised and in 1797 notes below £5.)

Some guide to the scale of private note issue can be given by using a figure from the early nineteenth century. The ratio of all private and joint stock bank issues to that of the Bank of England in the 1830s gives a figure of 30 per cent of the total (Pressnell, 1956: 160). That is, non-Bank issue was 50 per cent of Bank issue. This figure of around one-third was also used by Adie (1970) for the first half of the nineteenth century. When broken down into sub-periods, they were much higher at the start of the nineteenth century – 1.3 – but that was in wartime, when there would be an expectation of cash hoarding. Nevertheless, the ratio would undoubtedly have been slightly higher for the late eighteenth century and a figure of 50 per cent could be used as a lower bound. That would mean a note issue of £4 million at that point, something that had grown from close to zero in the course of the century.

The number of banks had grown from close to zero at the beginning of the period to 280 in 1790, though most of that came in the second half of the century. A note issue of £4 million, therefore, works out at an average of £14,000 per bank, a figure that seems entirely plausible and not out of line with the fragmentary evidence in some balance sheets of the time. Some indications can be found in the few surviving records of individual banks. Pressnell provides some of these for the second half of the eighteenth century. For example, the bankers Bell & Co. (Pressnell, 1956: 519) in the middle of the century had a note issue that was approximately half of all their liabilities. Thus notes, while still a small percentage of the total money stock, were nevertheless greater in size than deposits at this stage. Another example from the 1790s is that of Smith & Co. of Nottingham and Lincoln (Pressnell, 1956: 521). Note issue there was around 20 per cent of total liabilities (and deposits were roughly 45 per cent).

The figures, then, for the monetary base for the benchmark years are as shown in table 10.2: £8.5 million, £23 million, and £56 million. When the last is placed alongside the base for 1870 again it looks acceptable.

These rough estimates of the money stock do nevertheless raise some interesting questions and perhaps allow some answers. For example, there is much written on the use of bills of exchange as money in the period. Rondo Cameron went so far as to say that in the middle of the eighteenth century bills made up the bulk of the money supply. Our figures suggest this is impossible. With a money stock of £30 million and base of £23 million there is only £7 million of inside money. Some of this is undoubtedly bank deposits, leaving only a small fraction of the total money stock to be made up of bills.

Also, there are stories of the search for money in the eighteenth century perhaps suggesting that at least parts of the money stock were deficient. And while we have suggested that velocity should have been falling, it need not have been. If velocity remained unchanged across the century at a value of 3 then the money stock at the outset would have been £20 million, £30 million, in the middle, and £63 million at the end. Clearly the assumptions are critical. It is a matter of judgement to arrive at the figures we have. But taking all that into account, it would still seem that something was left to be done by bank credit.

What can be said of bank credit? If there were reliable representative figures on deposits, these would be a further guide to the composition of the total money stock. Bank deposits dominate the modern money stock. Trying to guess their magnitude in the eighteenth century is not a job for the faint-hearted. The principal indication possible is to use the growth of banks as a proxy for the growth of deposits. The main rationale for this, apart from there being a certain amount of information on the numbers of banks at different points, is that the banks were constrained in size. They were restricted to six partners, and so their balance sheets were unlikely to have grown greatly. At the beginning of the nineteenth century their main complaint was that they were under-capitalised, not having been able to grow in line with the needs of the economy. There is some evidence in support of this. Also as mentioned above, deposits were a much smaller part of the balance sheet in the eighteenth century.

There are some estimates of the scale of bank deposits at the beginning of the nineteenth century (Adie, 1970). These have been subjected to a variety of criticisms and hardly allow any possibility of backward extrapolation. This is dangerous territory and at this stage it seems wiser to concede defeat and accept that we cannot put a figure on deposits and must remain ignorant on the subject for most of the century. All that can be said is that they lie in the range between base and the total money stock.

There are some questions arising from these conjectures on the money stock. One such concerns the sufficiency of money. There was a very gentle inflation in the second half of the period. That being the case, then contrary to some accounts, there was no shortage of money. If anything, there was a slight excess of money. The composition of the money stock may not be known but a reasonable conclusion is that it was sufficient. The fact that there was no debasement of the coinage in the eighteenth century might add some support to this view. It may simply reflect better behaviour on the part of participants, but in any case that would probably point to greater confidence in the monetary system.

In general terms some support for the notion of a sufficiency of money can be found in the behaviour of interest rates. With almost no inflation, real and nominal rates are close to being identical. There are many influences on the rate of interest, but insofar as something can be read from them, the rate that matters is the market long-term rate. This can be found in the long-term bond yield, of which there are several examples. Such rates are remarkably stable and flat and if anything in slight decline across the century (Pressnell, 1960).

Other questions might include the reliability of the price indices, though there does seem to be general agreement that they are quite robust. But even if that is so, there could nevertheless have been alternating periods of scarcity and excess. Or there might have been a shortage of small-denomination coins in relation to the demand. This latter might explain the stories of manufacturers going around the country searching for currency to pay wages, or else producing their own token currency. If this practice indicated an increasing use of smaller denomination monies, then that in itself suggests an increasing use of money. But it is not one that is readily accommodated within our figures.

Some further light might be shed by a consideration of the money multiplier. The multiplier can be expressed as:

$$M = (1 + C/D)/(C/D + R/D)$$

The C/D ratio, and to some extent its reflection in the R/D ratio, shows the changing use of currency in relation to deposits. Any secular fall in those ratios indicates a growing use of banks, suggesting a growing confidence in the banking system. Unfortunately, there is still a great deal

Table 10.3 *Indicators of financial depth*

		1700			1750		1790	1870
M	1.4	1.76	2.3		1.3	1.12	1.36	3.8
M3/GDP	0.2	0.25	0.3	0.25	0.33	0.33	0.4	0.57
CIM	0.29	0.43	0.57	0.02	0.26	0.11	0.26	0.76

Sources: See text.

to do on this front. There is a tantalisingly titled article by Horsefield, 'The cash ratio in English banks before 1800' (Horsefield, 1949), which discusses some contemporary thought. However, it turns out to be of limited use. He is in fact referring to the R/D ratio in our money multiplier model, though even the definition of the phrase is unclear. As a result, all kinds of estimates of the ratio can be derived, ranging from as low as 5 per cent to as high as 70 per cent. There is no indication of trend or of the direction of change. It is difficult to use some figures, since in the period of private note issue it is not always clear where the liability for the note lies.

Scarcity of data on the components is a problem, but there is some information on the scale of these multipliers at different stages of monetary and economic development in different countries. Some speculation can therefore be introduced on the expected range within which the multiplier might have been expected to lie in England at this time. For example developing countries with nascent banking systems have multipliers in the region of 1.2–1.5. In itself a money multiplier that was increasing would reveal a certain amount about the contribution of banking in the period. A growing multiplier allows the monetary base to do more than it otherwise could.

Table 10.3 gives the multiplier found by dividing our estimates of M by our estimates of B. These highly tentative estimates give a money multiplier of around 1.7 at the beginning of the period and 1.3 for the middle and the end of the period. The size is in line with what is found in developing countries currently, but it is nevertheless surprising to find it higher at the beginning and not to find it rising in the second half of the century.

A related measure has been proposed by Mancur Olson and colleagues. They devised an 'objective measure', using money that captures the 'enforceability and the security of property rights', which they call 'contract intensive money', or CIM (Clague *et al.*, 1999: 186). When lending takes place it is in expectation of a later return. The parties involved need to be confident that the contract will be honoured. Low confidence will result in low levels of this kind of activity. There are no sophisticated capital markets in the absence of third-party enforcement of loan contracts: 'the extent to which societies can capture not only the gains from self-enforcing transactions but also those potential trades that are intensive in contract enforcement and property rights can be approximated by the relative use of currency in comparison with contract intensive money' (Clague *et al.*, 1999: 188). The definition of CIM is, the ratio of non-currency money to total money supply.

A high CIM indicates developed capital markets. And the higher CIM is, the greater are the gains from specialisation, and so the higher is the capital stock, productivity and per capita income. Thus better institutions – especially those that promote contractual enforcement – allow for the use of more sophisticated forms of money. CIM, they insist, is more than an indicator of financial development, since it is a general indicator of contractual and property rights. Nevertheless, if we wish to make use of this measure, we are still confronted with the problem of data availability. CIM should have been growing across the century (like a money multiplier) but attaching numbers to it is hazardous. Using the figures arrived at in table 10.1 gives CIM values for our benchmark years of .29, .26, and .26. Again there is the puzzle of decline rather than rise over the period.

It is not possible to make a serious comparison of English experience with the two other major continental European powers – France and the Netherlands – since the necessary research is lacking. However, some limited speculation can be made on the strength of what we do know. For example, a recent book on France opened up some of the territory. Hoffman *et al.* (2000) explored the scale of credit organised by Parisian notaries over the two centuries from 1660 to 1870. They have a wealth of a particular kind of data, and since Paris clearly dominated in French finance, they argue that some wider conclusions can be drawn. Notaries emerged as financial intermediaries as a consequence of the information to which they had access following the repeated government defaults at the end of Louis XIV's reign. They found that lending was taking place on a considerable scale in the seventeenth century and that was followed by spectacular growth in lending in the eighteenth century. Interestingly, they also note the absence of certain institutions that are normally associated with such activity – clearly defined property rights and secondary markets for the securities, to name just two. The essence of the French system was of brokers bringing parties together for long-term borrowing. They do not make any link with the real economy.

Of greater interest to us is why in France there was not more development in money itself. If, as we have argued, money was superior to credit in important informational aspects, then there were greater gains waiting to be achieved if money had spread at an earlier stage. Yet very little seems to be known of monetisation in the French economy at this time. There are suggestions that there was an insufficiency of money in the course of the eighteenth century. It is often remarked that one of the difficulties of raising taxes in eighteenth-century France was the limited extent of monetisation. In the period immediately following the one occupying our attention there were many experiments. These included extensive issue of paper money – the assignat – and of free banking. Considerable chaos ensued. It was 1801 before the Bank of France was established and later in the century before commercial banking became widespread.

A similar lack of data and of research means that little can be said of these aspects of the Netherlands. In the seventeenth century the Netherlands were the leading economic power. It was also the place where highly innovative measures in the field of finance were taking place. In fact any examination of the English financial revolution in the late seventeenth century reveals that many of the financial instruments and techniques in use had been imported directly from the Netherlands. Hart *et al.* (1997) set all this out in detail. They bring out the clear primacy of finance in the integration and economic development of the Netherlands.

What is clear is that at a very early stage the Dutch managed astonishingly high levels of public debt, and were burdened with extremely high levels of tax – several times that of their French or English counterparts at the time. (Having Spanish armies on their borders undoubtedly helps explain this.) The ability to manage such high debt levels is at the core of understanding the emergence of the fiscal/military state.

Yet again all too little is known of the monetary developments. It is true that at the beginning of the seventeenth century the Bank of Amsterdam was established – sometimes known as the Wisselbank or the Bank of Exchange. (This is sometimes misleadingly referred to as the first central bank.) But beyond that there seem to have been few strictly monetary developments of any significance in the course of the eighteenth century. It was the nineteenth century before the Bank of the Netherlands was founded.

Conclusion

The monetary system that had developed in England by the end of the eighteenth century still had some way to go before it reached the well-diversified and stable structure that prevailed for most of the twentieth century. There was still a lot of learning to do – on the lender of last resort for instance. That required changes in the usury laws, lessening the restrictions on the commercial banks, and so on. But the system that was in place at the end of the eighteenth century was still one of considerable sophistication. Many of the prerequisites had been in place since the seventeenth century. Trust and the rule of law had been developing and played some part. The importation of financial innovations from parts of Europe was also important. All these and the development of new instruments allowed the monetary system to develop the *potential* to make its own distinctive contribution to economic growth.

Is there a puzzle in that the evidence in the figures constructed here does not suggest great advances in the monetary sector? Or is it rather confirmation of the story told increasingly in the revisions of the Industrial Revolution, for example by Crafts and Harley (1992) and others of much slower development in the eighteenth century economy than was once believed? Faster growth comes in the nineteenth century, and the monetary system was well prepared to play its full part at that time and even be an instigating factor in the process.

Part V

War and hegemony

11 Naval power: what gave the British navy superiority?

Daniel A. Baugh

The common method of comparing the strength of one navy to another is to count the number and size of usable warships, and this is undoubtedly a valid way to begin because sooner or later an inferiority of warship strength had serious consequences. Yet tonnage alone did not signify naval power. This point is illustrated in the second half of the century, when the combined warship tonnage of the navies of France and Spain gradually rose to a figure well above that of the British navy, yet Europeans then feared British naval power more fervently than they had feared it during the first half of the century, when British tonnage exceeded that of any combination of rivals by a wide margin.[1] This came about, it will be seen, in consequence of a fundamental shift in British naval strategy.

The argument that underpins this chapter may be put crudely as follows. Building warships, even very good warships, was rather easy. Consistently repairing and replacing them over the years was harder. Manning them with competent seamen, feeding those men and preserving their health was harder still. And, finally, keeping squadrons operating at sea, especially for extended cruises and on distant deployments, was hardest (and most expensive) of all. The peculiarity of British naval power during the eighteenth century was that it was so steadily employed at sea, actively doing the work of seapower. It was this peculiarity in combination with a strategy truly aimed at command of the sea that gave Great Britain its formidable and growing advantages in seaborne commerce and financial prowess.

To compare across national lines the above capabilities – repairing, manning, feeding, sustaining ships at sea – while not ignoring such factors as leadership and strategic wisdom is a task that could not have been wisely attempted forty or even twenty years ago.[2] Moreover, the task

[1] The massive study by Jan Glete has made reliable comparisons possible (Glete, 1993).

[2] Because of space limitations specific references will mainly recognise sources that have provided information about the French and Spanish navies. For a bibliography of studies relating to the British navy on which this essay greatly depends see Baugh, in Hill, 1995: 453–5.

requires an appreciation of the interactions of administrative and operational naval history – easy to talk about in principle, but very hard to do systematically, and in fact almost never done.[3] In what follows these interactions are surveyed only at a general level. It is an approach suited to a brief essay but inevitably results in a degree of distortion. The plan has been to confine the scope to points of comparison that really mattered and to reveal that some aspects did not much matter.

The period under examination is approximately 1715–90. Before 1715 the British navy was primarily the servant of an allied grand strategy in Europe. Oceanic trade (unless one includes Spain's silver convoys) was of small account. By 1790 the value of the plantation production of Saint-Domingue, minuscule in 1715, was alone equal to the total value of exports from the United States of America. But the French Revolution intervened. Saint-Domingue's slave-based production soon collapsed – as time would tell, permanently. The French navy began in 1790 a period of prolonged decline. The Spanish navy, long allied with it, became its opponent. The great naval and maritime contest of the century did not immediately come to an end in 1790, but its political, financial and strategic form was never again quite the same.

The period from 1715 to 1790 is plainly unified by the growing importance of overseas commerce in European power calculations. Yet, it will be argued here, there was a significant divide within the period. The pivotal year was 1747, when an innovation in British naval strategy produced striking combat successes which, though little noticed in general histories, awakened France, and then Europe, to a new sort of awareness of British naval power and some fundamental recalculations of the capacities and limitations of national power. The motivation behind the enormous effort that France and Spain put into building up navies in the second half of the century cannot be understood without noticing the effects and perceived implications of Britain's new emphasis in naval strategy.

Geography and geopolitics

Did geography favour British seapower in the eighteenth century? Britain's location clearly threatened Holland's access to the Atlantic, but offered no such threat to France or Spain. In fact, the advantage was somewhat reversed. London merchantmen headed for the Mediterranean, Indian Ocean or Caribbean had to work their way down the Channel (where French privateers lurked) and then sail past the French

[3] An exception is Christian Buchet's remarkable study of the Caribbean theatre: Buchet, 1991.

naval base at Brest and the Spanish at Ferrol. In wartime convoys were indispensable. And if Portugal had not been kept friendly and independent, French warships and privateers might have operated out of Lisbon, magnifying the difficulties. France and Spain had easy access to both the Mediterranean and the Atlantic. Brest was farther west than Plymouth, closer to the Western Approaches. So long as Britain's commerce remained centred on southern England, French sea power enjoyed a geographical advantage.[4]

There were two ways, however, in which geography placed France at a disadvantage. One was the inaccessibility of Baltic naval stores and timber in wartime. Especially during the first half of the century when the Dutch were British allies, France could not rely on receiving wartime deliveries of hemp, tar and masts from the prime source, and after 1750, when the Dutch were neutral, the British navy could readily interdict supplies (though with diplomatic consequences, as will be seen further on). The second disadvantage pertained to the feasibility of conquering Britain by invasion. No country of Europe was geographically better situated to accomplish this than France, a fact that remained true in the twentieth century. Yet a closer look shows that an invasion attempt in the age of sail was extremely hazardous. The French Channel coast lacked a sheltered harbour deep and large enough for a battle-fleet; all the good places were on the English side. Troop transports and flat-bottomed boats could be assembled at Dunkirk, Le Havre or St Malo, but if a battle-fleet came into the Channel to cover them, it could not, in case of adversity, quickly find a safe roadstead; nor could it count on a favourable wind for retreating back down the Channel. French prospects for invading Britain would have been far less daunting if France had possessed the Scheldt estuary, and Britain's cost of naval defence would have been thereby greatly increased because a strong 'eastern squadron' in addition to a western one at the mouth of the Channel would have been necessary.

What about Great Britain's situation as an island? It was indeed a decisive factor, all the more so after the union with Scotland in 1707. Although the 'moat defensive', as Shakespeare's John of Gaunt termed it, was not of itself a guarantor of survival, its political implications were immense, because it made viable a maritime mode of national defence. Development of a large standing army could be restrained, a policy that harmonised with the English political class's fear of one. The maritime mode of defence obviously required a consistently strong navy and a

[4] Alfred T. Mahan's discussion of this subject is perceptive in many ways but suffers from excessive attention to the issue of fleet concentration and is insufficient regarding France (Mahan, 1918: 29–33).

treasury that could pay for it, for both of which seaborne commerce was deemed indispensable. Awareness of this nexus of power rose steeply during the first decade of the eighteenth century and the nation became wedded to it. No other nation of Europe had such clear-cut naval, commercial and financial priorities. In fact, there was a tendency to keep the British army too small. Much of the active part of the army was sent to garrison and fight overseas, leaving too few at home for island defence. It may be thought that the 'wooden walls' should have made a home army unnecessary, but a force of a certain size and mobility was needed to compel an enemy to make substantial and visible preparations so that the fleet would have time to be on guard.

Ships, dockyards, and supplies

The first category everyone looks at when comparing navies is warships. Undoubtedly, building warships signifies an aspiration to naval power and good ones were an expensive capital investment: a new 74-gun ship fully outfitted might typically cost almost £50,000 in the 1780s; the largest factory in Britain in the 1790s cost £5,000. Yet, aside from procuring the money, new construction was one of the easier naval challenges to meet. Designs could be copied, foreign shipwrights could be enticed to immigrate, timber imported, and so on. For instance, under the direction of Colbert France built up the largest battle-fleet in Europe in less than fifteen years; he obtained some ships from the Dutch, but France soon became self-sufficient in naval construction.

A ship of war was a wasting asset. At mid-century French naval authorities estimated an average lifetime of a ship of the line to be about twelve years. The average for British ships was somewhat longer, but regular repair was crucial. The sustaining of fleet numbers required not only steady maintenance of the ships laid up in reserve but a programme for regular replacement; this seems to have been a more difficult challenge than building a fleet in the first place.

Throughout the largely peaceful period from 1714 to 1739 the British maintained their fleet (active and reserve) at about 85 per cent of the wartime level of 1713, and did so even though there was no challenge from a rival. The French and Dutch battle-fleets had each been larger than the English in 1690, but there was hardly anything left of those French ships by 1720 and the Dutch navy was becoming a mere shadow of its great past. In the mid-1720s the Spanish laid foundations for a modern navy and built new ships, but France's fleet was preserved chiefly by maintenance. Of forty-seven French ships of the line listed in 1739, only thirteen were built after 1724; ten dated from the reign of Louis XIV. Because ships had not been discarded 'the French faced a block obsolescence problem'.[5] All the while, the government of Great Britain, supported by parliament and public, kept the Royal Navy strong. The impression given by histories published a century ago that the British navy fell into decay during the period from 1714 to 1739 was never supported by direct research and is completely false. In terms of relative numbers and tonnage there was no time during the century when British preponderance was greater. Jan Glete has described the period as 'the age of uncontested British naval supremacy'.[6]

It is often stipulated that French hull design was superior to British. French designs were somewhat influenced by theoretical science whereas British were derived from experience, yet when all factors are considered it is not clear that French designs were superior. What may be said with a measure of certainty is that French designers achieved their main goal: superior speed. Speed was only one concern of the British, who, except in the case of smaller cruisers, never lost sight of seaworthiness and endurance. Still, it is said, British designs were too conservative, hemmed in by 'establishments'. The establishments called for ships of 100, 90, 80, 70, 60 and 50 guns. The eighty-gun three-deckers were an absurdity; they were not large enough to keep the lowest tier sufficiently above water (perhaps the chief defect of the establishment system was what might be called an idolatry of round numbers). All in all, the British fleet suffered not so much from inferior design as from the conservatism inherent in a policy guided by a mandate for replacement. Too many three-decked ships, so much desired in the Anglo-Dutch wars, were preserved during the long period of peace; in 1740 they accounted for 44 per cent of British tonnage of ships of the line.[7] In the war that ensued their tremendous firepower was not really needed, and they were less seaworthy, less manoeuvrable, expensive to fit out and, perhaps worst of all, required lots of seamen (only one new three-decked ship was actually launched by war's end in 1748). Availability of useful sizes of ships mattered greatly, but hull design as a factor in naval success has been historically overemphasised.

When the great maritime contest of the century commenced in the 1740s, the French navy was at a marked disadvantage with respect to docks and dockyards. In 1739 the British navy had a total of sixteen dry-docks in six yards. The French navy had three in three yards – none at Toulon where the range of tide was insufficient to enable a dock to drain. Dry-docks allowed a reserve fleet to be more easily surveyed and

[5] Bourland, 1978: 172; Glete, 1993: I, 257. [6] Glete, 1993: I, 257.
[7] Based on Glete's figures (1993: I, 260).

maintained with less stress on the hull than careening entailed. Size was just one reason why the British fleet needed more docks; the main reason was that it was an active fleet that kept the sea and experienced a great deal of wear and tear. The wartime reality may be gauged by figures dated 3 November 1762: at that moment 305 British warships were in commission, fitted for sea, and manned (total 83,871 men); only fifty-eight of these were in port (11,455 men).[8] Such a ratio was characteristic of the British navy in the middle and later years of every war, and it is not surprising that cleaning, refitting and repairing held priority in British dockyards in time of war. A long-standing British tendency to invest in dockyard improvements escalated to a strong commitment after 1760. Money that might have been spent on shipbuilding was devoted to new docks, storehouses and roperies built of stone – very expensive but they lasted longer than ships and mitigated the consequences of a serious fire.[9] For a navy accustomed to keeping the sea, improved dockyards were a force multiplier, enabling an existing number of ships and seamen to perform more service at sea. After 1740 few new ships were built in royal dockyards; progress on them was slow, their main purpose being to employ the workforce in moments of slack demand for repairs.

Nearly all French ships of the line continued to be built in royal yards. The demands upon those yards for making repairs were considerably lower. It is an important fact that, until 1778, French naval power was commonly expressed either in the form of a 'fleet in being' in a protected harbour, ready for sea (or at least giving that appearance) or as a fleet in waiting – waiting for trade, supplies and reinforcements to assemble, and for an opportune time to take the convoy to sea with a chance of avoiding British interception. During the war of 1778–83 the French Atlantic fleet was much more active than in the preceding wars, and the serious inadequacies of the yard at Brest were exposed.[10]

Usually, the British navy found that it needed to add new ships in wartime, often in a hurry, but they were almost all built in merchant yards. The most serious emergency came in the later 1770s after the government had failed to match the vigorous shipbuilding programmes of France and Spain. The merchant yards were Britain's salvation. They had long been the main source of the navy's frigates, but on this occasion ships of the line were also needed. Between 1777 and 1782 inclusive, 44 out of 48 of the ships of 74 and 64 guns that were ordered for the British navy were assigned to merchant contracts.[11] These private shipyards that

[8] Gradish, 1980: 42, 46, 53.
[9] Coad, 1981: 17–21; 1983: 352–61.
[10] Meyer and Acerra, 1994: 133.
[11] Baugh, in Black and Woodfine, 1988: 153–4.

could build not only frigates but sturdy ships of the line were a very considerable naval asset.

The French dockyards had to worry about shortages of timber, masts, hemp and tar to a degree that, after 1714, the British did not. Wartime interruption of the French navy's supply of masts from the primary source, the Baltic, was sometimes very serious. It used to be thought that shortages of timber and masts troubled Britain as much as France, but by superior water transport and commercial advantages the British always solved their problems while the French could not. There were uneven deliveries of timber and naval stores to French dockyards even in peacetime, thanks to bouts of monetary starvation and clogged administration,[12] but in wartime the interruptions imposed by British seapower were troublesome. Only the peculiar political and strategic circumstances of the American Revolutionary War enabled the French navy to avoid the constraints experienced by its dockyards in the middle years of the Seven Years War.[13]

The French navy experienced, as the British navy did not, a shortage of heavy guns, particularly in the 1750s. During the long peace the number of French forges had diminished through lack of demand. Wartime losses in the 1740s coincided with incompetence of a great contractor to produce a crisis. A French entrepreneur bought 350 captured guns back from the British and sold them to the navy, but this was a meagre remedy. In May 1755 only nine of eighty-one new guns sent by the contractor to Rochefort dockyard were accepted for service. By 1759, however, after high-level intervention that brought in the army's ordnance expert, the problem was solved.[14] Operationally, the ordnance shortages of the first half of the Seven Years War were masked by the use of ships of the line *en flûte* as troop transports and by forbearing to send battle-squadrons to sea.

Institutional benefits of peacetime active service

During the period 1714–39 the British navy was active in protecting trade, and large squadrons were deployed a dozen times or more for diplomatic purposes. In the same period the French navy's seagoing activity was minimal. There was not enough sea service to encourage piecemeal administrative improvements; having missed the opportunity in the first half of the century, the French navy became susceptible in the second half to surges of reform that often involved sudden changes of direction. In the

[12] Pritchard, 1987: 165–7. [13] Bamford, 1956: 64–7, 207–11.
[14] Pritchard, 1987: 143–59.

British case the first half of the century marked the epoch in which the navy's institutional arrangements, under the guidance of practical experience, matured; after 1750 the challenge was to learn to use them more intelligently.[15]

Lack of sea service hurt the French naval officer corps, the problem being most severe in the decades after 1714.[16] It was not simply or even mainly a question of shipboard training. Unless younger officers had a chance to distinguish themselves at sea, positively or negatively, factors other than professional capability and dedication would inevitably dominate promotion. Such factors influenced promotion in the British navy too, but there were many more instances where professional merit could be noticed and advanced. The diminishing number of experienced French officers after 1714 produced in higher ranks 'a veritable gerontocracy', and during the war of 1744–8 a number of squadron commanders died on board.[17] Not surprisingly, the French navy needed more lieutenants with sea experience in the mid-1740s; it recruited them from commercial service, but institutional barriers limited their advancement.

The well-known divisions within the French officer corps stemmed mainly from path of entry; the tentacular connections of distinguished 'naval families' were prominent, but divisions also arose from geography. When the much-favoured duc d'Enville, who had spent what little there was of his active career in the Mediterranean galley service, arrived at Brest to command a major expedition in 1746, he had had no acquaintance with the Atlantic sailing navy nor with more than a handful of people connected with it.[18] Yet, aside from a tendency to provoke bitter finger-pointing after operational failures, not just between individual officers but groups of them conscious of special privilege or lack of it, the structure of the officer corps did not constitute a serious naval liability. Many French commanders were brave and brilliant (and some British commanders were the opposite). With few exceptions their duty was to shield a convoy or military expedition, to avoid combat if possible and to evade enemy forces – the last item sometimes involving brilliant feats of piloting executed in extremely hazardous situations. To be sure, the most energetic, resourceful and effective theatre commanders of the 1740s were Mahé de la Bourdonnais and Bouvet de Lozier, both risen in the service of the

15 After many years spent with this subject the present writer has reached the conclusion that the British navy achieved its institutional basis of success by 1750; see Baugh, in Hill, 1995: 156.

16 Meyer and Acerra, 1994: 95.

17 Vergé-Franceschi, 2000: 91–2; 1997: 253–69; 1991: 219; Pritchard, 1995: 31–2.

18 Pritchard, 1995: 29–32, 56.

French East India Company, but the challenges they faced were of an unusual kind.[19]

It has been observed that the French officers corps 'reacted to events that it did not influence'.[20] There was no central institution whereby such influence could be formally exercised. The functions of the Minister of Marine and Colonies did not begin to match those of the Board of Admiralty in London, which through an effective secretariat received copious correspondence from captains and lieutenants as well as flag officers. The Admiralty was thus in a position to guide the policies of its subordinate boards by information received directly from the sea service, not just the information reported by those boards. For the same reason, the First Lord could give well informed advice to the cabinet members who decided matters of strategy. In France, all this seems to have happened informally at best. The avenues of communication for naval planning were personal, subject to hazards of accident and ignorance. Britain's Admiralty office was not an expensive institution – its annual cost equivalent perhaps to that of two ships of the line – but it was much more than an administrative authority; it was a two-way channel of communication for officers of the sea service as well as a naval information centre. If, as the modern age holds, information is vital to success, the absence of such an institution put the French navy at a serious disadvantage.

Manning

Recruiting seamen in wartime was the most worrying and intractable of all eighteenth-century naval problems. None of the powers solved it. The French and Spanish monarchies created registries of all seafaring men, the aim being to make a listed reserve available for the navy, but British parliaments rejected proposals for such an arrangement. The register enabled the French to get a considerable naval force manned sooner than the British could. Although Britain's merchant marine provided a much larger national pool of seamen to draw upon, there was no system for bringing these skilled men into the navy other than the slow, dreadful method of impressment. At the end of about two years of war, however, the French and Spanish navies lost their manning advantage, while the British was starting to build up the large total it required (along the way both navies lost thousands to disease). In the long naval wars of the eighteenth century France faced a problem to which there was no

[19] When admiring these two, however, Lacour-Gayet (1902: 190–206) pointedly contrasted the performances of other French admirals of that decade.

[20] Pritchard, 1987: 55.

solution. Because of the heavy requirements the system of classes, which had aimed at allowing merchant seamen to take turns in performing naval service, was overwhelmed and had to be abandoned. The registry organisation became an agency of conscription; rivers were scoured far upstream to gather in boat and bargemen.[21] Lacking sea experience and gunnery skills, such men could not compare to the landsmen who had spent years in the British navy, and the well-known British combat advantage of faster rate of fire thus became even more pronounced.

There is not space here to give the problem of naval manning the treatment it deserves, but two broad questions that are of special relevance to economic history should be asked. First, how did the British manage to succeed as well as they did (setting aside the problem of initial mobilisation, which they never conquered). Second, did a basic insufficiency of seamen represent an absolute barrier to French and Spanish naval aspirations?

To appreciate Britain's relative success one must grasp the full measure of its problem. Statistics indicate a total of 58,231 British seamen employed just before the Seven Years War (17,369 naval) and a total of 115,641 (74,711 naval) during the war.[22] These are annual averages; by war's end the naval figure was over 80,000. If upon the outbreak of war the navy had simply tried to co-opt the existing merchant pool, few seamen would have been left to carry on Britain's vast seaborne trade. Without a continuing high level of trade, support for the war would have diminished and war finances would have faltered. The pattern of the preceding century, where merchant vessels could be manned by men discharged between campaigning seasons, no longer operated; the navy was now mobilised year round. Yet, as the figures show, the total number of seamen increased enormously.

How did the British do it? Partly by allowing foreign seamen to sign on to British merchant ships (the Navigation laws prohibiting this were suspended in time of war). Yet it needs to be recognised that the navy itself trained up large numbers of seamen by welcoming able-bodied landsmen. A desperate need to acquire some skilled seamen (without whom navigation was unsafe and landsmen could not have been trained) has obscured this important fact.[23] One other point should be mentioned: whereas losses from disease were irreparable, British seamen who deserted

[21] Pritchard, 1987: 71–88; this is a detailed and informative chapter, but while accepting Pritchard's point that more reliable pay could have mitigated the problem during the mid-century years, one must question whether pay could have had much effect on the problem of the 1780s.

[22] Starkey, in Fisher and Nordvik, 1990: 29.

[23] Rodger, 1986: 155–9; Rodger, in Duffy, 1992: 82–92.

usually wound up in the British merchant service, until the American Revolution.

In answering the second question it should be noted that the French government tried to mitigate the national shortage of seamen by allowing neutral shipping to carry France's wartime trade. Despite all the difficulties, this plan, decreed in 1756, had the effect of reducing demand. It was also aimed at reducing losses of seamen to British capture.[24] Yet these losses remained very large. An account of May 1757 showed that of the 47,000 French seamen in the Atlantic sphere, 19,000 were in the navy and 10,000 were prisoners of war in England. At war's end there were 25,793 unexchanged French mariners in British hands. Such losses were greatest in the Seven Years War, when the impact of British naval power was greatest, but in all three wars from the 1740s to 1780s the French lost many more seamen to capture than the British did.[25]

Thus, the French manning problem was directly affected by British seapower. When peace came in 1763 the French fisheries and merchant marine recovered, but merchant vessels were becoming more efficient so the number of French seamen scarcely increased, remaining at about 60,000.[26] In the American Revolutionary War the French kept launching ships, but towards the end they could not be manned. When the French government sought peace in 1782 shortage of seamen joined exhaustion of finances as a key consideration.[27] Of course, the Spanish navy was in alliance. Statistics show that until 1790 Spain managed to man its large navy without undue strain by use of a coercive register,[28] but how well trained those men were is another issue.

The challenge of distant deployments

Throughout the century the theatre of prime naval importance was composed of the Channel, its western approaches, and the bay of Biscay. It will be considered in the next section. The remaining principal zones were the Mediterranean, Indian Ocean and Caribbean.

The geographical advantages of France and Spain in the Mediterranean over Britain were considerably offset by the bases Britain established at Gibraltar (1704) and Port Mahon (1708). When Britain had reason to send a large fleet in the 1740s, Port Mahon proved to be indispensable. By the 1750s, however, the region had declined from its former high importance, thanks to the European diplomatic realignment of 1756 and a

[24] Pares, 1936: 359–75.
[25] Le Goff, 1990: 225; Pritchard, 1987: 82; Le Goff, in Acerra *et al.*, 1985: esp. 108.
[26] Le Goff, in Van Royen *et al.*, 1997: 287–387. [27] Dull, 1975: 316.
[28] See Phillips, 2001: 436–40; also Phillips, in Van Royen *et al.*, 1997: 334–6.

declining presence of British shipping.[29] While Britain continued to send warships to the Mediterranean after Port Mahon was lost to a surprise French assault in 1756, British strategists waited for peace negotiations to recover it, turning their attention elsewhere.

The Indian Ocean became a region of naval contention from the 1740s onwards, when France and Britain deployed naval squadrons to support their respective East India companies. In the early 1750s a dry-dock capable of receiving a fifty-gun ship was built at Bombay. Larger docks were completed in 1762 and 1773, both capable of receiving 74-gun ships of the line. As Admiral Sir Edward Hughes remarked in 1784 after wartime experience of the Bombay base, it was the only place where the ships of his squadron could 'be even properly refitted, much less repaired'. Suffren, his opponent, like La Bourdonnais before him, was a tenacious and resourceful commander, but he lacked the nearby repair facility that was available to Hughes. The dockyard at Bombay, under management of the East India Company, with masts and other naval stores on hand, 'expert native artificers', and a large, well-defended harbour, was a formidable asset; early in the next century British warships durably built of teak were constructed there.[30]

Any account of the French navy in the Caribbean after 1714 must emphasise its absence. Although French sugar and coffee production and profitability grew substantially at Martinique and Guadeloupe, and very rapidly at Saint-Domingue after 1730, the flag of the French navy did not follow. This trade speedily became extremely valuable, not least because so much of the produce was re-exported to other parts of Europe; by mid-century it accounted for half of total French external trade.[31] Yet cruisers were not stationed in the islands except sporadically, nor was any step taken toward constructing a Caribbean repair base to serve naval needs. To be sure, until 1744 there was no urgency: the British navy looked after suppressing the pirates, and Spanish *guarda costas* rarely troubled French vessels. For emergencies there were private repair facilities. Still, it is amazing that nothing was done to establish a royal yard in the Caribbean until 1787 (at Fort Royal, Martinique).[32]

In contrast, the British established naval bases at Antigua and Jamaica about 1730. Defence of trade against the *guarda costas* was the immediate reason, but it is obvious that the Admiralty expected these bases to be permanent. Careening wharves with specialised capstans were built, essential not just for cleaning hulls, but destroying the 'worm' (*teredo navalis*) and thus allowing ships to remain in the region for two or three

[29] Davis, 1962b: 17. [30] Lambert, in Digby, Bowen and Lincoln, 2002.
[31] Blackburn, 1997: 445. [32] Vergé-Franceschi, 2000: 232.

years. Enlargements and improvements to the repair and storage facilities at these bases continued throughout the century. Equally important was reliable victualling. In this sphere an important advantage was the ease and low cost of obtaining food from British North America. Although provisions spoiled rapidly in the West Indies, a genuine effort was nevertheless made to keep reserves in store, whether the responsibility lay with a private contractor or the victualling department. The British navy in the West Indies never experienced desperate food shortages of the kind that so often forced French squadrons to return home.[33]

In view of this markedly superior logistical support, why did British naval power achieve so little in the Caribbean until the later years of the Seven Years War? Failed attempts at conquest, beginning with the huge debacle at Cartagena in 1741, account for the impression of futility. The origins of these failures lay in England. Mounting a successful assault on a Spanish or French stronghold required a large combined military and naval force. Preparations were complex and always delayed; the ships were overcrowded because losses to disease were anticipated; some of the men, many of them impressed and recently congregated, became ill before leaving; the voyage down the Channel was often halted by adverse winds; and the transatlantic passage by convoy was slow (the British habit of stopping at Madeira for wine made the time of passage about ten days longer than the French). Upon arrival there was an understandable temptation to give the men coming down with scurvy a chance to recuperate at Antigua or Jamaica; there they might contract dysentery or some other tropical disease (in this regard the bases may actually have done harm). Departure from England commonly occurred in the spring. Thus the expedition would end up attacking on the eve of the rainy season with its mosquitoes and be defeated by yellow fever. Not without cause did the Spaniards of the Caribbean speak of yellow fever as the 'patriotic fever'.[34] The keys to success from 1759 onwards lay in leaving England in the severe weather of November or December with a good plan, in bringing some of the troops and victuals from British North America, and in attacking without delay.[35]

Yet it is a mistake to suppose that the history of British seapower in the Caribbean prior to 1759 was simply one of failure. In the wars of 1744–8 and 1756–63 British warships on station not only ruined French inter-island trade but often stifled French privateers. The price of

[33] Buchet, 1991: II, 905–18, 1,067–83; Buchet, 1999: 191.
[34] Buchet, 1997b: 191.
[35] All this was brought to light and laid out by Christian Buchet in 1991 and summarised by him in Buchet, 1994. The role of disease in the sieges of Louisbourg and Havana is compared in McNeill, 1985: 80–105.

French pre-war neglect was evident in 1744. Within months the governor at Martinique was reporting to the Minister of Marine that the nearby waters were swarming with British privateers (many of them from North America) and begged him to station a few cruisers and establish a repair base. The minister, the comte de Maurepas, provided neither; he used what ships he had for transatlantic convoys. At Saint-Domingue, which depended upon sea communications between its regions, nothing involving both bulk and value dared to move.[36] The principal limitation on French naval presence in the islands was inadequate victualling. Victualled at home for seven months without prospect of resupply in the islands (as had been the case before 1714), the convoy escorts of the 1740s were obliged to return to Europe almost immediately. In the Seven Years War arrangements were made, at great hazard and expense, to enable these warships to linger for three or four months, but French commanders found excuses for not cruising against the enemy.

During the wars of 1744–8 and 1756–63 the British stationed forces in the Caribbean were not large enough to undertake systematically the mission of intercepting incoming convoys from France. Besides, the commanders-in-chief were never in doubt that their first responsibility was to protect trade; this was spelled out in their orders and reinforced by the propensity of island assemblies and the West India interest in the House of Commons to bring them under investigation.[37] In these mid-century wars, the French convoys were seriously harassed by the British navy at the time of departure (as will be seen in the next section). This was not the case in the American Revolutionary War, when the British could not inhibit French departures but did maintain a considerable force in the Caribbean. In that war the French brought large naval forces to the West Indies and went on the offensive, but their operations depended absolutely on the incoming convoys that brought troops and supplies from France each spring. Again and again, the British West Indian squadrons failed to intercept these convoys as they approached Martinique from the Atlantic. In each case, the particular cause of failure was slightly different, but they all may be traced to a lack of strategic resolve and care.[38] As a result, much of the logistical advantage that enabled British forces to maintain a presence in the islands was thrown away.

[36] Taillemite, 1988: 139–49. The requests of early August 1744 were made by Governor Champigny. His successor, Caylus, repeated the request for stationed cruisers; just two of them, he claimed, would make a great difference. For Saint-Domingue, see Pares, 1936: 301.

[37] Pares, 1936: 320.

[38] Jonathan Dull highlights this important series of failures; see Dull, 1975: 283.

The transformation of strategy

From 1715 to 1745, whenever the British battle-fleet was deployed, its purpose was deterrence or containment. Fleets were sent to particular locations, often within confined seas. Whether assisting diplomacy in time of peace or defending trade and preventing invasion in time of war, naval strategy was reactive. To this pattern there were three exceptions: the sending of a large squadron to the West Indies in support of an assault on Cartagena in 1740–1; a fleet in the Mediterranean in the 1740s to help the Austrians in Italy by disrupting Spanish supply lines; an expedition to capture Louisbourg in 1745 (though this was planned and carried out by New Englanders, aided by a few ships of the Royal Navy already in American waters). Many of the twenty-nine ships of the line at Cartagena remained too long in the Caribbean after the assault was abandoned, causing temporary naval weakness in European waters, but naval strength was soon restored both in the Mediterranean and at home, and after the Jacobite rebellion was crushed in April 1746 the Admiralty adopted the strategy of the Western Squadron. The aim was to keep a strong battle-squadron cruising off the French Atlantic coast for as long as possible. In due course the success of this strategy generated apprehensions that profoundly altered European power politics.

Autumn 1746 marks the beginning of the Western Squadron strategy. Rear-admiral George Anson commanded the squadron and repeatedly took it back to sea from Plymouth despite increasingly harsh weather.[39] His principal object at the time was to intercept a returning French squadron – always the hardest thing to do, even in good weather, and he failed. The following spring, however, with the squadron poised in readiness at Plymouth, reliable intelligence was received of the imminent departure of a large French convoy. Anson hurried to Plymouth, raced southward and overtook his quarry off Cape Ortegal. In the resulting battle of Ortegal (First Battle of Cape Finisterre in British usage) he destroyed the naval escort, capturing six of the line and three East Indiamen. Admiral Edward Hawke's mission was similar when he took the Western Squadron to sea in early August. Hawke's cruise was a true test. He stayed at sea until mid-October, when, by strategic cunning, he brought about a major encounter.[40] In this Second Battle of Cape Finisterre (fought in the longitude of that cape but about 300 miles north of it) Hawke's squadron captured six out of the eight escorting ships of

[39] Some would place the beginning in 1745, but the squadron then was too weak and too easily distracted from remaining off the coast of France; see Richmond, 1920: III, 5–22, 38–42.

[40] Hawke's strategic imagination is displayed in Mackay, 1965: 54–68.

the line; the other two, heavily damaged, turned back, leaving the huge outbound convoy to proceed unprotected.

Successes of this kind were uncommon, not just because France's avenue to the open Atlantic was 400 miles wide, but because the French often waited in port until sickness or adverse weather forced the British squadron to leave. The strategy did not attempt blockade; it was expected that enemy warships and convoys would sail.[41] In fact, the Western Squadron was not really stationed; it moved north and south according to intelligence received. By remaining well offshore it not only enjoyed greater safety but kept the enemy in the dark as to its location, an important attribute of its power. Under its protection, from 1758 to 1761 smaller warships and privateers lurked inshore, thereby tightening the watch on the coast so that the strategy progressively amounted to blockade.

The Western Squadron took a terrible beating from storms, and the crews fell down with scurvy. The nearest naval base was Plymouth, only developed within the last half-century.[42] A force at least one and a half times that of the squadron at sea was required so that piecemeal detachments could be made for repairs and refreshment. In short, there was great difficulty in carrying out the strategy and therefore in resolving to do it. Yet despite the suffering from and losses to sickness, the battering of storms and the regularity of disappointment, the strategy was not abandoned; in fact, it was reinstituted in 1755 even before war was declared. One man deserves the credit for this, Anson, the only active seaman on the Board of Admiralty in 1746 and First Lord in 1755. A steady, almost stolid, man, he was convinced that a Western Squadron should be kept cruising as many months of the year as possible, whatever it took.

The reason is clear: beyond argument this was the most efficient strategy available, because it could accomplish so many goals at once. Interception of outbound convoys and expeditionary forces, or at least destruction of the naval escort, obviated the need for deploying strong squadrons across the oceans, whether to the Caribbean, North America or East Indies. And, given the French navy's lack of a commodious safe harbour in the Channel, the strategy made a strong Channel fleet (or 'Eastern Squadron') unnecessary. The above attributes are widely recognised. Less often remarked but realised by the Admiralty at the time was the benefit of possibly welcoming and shielding an incoming British trade convoy before French predators could reach it. Moreover,

41 Ryan, in Acerra *et al.*, 1985, is tremendously informative, but its theme, 'the blockade of Brest', is not appropriate to the mid-century formative years of the strategy.

42 The best discussion of the development of the Western Squadron is Duffy, in Duffy, 1992.

the squadron cruised near the common track of trade headed for Lisbon, the Mediterranean and the Caribbean. Its presence deterred French commerce raiders from attacking in squadrons (as they had done with such notable success in the time of Queen Anne). Dramatic and massive trade losses were thus rendered a thing of the past and piecemeal losses were diminished. What is too easily forgotten in historical discussion of the Western Squadron is its role in protecting trade; the Admiralty's concern about this was intense, since it had reason to fear that a committee might be appointed by parliament to take over the assignment of cruisers.[43]

Yet the most significant attribute of the Western Squadron for the future was its utility as an offensive weapon. By being positioned well offshore, it might have the good fortune to intercept richly laden incoming French merchant vessels before they picked up warnings to evade. But its primary offensive function was disruption of convoy departures. It curtailed, by interception or prolonged delay, metropolitan France's ability to trade with its plantation colonies and to defend them from British conquest. To the customary naval missions of defence of the realm and trade, the strategy added a war-winning component.

The impact on Europe

It may be difficult to accept that a dozen and a half ships of the line cruising off the French coast could have set in motion a major shift in the assumptions upon which European power politics rested. Of course, the new British naval strategy did not stand alone but worked in combination with an ever-increasing belief throughout Europe in the importance of seaborne commerce to a state's financial power. When France's plantation trade fell under threat of annihilation, the monarchy awakened to its importance. It could no longer ignore the menace of British naval power, now highly visible.

Yet at first, to all appearances the court seemed unconcerned when the news of the October 1747 defeat reached Fontainebleau. According to the marquis d'Argenson the episode was treated as a joke![44] True or not, there was official silence. All this might be taken as indicating that the French monarchy did not much care about the fate of its navy. But in naval circles the reality was quickly perceived: most of the warships lost in 1747 were of recent construction, and so an ambitious naval building programme – eight ships of the line a year – was adopted in 1748. But the recovery was

[43] In the early 1740s there were stirrings in the House of Commons to reinstitute something like the Cruisers and Convoys Act of 1708.
[44] D'Argenson, 1857: V, 96–100.

slow, because twenty-seven older ships had to be declared unfit, which meant that only thirty of the line, out of sixty-nine in 1744, remained of use. Although the building programme was carried on vigorously for the next three years, it was temporarily choked off by a government financial crisis in 1752.[45]

A great naval and colonial contest with Britain lay only three years in the future. Both the British and French governments were unyielding with regard to unsettled colonial issues, and these proved to be the immediate cause of the hostilities that erupted in 1755. Although Louis XV soon allowed France to be drawn into a German war, popular opinion continued to focus on the naval and colonial contest with Britain. There was inaugurated in France a patriotism that was national in character, and distinctly anglophobic. England was the 'new Carthage'.[46] After 1757 this patriotism was sorely tested by repeated naval disappointments but it remained alive and found expression near war's end in the form of real currency. Of the twenty-two French ships of the line launched between 1762 and 1768 to restore the French navy's losses only five were paid for by the state treasury. Funds for the rest came from direct grants provided by provincial authorities, cities, chambers of commerce, bankers and financiers. It was all coordinated by the leading minister, the duc de Choiseul, who well knew that the treasury was empty.[47] In the peacetime years that followed, Louis XV's German war was regarded as a great mistake and Spain came to be considered the principal ally. The French monarchy now looked to the oceans.[48]

Although the French reacted first and continued to react most earnestly, the new naval strategy entailed further requirements that affected much of Europe. These requirements arose because the French, conscious of the extreme vulnerability of their shipping when war recommenced, turned to neutral vessels, chiefly Dutch. At first, Dutch vessels happily carried naval stores from the Baltic to France and were soon bringing French plantation goods across the Atlantic. Seeing the offensive aspect of their naval strategy thus thwarted, the British devised a legal formula in 1756 for authorising the arrest of such vessels and confiscation of their cargoes.[49] The neutral countries were incensed, but none had sufficient naval force to prevent the British from doing it, and in any case, a nation that contested British seapower invited economic suffering. Before the late 1740s the British navy had been used in ways that

[45] Meyer and Acerra, 1994: 100–3; Pritchard, 1987: 126–7.
[46] Dziembowski, 1998: 51–110.
[47] Meyer and Acerra, 1994: 114; Scott, 1979: 17–35.
[48] Baugh, 1998: 14–15. [49] Pares, 1938: esp. 180–204.

aided some European states while afflicting others. The new strategic emphasis by requiring the detention of neutral shipping provoked universal resentment, however, and the more successful the strategy became the more it appeared that Britain would end by monopolising all seaborne commerce. The resulting financial supremacy, it was anxiously imagined, would probably render Britain the 'arbiter of Europe'.

To the French court and public the prospect of all this became increasingly unbearable. The French building programme of the 1760s, despite substantial losses to British capture during the war, narrowed Britain's lead. Nevertheless, on the eve of war in May 1775 the British navy outnumbered the French 95 to 63 in ships of the line and 75 to 37 in frigates. At this point, however, the British navy suffered a catastrophe, self-inflicted by a government that was so intent in 1775–7 on militarily crushing the American Revolution that it utterly neglected the fleet. The French government, guided by the comte de Vergennes, seized the moment: there was a cascade of new construction. No less than twenty French ships of the line and frigates were launched in 1778, the year that war with Britain commenced, and many more followed.[50] Even so, Vergennes knew that France alone could not cope with the British navy.[51] He looked immediately to Spain.

The rise of the Spanish navy in the eighteenth century began quite early. The truly permanent foundations were laid in the 1720s under the guidance of José Patiño. At that time the main object was to support campaigns in Sicily, Sardinia and Italy, but in the 1730s quarrels over British trading access to the Spanish Empire culminating in the war of 1739–48 shifted the emphasis to the Atlantic and West Indies, where it stayed. When the war ended the peace-loving Ferdinand VI (1746–59) authorised his leading minister, José de Carvajal y Lancaster, to pursue an ambitious naval build-up.[52] The purpose was not revenge against Britain, but to provide an instrument strong enough to secure independence from both British and French high-handedness (Madrid had a long-standing mistrust of French naval 'help' in defending its American empire). Carvajal relaxed the strict colonial mercantilism that had been hitherto favoured. This benefited Britain and he was proud of his ancient English lineage, but his policy owed nothing to sentiment: he saw the strict policy as fruitless, expensive and unnecessary.[53] The anglophobic Carlos III (1759–88) overthrew Carvajal's policy, however, and encouraged what may be

50 Meyer and Acerra, 1994: 119. 51 Dull, 1975: 97–101.

52 Black, 1991: 252. Six ships a year were to be built in Spain, three at Havana. The schedule at Havana was not carried out; in the three preceding decades, however, twenty-seven ships of the line had been built there (Inglis, 1985: 52).

53 McLachlan, 1938: 457–77.

termed an enlightened mercantilism.[54] The revenues from Spanish America rose, but the naval cost of the policy consumed them. Nevertheless, without those revenues the vast fleet that by 1775 actually matched the tonnage of the French navy could not have been built.[55]

Back in the 1720s and 1730s Ambassador Benjamin Keene at Madrid had repeatedly advised his government not to take Patiño's navy at face value,[56] but in 1779, when Spain went to war alongside France, Britain's situation was extremely serious. Combined Bourbon naval tonnage was nearly 40 per cent greater than the British.[57] If the French and Spanish navies had cooperated better and Spain's had been manned with more skilled men (always a big 'if' during the century), Britain might not have been able to catch up. Even with the timely introduction of copper sheathing – a significant force multiplier by reducing dockyard visits[58] – Britain did not have enough ships to maintain a Western Squadron, and British strategy fell into reactive confusion. The British navy finally recovered superiority in 1782 (though total Bourbon tonnage remained larger). Vergennes, judging that France would run out of seamen and money before Britain did, pressured Carlos III into accepting peace.[59]

Yet the French and Spanish monarchies did not abandon the maritime struggle. It is not generally realised that large budgetary allocations for the French navy continued in the decade after 1783, notwithstanding the huge government debt that had resulted from the unprecedented level of naval expenditure during the war just ended. In 1787 the keepers of the purse reduced the maréchal de Castries' budget, citing a financial crisis (that, as posterity knows, led to the French Revolution). Dissatisfied by this explanation, he quit. Still, in 1790 French warship tonnage was 20 per cent greater than in 1780. As Jan Glete has observed, here is 'a major political mystery – an enormous peace-time shipbuilding program undertaken by an insolvent regime which faced political ruin'.[60] Funds were also lavished on the Spanish navy at this time; in 1790 the combined French and Spanish navies retained a 30 per cent tonnage superiority over the navy of Britain.[61] There can be only one rational explanation of the 'mystery': these Old Regime monarchies were thoroughly convinced that maritime commerce was the key to national power and understood that naval power was its necessary guarantor.

[54] Liss, 1983: 61–74, esp. 70.
[55] Barbier, 1984: 173, 179, 182, 188; Glete, 1993: I, 276. [56] Black, 1991: 243–8.
[57] The 40 per cent figure is for 1780; Glete, 1993: I, 276.
[58] Rodger, 1993: 296; Knight, 1987: lvi.
[59] Dull, 1975: 279, 304, 316–7, 321–4, 327, 334. [60] Glete, 1993: 277.
[61] Glete, 1993: I, 276. During the period of peace after 1783 practically all European states with sea access were building up their navies.

Conclusion

Although the British put a strong, intelligent effort into keeping up and improving the efficiency of their navy after 1783, it seems possible that the trend was not in their favour. They were undoubtedly losing the shipbuilding contest to the Bourbon combination, and under the guidance of Castries the French navy was improving its dockyards and reforming its administration. Louis XVI's interest in the maritime sphere was unmistakable. The escalation of naval rivalry would have continued if financial catastrophe and revolution had not ended it.

Nevertheless, one must doubt whether the French navy, even if abetted by the Spanish, could have overtaken the British. In the 1780s, when important French improvements and reforms were finally being advanced, the British navy's material and institutional advantages had been in place for a long time. Those advantages stemmed from steadiness of financial support, commitment to maintaining a large reserve of seamen through peacetime enforcement of the Navigation Acts, and an assumption that there would be extensive and sustained active service at sea. For a century, governments of Great Britain had been unwaveringly committed to these fundamentals of naval policy, however painful the cost. The singular exception was registered in the mid- and later 1770s, as noted above, and when naval superiority was lost, the Admiralty and its theatre commanders fell into strategic confusion.

The monarchies of France and Spain had lavished large sums on building great fleets, but their financial support was less consistent and assured, and their potential for augmenting the national supply of mariners was unequal to Britain's, a situation that could not be easily or quickly transformed. As for attaining a high level of active service at sea, such a policy invariably magnified naval expenditures, and it must be doubted whether the cost could have been sustained. A long and impressive list of well-designed warships was one thing; operating them was quite another. French naval expenditures in the American war were four times those in each of the two earlier wars, mainly for this reason.

Yet it was active service in peace and war, particularly in the first half of the century, which had provided the challenges that rendered the British navy superior as a fighting instrument. Its officers became more generally proficient, its seamen more numerous, better sailors, and better gunners, its dockyards and overseas bases more numerous and better equipped for making timely repairs, its guns more plentiful, its ordnance stores more regularly supplied even to distant stations. These were not easy advantages for the French or Spanish to overcome, and there is one more, ignorantly criticised in the popular historical literature yet probably the most important triumph of eighteenth-century British naval administration: the victualling service.

When Sir Edward Hawke caught the French fleet off Quiberon Bay in mid-November 1759, his Western Squadron had been at sea for five months with only two very brief returns to Plymouth and Torbay, yet there was scarcely a sick seaman aboard the squadron. Anson, the First Lord, had responded to Hawke's requests for fresh provisions with a resolve that would accept no excuses. Fresh beef and greens were sent by hired vessels to the rendezvous, the live cattle being hoisted aboard in slings in open sea. And yet the total cost of victualling the entire British navy for the year 1759 – everywhere, including the special expense of fresh beef – was scarcely greater than it had been in 1710 for a smaller, less active, less widely deployed navy.[62] Unfortunately, other men at the head of the Admiralty did not take the same pains to fend off scurvy as Anson and Hawke did for the Western Squadron in 1759. Partly for this reason, the achievement of the Victualling Board in the eighteenth century has been obscured, but its contribution is demonstrable[63] – a fact that should not be relegated to social or medical history but positioned at the very centre of strategic history, since British naval strategy relied so heavily upon remaining on station.

The accent on active service, on keeping the ships on station performing the tasks of seapower, had significant consequences for seaborne commerce and more broadly for success in Britain's eighteenth-century wars, which were in reality contests of financial attrition. The short-run commercial consequences of West Indian naval protection have been measured: during the wars of 1744–8 and 1756–63 British trade profits attained high levels while French suffered; during the American Revolutionary War, however, when British naval protection in the region was deficient, French profits held up while British descended to their lowest level of the century.[64] It is surely over the long run, however, that British naval power had the most significant commercial and economic effects. Whether reliable access to distant markets helped to foster British manufacturing efficiency is a controversial issue, but continuity in overseas trade furnished a considerable economic advantage and British trade suffered far less from wartime disruption during the century than French.

Clearly, French sugar and coffee (but not tobacco) dominated European markets, more than ever in the 1780s, but in general British export goods were widely favoured, as they had been throughout the

[62] Buchet, 1999: 330. The expense for victualling in 1758, when 70,000 men were fed instead of the 84,464 of 1759, was actually less than the expense for 1710.

[63] Buchet's research establishes this point.

[64] See Blackburn, 1997: 420, based on Ward, 1978: 204–7.

century. British manufacturers did not need a captive market in the thirteen colonies, a point that was plainly demonstrated when, notwithstanding the wartime alliance, French merchants and goods did not succeed in the American market. Spanish statesmen in the 1780s were perplexed by the high level of British (and now American) commercial penetration of their transatlantic empire.[65] It was not just superior manufacturing productivity that gave British goods their competitive advantage in transatlantic markets; it was relatively uninterrupted delivery, fewer shipping losses in time of war, reliable and familiar modes of credit and also the dynamic competitiveness of the multilateral British Atlantic commercial system – all of which were safeguarded by the Royal Navy.[66]

[65] Liss, 1983: 147–8.
[66] On the character of the British Atlantic system see Baugh, in Stone, 1994: 196–9.

Conclusions

Institutional change and British supremacy, 1650–1850: some reflections

Stanley L. Engerman

1 Introduction

We have all long been fascinated with understanding the 'European Miracle' and more specifically the 'British Miracle' of the seventeenth and eighteenth centuries. The growth of Britain from a small island with internal discord to become Europe's and the world's leading economic and political power by the start of the nineteenth century has had many explanations, reflecting in some measure the present-day views of economists, historians and other scholars. In the years after 1500, western European per capita incomes grew at a more rapid rate than did those in the rest of the world. Within Europe the Netherlands and Britain grew most rapidly before 1820, but at rates about one-fifth of the British rate between 1820 and 1870. With this early, but relatively slow, start it was in the period 1820–70 that British growth accelerated and its position improved vis-à-vis the rest of Europe, even western Europe, and the rest of the world. From a relative per capita income twice that of the rest of the world in 1700, the UK relative rose to 2.6 in 1820, and then to 3.7 in 1870. Thus, while British growth began to accelerate after 1700, it was not until the middle of the nineteenth century that Britain developed its large lead.[1] Not only did the British metropolis develop economically, but this growth occurred with the acquisition of an extensive overseas empire consisting of a rather diverse set of colonies.

It is not necessary here to try to catalogue the full set of explanations that have been given – numerous books and articles have clearly done

This is a revised version of the paper presented at the Madrid conference. I wish to thank the conference attendees for many useful comments and suggestions. In addition, I benefited from the insights of Patrick O'Brien, as I have done so many times in the past and will, hopefully, do so in the future.

[1] The growing importance of the United Kingdom as an economic power is indicated by its increased share of world GDP, from 2.9 per cent in 1700, to 5.2 per cent in 1820, and 9.1 per cent in 1870 (Maddison, 2001: 263). More dramatic, of course, was the rise in the share of world manufacturing output, from 1.9 per cent in 1750, to 9.5 per cent in 1830, and 19.9 per cent in 1860 (Bairoch, 1982). Note that in both cases the British lead grew most rapidly in the mid-nineteenth century.

that – but for present purposes we might note a present-day transition from an exclusive concentration on the role of narrowly defined economic factors to a focus including attention to cultural factors and societal institutions in providing the conditions leading to British economic growth. The claim that Britain grew because it had favourable natural resources with which to meet the needs of the Industrial Revolution has been replaced (or supplemented) by the argument that it was Britain's superior political and cultural institutions that permitted the process of industrialisation to take place.

The recent work in economic history on institutions owes much to the basic analysis of Douglass North.[2] To North, institutions represent humanly devised constraints on behaviour that structure human interactions by the providing of rules of the society as well as the incentives that shape economic, political and social organisation. Both formal rules and informal constraints influence transaction and production costs within society. Important aspects of rules include the defining and enforcement of property rights and the definition of enforcement provisions between two parties as well as those between these and potential third parties. Appropriate institutions reduce the costs of production and distribution and permit societies to gain from the presence of trade among individuals. Changing institutions may be relatively costless economically, but they may impose rather high costs in terms of political causes or consequences. Institutions, as human-imposed constraints, are not the only set of constraints faced within the economic sphere; there are also those due to nature, including climate, topography, soil type and demographic forces, which influence the amounts and types of outputs produced.

2 Historiographic issues

Before discussing the arguments relating to institutional change and British supremacy, I want to note several key issues underlying studies of economic growth. While this section will be rather general, the issues discussed have greatly influenced the manner in which the roles of institutions and of resources have been analysed.

This and the following sections will discuss four key questions:

1. Is it better, in the long run, for a society to have things easy or difficult?
2. Is it better, in the long run, to be a leader or a follower?
3. What is the role of cultural factors in economic development relative to environmental forces?

[2] See, in particular, North, 1990.

4. What is the relationship between institutions in the metropolis and institutions in the colonies?

Among the major questions of economic and historical interpretation, important for examining the past, is the question of whether it is better for a society to have had it easy (with lower costs of labour and of mineral resources, which yield high profits, but this positive aspect may be offset by the complacency or inertia that ease of meeting economic needs can lead to) or difficult (challenges may be a spur to achievement, technically and otherwise, but they could be too great to permit a favourable outcome).[3] Examples of these arguments about optimum challenges and responses can be found for many times and places including explanations for British and colonial economic growth. When, for example, does labour scarcity bring about an innovative society, as argued for the US by North, when does a challenge lead to different forms of labour organisation (such as serfdom, slavery or free labour), and when, instead, is labour scarcity too severe to permit any outcome except economic failure? In the nineteenth-century debate on the economic backwardness of the tropics, it was asked whether tropical lands provided too much consumption for too little effort, so that only areas with temperate climates can provide the high levels of input and output needed to sustain long-term development.

In examining differential growth paths we should remember that not all societies have been interested solely in wealth maximisation. Some were preoccupied with politics, others with the spread of religion, and still others with maximisation of equality. Some were concerned with power in Europe, others with control in the Americas or in Asia, including the East Indies.

3 European settlements overseas

Is it better for long-term economic growth to be first or to be a follower, and, if a follower, what is the optimum number to be behind the leader? As China indicates, leadership in innovation, technologically and organisationally, need not guarantee protracted leadership in production and consumption. Was learning from the leaders the more efficient way to grow relative to being first to undertake some activity and having to pay the costs of learning by yourself?[4] For a time, Spain seemed richer than

[3] Arnold J. Toynbee (1946) was the leading proponent of a challenge-and-response model to explain the rise and fall of civilisations. He points to a 'Golden Mean' and discusses when challenges are 'enough' or 'too much', or excessive. He also comments that 'every challenge that has eventually evoked a victorious response turns out, on inquiry, to have baffled or broken one respondent after another'. See Toynbee, 1946: 140–5.

[4] For a useful discussion of technological leadership and economic growth, raising the prospect of 'the handicap of the early start', see Ames and Rosenberg, 1963.

was the United Kingdom. The Spanish settled in the Americas about one century prior to the British arrival there, a lead that permitted the Spanish to follow the Willie Sutton rule (of going where the money was), leaving the British with an area that was considered by many to be undesirable. Areas settled by the British had relatively few native-Americans, and these had lower population densities and less complex agricultural systems than was found among the Indians in Spanish-America. Not only did the Spanish have an economic lead over the British, French and Dutch, but the Portuguese had early settled in, and controlled, the relatively wealthy country of Brazil, in addition to having several Asian outposts. The Netherlands had modernised in Europe before the British, and became a major trading (and settling) nation in both the Americas and Asia, before losing out to the British.[5] The British arrived in the New World at about the same time as the French, but the French colonies, particularly Saint-Domingue, were extremely productive areas. Before the Haitian Revolution of 1791, output in the French islands of the Caribbean exceeded that in the British.[6] Thus, in terms of the chronology of colonial development, the British were, at best, tied for fourth. The British did not initially have a lead in Europe, in the American colonies or in the Asian regions. Not being first anywhere did not, however, stop the British from ultimately rising to world economic and political power, leaving the European nations that had been first and second to settle in the Americas, Spain and Portugal, far behind and in rather disadvantageous positions for several centuries.

The third traditional 'big-think' issue, one that has been experiencing a recent scholarly comeback, concerns the relative importance of cultural background and of environmental factors in determining the range of institutions and patterns of behaviour in new (and old) nations.[7] Some argue that the important institutions were carried from the Old World and imposed on the New World colonies, not just initially, but for a protracted period of time and with limited changes. This argument has been supported by the claim that the relative success of the metropolis in Europe was consistent with the success (or lack of same) of colonies in America or in Asia. While such a comparison might, at first, seem consistent with the argument for the importance of cultural background, it does raise questions about whether the same institutions existed in all cases and were equally useful in different circumstances. The argument against attributions of the overriding claims of culture is the contention

[5] See de Vries and van der Woude, 1997: 699–710. A similar ranking was made at times by various contemporary observers, including William Petty and Adam Smith. See also Mokyr, 2000: 503–20.

[6] Eltis, 1998: 105–37.

[7] See Engerman, 2000, and Engerman *et al.*, 2000.

that in the settlement process environmental factors played a critical role in shaping economic and social structures and institutions.[8] Thus, the Old World cultural patterns were not adopted without substantial revisions in the New World colonies of European powers.

Examining the dramatic changes over time of the American regions first settled by native-Americans and later settled by the British and other Europeans, as well as the changes in economic performance on the European continent itself, raises a significant issue: the link of climate, geography, resources, productivity and economic development. Until *c.* 1500, the wealthier areas of Europe and the Americas were in the warmer climates, often semi-tropical or tropical zones: Italy, at least its most southern parts, Spain, and Portugal were among the highest-income nations of Europe, while those areas to become Mexico and Peru were the most highly developed regions of the Americas. The Aztecs and Incas, accounting for nearly 60 per cent of New World Indians, were well-developed societies, modern in many ways, with relatively large urban populations and military forces, suggesting that rural areas could produce more than enough foodstuffs to feed themselves. They also had, as developed societies, political hierarchies, slavery and imperialism. Southern Europe and the southern part of the Americas were, before Columbus, independently developing, but there were some similarities in their ability to achieve economic success. And for the next two centuries, the richest areas of the Americas remained tropical, being Latin America and the French and British Caribbean islands. The former's wealth came primarily from exports of gold and silver, first to Iberia, and then redirected to balance trade with Europe and with Asia.[9]

By the mid-eighteenth century, however, things had changed. It was now the temperate zones that were economically advantaged, in terms of production, innovation, and income, while the tropical areas suffered from an increasing relative decline as well as limited innovation. How did England, the Netherlands and the thirteen colonies that became the United States create this change in the relation between climate and growth, or, at the least, what were the conditions under which they could benefit from whatever caused the change in this relation?

[8] This statement is based upon the observations that different colonies of the same European nations have rather different patterns of success, and that in some cases the developments in the colonies actually preceded the period of rapid industrialisation in Europe.

[9] See Attman, 1986. It is estimated that between 1500 and 1800 the New World colonies of Spain and Portugal accounted for about 85 per cent of the world's production of silver and about two-thirds of the gold. See Cross, 1983.

Estimates of the regional allocation of the native American population of the Americas are in William Denevan, 1976: 289–92. The area of Spanish settlement included about 85 percent of the New World's native-Americans.

While not the first in terms of European and American economic success, the British did ultimately gain a large advantage. This was influenced by its military power and its ability to successfully pursue wars against other nations. For much (about 60 per cent of the years between 1650 and 1815) of the period before, and including, the Industrial Revolution, the British were at war with countries including Spain, the Netherlands, France, several other nations in Europe, and various parts of the Americas.[10] Their military actions also included a long Civil War, the American Revolution and uprisings in India. As a military power, the British were generally quite successful. (And a loss such as that in the American Revolution, both by reducing British military expenses and because of the limited trading possibilities that were open to the newly independent nation, may have actually benefited the British in terms of foreign trade and national income.)

This successful British experience raises some familiar questions about the nature of the basic policy pursued by all European nations – mercantilism. Was the aim of mercantilism power or plenty? Wars were expensive in terms of resources and manpower, and for this reason sophisticated observers, including Edmund Burke and Adam Smith among others, advocated British granting independence to the mainland North American colonies rather than fight a war against the thirteen colonies in revolt. Jeremy Bentham used the case of US independence from the British to argue that Spain would benefit from the freeing of its colonies then in revolt.[11] He claimed, based on US trade statistics, that the same trade patterns but at higher levels would emerge if independence was granted.[12] There would be no need to pay the high naval and military costs of attempting to retain these areas as colonies if the benefits of independence were to be similar to those in the British-American trade. While Adam Smith claimed that defence was more important than opulence, he provided no estimates of the higher shipping costs, at least initially, resulting from the shift from low-cost Dutch to higher-cost British shipping.[13] He, thus, defined the trade-off between defence and opulence in only the most general of terms. This is surprising for someone who often explained actions, including the morality of the Quakers in Pennsylvania

[10] While there were few changes in the land ownership in Europe at this time, there was considerable turnover of ownership in the colonies in the Americas and in Asia. For information on warfare and changes in possession in the Caribbean, see Watts, 1987: 240–58, and Ashdown, 1979: 20–1, 64–81.

[11] Bentham, 1995.

[12] Bentham's data for US trade was taken from Seybert, 1818.

[13] Smith [1776] 1976: I, 464–5. Smith points out that the acts had raised the prices of foreign goods and lowered the prices received for British exports.

in freeing their slaves, in terms of relative costs.[14] He also pointed to the negative effects of trade regulations on the development of British income and manufactures.[15] The British achievement of world power (which lasted about one century) may have been worth it, at least to some of the British (and to others in the Empire), but to many others in Britain and elsewhere it did not come cheap.

It is clear that the British colonies of New England had rather different economic and demographic structures and institutions than did British colonies in the Caribbean (and also from Britain). Similarly, French Canada was quite different from the French West Indies (and also from France). Indeed, the French and British West Indies were rather similar in production patterns, demography and wealth, certainly more so than were the two metropolitan areas or the colonies elsewhere. French Canada rather easily became British Canada after 1763, although some minor problems were to arise over the next two centuries. And in some cases, particularly with the Spanish, those institutions that developed regarding native-American labour in mining and agriculture were as much carry-overs of prior Indian methods than they were methods brought over from Spain. This suggests that the same environment may generate somewhat similar institutions, despite dramatic cultural difference among European societies.

Perhaps the crucial form of cultural carry-over to be considered was the ability to adapt to different conditions and to adjust as seemed necessary, rather than the retention of any specific set of institutions. The ability to adjust, based, in part, on education, political liberty and scientific abilities, may ultimately have been more significant than were the continuation of any particular set of beliefs and behaviour, particularly given that the movement was to a rather different environment, with variations in climate, soil and natural resources. Even if some specific European cultural carry-overs had played a role in the early settlement process, it is not clear that these cultural factors were immutable for long periods despite confrontation with new environments and different forms of economic conditions, as well as the changes brought about by new groups via in-migration and population intermixture.[16]

14 Smith [1776] 1976: I, 388. Smith claimed that 'had they [slaves] made any considerable part of their property, such a resolution could never have been agreed to'.

15 Smith [1776] 1976: II, 881: 'That the mercantile system has not been very favourable to the revenue of the great body of the people, to the annual produce of land and labour of the country, I have endeavored to show . . . It seems not to have been more favourable to revenue of the sovereign.' See also Smith [1776] 1976: II, 610.

16 Nevertheless, the immutability of culture has long been used to account for the continued economic backwardness that persists in parts of the world today. See, most recently, Landes, 1998: esp. 512–24.

4 Explanations of British growth

A basic categorisation of explanations of British economic growth would include those based on economic, cultural, political and institutional factors. Among the numerous economic factors that have been considered are: natural resources, including the presence of coal and iron; the opportunities to trade with foreign nations, both to provide markets for British exports and to benefit from imports of goods that Britain were incapable of producing, at least at relatively low prices; the opportunities and profits created by the colonial trade in slaves and in slave-produced commodities; and the role of population change. Some argue that high population growth was beneficial, leading to a greater labour supply and the advantages of scale effects from higher demand; others argue, however, that it was the relatively slow rate of population growth, providing for a lower population density and higher ratios of land and capital to labour, that permitted British growth.

The nature of cultural factors considered include religion, particularly the impact of non-conformists in the development of technology and entrepreneurship in the British economy; the expansion of knowledge, including the willingness to search out new methods and techniques; and an education system that permitted a wide diffusion of information and skills among the population.[17] Culture has been defined to include family and kinship patterns; tastes and preferences regarding work versus leisure; the determination of appropriate levels of savings and consumption; and a widespread desire to financially profit-maximise rather than follow customary, non-economic, behavioural patterns. Some distinguish between economic and non-economic aspects of human behaviour, with non-economic behaviour considered to be based on culture. This distinction is perhaps best explained in terms of understanding the costs of different patterns of behavior, and the incomes people were willing to forego to obtain other ends, rather than regarding the economic and non-economic considerations as distinct.

The nature of the appropriate political system to allow for economic growth also has been debated, and there have been several alternative views of the necessary characteristics in the form and use of governmental power. Some argue that Britain was a weak state, its society based on *laissez-faire* principles, with a limited role for the government, and that this restraint upon interference with the private sector had been crucial to the process of economic growth. The British government probably imposed

[17] The classic on these issues remains Max Weber, 1958. On the British case, see McClelland, 1961: 132–49. See also François Crouzet, 1985.

fewer constraints on entrepreneurial, landowner and worker behaviour, at least relative to the continental countries, and it is argued this limited government led to British expansion. To others it was a strong central state that permitted economic growth. The exercise of power by the ruling elite often meant, however, some rather savage repression and violence undertaken against the lower orders. Further controls were introduced by legislation such as the Poor Laws and Masters and Servants Acts. Nevertheless, England had ended serfdom much earlier than did continental nations. And while voting rights and the percentage of males voting were limited until the twentieth century, the percentage voting tended to be higher than elsewhere in Europe. From the start there were apparent differences in the mix of private vs. government activities in Britain from elsewhere. Private actions were the basis of most market activities, even with a state-directed mercantilism. It was probably the importance of private activities internally, in combination with a strong state externally, based on a large and successful naval and military and extensive controls over foreign trade and shipping, that led to the British rise to power in a very competitive world.

Not all contemporaries regarded eighteenth-century Britain as a growing economy, and the mid-century debate as to whether the British population was increasing or decreasing provided several different answers. Richard Price,[18] arguing for a decrease in population over the course of the century, pointed to such contributing factors as the long and destructive wars on the continent, at sea and in the colonies, the required increased size of the army and navy with their demands for manpower and the increases in luxury spending, and public taxes and debts. While Price was clearly incorrect in describing the changing population size, his reasoning does point to the costs of military activities. All nations of Europe at this time were following the economic and political rubrics of what has come to be called mercantilism, with regulations regarding labour, trade, colonies, specie, settlement, migrations, production, etc., in the interests of the metropolitan power. Although for many years mercantilism has been treated as it was by Adam Smith, as a negative influence on economic growth, recent attention to the British success in military and economic conflict both due to and contributing towards the development of a strong centralised state has led to some re-evaluation of the argument. More attention is now being paid to the importance of the distinction between the rules regarding external relations and those applied to internal transactions. Relatively unconstrained internal trade, even more than the rules governing international matters, distinguished

[18] Richard Price, 1780.

British mercantilism from that of other nations, and was the basis for the apparent greater success of British policy during the mercantile era.

5 Institutional factors in British growth

In recent years, economists and economic historians have become more concerned with the role of institutions in the economy. In some ways, the term institutions suggests a return to a term used in earlier historical writings meant to describe different institutions and their evolution, but the present writings deal in considerably more detail with the analysis of the causes and consequences of institutions, their changes and their impacts on the economic sphere. The concept of institutions is not easily defined, but in general terms, as noted above, it refers to specific organisations or rules that constrain or influence human behaviour. These may be fixed or they may be flexible over time in response to changing conditions. One set of institutions considered essential to economic growth has been the establishment of legal order, providing for stability in dealings between two parties (e.g., contract law) as well as setting social controls that influence the behaviour of all parties in society (e.g., criminal law). Legal codes serve to limit the disruptions of society, since the increased undertaking and enforceability of contracts and agreements with their greater certainty makes for a greater willingness and ability of all parties to transact and meet the terms of provisions agreed upon. Transactions covered include those regarding labour, such as the terms of employment, the manner of leaving work and the ability to organise. The Masters and Servants Acts, from the early eighteenth century to the late nineteenth century, provided an important aid to British capitalists, and possibly, by increasing certainty in regulations, also to workers.[19] Similarly, changing provisions regarding labour standards and the right to organise unions had major impacts on economic activity, by determining the availability of the labour supply and the profitability of business firms.

Among the more important laws and institutional arrangements discussed have been those concerning property rights in physical goods and in intellectual capital. Of primary importance is the degree of certainty of ownership rights in the future and whether the asset can be sold by the owners or must be retained. Certainty of property rights, which increases asset values, will influence investments, and this could involve both actions taken within the private sector and relations between the government and private individuals. An important impact upon the issuance of public debt is called credible commitment. This enhanced

[19] See Steinfeld, 2001.

ability of the government to borrow meant a stronger central government was possible, but whether this promoted growth depended upon the use to which the funds were put.[20] The size of the British public debt was, however, regarded by some contemporaries as a negative influence on British economic growth in the eighteenth century. At the time the French monarchy also kept their commitments, unlike in the seventeenth century, when there were defaults and confiscations. The frequency of wars and the demand for funds made the cost of borrowing expensive and resulted in a heavy debt burden, affecting private expenditure. Are there conditions under which a government can commit itself not to seize property belonging to residents, and, if it does so, to do so with payment of adequate compensation? And how can the government convince individuals that it will honour its self-enforcing ordinances permanently?

Discussions of the impact of changes in government legislation upon the private sector have had a rather long and complex history. It will be useful to note several different examples of historical cases in which the nature of the government commitment has been discussed. In some cases the government deemed it necessary to pay compensation to individuals who suffered losses in wealth due to legal or administrative changes, but in most cases it did not. Government seizures of land under the property of eminent domain generally required payment to owners, and in the British (and most other) emancipations of slaves there was compensation in cash and labour time paid to the slave-owners, and in most cases (but not the British) compensation was paid for ending serfdom as well.[21]

Respect for the holders of property rights did not apply in all the cases in which laws were changed. Despite the claims of owners of slave-trading vessels that they had entered the industry when it was legal and had even been given encouragement by the government, their calls for compensation in response to Dolben's Act of 1788 were not met.[22] Rather, as Burke argued in 1789, compensation was not necessary for ending the slave trade, since slavery was 'a system of robbery', but also, more generally, that those in the slave trade always knew that the government has the right to withdraw its approval from that which it had previously 'authorised and

[20] See, for example, North and Weingast, 1989. See also Wright, 1999: 355–61, and Williamson, 1985, and the ensuing debates with Crafts, Mokyr and Harley.

[21] So firm was the belief in property rights in these cases that, while slave-owners and serf-owners generally received some compensation, in no case did slaves or serfs receive compensation. Compensation could be paid via cash, bonds or guaranteed labour time, but was not always for the full price or value of the asset. Earlier English discussions of compensation concerned the confiscation of the monasteries.

[22] In the case of Dolben's Act of 1788, which reduced the numbers of slaves carried per ton by a vessel from Africa, some compensation was paid, but only for damages on those ships that had been already fitted out. Porter, 1970: 41–9.

protected'.[23] Pitt, in 1792, pointed out that all people were affected by trade regulations, and if compensation were required to limit the slave trade, no new taxes, expenditures or legislation, could ever be introduced by parliament.[24] The Earl of Sheffield, in 1790, claimed that the demand for compensation was a 'new doctrine' (the precise settlement over the church lands at the time of the Restoration seems uncertain) and 'that compensation is not to be made for private property, diminished or destroyed for public views, by act of Parliament'.[25] Those dismayed at the absence of compensation for ending the slave trade or what was regarded as inadequate compensation for ending slavery claimed that this could lead to government confiscation and 'an end of all property'.[26] What is the optimum between the payment of no compensation and the payment of full compensation is not obvious, but it might be noted that neither of these actions (the failure to compensate slave traders or the compensation paid to slave-owners) seemed to have had much impact on British rates of economic growth in the long run.

In discussing the role of institutions, knowledge of the factors which determine their establishment is important. Are the institutions to be regarded as exogenous or as endogenous to the economy, and, if endogenous, to what forces did they respond? Or, to return to an earlier question, to what extent were they set by cultural background and in what way were they influenced by natural and environmental factors? What is the optimum size of the governing unit, and would it be better to have centralised or decentralised governments impose new institutions to advance the process of economic growth? The analysis of the appropriate institutional arrangements may indicate that only one unique set can provide a favourable outcome but, alternatively, it may be that there is more flexibility in allowing for different possible institutions to achieve the same desired growth rate. And, even if the institutional framework is not optimal, it may be that the growth potential is sufficient so that even a shortfall from the maximum possible still yields high growth.

The political power that can determine which institutions are adopted may be all-inclusive, in terms of being the outcome of a broad suffrage and strong legislative power. Or the suffrage may be restricted, with only a small minority of the population able to vote and directly influence

[23] Cobbett, 1816, 96–7. [24] Cobbett, 1817, 1,145–6.

[25] Sheffeld, 1790. In the Minutes of the West Indian Planters and Merchants, 19 May 1789, it was claimed 'that the prime Minster's declaration, that no compensation could be paid for abolition, is so repugnant to every principle of justice that it will destroy all faith in Royal Charters and in Parliament' (Porter, 1970: 54–66).

[26] Some later claimed that if slaves were confiscated, default on the public debt was the obvious next step. Hansard, *Parliamentary Debates*, vol. 12, 630.

legislative policy. If such limited political powers for some members of society existed, then the group that establishes institutions, legal codes and property rights regimes, presumably in their own interest, will be able to exclude other members of society from benefits and influence. Thus there may be a well-defined and enforced set of property rights, but these may leave powerless a large element of the population, who can be considered to be outsiders to the decision-making society. At an extreme, slave-owners may have been able to establish a finely operating set of institutions, one that permitted rapid economic growth, but this meant a significant component of the nation's population was considered to be outsiders without rights. The political (or military) determination of the size of the elite group is a critical issue for institutional analysis. A small group may directly benefit from particular institutional patterns. While this may lead to measured increases in income for them but also other members of society, the limited nature of the decision-making group would still raise problems for understanding the distribution of the rewards from economic growth and for the interpretation of the growth process.

6 British growth and the government

Although there may have been more economic decisions left to the private sector in Britain than elsewhere in pre-nineteenth century Europe, clearly the government played a major role in the shaping of British growth. The monarchy often found it necessary to share some of its power, or at least to permit economic benefits to accrue to others in society. It made available, for a price, monopoly charters to the wealthy in society. Political power influenced the size of the electorate. The ruling elite could determine the benefits that might be permitted to those without any direct political power, but who would be able to gain benefits because of threats of political and/or economic instability, or because some benefits to them might increase the gains to the elite. Given the nature of economic forces, as well as of threats to stability, those who benefit from governmental decisions need not be those with a direct political voice. It would, be expected, however, that with the greater influence due to expanded suffrage, a broadening of the benefits of policies would result. Nevertheless, the breakdown of British serfdom after the Black Death reflected more changing economic conditions for landowners than it did any pronounced shifts in political and legal powers, while the limited political power of the ex-serfs did impose constraints on the magnitude of subsequent changes.[27] Similarly, Poor Laws and factory legislation

[27] See Hilton, 1983.

were imposed, even with limited political changes favouring lower classes, although as suffrage expanded, so did the benefits provided to the poor and to the labour force.[28] Even though the ruling elite, the governmental decision-makers, may have been narrow, and operated in their own perceived self-interest, the implied threat to stability or feelings of morality, meant that the emerging institutions provided a broader diffusion of benefits than was initially intended or would seem to be short-run profit maximising for the elite. This does not, of course, help answer questions of how or why suffrage rules changed over time, and why the electorates were ultimately broadened, surely an essential aspect of any study of institutional development and change.

One of the more dramatic developments in the era of rising British supremacy was the changing view of the individual vis-à-vis the state, reflecting either religious or secular (Enlightenment) ideals. Earlier views, captured in interpretations of mercantilism and cameralism, as well as in the belief that the monarchy was the state, focused on the total income of the nations, indicative of national power. Accepting this as a goal of policy placed a premium on the total numbers of people, not the conditions of these individuals (except insofar as these influenced changes in total numbers). This concern with total population led to policies such as public health measures that aided individuals, as well as to measures that helped increase the size of the state, such as limitations on emigration, but with encouragement of immigration. After the Enlightenment, however, there was a greater concern with individual welfare, even when political rights were not broadly extended. It did take a prolonged period of time, but in due course such basic changes as the abolition of serfdom and slavery were introduced in Europe and its overseas offshoots in the Americas, although with more delay elsewhere in the world. Such social and political transitions were never easy, no matter what factions were involved. Britain's Civil War preceded those of most European nations, and while costly in terms of loss of life and property, may have been less costly than those elsewhere. Thus the British had some advantage in having had its major revolution earlier and less disruptive than those in many other European nations.

The late seventeenth-century consolidation of centralised political power in England permitted a more successful accomplishment of external power. The introduction of the Navigation Acts, enforced at the expense of the Dutch, various segments of British society and colonists in America, was a key measure in the expansion of the British shipping

[28] On the Poor Laws, see Slack, 1990 and on the Factory Acts, see Hutchins and Harrison, 1966.

industry, although not without continued (but as of yet unmeasured) economic costs. As late as the 1770s and 1780s there were complaints about the need to pay high prices in Britain for sugar produced in the British West Indies, relative to the prices of French West Indian sugar.[29] It was argued that French West Indian sugar sold at lower prices in world markets because of the greater effectiveness of French planters and their better ability to manage their slave labour force.

British naval power was increased as part of its 'Blue Water' policy, introduced by the Commonwealth during the English Revolution, which meant a British focus on oceanic and overseas control, with a lessened continental involvement on Europe. The military costs of wresting power from the Dutch, Spanish and French were not insignificant, with costs in terms of manpower lost or diverted, investible funds diverted, higher taxes paid by producers and consumers, trade reduced or diverted and necessary readjustments of the institutional structure. It may, of course, be argued that such costs did yield high benefits, economic and otherwise, to the British, and were definitely worth paying for their approximately one century of glory. It is still debated whether the favourable institutional development for growth came about mainly due to the external power achieved by the British; or whether the institutions that had developed internally were the cause of the British success, militarily and economically, permitting the expansion of power externally. Or were internal institutional changes and the achievement of external power entwined in a non-separable manner, both being part of the same overall growth process?

7 Changing institutions

One major problem in the linking of specific economic institutions to economic growth arises from the possibilities of substituting different institutional arrangements to meet the same target. Were there alternative measures possible to achieve the same goal, and what were the efficiency differences between alternative institutions?[30] Given the many changes over time in Britain in the financial sector, labour controls, trade policy, tax rates and structure, religious beliefs, educational systems, etc., often without dramatic impacts on the overall growth rate of the economy, establishing the importance of any one specific institution may seem problematic. Perhaps the most important contribution of the institutional framework and the belief structure of participants in the economy was in

[29] See the discussion of this point in Engerman, 2000: 227–49.
[30] See Davis and North, 1973, for a discussion of alternative possible arrangements.

the setting of rather general provisions and the ability to flexibly adjust to new and changing circumstances, rather than maintenance of fixed sets of rules, firmly and without change. Certainly the fixed pattern of some British institutions have long been considered to have been the cause of its relative decline in the late nineteenth century. And the current ability of the United States to delay a similarly long-expected relative decline may reflect its ability to adapt to different sets of circumstances, and not a willingness to hold firm to earlier successful policies, at high costs, as did the British in the late nineteenth century.

A somewhat similar set of questions about the optimum arrangements of institutions concerns the often-proclaimed link between political democracy and economic growth. As argued for the nineteenth-century United States, a wider suffrage led to broader education, a wider availability of land to families and relatively greater income and wealth equality, all consistent with rapid economic growth.[31] Certainly suffrage in the United States was broader than in Britain at this time, but in some circumstances the relation between the widespread ability to vote and economic growth may not be clear. In the twentieth century, expansion of the franchise has led to increasing concern with income redistribution, regulation of economic activity and the promoting of environmental and other limits that lower growth. Even earlier a similar outcome had been predicted. Sir Henry Sumner Maine argued in 1886, in his *Popular Government*, that if workers had been given universal suffrage and permitted to vote on the introduction of machines, such as the spinning jenny, the power-loom and the threshing machine, these would never have been introduced.[32] Maine also pointed to other possible undesirable social and political outcomes that could arise with a broadened franchise, posing further problems for analysing the impact of changing political rules.

The basic claims for the initiating importance of institutions ultimately rests on the belief in the exogeneity of their determination. Nevertheless, granting the critical importance of institutions in shaping economic change, some of the more interesting questions relate to the forces underlying the origins and evolution of institutions, and how they were influenced by various circumstances.

Political change within a society will often lead to changes in institutions, and cause shifts in the expected beneficiaries of policy measures. The reasons for such political changes, whether the outcome of foreign warfare, internal revolutions, voting upheavals or palace coups, are many. They may also be based, not on any dramatic shock to the system, but merely on the attempt of one party to get the economic gains currently

[31] See the sources cited in footnote 7. [32] Maine, 1886: 112.

received by another party. While directly concerning the presumed transition from feudalism to capitalism – itself a rather significant institutional change – the Sweezy-Dobb debate of the 1940s examined the relative importance of external trading relations in contrast with internal conditions of production in explaining these changes in European economic growth and structure. In its more recent guise, as the Brenner debate, the contending forces are now demographic changes and shifts in political power (whatever their cause). While there presently seem few detailed accounts of the economic costs of the English Revolution, it is of interest that in several of the earlier revolutions or independence movements for which we have some data, such as the American Revolution, the French Revolution, the Spanish-American revolutions of the first decade of the nineteenth century and the independence of Brazil, there were declines in per capita income for one or more decades before economic growth resumed. The one major exception to this pattern of recovery was the case of Haiti, where the inability to recover has persisted for two centuries.

An influence on institutions, emphasised by Montesquieu in the 1740s, was the role of climate and resources and their impact on settlement patterns and economic and social structures. Certain parts of the world were unable to sustain populations (at least at then present means of technology), while others had both livable climates and the soil and resources to produce adequate amounts in excess of subsistence. At past and present scientific (and non-scientific) levels of knowledge, certain crops and livestock types can only be grown, or can be grown only inexpensively, in specific climatic conditions. Similar arguments arose in the debates on colonisation of the New World.[33]

When peoples of similar background and culture migrate to areas with similar climate, the nature of the institutions in the areas of in-migration tend to resemble those in the area of out-migration. But if the movement is to areas with rather different climate and crop conditions, there will be adjustments made to adapt to the new circumstances. This was obviously the case in the European settlement of the Americas. No European power maintained unchanged institutional patterns in new areas of settlement. Further, the same settling nation looked quite different depending on the location of their colonies. The British West Indies became slave colonies producing sugar, and were about 90 per cent black slave, with

[33] Some Frenchmen did not think Canada worth settling. Richelieu's finance minister, the duc de Sully, was against this, arguing that no region north of 40° latitude could ever be economically successful. Nor, to Voltaire, was Canada even worth defending. He claimed that the war over Canada between the British and French was obviously not worth it, being a fight over a few acres of snow, and argued that the war would cost more than Canada was worth. See Lokke, 1932: 15–8; Voltaire, 1947: 110.

slaves working mainly in units of 150–250. For almost the entire first century of British migration, more migrants went to the Caribbean than to the North American mainland. The mainland was quite different, about 90 per cent white, mainly producing grains on relatively small, family-sized farms, and before 1776, slavery was important only for southern US tobacco and rice production. Relative to the West Indies, the thirteen mainland colonies received few slaves, but whereas both whites and blacks probably suffered rates of natural decrease in the West Indies, both groups on the mainland grew at unusually high rates by any standards.[34] Yet with all these demographic, economic and political differences, *c.* 1770, the three major regions of the British mainland colonies, and the largest West Indian colony, Jamaica, had roughly the same wealth per capita (of the total population).[35] And despite what some thought (and still think) to be the superiority of British institutions, in the Caribbean French colonial output and productivity exceeded that of the British.[36]

Also of interest in examining the link between institutions, cultures and environmental factors (here defined to include both natural resources and population density) is the analysis of what happened in the British West Indies when slavery ended after 1834. The compensation paid to slave-owners did not cover their losses, since it was not clear what slave prices it should be based on, and nothing was paid to offset the loss in land values due to emancipation. Compensation was paid to slave-owners, in cash and in required labour time, but not to slaves. Nowhere in Africa, the Americas, Asia or Europe were slaves and serfs given anything but freedom, although in most cases owners were compensated, generally by the government.[37]

The post-emancipation output pattern in the British West Indies was of a very sharp decline in the plantation sector and in sugar output, with it taking a long time (if ever) for some areas to re-achieve pre-emancipation levels of sugar output. The British West Indies really had three distinct experiences. In Barbados and Antigua there was a very high population density, with low wages (following low slave prices), so that the plantations were maintained. Antigua did not even want or need coerced apprenticeships to bind labour. In Trinidad and British Guiana, areas still expanding under slavery, there was underpopulation and labour scarcity, leading to the importation of contract labor, from Asia and Africa, to maintain sugar production. In Jamaica, and most other islands, there were declines in the plantation sector, which meant they were unable to pay for indentured

[34] See Fogel, 1989: 17–40. [35] Coclanis, 1990: 245–60. [36] See Eltis, 1998.

[37] See the discussion in Engerman, 2002. In one unusual case the ex-slaves of Haiti were to pay compensation to their former owners in France.

labor, and these islands suffered prolonged economic declines. Some of the patterns of demographic and economic change by colony experienced under slavery continued after the ending of slavery, even with a quite different set of institutional arrangements regarding the labour force.[38]

8 Implications

Clearly institutions were important in the establishment of British economic and political supremacy in the eighteenth century, and the recent attention to institutions, legal rules and judicial and legislative enforcement has been most useful in understanding and explaining the process of growth. It remains of interest, however, to see if we can better understand how specific institutions developed, how they changed over time, and why, sometimes, they did not change. Institutions are a product of human interactions with other humans and with non-human forces, and to understand the causes and consequences of institutions more needs to be learned not only about the historical actors, but also about the influence of other aspects of the economy and society.

The essays in this volume provide major contributions to the history and the historiography of British economic change, and to the debates on the question of British exceptionalism in modern times. There are some new facts and interpretations, and some new questions are asked, although some of the broad outlines familiar from the earlier literature remain.

Whether described as an Industrial Revolution or not, the British economy by 1820 was about the richest in the world (except for perhaps the Netherlands). From the middle of the pack of western European per capita income in 1600 and 1700, British eighteenth-century growth eclipsed that of the other western European nations, and also (with the exception of the United States) of the other nations of the world. The eighteenth century saw the rise of British economic, political and military power to world leadership.

Underlying the economic basis of this growth in income was the dramatic shift from the agricultural sector to industry and services, made possible by the rapid increase in agricultural productivity and the availability of urban and industrial occupations for the labour freed from the agricultural sector. The basis of this agricultural improvement is seen to be the onset of capitalist agriculture, based on large farms with hired wage-earners, but, it is argued, the gains were made by all sizes of farms,

[38] A similar pattern of changes, based on the land–labour ratios, also characterised that of the other European powers in the Caribbean.

not just large farms or those that had experienced enclosures. It is this focus on the broad diffusion of change, not just in agriculture but also in industry, that points to new questions in understanding British society. These changes in agriculture, or the agricultural revolution, were earlier discussed but with attention given only to large farms, as were their effects in redistributing income to landowners, with impacts upon national patterns of consumption and savings and investment behavior.

Another important recent contribution to the analysis of British growth has been the attention given to British military power and the efficient centralised government that was able to develop a strong navy and army. The need to finance a strong central government and to provide adequate military equipment points to a reinterpretation of the role of taxation and public debt in the British economy, one in which Patrick O'Brien has played a major role. That Britain had higher taxes than its neighbours, and a significantly larger national debt were, in earlier discussions, seen as major problems for the economy, not as the source of its strength. Yet given that the expenditures were for military purposes the long-term effects are now seen as central to the establishment of the British economy and empire with its possible large economic payoff. The control of the seas by the navy also served, in wartime and in peace, to support British international trade with its colonies and with other nations. Power and plenty came together; indeed, power led to plenty according to several of the interpretations in this volume, and without the control of the seas the growth of the economy would have been limited and some other European power possibly become dominant. This being said, a fuller benefit-cost examination of not just the benefits of war and a strong military, but also the costs to the economy in resources and lives should be considered. Even if we accept that the priority of the society, or at least of its elite, was to secure military and economic dominance over its rivals, the evaluation of the costs paid to achieve such benefits remains an interesting historical issue. This focus on naval power externally, maintained by a strong central government, does not mean that, internally, the economy did not allow freedom to individual decision-makers. The central government provided for and enforced various provisions for maintaining legal stability and property rights enforcement, and within these frameworks a greater role for individuals in the economy was possible.

Another important aspect of the growth process discussed was the wide diffusion of inventive skills and productivity improvement in both industry and agriculture. Despite a frequent concentration by writers on the growth of large farms and large firms, small farms and small firms were able to benefit from the technological and organisational changes and contribute to economic growth. Heroic innovators and entrepreneurs there were, but their contribution to economic growth would have been limited without the role played by the larger numbers of smaller economic actors. Change in a much larger component of the economy than just cotton textiles and coal and iron is now being considered in examining British industrialisation and exceptionalism. That growth required a larger pool of entrepreneurs than customarily claimed suggests the importance of a more open society with considerable social, regional and occupational mobility, as well as the significance of flexibility and adaptability as an essential part of the growth process.

The study of the British Industrial Revolution, which at times has seemed to focus on Britain alone, is now written to include a broader, international perspective. The role of ideas and innovations is not seen as solely British. Britain was dependent upon transfers from elsewhere in Europe and Asia, as well as Africa and the Americas. Britain at this time was an open economy, open not only for trade in goods, people and capital, but also for ideas and intellectual attitudes from elsewhere. Britain did not invent everything it used, but it did provide an excellent system to make things discovered elsewhere into productive assets. Nor were the key aspects of the banking and financial systems created anew by the British. Many of the methods and techniques used had first succeeded in the Netherlands. The payoff was not to the first inventor, but to the society that was first able to make things productive and profitable. As seen in later centuries, when the United States adapted British technology, and Japan later adapted American technology, global interaction includes more than just trade in produced goods. The more frequently discussed and controversial question of the importance of foreign trade in promoting British economic growth has been examined on the basis of some newly prepared data, arguing for the key roles of India and the West Indies as markets for British manufacturers. The suggested linking of internal and external markets, and the ability of the internal economy to respond to external conditions, should be useful in analysing the relative importance of each of these demand sources.

9 Concluding reflections

There are several important questions, often only touched on or not fully discussed, that seem to be worth more attention for the study of British exceptionalism. The comparison of the growth rates of per capita income for Britain and elsewhere in western Europe indicates, as is well known, that between 1500 and 1800 the economic power shifted from Italy, Spain and Portugal in Southern Europe to Britain and the Netherlands in the north. It is interesting that during this period, with the geographic relocation of the growing areas, there was a similar movement from south to north in the Americas, with growth now being much higher in the more temperate zones. Whether these movements in America and in Europe are related is not clear, but more attention to the economic role of climate and resources in shaping production and institutions would be useful.

While there is a greater concern with political factors and the government in explaining British growth, there remain some missing aspects possibly worth more examination. As with most discussions of the British Industrial Revolution, the starting date is 1688, but little is said about the implications of the Civil War, its costs and consequences. Similarly, little has been said about the effects on one of Britain's major rivals, France, of the French Revolution and the Haitian Revolution on the relative rankings of the two nations before and after 1789. These two revolutions imposed severe costs on the French economy, which had previously been growing at a reasonably rapid rate. The American Revolution, winning independence, apparently had a smaller economic impact on Britain than the Haitian Revolution had upon France, since Haitian output and exports drop dramatically for a rather prolonged time, while the United States experienced a smaller decline and a quicker recovery and remained a major market for British exports. Finally, these essays basically assume the structure of British society, little being said about religion, culture, preferences regarding work and leisure and savings and consumption, and the evolution of the power structure and the political elite. But, as Adam Smith argued, there are great advantages to be gained from a division of labour, so we must appreciate what we have learned, and look forward to subsequent publications to fill remaining gaps.

Laudatio patritii: Patrick O'Brien and European economic history

Gianni Toniolo

A tradition going back to the Middle Ages prescribes that symposia celebrating a distinguished scholar end with the latter's *laudatio*. It is for me both an honour and a pleasure to perform this task. My friendship with Patrick dates back to 1977 when he introduced me to St Antony's, my intellectual home for years to come.

Unfortunately, this *laudatio* will be the least original of all the papers collected in this book. We are all members of a community that has long drawn upon Patrick's intellectual and personal gifts. We all have studied his books and papers, learned from his lectures and seminars, benefited from his advice, relished his wit, delighted in his company. And many of us have experienced the warmth of his loyal friendship. Can I possibly add anything new to all this?

My task is made even more difficult by the fact that I am no expert of British economic history. I am, however, encouraged by the width of Patrick's scholarship, his contribution to our understanding of economic history being by no means confined to his country of origin. Even so, a full, if cursory, review of Patrick O'Brien's work is beyond my capability. The sheer quantity of his production – fifty-three papers in the last decade alone – defies any attempt by this *laudatio* to systematically analyse Patrick's work. Let me just recall that Patrick's first published papers dealt with the economic history of Britain and Egypt. Such a diversity in scholarly interests, particularly unusual in a young D.Phil., was to characterise the whole of O'Brien's career. Comparative, and later 'global', analysis is the hallmark of his entire scholarship, all the way to his contributions to global history and his well-deserved appointment as 'centennial' professor at the London School of Economics.

I have *not* tried, in preparing this *laudatio*, to read the books and papers by Patrick I haven't had the opportunity, or simply was too lazy, to read over the three decades of my life devoted to economic history. I knew from the start that it would be presumptuous of me to try and grasp even the basics of the Egyptian economy, of the consequences of the

American Civil War, of Dutch mercantilism, of the British aristocracy and of the other topics over which Patrick's scholarship has roamed that remain outside my professional interests. I just went through my notes, my memories and my own work to see what *I* have learned from Patrick, how he has shaped my own approach to the discipline, what influence he exercises on my teaching of European economic history, particularly on topics in which I am no expert, such as the origin, unfolding and consequences of the British Industrial Revolution.

Not on markets alone . . .

In the beginning was the Royal Navy. This might be the opening sentence of an O'Brien Bible on the Industrial Revolution. Except that he is too sophisticated a historian to fall into the trap of single-cause explanations of complex events. Yet, his emphasis on the economic fallout of sails and guns has provided a new perspective on the origin, in the British Isles, of modern economic growth.

Patrick's chapter in the Floud-McCloskey *Economic History of Britain* (O'Brien, 1994) is a masterpiece in modern institutional history. The list of the institutions examined in order to assess their impact on British economic development might have been drawn up by a 'new-growth' theorist. The treatment of this complex issue is intriguing both to the economist and the historian. The former is attracted by the rigour of the exposition, even in the absence of formal equations, the latter by the interaction of the various forces and actors at play as well as by the *longue durée* perspective. Everywhere in Patrick's writings one can find careful evaluations of the influence of long-run social, ideological, religious, demographic and geographical forces on economic outcomes. This is a distinctive feature of his discourse. In the case of institutions, the point is well illustrated, among other instances by Patrick's approach to social order and the protection of property. 'The Hanoverian state', he argues, 'provided good order on the cheap for an economy on its way through an industrial revolution . . . because respect for property rights and hierarchy permeated all ranks of an increasingly cohesive nation' (O'Brien, 1994: 227). Law and order were provided to an acceptable degree, contracts were passably enforced, mostly through arbitration and reputation, labour markets slowly liberalised. There was, relative to most countries on the continent, an early shift from the mercantilist state's emphasis on the minute regulation of every aspect of economic life to the provision of public goods. If there were institutional failings, Patrick finds, they regarded corporate laws, money supply and the inadequate provision of social overhead capital.

Several historians simply see high taxation as a retarding factor in the economic development of the Hanoverian state. Most new-growth economists would *a priori* concur. Moreover, many argue that the high level of wartime expenditure, partly met by borrowing, crowded out private investment at a crucial moment in the Industrial Revolution. Patrick knows better: he carefully weighs the burden of taxation against the benefits derived from the goods bought with tax revenue.

In the first place he points to the efficiency of the British state in providing defence, the most important of all public goods. In contrast to the inhabitants of most areas in continental Europe, those of the British Isles felt secure in the continuation of their self-government, in the preservation of their own institutions and, more basically, did not have to fear the periodic expropriation of their harvests and properties at the hand of hostile armies passing through their territories, as was the case with so many Europeans up to the Congress of Vienna and beyond. The economic benefits of security are difficult to measure but are probably considerable. More important still, Patrick maintains that the navy was crucial 'in securing for British business disproportionate shares of world trade, shipping, shipbuilding and commercial services' (O'Brien, 1986: 296). If it is true that the early success of the British economy is based upon a precocious realisation of the advantages of the international division of labour, then – Patrick convincingly argues – the navy played a strategic role in the transformation of the economy that goes under the label of Industrial Revolution.

This is a novel approach to the long-standing issue of the contribution made by the mercantilist state to the origin of 'modern economic growth'. Since Heckscher's famous study, few scholars have held an entirely negative view of mercantilism. Its endeavour to actively promote economic development, albeit mostly for the wrong reasons and often by way of suboptimal policies, signalled a departure from the previous neglect of the economy by most medieval rulers. It constitutes an important element in the transition from the 'traditional economy' to 'modern economic growth'. The benefits of an active stance of the state in economic matters derived, in most scholars' view, from subsidies, tax exemptions, regulations for the encouragement of industry, commerce and finance, from a more effective central organisation of state revenue and expenditure, from the provision for social overhead capital, from the reorganisation of weights and measures, and of the mint. Patrick showed that in some of these matters the Hanoverian state was a step ahead of its continental competitors, while in other areas it was not as advanced as, for instance, France. What made the difference was the particular nature of the military expenditure to which geography obliged the British Isles. While continental armies represented essentially a drag on productive resources, often being unable to create expectations of security even within the national borders, things were intrinsically different across the Channel. The strategic, mercantilist and imperialistic ambitions of the Hanoverian state were, almost by definition, sea-bound. They 'generated virtuous circles and cycles of capital accumulation and technological progress that led the economy forward and upward to a plateau of possibilities from where the First Industrial Revolution eventually emerged' (O'Brien, 2000a: 7). It was relatively easy for the state to command the resources required to mobilise the naval force necessary to protect and enhance British overseas interests, not only because of the efficiency of the state itself but also 'because it was widely recognised and appreciated that public investment in the Royal Navy could be profitable for the economy at large'. The navy 'preserved the security of the Realm; protected Britain's growing share in international trade and profits; . . . destroyed and degraded competitors for commercial and imperial supremacy' (O'Brien, 2000a: 7). Far from being unproductive, or productive only through seizure of enemy territory, as in the case of its competitors, the British idiosyncratic military expenditure 'generated all manner of externalities for industry, foreign trade, commercial services and the growth of maritime cities' (O'Brien, 2000a: 7).

Costs and benefits of imperialism

My generation is probably the last one educated to be sanguine about imperialism. And to pass on it a judgement without appeal. I still regard it as a commendable moral and political stance. However, more often than not, emotions and outrage overflowed into the realm of research. This was understandable, but hardly conducive to serious scholarship. In my young days, most historians and economists took for granted that prosperity in the most advanced western countries was to a large extent based upon large-scale exploitation of the less-developed world. This view was not quite the same as Lenin's: it simply held that colonialism, and neo-colonialism after it, were *the* pillars of the economic success of the first comers to industrialisation thanks to a cheap supply of raw materials and captive markets for metropolitan products. A long-run decline in the terms of trade of primary producers seemed to validate this view.

Patrick O'Brien, the scholar who drew our attention to the crucial role played by the Royal Navy in pushing the British economy ahead, was also the one who showed that the Empire did not pay. There is no contradiction in simultaneously holding both these views. The economic value of the Royal Navy consisted in the efficient production of defence as a public good, in securing safe navigation for merchant vessels, and when necessary, in bullying reluctant traders (in showing the flag, as the euphemism went). The Royal Navy was not, Patrick argues, efficiently employed in preserving British home rule over vast overseas territories.

Patrick has carefully examined and confuted the main supposed benefits accruing to Victorian and Edwardian Britain from its formal Empire. On commodity trade he agrees that 'Britain's dependence on overseas markets for the sale of manufactured exports and upon foreign and imperial sources of supply for foodstuffs and raw materials was unique among European nations' (O'Brien, 1988a: 166) but sees no reasons why an independent India should have 'withdrawn from trade with the United Kingdom' (O'Brien, 1988a: 169). Moreover, even in the presence of infant industry protection from counterfactually independent colonies, there is no reason to believe that a mature and diversified economy such as Britain's would have been incapable of adjusting to changes in the tariff policies of relatively small foreign countries. On the contrary, an 'early delinking of the economy from commerce with the empire may have promoted faster productivity growth and the structural changes required by the British economy to meet the challenges of the twentieth century' (O'Brien, 1988a: 170). Similar arguments apply even more forcefully to capital movements. The share of private foreign investment going to the Empire did not exceed 20 per cent and – while some highly profitable imperial enterprises existed, presumably exploiting their privileges as local monopolies – most lines of investment did not secure higher returns in the colonies than elsewhere (O'Brien, 1988a: 170). Again, it is unlikely that an early withdrawal from the Empire might have significantly changed the pattern of British investment overseas, except for legal monopolies, in which case, however, financial resources could arguably have been more profitably employed at home.

The Empire was also a drag on public finances. Patrick's early work, his D.Phil. dissertation under Habbakuk and Hartwell, focused on taxation and financial policy, and he later made substantial contributions to the history of public revenue and expenditure. He showed that, rather than deriving net benefits from the colonies, the British taxpayer subsidised the Empire to a considerable extent (O'Brien, 1988a: 189). In particular, apart from India, the dominions and colonies spent insignificant shares of their budgets on defence, while over half of total military spending was voted by the Westminster parliament to sustain troops located outside the British Isles.

With these findings, Patrick pioneered the *now* increasingly large group of historians who argue that the Empire did not pay. In his comparative view of the factors in the long-run economic growth of the main European countries, the Empire and British decline – two among the most important issues in British historiography – appear to be closely intertwined. On the eve of the First World War, British citizens were twice as heavily taxed as those of Britain's closest competitors. Patrick's conclusion is straightforward: an alternative 'Cobdenite' policy, contemplating an early granting of independence to the British colonies, would have done much to reverse the country's decline relative to the rest of western Europe and the United States.

If the Empire was, on balance, a liability rather than an asset for the British economy, why did Victorian and Edwardian governments 'simply ignore that vociferous and percipient minority of radicals crying out from the wilderness against the waste and futility involved in sustaining high levels of public expenditure to defend and extend the empire' (O'Brien, 2000a)? Patrick's answer is a text-book illustration of a well-known case in political economy. The costs were spread thinly over the vast majority of British citizens, while a small minority drew substantial economic and social benefits from the Empire. 'Benefits', Patrick says, 'accrued disproportionately to the untaxed white settlers of the dominions and colonies, and to those at the top end of the income and social scales in British society' (O'Brien, 1988a: 194). As late as 1903–6, those in receipt of about 40–45 per cent of the national income contributed only to about 11 per cent of total tax revenue. This was the minority who benefited most

> directly and tangibly from military and other governmental expenditures allocated to support imperial rule, to foster imperial trade and to mitigate the risks of private investment in the dominions and colonies. Britain's 'gentlemanly capitalists', resident in large part in the home counties . . . derived the largest gains (net of taxes) from military and other forms of imperial subsidy. Meanwhile the majority of the English people cheerfully and even proudly shouldered the tax bill of an empire. (O'Brien, 1988a: 195)

It is typical of Patrick to try to see if his research findings on Britain would also hold true in the case of other countries and geographic areas. A bold comparative assessment of the costs and benefits of imperialism in various countries showed that, by and large, empires were not as profitable as they were, so far, believed to be (O'Brien and Prados de la Escosura, 1998).

The comparison headache . . .

It is surely not by chance that Patrick was made a Centennial professor at LSE, in charge of a global history project. Comparative history is where – for all his amazing contributions to British economic history – Patrick's absolute advantage over most of us has always been. Surely, his being one of the most active and innovative scholars in comparative economic history, is one of the reasons why he attracted so many students to Oxford.

Again, his works in the field are too numerous to be even cursorily covered here. I shall therefore mention only two areas where his contribution has been particularly fruitful: comparative quantification and the diffusion pattern of modern economic growth (*à la* Kuznets) in Europe.

Among the European scholars of his generation, Patrick stands out as one of the few true believers in quantification. At a time when the very word cliometrics was almost anathema in several continental European universities, and regarded as yet another passing intellectual fashion in others, he wrote a paper 'in praise of new economic history' (O'Brien, 1982b). His presentation at this conference is just the latest confirmation of Patrick's interest in, and command of, quantitative historical research.

The way Patrick deals with quantification is rooted more in O'Brien the historian than in O'Brien the economist, in that it is refreshingly cautious. One will never see Patrick jumping to conclusions out of regressions based upon numbers innocently grabbed from one of the many website databases. The historian in him rejects the very idea of relying on 'data', if etymologically defined as 'given'. He has taught us that numbers must be drawn from original sources, carefully checked against all other available evidence, and employed only within the limits of their ascertained validity. Moreover, the numbers thus obtained must be handled with care, bearing in mind the theoretical and statistical assumptions implicit in their collection and use. All-purpose, wholesale quantification does not belong to Patrick's historical analysis.

In particular, Patrick's work is a constant caveat against contravening 'important precepts of index number theory' (O' Brien, 1986: 331). There is a revealed preference in his work for binary comparisons and for showing estimates of output, consumption and related variables in two sets of relative prices. His early work on comparing the growth patterns of Great Britain and France in the nineteenth century is an excellent illustration of the fruits such methodology can bear in the hands of a refined historian (O'Brien and Keyder, 1978). The findings of O'Brien and Keyder were at the time quite revolutionary. They showed how French industry, finding its overseas markets restrained by an international economy dominated by Britain, quite successfully reacted by concentrating on high-quality products and the finishing end of manufacturing activity. The traditional assumption about the backwardness of the French economy had to be qualified, if not entirely revised.

Other binary comparisons followed, involving, in particular, countries, such as those on the Mediterranean, whose growth patterns most differed from that of Britain. This line of research yielded copious fruits. From the methodological standpoint, it carried the important message that a certain degree of indeterminacy is intrinsically inherent in any comparative exercise. Patrick's work reminds us that the search for meaningful comparisons will remain a major headache for the economic historian, which no amount of technical sophistication can entirely cure. Solutions for comparative quantitative problems are mostly found on a case-by-case basis, drawing as much from the technical toolbox as from the deep understanding of the issues at hand that only good historians can master.

. . . and the European diffusion 'pattern'

From a substantive, as opposed to methodological, point of view, Patrick's huge comparative efforts have greatly contributed to our understanding of the diffusion pattern of modern economic growth from the British Isles to the rest of the European continent.

In the debate about the diffusion pattern, Patrick sides with those who see the United Kingdom as 'special' rather than paradigmatic case (e.g., O'Brien, 1997a).

In searching for factors accelerating or retarding the diffusion process, O'Brien places considerable emphasis on agriculture, as shown by his comparative study of the agrarian economies of Britain and France (O'Brien, 1996), a masterful show-piece of his scholarship. Geography, resource endowment, demographic trends, urban development, institutional arrangements dating back several centuries and international trade are all called upon to explain the capability of agrarian economies to generate or retard the onset of modern economic growth. In all these dimensions, Britain was superior to its competitors on the eve of the Industrial Revolution. And it is to these dimensions that Patrick turns over and again to explain the timing and success of the individual countries and regions of Europe in producing their own 'modern economic growth'. In analysing diffusion, his first interest is to explain why some agrarian economies were more successful than others in sustaining the long transition to urban industrial societies. His works on France, Italy, Spain and on the so-called periphery at large (O'Brien and Prados de la Escosura, 1992) always move from the agrarian perspective.

The ability of agriculture to induce structural change, or lack thereof, is for Patrick the cornerstone variable in modern economic growth and its diffusion. From this general point of view, he is securely anchored to a time-honoured mainstream tradition. But he departs from that tradition in several ways, the most important of which being that he by no means considers structural change in agriculture a necessary precondition for growth. The study of Spain and Italy leads him to believe that industrialisation is indeed possible in the absence of major agricultural changes, in which case, however, industrialisation will take particular connotations and lead to a less balanced, and possibly weaker, growth pattern.

When considering other variables in the diffusion process – for instance major innovations such as railways – Patrick consistently takes the structural approach. The size of benefits accruing to a given area from the diffusion of the iron horse typically depend on a number of variables ultimately related to income levels. 'There were', he writes 'many parts of Europe . . . whose people remained too poor to take advantage of cheaper and more variegated consumption provided by railways. Their capacity to respond to the widening of markets continued to be restrained by unfavourable resource endowment' (O'Brien, 1983). The same goes, on the supply side, for the ability of an economy to internalise, through linkages and spillovers, the benefits of railway building.

While greatly contributing to the search for a new typology of the European diffusion pattern, particularly with his research agenda on productivity, Patrick is convinced that we do not as yet know enough to convincingly narrate the continent's economic history within a single European frame of reference. To start with, 'economic historians are simply not yet in a position to appreciate the scale of variations among European countries in terms of per capita income and consumption levels' (O'Brien, 1986: 331).

Patrick is obviously not a Gerschenkronian. While admiring Gerschenkron's awesome learning and capacity for generalisation (O'Brien, 1986: 325), he sees too many pitfalls in his attempt at explaining Europe's growth pattern in the nineteenth century. Yet, there are at least three Gerschenkronian traits in O'Brien's understanding of diffusion: (i) Britain is not the paradigm; (ii) income levels in agriculture go a long way towards explaining growth diffusion; (iii) industrialisation does nevertheless take place in the absence of structural change in agriculture. What Patrick drops from the original Gerschenkron construction is the idea of industrialisation spurt engineered by 'agents' such as the universal banks and the state.

Both what he retains and what he drops look like excellent starting points for reconstructing a diffusion typology.

Two clearly discernible red threads

As I said in the beginning, this *laudatio patritii* is simply meant to account for what I have personally learned, and it is a great deal, from my friend's contribution to the discipline. A number of his insightful findings and interpretations have long been incorporated into my graduate and undergraduate teaching. But my intellectual debt to him goes further than that. Patrick's *opus* is one of those felicitous cases where the whole is greater than the sum of its parts. Patrick's papers and books unveil two clearly discernible *fils rouges*, showing a remarkable consistency in his approach to research in economic history.

The first red thread relates to the very nature of our discipline. Economic history, Patrick implies without explicitly saying so, has a potentially powerful message for both economics and history. But this message constantly runs the risk of getting lost. On the edge of the two most established and respected of the social sciences, economic history frequently leans too much one way or the other, thus running the risk of losing its own identity.

Patrick, the eclectic and sophisticated scholar, abhors methodological Manicheism. He appreciates, and practises, both kinds of discourse in the discipline: the economic and the historical. He knows that good economic history may be found in sophisticated cliometrics as well as in refined anecdotal story-telling. His work and teaching, however, convey the belief that economic history has its own strong idiosyncratic character. It is the *combination* of state-of-the art applied economics with archival research and broad historical knowledge that provides the deepest understanding of past economic events. The few, like Patrick, who master the art of this combination to standards of excellence have established economic history as a stand-alone discipline, which, like Janus, looks both ways, to economics and to history without being absorbed by either of them. It is this fascination with these two sciences merging to create a new discipline that has attracted so many of us to economic history.

In this light, I see Patrick's scholarship as conveying a message to both the historian and the economist. The message to the historian is on the one hand that quantification matters more and requires more sophisticated tools than most are ready to accept, and on the other hand that there is no substitute for solid theory as a compass to direct historical research. In reading the books and papers by Patrick O'Brien, one seldom finds explicit theorising. But the economics-literate can easily read in his arguments how economic theory has shaped his research agenda, his selection of evidence and the search for causality.

The message to the economist is that time matters. It matters a lot. If pure economic theory, as a subset of the discipline, can either ignore time or shape it according to its heuristic needs, economics as a whole cannot afford to do so. It must take time seriously or else accept a considerable loss in relevance. If it takes time for markets to clear and for monetary and fiscal policies to produce their effects, if employment and output fluctuations will ever be with us, if path dependence normally results in multiple equilibria, then time is possibly the single most important dimension of economic life. And time is the realm of the historian.

The second *fil rouge* running through Patrick's work has already been indirectly mentioned. It consists in the endless search for comparison. If we randomly select any one of Patrick's pages we are more likely than not to encounter sophisticated comparative analyses. This does not apply to his numerous explicitly comparative essays only. It is a striking, peculiar feature of O'Brien's contributions to the economic history of Britain that they are framed in comparative terms. Comparisons flow constantly and easily from Patrick's pen: they illuminate complex issues, provide measuring rods, add new perspectives, allow tentative 'lessons' to be drawn from the past.

Patrick seems to tell us: 'He who does not compare, understands little.' The message is neither obvious nor banal. It is surely not redundant. Constant search for intelligent comparison is not in large supply, it is not one of the main features of economic history as it is written today.

In this brief *laudatio* I have left unconsidered most of Patrick's relevant contributions to our stock of knowledge. Some of the gaps have been filled by the essays collected in this book. The latter will, I am sure, in due time produce further analyses of Professor O'Brien's outstanding scholarship. Gerschenkron, whom Patrick admired while disagreeing with him, used to say that there is no better reward for scholarly research than its ability to inspire and stimulate new research. If this is true, then Patrick has already received a more important, and lasting, tribute than the one paid by this *laudatio*.

References

Abel, Wilhelm 1980, *Agricultural Fluctuations in Europe from the Thirteenth to the Twentieth Centuries*, London: Methuen.

Abel, Wilhelm 1996, *Agrarkrisen und Agrarkonjunktur*, Berlin: Paul Parey Verlag.

Acemoglu, Daron, Johnson, Simon and Robinson, James 2002, 'The rise of Europe: Atlantic trade, institutional changes and economic growth', NBER Working Paper 9378.

Acerra, Martine 1997, 'Le Matériel de la marine de guerre française: effectifs, arsenaux et approvisionnements au XVIIIe siècle', *Le Bulletin de la Société d'Histoire Moderne et Contemporaine: Européens et espaces maritime au XVIIIe siècle*, 64–80.

Acerra, Martine, Merino, José and Meyer, Jean (eds.) 1985, *Les Marines de guerre européennes au XVII–XVIIIe siècles*, Presses de l'Université de Paris-Sorbonne.

Adie, Douglas 1970, 'English bank deposits before 1844', *Economic History Review* 23, 2: 285–97.

Adler, Ken 1997, 'Innovation and amnesia: engineering rationality and the fate of interchangeable parts manufacturing in France', *Technology and Culture* 38: 273–311.

Ågren, M. (ed.) 1998, *Iron-Making Societies. Early Industrial Development in Sweden and Russia, 1600–1900*, Providence: Berghahn Books.

Aldcroft, D. H. and S. P. Ville (eds.) 1994, *The European Economy 1750–1914*, Manchester University Press.

Allen, Robert C. 1988, 'The growth of labour productivity in early modern English agriculture', *Explorations in Economic History* 25: 117–46.

Allen, Robert C. 1992, *Enclosures and the Yeomen, the Agricultural Development of the South Midlands 1450–1850*, Oxford: Clarendon Press.

Allen, Robert C. 1994, 'Agriculture during the Industrial Revolution', in Floud and McCloskey (eds.), pp. 96–122.

Allen, Robert C. 1999, 'Tracking the Agricultural Revolution', *Economic History Review* 52: 209–35.

Allen, Robert C. 2000, 'Economic structure and agricultural productivity in Europe, 1300–1800', *European Review of Economic History* 4: 1–25.

Allen, Robert C. 2001, 'The Great Divergence in European wages and prices from the Middle Ages to the First World War', *Explorations in Economic History* 38: 411–47.

Allen, Robert C. and Ó'Gráda, Cormac 1988, 'On the road again with Arthur Young: English, Irish, and French agriculture during the Industrial Revolution', *Journal of Economic History* 38: 93–116.

Ambrosoli, M. 1997, *The Wild and the Sown, Botany and Agriculture in Western Europe, 1350–1850*, Cambridge University Press.

Ames, Edward and Rosenberg, Nathan 1963, 'Changing technological leadership and industrial growth', *Economic Journal* 73: 13–31.

Antrás, Pol and Hans-Joachim Voth 2003, 'Factor prices and productivity growth during the British industrial revolution', *Explorations in Economic History* 40, 1: 52–77.

Armytage, Frances 1953, *The Free Port System in the British West Indies. A Study in Commercial Policy, 1766–1822*, London: Longmans, Green & Co.

Arrighi, Giovanni 1994, *The Long Twentieth Century: Money, Power, and the Origins of Our Time*, London: Verso.

Ashdown, Peter 1979, *Caribbean History in Maps*, London: Longman.

Asselain, Jean-Charles 1984, *Histoire économique de la France du XVIIIe siècle à nos jours*, 2 vols., Paris.

Aston, T. H. and Philpin, C. H. E. (eds.) 1985, *The Brenner Debate*, Cambridge University Press.

Attman, Artur 1986, *American Bullion in the European World Trade, 1600 – 1800*, Gothenburg: Kungl, Vetenskaps-och Vitterhets-Samhället.

Bairoch, Paul 1968, *The Working Population and Its Structure*, Brussels: Institut de Sociologie de l'Université Libre.

Bairoch, Paul 1982, 'International industrialization levels from 1750 to 1980', *Journal of European Economic History* 11: 269–332.

Bairoch, Paul 1988, *La Population des villes européennes, 800–1850: banque de données et analyse sommaire des résultats*, Geneva: Droz.

Bairoch, Paul 1989, 'Les trois révolutions agricoles du monde développé: rendements et productivité de 1800 à 1985', *Annales ESC* 2: 317–53.

Bamford, Paul W. 1956, *Forests and French Sea Power, 1660–1789*, University of Toronto Press.

Banken, R. 2000, *Die Industrialisierung der Saarregion 1815–1914*, Stuttgart: Franz Steiner.

Barbier, Jacques A. 1984, 'Indies revenues and naval spending: the cost of colonialism for the Spanish Bourbons, 1763–1805', *Jahrbuch für Geschichte von Staat, Wirtschaft und Gesellschaft Lateinamerikas* 21: 171–88.

Barbier, Jacques and Kuethe, A. (eds.) 1984, *The North American Role in the Spanish Imperial Economy, 1776–1819*, Manchester University Press.

Barnes, D. G. 1961, *A History of the English Corn Laws, 1660–1846*, New York: Kelley.

Barro, Robert J. 1997, *Determinants of Economic Growth: A Cross-Country Empirical Study*, Cambridge, MA: MIT Press.

Barro, Robert 2000, 'Rule of law, democracy and economic performance', in O'Driscoll, Holmes and Kirkpatrick (eds.) 2001, pp. 31–49.

Bates, D. L. 1998, 'Cotton-spinning in Northampton: Edward Cave's Mill, 1742–1761', *Northamptonshire Past and Present* 9: 237–52.

Baugh, Daniel A. 1988, 'Why did Britain lose command of the sea during the war for America?', in Black and Woodfine (eds.), pp. 149–69.

Baugh, Daniel A. 1994, 'Maritime strength and Atlantic commerce: the uses of a grand marine empire', in Stone (ed.), pp. 185–223.

Baugh, Daniel A. 1995, 'The Eighteenth-Century Navy as a national institution, 1690–1815', in Hill (ed.), pp. 120–60.

Baugh, Daniel A. 1998, 'Withdrawing from Europe: Anglo-French maritime geopolitics, 1750–1800', *International History Review* 20: 1–32.

Beck, L. 1897, *Die Geschichte des Eisens. Dritte Abteilung. Das XVIII. Jahrhundert*, Brunswick: Friedrich Vieweg.

Behrendt, Stephen D. 1993, 'The British slave trade, 1785–1807: volume, profitability, and mortality', Ph.D. thesis, University of Wisconsin.

Behrendt, Stephen D. 1997, 'The annual volume and regional distribution of the British slave trade, 1780–1807', *Journal of African History* 38: 187–211.

Behrendt, Stephen D. 2001, 'Markets, transaction cycles, and profits: merchant decision making in the British slave trade', *The William and Mary Quarterly* 3rd series, 58: 170–204.

Belhoste, J.-F. *et al.* 1994, *La Métallurgie comtoise XVe–XIXe siècles*, Besançon: Asprodic.

Bentham, Jeremy 1995, *Colonies, Commerce, and Constitutional Law: Rid Yourselves of Ultramaria and Other Writings on Spain and Spanish America*, Oxford: Clarendon Press.

Berg, Maxine 1994, *The Age of Manufactures, 1700–1820*, 2nd edn, London: Routledge.

Berg, Maxine and Bruland, Kristine (eds.) 1998, *Technological Revolutions in Europe: Historical Perspectives*, Cheltenham: Edward Elgar.

Berg, Maxine and Clifford, Helen 1999, *Consumers and Luxury: Consumer Culture in Europe, 1650–1850*, Manchester University Press.

Berg, Maxine and Hudson, Pat 1992, 'Rehabilitating the Industrial Revolution', *Economic History Review* 45: 24–50.

Bergeron, L. 1981, *France under Napoleon,* Princeton University Press.

Bernal, A. M. 1988, *Economía e historia de los latifundios*, Madrid: Instituto de España/Espasa Calpe.

Beveridge, W. H. 1939, *Prices and Wages in England from the Twelfth to the Nineteenth Century*, London: Longmans.

Black, Jeremy 1991, 'Anglo-Spanish naval relations in the eighteenth century', *Mariner's Mirror* 77: 235–58.

Black, J. M. 1999, *From Louis XIV to Napoleon. The Fate of a Great Power*, London: University College London Press.

Black, J. M. 2001, *Walpole in Power*, Stroud: Sutton Publishing.

Black, J. M. 2002, *European International Relations,* Basingstoke: Palgrave.

Black, Jeremy and Woodfine, Philip (eds.) 1988, *The British Navy and the Use of Naval Power in the Eighteenth Century*, Leicester University Press.

Blackburn, Robin 1997, *The Making of New World Slavery: From the Baroque to the Modern, 1492–1800*, London: Verso.

Blanchard, Ian 2000, 'Russian railway construction and the Urals charcoal iron and steel industry, 1851–1914', *Economic History Review* 53: 107–26.

Blaug, Mark *et al.* (eds.) 1995, *The Quantity Theory of Money*, Cheltenham: Edward Elgar.
Bloch, Marc 1966, *French Rural History*, London: Routledge & Kegan Paul.
Blum, Jerome 1978, *The End of the Old Order in Europe*, Princeton University Press.
Boëthius, B. 1957, 'Swedish iron and steel, 1600–1955', *Scandinavian Economic History Review* 5: 144–75.
Bonney, M. M. and R. J. 1993, *Jean-Roland Malet: premier historien des finances de la monarchie française*, Paris: Comité pour l'histoire économique et financière de la France.
Bonney, R. J. (ed.) 1995a, *Economic Systems and State Finance*, Oxford: ESF/Clarendon Press.
Bonney, R. J. 1995b, *The Limits of Absolutism in Ancien Régime France*, Aldershot: Edward Elgar.
Bonney, R. J. 1995c, 'The Eighteenth Century. II. The struggle for great power status and the end of the Old Fiscal Regime', in Bonney (ed.) 1995a, pp. 315–90.
Bonney, R. J. 1998, 'What's new about the new French fiscal history?', *Journal of Modern History* 70: 639–67.
Bonney R. J. (ed.) 1999, *The Rise of the Fiscal State in Europe, c.1200–1815*, Oxford University Press.
Bonney, R. J. 2001, 'France and the first European paper money experiment', *French History* 15: 254–72.
Bordo M. D. and Capie, F. H. (eds.) 1994, *Monetary Regimes in Transition*, Cambridge University Press.
Bordo; Michael D. and Cortés-Conde, Roberto (eds.) 2001, *Transferring Wealth and Power from the Old to the New World. Monetary and Fiscal Institutions in the 17th through the 19th Centuries*, Cambridge University Press.
Bordo, Michael and Jonung, Lars 1987, *The Long-Run Behaviour of the Velocity of Circulation: the International Evidence*, Cambridge University Press.
Bordo M. D. and White, E. N. 1991, 'A tale of two currencies: British and French finance during the Napoleonic Wars', *Journal of Economic History* 51: 303–16
Bordo M. D. and White, E. N. 1994, 'British and French finance during the Napoleonic Wars', in Bordo and Capie (eds.), pp. 241–73.
Boserup, E. 1965, *The Conditions of Agricultural Growth*, New York: Aldine.
Bosher, J. F. 1970, *French Finances 1770–1795: From Business to Bureaucracy*, Cambridge University Press.
Bosher, J. F. 1972, 'The French Crisis of 1770', *History* 57: 17–30.
Boulle, Pierre H. 1975, 'Marchandises de traite et développement industriel dans la France et l'Angleterre du XVIIIe siècle', *Revue Française d'Histoire d'Outre-Mer* 62, 226/227: 309–30.
Bourde, A. J. 1953, *The Influence of England on the French Agronomes, 1750–1789*, Cambridge University Press.
Bourde, A. J. 1967, *Agronomie et agronomes en France au XVIII siècle*, 3 vols., Paris: SEVPEN.
Bourgadé, Jacques Marquet de 1997, *L'Administration des finances sous l'Ancien Régime*, Paris: Comité pour l'histoire économique et financière de la France.

Bourland, R. D. 1978, 'Maurepas and his administration of the French navy on the eve of the War of the Austrian Succession, 1732–1742', Ph.D. thesis, University of Notre Dame.

Bowen, H. V. 2002, 'Sinews of trade and empire: the supply of commodity exports to the East India Company during the eighteenth century', *Economic History Review* 55: 466–86.

Bowden, P. J. 1985, 'Agricultural prices, wages, farm profits, and rents', in Thirsk (ed.), pp. 1–118.

Braudel, Fernand 1981–4, *Civilization and Capitalism: 15th–18th Century*, London: Collins.

Brennan, T. 1997, *Burgundy to Champagne. The Wine Trade in Early Modern France*, Cambridge University Press.

Brenner, Robert 1985, 'Agrarian class structure and economic development in pre-industrial Europe', in Aston and Philpin (eds.), pp. 10–63.

Brewer, John 1989, *The Sinews of Power: War, Money and the English State, 1688–1783*, New York: Knopf.

Brewer, John and Porter, Roy 1993, *Consumption and the World of Goods*, London: Routledge.

Brezis, Elise S. 1995, 'Foreign capital flows in the century of Britain's industrial revolution: new estimates, controlled conjectures', *Economic History Review* 48, 1: 46–67.

Brezis, Elise S. and Crouzet François H. 1995, 'The role of *assignats* during the French Revolution: an evil or a rescuer?', *Journal of European Economic History* 24: 7–40.

Brezis, Elise S., Krugman, Paul R. and Tsiddon, D. C. 1993, 'Leapfrogging in international competition: a theory of cycles in national technological leadership', *American Economic Review* 83: 1,211–8.

Broadberry, S. N. 1997, *The Productivity Race: British Manufacturing in International Perspective, 1850–1990*, Cambridge University Press.

Bruguière, M. 1969, *La Première Restauration et son budget*, Hautes études medievales et modernes, 10, Geneva: Droz.

Brunt, Liam 1997, 'Nature or nurture? Explaining English wheat yields in the agricultural revolution', University of Oxford, Discussion Papers in Economic and Social History, Number 19.

Brunt, Liam 1999, 'Estimating English wheat yields in the Industrial Revolution', University of Oxford, Discussion Papers in Economic and Social History, Number 29.

Buchet, Christian 1991, *La lutte pour l'espace caraïbe et la façade atlantique de l'Amerique Centrale et du Sud 1692–1763*, 2 vols., Paris: Librairie de l'Inde.

Buchet, Christian 1994, 'The Royal Navy and the Caribbean, 1689–1763', *Mariner's Mirror* 80: 30–44.

Buchet, Christian, (ed.) 1997a, *L'homme, la santé et la mer*, Paris: Honoré Champion.

Buchet, Christian 1997b, 'Quantification des pertes dans l'espace caraïbe et retombées stratégiques', in Buchet (ed.), pp. 177–94.

Buchet, Christian 1999, *Marine, économie et société: Un exemple d'interaction: l'avitaillement de la Royal Navy durant la guerre de sept ans*, Paris: Honoré Champion.

Buist, M. G. 1974, *At Spes Non Fracta: Hope & Co., 1770–1815*, The Hague: Martinus Nijhoff.

Burda, Michael and Wyplosz, Charles 1997, *Macroeconomics: A European Text*, Oxford University Press.

Burnard, T. G. 2001, '"Prodigious riches": the wealth of Jamaica before the American Revolution', *Economic History Review* 54, 3: 506–24.

Buron, Edmond 1931–2, 'Statistics on Franco-American Trade, 1778–1806', *Journal of Economic and Business History* 4: 571–80.

Burt, Roger 1995, 'The transformation of the non-ferrous metals industries in the seventeenth and eighteenth centuries', *Economic History Review* 48, 1: 23–45.

Cameron, Rondo 1961, *France and the Economic Development of Europe 1800–1914*, Princeton University Press.

Cameron, Rondo (ed.) 1967a, *Banking in the Early Stages of Industrialization*, Oxford University Press.

Cameron, Rondo 1967b, 'England, 1750–1844', in Cameron (ed.), pp. 15–59.

Campbell, Bruce M. S. 1983, 'Arable productivity in medieval England: some evidence from Norfolk', *Journal of Economic History* 43: 379–404.

Campbell, Bruce and Overton, Mark (eds.) 1991, *Land, Labour and Livestock: Historical Studies in Agricultural Productivity*, Manchester University Press.

Capie, Forrest and Webber, Alan 1983, 'Total coin and coin in circulation in the United Kingdom, 1868–1914', *Journal of Money Credit and Banking* 15, 1: 24–39.

Carmona, Juan and Simpson, James 2003, *El laberinto de la agricultura española. Instruciones, contratos y organización entre 1850 y 1936*, Zaragoza: PUZ.

Carrier, E. H. 1932, *Water and Grass. A Study of the Pastoral Economy of Southern Europe*, London: Christophers.

Castaign, John and Wetenhall, Edward 1697–1817, *The Course of the Exchange*, Goldsmiths Library, University of London.

Chabert, Alexandre 1945–9, *Essai sur les mouvements des prix et des revenus en France . . . de 1798 à 1820*, Paris: Librairie de Médicis, Editions M-Th. Genin.

Chalklin, Christopher 2001, *The Rise of the English Town, 1650–1850*, Cambridge University Press.

Challis, C. E. (ed.) 1992, *A New History of the Royal Mint*, Cambridge University Press.

Chambers, J. D. and Mingay, G. E. 1966, *The Agricultural Revolution 1750–1880*, London: Batsford.

Chapman, Stanley D. 1966, 'The Midlands cotton and worsted spinning industry, 1769–1800', Ph.D. thesis, University of London.

Chapman, Stanley D. 1987, *The Cotton Industry in the Industrial Revolution*, 2nd edn, London: Macmillan.

Chapman, Stanley D. and Chassagne, S. 1981, *European Textile Printers in the Eighteenth Century*, London: Heinemann.

Chenery, Hollis and Syrquin, Moshe 1975, *Patterns of Development*, Oxford University Press.

Church, R. A. (ed.) 1994, *The Coal and Iron Industries*, Oxford: Blackwell.

Clague, Christopher, Keefer, Philip, Knack, Stephan and Olson, Mancur 1999, 'Contract intensive money: contract enforcement, property rights, and economic performance', *Journal of Economic Growth* 4: 185–211.

Clark, Gregory 1993, 'Agriculture and the Industrial Revolution, 1700–1850,' in Mokyr (ed.), pp. 227–66.

Clark, Gregory 1998, 'Commons sense: common property rights, efficiency, and institutional change', *Journal of Economic History* 58: 73–102.

Clark, Gregory 1999, 'Too much revolution: agriculture in the Industrial Revolution, 1700–1860', in Mokyr (ed.), pp. 206–40.

Clark, G. 2001, 'The secret history of the Industrial Revolution', University of California, Davis (mimeo).

Clark, Gregory, Huberman, Michael and Lindert, Peter 1995, 'A British food puzzle', *Economic History Review* 48: 215–37.

Coad, Jonathan 1981, 'Historic architecture of H. M. naval base Portsmouth, 1700–1850', *Mariner's Mirror* 67: 3–59.

Coad, Jonathan 1983, 'Historic architecture of H. M. naval base Devonport, 1689–1850', *Mariner's Mirror* 69: 341–92.

Cobbett, W. 1816, *The Parliamentary History of England from the Earliest Period to the year 1803, Vol. XXVIII Comprising the Period from the Eighth of May 1789 to the Fifteenth of March 1791*, London: T. C. Hansard.

Cobbett, W. 1817, *The Parliamentary History of England from the Earliest Period to the year 1803, Vol. XXIX Comprising the Period from Twenty-second of March 1791 to the Thirteenth of December 1792*, London: T. C. Hansard.

Cochran, Thomas C. 1981, *Frontiers of Change: Early Industrialism in America*, Oxford University Press.

Coclanis, Peter A. 1990, 'The wealth of British America on the eve of the Revolution,' *Journal of Interdisciplinary History* 21: 245–60.

Cohen, J. S. and Weitzman, M. L. 1975, 'A Marxian model of enclosures', *Journal of Development Economics* 1: 287–336.

Coleman, D. C. 1983, 'Protoindustrialization: a concept too many', *Economic History Review* 36: 435–48.

Coleman, D. C. 1992, *Myth, History and the Industrial Revolution*, London: Hambledon Press.

Collins, Michael 1979, 'English bank deposits before 1844: a comment', *Economic History Review* 32, 1: 114–7.

Crafts, N. F. R. 1976, 'English economic growth in the eighteenth century: a re-examination of Deane and Cole's estimates', *Economic History Review* 29: 226–35.

Crafts, N. F. R. 1977a, 'Determinants of the rate of parliamentary enclosure', *Explorations in Economic History* 14: 227–49.

Crafts, N. F. R. 1977b, 'Industrial revolution in Britain and France: some thoughts on the question "Why was England first?"', *Economic History Review* 30: 429–41.

Crafts, N. F. R. 1981, 'The eighteenth century: a survey', in Floud and McCloskey (eds.), pp. 1–16.

Crafts, N. F. R. 1984, 'Economic growth in France and Britain, 1830–1910: a review of the evidence', *Journal of Economic History* 44: 49–67.

Crafts, N. F. R. 1985, *British Economic Growth during the Industrial Revolution*, Oxford: Clarendon Press.

Crafts, N. F. R. 1989, 'British industrialization in an international context', *Journal of Interdisciplinary History* 19: 415–28.

Crafts, N. F. R. 1996, 'The First Industrial Revolution: a guided tour for growth economists', *American Economic Review* 86, 2: 197–201.

Crafts, Nicholas 1998, 'Forging ahead and falling behind: the rise and decline of the First Industrial Nation', *Journal of Economic Perspectives* 12, 2: 193–210.

Crafts, Nicholas F. R. 2000, 'Development history', LSE Working Papers in Economic History, 54/00.

Crafts, Nicholas 2003, 'Productivity growth in the Industrial Revolution: a new growth accounting perspective', LSE (mimeo).

Crafts, N. F. R. and Harley, C. K. 1992, 'Output growth and the British Industrial Revolution: a restatement of the Crafts-Harley view', *Economic History Review* 45: 703–30.

Cross, Harry E. 1983, 'South American bullion production and export, 1550–1750', in Richards (ed.), pp. 397–423.

Crouzet, François 1972, 'Editor's introduction', in Crouzet, François (ed.), *Capital Formation in the Industrial Revolution*, London: Methuen, pp. 1–69.

Crouzet, François 1980, 'Toward an export economy: British exports during the Industrial Revolution', *Explorations in Economic History* 17, 1: 48–93.

Crouzet, François 1985, *The First Industrialists: The Problem of Origins*, Cambridge University Press.

Crouzet, François 1987, *L'Economie britannique et le blocus continental 1806–1813*, Paris: Presses Universitaires de France.

Crouzet, François 1990a, 'Angleterre-Brésil, 1697–1850: un siècle et demi d'échanges commerciaux', *Histoire, Economies, et Sociétés* 9, 2: 287–317.

Crouzet, François 1990b, *Britain Ascendant: Comparative Studies in Franco-British Economic History*, Cambridge University Press.

Crouzet, François 1990c, 'Variations on the North-Atlantic triangle from Yorktown to Waterloo', in Crouzet 1990b, pp. 318–40.

Crouzet, François 1993, *La grande inflation. La monnaie en France de Louis XVI à Napoléon*, Paris: Fayard.

Cuenca Esteban, Javier 1984, 'The United States balance of payments with Spanish America and the Philippine Islands, 1790–1819: estimates and analysis of principal components', in Barbier and Kuethe (eds.), pp. 198–209.

Cuenca Esteban, Javier 1987, 'Fundamentos para una interpretación de las estadísticas comerciales francesas, 1787–1821, con referencia especial al comercio franco español', *Hacienda Pública Española* 108/9: 221–51.

Cuenca Esteban, Javier 1994, 'British textile prices, 1770–1831: are British growth rates worth revising once again?', *Economic History Review* 47, 1: 66–105.

Cuenca Esteban, Javier 1997, 'The rising share of British industrial exports in industrial output, 1700–1851', *Journal of Economic History* 57, 4: 879–906.

Cuenca Esteban, Javier 2001, 'The British balance of payments 1772–1820. India transfers and war finance', *Economic History Review* 54, 1: 58–86.

d'Argenson, marquis 1857, *Journal et mémoires du marquis d'Argenson*, ed. E. J. B. Rathery, 9 vols., Paris: Mme Ve Jules Renouard.

Darity, William 1992, 'A model of "original sin": rise of the west and lag of the rest', *American Economic Review* 82, 2: 162–7.

Davenant, C. [1771] 1967, *The Political and Commercial Works*, collected and revised by Sir Charles Whitworth, 5 vols., Farnborough: Gregg Press.

David, Paul A. and Wright, Gavin 1997, 'Increasing returns and the genesis of American resource abundance', *Industrial and Corporate Change* 6, 2: 203–45.

Davis, Lance E. and North, Douglass C. 1973, *Institutional Change and American Economic Growth*, Cambridge University Press.

Davis, Ralph 1954, 'English foreign trade, 1660–1700', *Economic History Review* 7, 2: 150–66.

Davis, Ralph 1962a, 'English foreign trade, 1700–1774', *Economic History Review* 15, 2: 285–303.

Davis, Ralph 1962b, *The Rise of the Shipping Industry in England in the Seventeenth and Eighteenth Centuries*, London: Macmillan.

Davis, Ralph 1979, *The Industrial Revolution and British Overseas Trade*, Leicester University Press.

Day, L. and McNeil, J. 1996, *Biographical Dictionary of the History of Technology*, London: Routledge.

Deane, Phyllis 1957, 'The output of the British woollen industry in the eighteenth century', *Journal of Economic History* 17: 207–23.

Deane, P. and W. A. Cole 1962, *British Economic Growth, 1688–1959: Trends and Structure*, Cambridge University Press.

Defoe, Daniel 1728, *A Plan of the English Commerce*, London.

Dehing, Pit and Hart, Marjolein 't 1997, 'Linking the fortunes: currency and banking, 1550–1800', in Hart *et al.* (eds.), pp. 37–61.

de Korte, J. P. 1983, *De Financiele Verantwoording in de Verenigde Oostindische Compagnie*, The Hague: Nijhoff.

Demonet, M. 1990, *Tableau de l'agriculture française au mileu du 19e siècle: l'enquête agricole de 1852*, Paris: EHESS.

Denevan, William 1976, 'Epilogue', in Denevan, William (ed.), *The Native Population of the Americas in 1492*, Madison: University of Wisconsin Press.

Denison, Edward F. 1962, *The Sources of Economic Growth in the United States and the Alternatives Before Us*, New York: Committee for Economic Development, Supplementary Paper No. 13.

Dercon, S. 1998, 'Wealth, risk and activity choice: cattle in western Tanzania', *Journal of Development Economics* 55: 1–42.

de Vries, Jan 1974, *The Dutch Rural Economy in the Golden Age, 1500–1700*, New Haven: Yale University Press.

de Vries, Jan 1975, 'Peasant demand patterns and economic development: Friesland, 1550–1750', in Parker and Jones (eds.), pp. 205–65.

de Vries, Jan 1984, *European Urbanization, 1500–1800*, London: Methuen.

de Vries, Jan 1994, 'The Industrial Revolution and the Industrious Revolution', *Journal of Economic History* 54: 249–70.

de Vries, Jan and van der Woude, A. M. 1997, *The First Modern Economy: Success, Failure, and Perseverance of the Dutch Economy, 1500–1850*, Cambridge University Press.

Dickson, P. G. M. 1967, *The Financial Revolution in England: A Study in the Development of Public Credit, 1688–1756*, London: Macmillan.

Dickinson, H. T. (ed.) 1989, *Britain and the French Revolution, 1789–1815*, Basingstoke: Penguin.

Digby, Nigel, Bowen, H. V. and Lincoln, Margarette (eds.) 2002, *The Worlds of the East India Company*, Woodbridge: Boydell and Brewer.

Dormois, J.-P. 1997, *L'Economie française face à la concurrence britannique à la veille de 1914*, Paris: Harmattan.

Doyle, W. 1996, *Venality. The Sale of Offices in the Eighteenth Century*, Oxford University Press.

Duffy, Michael (ed.) 1992a, *Parameters of British Naval Power, 1650–1850*, University of Exeter Press.

Duffy, Michael 1992b, 'The establishment of the western squadron as the lynchpin of British naval strategy', in Duffy (ed.), pp. 60–81.

Dull, Jonathan R. 1975, *The French Navy and American Independence: A Study of Arms and Diplomacy, 1774–1787*, Princeton University Press.

Dziembowski, Edmond 1998, *Un Nouveau Patriotisme français, 1750–1770: La France face à puissance anglaise à l'époque de la guerre de Sept Ans*, Voltaire Foundation, Oxford University Press.

Ellis, G. 1981, *Napoleon's Continental Blockade: The Case of Alsace*, Oxford University Press.

Ellis, Joyce 2001, *The Georgian Town, 1680–1840*, Basingstoke: Palgrave.

Eltis, David 1998, 'The slave economies of the Caribbean structure: performance, evolution, and significance', in Knight (ed.), pp. 105–37.

Eltis, David and Stanley L. Engerman 2000, 'The importance of slavery and the slave trade to industrializing Britain', *Journal of Economic History* 60, 1: 123–44.

Eltis, David and Richardson, David 1995, 'Productivity in the transatlantic slave trade', *Explorations in Economic History* 32: 465–84.

Eltis, Walter 1995, 'John Locke, the quantity theory of money and the establishment of a sound currency', in Blaug (ed.), pp. 4–26.

Engerman, Stanley L. 1972, 'The slave trade and British capital formation in the eighteenth century: a comment on the Williams thesis', *Business History Review* 46, 4: 430–43.

Engerman, Stanley L. 1998, 'British imperialism in a mercantilist age, 1492–1849', *Revista de Historia Económica* 16, 1: 195–225.

Engerman, Stanley L. 2000, 'France, Britain, and the economic growth of colonial North America', in McCusker and Morgan (eds.), pp. 227–49.

Engerman, Stanley L. 2002, 'Pricing freedom: evaluating the costs of emancipation and of manumission', in Shepherd (ed.), pp. 273–302.

Engerman, Stanley L., Haber, Stephen H. and Sokoloff, Kenneth L. 2000, 'Inequality, institutions and differential paths of growth among New World economies', in Ménard (ed.), pp. 108–34.

English, W. 1973, 'A technical assessment of Lewis Paul's spinning machine', *Textile History* 4: 68–83.

Evans, C. 2000, *Coal, Iron and the Industrial Revolution In Britain*, unpublished paper, University of Glamorgan.

Evans, C. and Ryden, G. 1998, 'Kinship and the transmission of skills: bar iron production in Britain and Sweden, 1500–1860', in Berg and Bruland (eds.), pp. 188–206.

Faure, Edgar 1977, *Le Banqueroute de Law,* Paris: Gallimard.

Feinstein, Charles H. 1978, 'Capital formation in Great Britain', in Mathias and Postan (eds.), vol. VII, part I, pp. 28–96.

Feinstein, Charles H. 1981, 'Capital accumulation and the Industrial Revolution', in Floud and McCloskey (eds.), vol. I, pp. 128–42.

Feliu, Gaspar 1991, *Precios y salarios en la Cataluña moderna*, 2 vols., Madrid: Banco de España.

Félix, J. 1999, *Finances et politique au siècle des Lumières. Le ministère L'Averdy, 1763–1768*, Paris: Comité pour l'histoire économique et financière de la France.

Findlay, Ronald 1982, 'Trade and growth in the Industrial Revolution', in Kindleberger and di Tella (eds.), vol. I, pp. 178–88.

Findlay, Ronald 1990, 'The "triangular trade" and the Atlantic economy of the eighteenth century: a simple general-equilibrium model', *Essays in International Finance*, No. 177, Princeton University.

Finberg, H. P. R. (ed.) 1967, *The Agrarian History of England and Wales*, vol. IV, Cambridge University Press.

Fisher, F. J. 1935, 'The development of the London food market, 1540–1640', *Economic History Review* 5: 46–64.

Fisher, F. J. (ed.) 1961, *Essays in the Economic and Social History of Tudor and Stuart England*, Cambridge University Press.

Fischer, Lewis R. and Nordvik, Helge W. (eds.) 1990, *Shipping and Trade, 1750–1950: Essays in International Maritime Economic History*, Pontefract: Lofthouse Publications.

Fitton, R. S., 1989, *The Arkwrights: Spinners of Fortune*, Manchester University Press.

Flinn, Michael 1984, *The History of the British Coal Industry, Volume 2, 1700–1830: The Industrial Revolution*, Oxford University Press.

Florén, A. *et al.* 1998, 'The social organisation of work at mines, furnaces and forges' in Ågren (ed.), pp. 61–138.

Floud, Roderick and McCloskey, Donald N. (eds.) 1981, 1994, *The Economic History of Britain Since 1700. Volume 1: 1780–1860.* Volume 2: 1860–1939. Volume 3: 1939–1992, Cambridge University Press.

Fogel, Robert William 1989, *Without Consent or Contract: The Rise and Fall of American Slavery*, New York: W. W. Norton.

Fogel, Robert William 1991, 'The conquest of high mortality and hunger in Europe and America: timing and mechanisms', in Higonnet *et al.* (eds.), pp. 33–71.

Fontana, J. 1985, 'La desamortización de Mendizábal y sus antecedentes', in García Sanz and Garrabou (eds.), pp. 219–44.

Forbonnais, F. Véron de 1758, *Recherches et considerations sur les finances de France depuis l'année 1595 jusqu'à l'année 1721*, 2 vols., Basle.
Forrest, A. and Jones, P. M. (eds.) 1991, *Reshaping France: Town, Country and Region during the French Revolution*, Manchester University Press.
Fortrey, Samuel 1663, *Englands Interest and Improvement*, Cambridge: John Field.
Fourastie, Jean 1958, *Documents pour l'histoire et la théorie des prix. Séries statistiques réunies et elaborées*, 2 vols., Paris: Librairie Armand Colin.
Fox R. (ed.) 1996, *Technological Change: Methods and Themes in the History of Technology*, Amsterdam: Harwood.
Francis, A. D. 1972, *The Wine Trade*, London: Adam & Charles Black.
Frank, A. G. 1978, *World Accumulation, 1492–1789*, London: Macmillan.
Frank, A. G. 1998, *ReOrient: Global Economy in the Asian Age*, Berkeley: University of California Press.
Fremdling, Rainer 1986, *Technologischer Wandel und Internationaler Handel im 18. und 19. Jahrhundert: Die Eisenindustrien in Großbritannien, Belgien, Frankreich und Deutschland.* Berlin: Duncker & Humblot.
Fremdling, Rainer 1991a, 'Foreign competition and technological change: British exports and the modernisation of the German iron industry from the 1820s to the 1860s', in Lee (ed.), pp. 47–76.
Fremdling, Rainer 1991b, 'The puddler. A craftsman's skill and the spread of a new technology in Belgium, France and Germany', *Journal of European Economic History* 20: 529–67.
Fremdling, Rainer 1998, 'The French iron industry, 1820–1860. The change from charcoal to mineral-fuel based technology', in Merger *et al.* (eds.), pp. 712–24.
Fremdling, Rainer 2000, 'Transfer patterns of British technology to the continent: the case of the iron industry', *European Review of Economic History* 4: 195–222.
Fremdling, Rainer and Gales, Ben 1994, 'Iron masters and iron production during the Belgian Industrial Revolution: The "Enquete" of 1828', in Klep and van Cauwenberghe (eds.), pp. 247–58.
Fritschy, W. 1990, 'Taxation in Britain, France and the Netherlands in the eighteenth century', *Economic and Social History in the Netherlands* 2: 57–79.
García Sanz, Ángel 1974, 'Agronomía y experiencias agronómicas en España durante la segunda mitad del siglo XVIII', *Moneda y Crédito* 131: 29–54.
García Sanz, Ángel and Garrabou, Ramon (eds.) 1985a, *Historia agraria de la España contemporánea. 1. Cambio social y nuevas formas de propiedad 1800–1850*, Barcelona: Crítica.
García Sanz, Ángel 1985b, 'Crisis de la agricultura tradicional y revolución liberal', in García Sanz and Garrabou (eds.), vol. I, pp. 7–99.
García Sanz, Ángel 1994, 'Los privilegios de la Mesta: contexto histórico y económico de su concesión y de su abolición, 1273–1836', in *Quaderno de leyes y privilegios del honrado Concejo de la Mesta* (facsimile edition), Valladolid: Lex Nova.
Gelder, H. E. van 1978/9, 'De Nederlandse manualen 1586–1630', *Jaarboek voor Munt- en Penningkunde*, 65/66: 39–79.

Gilboy, Elizabeth W. 1934, *Wages in Eighteenth Century England*, Cambridge, MA: Harvard University Press.

Gille, Bertrand 1968, *La Sidérugie française au XIXe siècle*, Geneva: Droz.

Glete, Jan 1993, *Navies and Nations: Warships, Navies and State Building in Europe and America, 1500–1860*, 2 vols., Stockholm: Almqvist and Wiksell International.

Glover, Richard 1963, *Peninsular Preparation: the Reform of the British Army, 1795–1809*, Cambridge University Press.

Goldstone, J. 1986, 'The demographic revolution in England: a re-examination', *Population Studies* 49: 5–33.

Gouk, P. (ed.) 1995, *Wellsprings of Achievement: Cultural and Economic Dynamics in Early Modern England*, Aldershot: Ashgate.

Gradish, Stephen F. 1980, *The Manning of the British Navy during the Seven Years' War*, London: Royal Historical Society.

Grantham, George 1978, 'The diffusion of the new husbandry in northern France', *Journal of Economic History* 38: 311–37.

Grantham, George 1980, 'The persistence of open field farming in nineteenth century France', *Journal of Economic History* 40: 515–31.

Grantham, George 1989, 'Agricultural supply during the Industrial Revolution: French evidence and European implications', *Journal of Economic History* 49: 43–72.

Grantham, George 1991, 'The growth of labour productivity in the production of wheat in the cinq grosses fermes of France, 1750–1929', in Campbell and Overton (eds.), pp. 340–63.

Grantham, George 1999, 'Contra Ricardo: on the macroeconomics of pre-industrial economics', *European Review of Economic History* 3: 199–232.

Greene, J. P. 2000, 'How the winners lost command' [review of F. Anderson, *Crucible of War. The Seven Years' War and the Fate of Empire in British North America, 1754–1766* (2000)], *Times Literary Supplement*, 25 August, 8–9.

Griffiths, S. 1873, *Griffiths' Guide to the Iron Trade of Great Britain*, London: Newtown Abbot.

Griffiths, Trevor, Hunt, David and O'Brien, Patrick 1992, 'Inventive activity in the British textile industry, 1700–1800', *Journal of Economic History* 52: 881–906.

Griffiths, Trevor, Hunt, David and O'Brien, Patrick 1998, 'The curious history and imminent demise of the challenge and response model', in Berg and Bruland (eds.), pp. 119–38.

Grossman, Herschel I. 2001, 'The state in economic history', in Bordo and Cortés-Conde (eds.), pp. 453–63.

Habakkuk, John 1940, 'English landownership, 1680–1740', *Economic History Review* 10: 2–17.

Hamilton, Earl J. 1929, 'American treasure and the rise of capitalism', *Economica* 9: 338–57.

Hanauer, Charles Auguste 1876–8, *Etudes économiques sur l'Alsace ancienne et moderne*, 2 vols., Paris: Durand et Pedone-Lauriel.

Hardin, G. J. 1998, *Managing the Commons*, Bloomington: Indiana University Press.

Harley, C. Knick 1993, 'Reassessing the Industrial Revolution: a macro view', in Mokyr (ed.), pp. 171–226.

Harley, C. Knick 1994, 'Foreign trade: comparative advantage and performance', in Floud and McCloskey (eds.), pp. 300–31.

Harley, C. K. and Crafts, N. F. R. 2000, 'Simulating the two views of the Industrial Revolution', *Journal of Economic History* 60: 819–41.

Harris, J. R. 1988, *The British Iron Industry, 1700–1850*, Basingstoke: Macmillan.

Harris, J. R. 1997, *Industrial Espionage and Technology Transfer: Britain and France in the Eighteenth Century*, Aldershot: Ashgate.

Harris, J. R. 1998, *Industrial Espionage and Technology Transfer: Britain and France in the Eighteenth Century*, Aldershot: Ashgate.

Harris, R. D. 1976, 'French finances and the American War, 1777–1783', *Journal of Modern History* 48: 247–50.

Harris, Ron 2000, *Industrializing English Law: Entrepreneurship and Business Organization, 1720–1844*, New York: Cambridge University Press.

Hart, Marjolein 't 1993, *The Making of a Bourgeois State: War, Politics and Finance during the Dutch Revolt*, Manchester University Press.

Hart, Marjolein 't, Jonker, Joost and van Zanden, Jan Luiten (eds.) 1997, *A Financial History of The Netherlands*, Cambridge University Press.

Harte, N. B. (ed.) 1997, *The New Draperies in the Low Countries and England, 1300–1800*, Oxford University Press.

Hartmann P. C. (ed.) 1979, *Das Steuersystem der Europäischen Staaten am Ende des Ancien Régime. Eine offizielle französische Enquête, 1763–8* . . . Munich: Artemis.

Hartwell, R. Max 1971, *The Industrial Revolution and Economic Growth*, London: Methuen.

Hatton, Timothy J., Lyons, John S. and Satchell, S. E. 1983, 'Eighteenth-Century British trade: homespun or empire made?', *Explorations in Economic History* 20, 2: 163–82.

Hauser, Henry (ed.) 1936, *Recherches et documents sur l'histoire des prix en France, de 1500 à 1800*, Paris: Imprimerie Les Presses Modernes.

Hayami, Yujiro and Otsuka, Keijiro 1993, *The Economics of Contract Choice: An Agrarian Perspective*, Oxford: Clarendon Press.

Higonnet, Pierre, Landes, David S. and Rosovsky, Henry (eds.) 1991, *Favourites of Fortune. Technology, Growth and Economic Development since the Industrial Revolution*, Cambridge, MA: Harvard University Press.

Hilaire-Pérez, Liliane 2000, *L'Invention technique au Siècle des Lumières*, Paris: Albin Michel.

Hildebrand, K.-G. 1958, 'Markets for Swedish iron in the 18th century', *Scandinavian Economic History Review* 6: 3–52.

Hildebrand, K.-G. 1992, *Swedish Iron in the Seventeenth and Eighteenth Centuries. Export Industry Before the Industrialization*, Södertälje: Bröderna Ljungsbergs Trykerei.

Hill, J. R. (ed.) 1995, *The Oxford Illustrated History of the Royal Navy*, Oxford University Press.

Hills, R. L. 1970, *Power in the Industrial Revolution*, Manchester University Press.

Hilton, Rodney 1983, *The Decline of Serfdom in Medieval England*, 2nd edn, Houndsmills: Macmillan.

Hobsbawm, Eric and Rudé, George 1985, *Captain Swing*, Harmondsworth: Peregrine Books.

Hoffman, E. and Mokyr, J. 1984, 'Peasants, potatoes, and poverty: transactions costs in prefamine Ireland', *Research In Economic History* 3: 115–45.

Hoffman, Philip T. 1988, 'Institutions and agriculture in Old-Regime France', *Politics and Society*, 16: 241–64.

Hoffman, Philip T. 1996, *Growth in a Traditional Society: The French Countryside, 1450–1815*, Princeton University Press.

Hoffman Philip T. and Norberg, Kathryn (eds.) 1994, *Fiscal Crises, Liberty, and Representative Government, 1450–1789*, Stanford University Press.

Hoffman, Philip T., Postal-Vinay, Gilles and Rosenthal, Jean-Laurent 2000, *Priceless Markets: The Political Economy of Credit in Paris, 1660–1870*, University of Chicago Press.

Hoffman, Philip T. and Rosenthal, Jean-Laurent 1995, 'Redistribution and long-term private debt in Paris, 1660–1726', *Journal of Economic History* 55: 256–84.

Holderness, B. A. 1997, 'The reception and distribution of the New Draperies in England', in Harte (ed.), pp. 217–43.

Horrell, S. 1996, 'Home demand and British industrialization', *Journal of Economic History* 56: 561–604.

Horsefield, J. K. 1949, 'The cash ratio in English banks before 1800', *Journal of Political Economy* 57: 70–4.

Horsefield, J. K. 1952, 'Banking practices', *Economica* 19: 308–21.

Hume, David 1751, 'Of the balance of trade', reprinted in Munroe, 1965, pp. 323–38.

Humphries, Jane 1990, 'Enclosures, common rights, and women: the proletarianization of families in the late eighteenth and early nineteenth centuries', *Journal of European Economic History* 50: 17–42.

Hunter, W. A. 1951–3, 'James Hargreaves and the invention of the Spinning Jenny', *Transactions of the Newcomen Society* 28: 141–51.

Hutchins, B. L. and Harrison, A. 1966, *A History of Factory Legislation*, 3rd edn, New York: Augustus M. Kelley.

Hyde, C. K. 1977, *Technological Change and the British Iron Industry, 1700–1870*, Princeton University Press.

Inglis, G. Douglas 1985, 'The Spanish naval shipyard at Havana in the eighteenth century', in Department of History (ed.), *Fifth Naval History Symposium*, Baltimore: Nautical and Aviation Publishing Co. of America, pp. 47–58.

Inikori, J. E. 1989, 'Slavery and the revolution in cotton textile production in England', *Social Science History* 13, 4: 343–79.

Inkster, Ian 1990, 'Mental capital: transfers of knowledge and technique in eighteenth century Europe', *Journal of European Economic History* 19, 2: 403–41.

Inkster, Ian 1991, *Science and Technology in History: An Approach to Industrial Development*, Basingstoke: Macmillan.

Inkster, Ian 1996, 'Discoveries, inventions and industrial revolutions: on the varying contributions of technologies and institutions from an international historical perspective', *History of Technology* 18: 39–58.

Irwin, Douglas A. 1988, 'Welfare effects of British trade: debate and evidence from the 1840s', *Journal of Political Economy* 96: 1,142–64.

Irwin, Douglas A. 1991, 'Mercantilism as strategic trade policy: The Anglo-Dutch rivalry for the East India trade', *Journal of Political Economy* 99, 6: 1,296–314.

Israel, Jonathan 1989, *Dutch Primacy in World Trade, 1585–1740,* Oxford University Press.

Jackson, R. V. 1985, 'Growth and deceleration in English agriculture, 1660–1790', *Economic History Review* 3: 333–51.

Jacob, Margaret C. 1997, *Scientific Culture and the Making of the Industrial Revolution*, Oxford University Press.

Jobert, Pierre 1979, 'Paul Thoureau: échec d'une concentration métallurgique en Côte-d'Or 1840–1861', *Annales de Bourgogne* 51: 5–30.

John, A. H. 1954–5, 'War and the English economy, 1700–1763', *Economic History Review* 7: 329–44.

Jones, D. W. 1988, *War and Economy in the Age of William III and Marlborough,* Oxford University Press.

Jones, Eric L. 1981, *The European Miracle*, Cambridge University Press.

Jörberg, Lennart 1972, *A History of Prices in Sweden 1732–1914*, Lund University Press.

Kaiser, Thomas E. 1991, 'Money, despotism and public opinion in early eighteenth-century France: John Law and the debate on royal credit', *Journal of Modern History* 63: 1–28.

Kanefsky, John and Robey, John 1980, 'Steam engines in 18th-century Britain: a quantitative assessment', *Technology and Culture* 21: 161–86.

Kindleberger, Charles P. 1993, *A Financial History of Western* Europe, 2nd edn, New York: Oxford University Press.

Kindleberger, Charles P. and di Tella, Guido (eds.) 1982, *Economics in the Long View. Essays in Honour of W. W. Rostow*, 3 vols., New York: Oxford University Press.

Klep, P. and van Cauwenberghe, E. (eds.) 1994, *Entrepreneurship and the Transformation of the Economy*, Leuven University Press.

Knight, Franklin W. (ed.) 1998, *General History of the Caribbean, Volume III. The Slave Societies of the Caribbean*, Paris: UNESCO.

Knight, R. J. B. 1987, *Portsmouth Record Series, Portsmouth Dockyard Papers 1774–1783: The American War*, City of Portsmouth.

Komlos, J. 2000, 'The Industrial Revolution as the escape from the Malthusian Trap', *Journal of European Economic History* 29, 2–3: 307–31.

Kussmaul, A. 1981, *Servants in Husbandry in Early Modern England*, Cambridge University Press.

Kussmaul, A. 1990, *A General View of the Rural Economy of England, 1538–1840*, Cambridge University Press.

Kuznets, Simon 1971, *Economic Growth of Nations: Total Output and Production Structure*, Cambridge, MA: Belknap Press.

Kwass, M. 2000, *Privilege and the Politics of Taxation in Eighteenth-Century France*, Cambridge University Press.

Labrousse, Camille Ernest 1933, *Esquisse du mouvement des prix et des revenus en France au XVIIIè siècle*, 2 vols., Paris: Librairie Dalloz.

Lacour-Gayet, G.1902, *La Marine militaire de la France sous le règne de Louis XV*, Paris: Honoré Champion.

Lambert, Andrew 2002, 'Strategy, policy and shipbuilding: the Bombay dockyard, the Indian Navy and imperial security in eastern seas, 1784–1869', in Digby, Bowen and Lincoln (eds.), pp. 137–52.

Landes, David S. 1969, *The Unbound Prometheus: Technological Change and Industrial Development in Westen Europe from 1750 to the Present*, Cambridge University Press.

Landes, David S. 1998, *The Wealth and Poverty of Nations: Why Some Are so Rich and Some Are so Poor*, New York: W. W. Norton.

Langley, L. 1996, *The Americas in the Age of Revolution 1750–1850*, New Haven: Yale University Press.

Law, John 1934, *Oeuvres complètes*, ed. P. Harsin, 3 vols., Paris.

Le Goff, T. J. A. 1985, 'L'impact des prises effectuées par les Anglais sur la capacité en hommes de la marine française au XVIIIe siècle', in Acerra, Merino and Meyer (eds.), pp. 103–22.

Le Goff, T. J. A. 1990, 'Problèmes de recrutement de la marine française pendant la Guerre de Sept Ans', *Revue historique* 283: 205–33.

Le Goff, T. J. A. 1997a, 'Les caisses d'amortissement en France (1749–1783)', in *L'Administration des finances sous l'Ancien Régime*, Paris: Comité pour l'histoire économique et financière de la France, pp. 177–93.

Le Goff, T. J. A. 1997b, 'The Labour market for sailors in France', in van Royen, Bruijn and Lucassen (eds.), pp. 287–327.

Le Goff, T. J. A. 1999, 'How to finance an eighteenth-century war', in Ormrod *et al.* (eds.), pp. 377–413.

Le Goff, T. J. A. and Sutherland, D. M. G. 1991, 'The Revolution and the rural economy', in Forrest and Jones (eds.), pp. 53–85.

Lee, W. R. (ed.) 1991, *German Industry and German Industrialisation*, London: Routledge.

Le Roy Ladurie, E. 1974, *The Peasants of Languedoc*, Urbana: University of Illinois Press.

Le Roy Ladurie, E. 1976, *The Peasants of Languedoc*, Urbana: University of Illinois Press.

Levasseur, E. 1911, *Histoire du Commerce de la France*, 2 vols., Paris.

Lévy, C.-F. 1969–80, *Capitalistes et pouvoir au siècle des lumières*, 3 vols., The Hague: Mouton.

Lindert, P. 1987, 'Who owned Victorian England?: the debate over landed wealth and inequality', *Agricultural History* 61: 25–51.

Lindert, P. 1991, 'Historical patterns of agricultural policy', in Timmer (ed.), pp. 29–83.

Liss, Peggy K. 1983, *Atlantic Empires: The Network of Trade and Revolution, 1713–1826*, Baltimore: Johns Hopkins University Press.

Llopis, E. 1983, 'Algunas consideraciones acerca de la producción agraria castellana en los veinticinco últimos años del Antiguo Régimen', *Investigaciones Económicas* 21: 135–51.

Llopis, E. 1989, 'El agro extremeño en el setecientos: crecimiento demográfico, "invasión mesteña" y conflictos sociales', in *Estructuras agrarias y reformismo ilustrado en la España del siglo XVIII*, Madrid: MAPA, pp. 267–90.

Lokke, Carl Ludwig 1932, *France and the Colonial Question: A Study of Contemporary French Opinion, 1763–1801*, New York: Columbia University Press.

Lucassen, Jan 1987, *Migrant Labour in Europe, 1600–1900*, London: Croom Helm.

Mackay, Ruddock F. 1965, *Admiral Hawke*, Oxford: Clarendon Press.

MacLeod, Christine 1988, *Inventing the Industrial Revolution. The English Patent System, 1660–1800*, Cambridge University Press.

MacLeod, Christine 1992, 'Strategies for innovation: the diffusion of new technology in nineteenth-century British industry', *Economic History Review* 45: 285–307.

Maddison, Angus 1995, *Monitoring the World Economy, 1820–1992*, Paris: OECD.

Maddison, Angus 2001, *The World Economy: A Millennial Perspective*, Paris: OECD.

Mahan, Alfred T. 1918, *The Influence of Sea Power upon History, 1660–1783*, 12th edn, Boston: Little Brown.

Maine, Sir Henry Sumner 1886, *Popular Government*, New York: H. Holt.

Manger, Johannes B., Jr. 1923, *Recherches sur les relations économiques entre la France et la Hollande pendant la Revolution française 1785–1795*, Paris.

Marino, John A. 1988, *Pastoral Economics in the Kingdom of Naples*, Baltimore: Johns Hopkins University Press.

Marshall, P. J. (ed.) 1998, *The Oxford History of the British Empire, Vol. 2, The Eighteenth Century*, Oxford University Press.

Martin, Luc 1997, 'The rise of the New Draperies in Norwich', in Harte (ed.), pp. 245–74.

Mathias, Peter 1979, *The Transformation of England: Essays in the Economic and Social History of England in the Eighteenth Century*, London: Methuen.

Mathias P. and O'Brien, P. K. 1976, 'Taxation in England and France, 1715–1810', *Journal of European Economic History* 5: 601–50.

Mathias, Peter and Postan, Michael M. (eds.) 1978, *Cambridge Economic History of Europe*, Cambridge University Press.

Mathon de la Cour, C.-J. (ed.) 1788, *Collection des Comptes-rendus, pièces authentiques, états et tableaux concernant les finances de France depuis 1758 jusqu'en 1787*, Lausanne and Paris.

Mayhew, N. J. (1995), 'Population, money supply, and the velocity of circulation in England, 1300–1700', *Economic History Review* 48, 2: 238–57.

McClelland, David C. 1961, *The Achieving Society*, Princeton: D. Van Nostrand.

McCloskey, D. N. 1975, 'The economics of enclosure: a market analysis', in Parker and Jones (eds.), pp. 115–34.

McCloskey, D. N. 1980, 'Magnanimous Albion: free trade and British national income, 1841–1881', *Explorations in Economic History* 17: 303–20.

McCloskey, D. N. 1981, 'The Industrial Revolution: a survey', in Floud and McCloskey (eds.), vol. I, pp. 103–27.

McCloskey, D. N. 1995, '1066 and a wave of gadgets: the achievements of British growth', in Gouk (ed.), pp. 114–32.

McCusker, J. J. 1978, *Money and Exchange in Europe and America, 1600–1775*, Williamsburg, VA: University of North Carolina Press.

McCusker, John J. and Morgan, Kenneth (eds.) 2000, *The Early Modern Atlantic Economy*, Cambridge University Press.

McEvedy, C. and Jones, R. J. 1978, *Atlas of World Population History*, Harmondsworth: Penguin.
McGowen, Randall 1999, 'From pillory to gallows: the punishment of forgery in the age of the financial revolution', *Past and Present* 165: 107–40.
McKendrick, Neil, Brewer, John and Plumb, J. H. 1982, *The Birth of a Consumer Society: The Commercialization of Eighteenth-Century England*, London: Europa.
McLachlan, Jean 1938, 'The Seven Years' Peace, and the West Indian policy of Carvajal and Wall', *English Historical Review* 59: 457–77.
McNeil, Ian 1990, *An Encyclopedia of the History of Technology*, London: Routledge.
McNeill, John Robert 1985, *Atlantic Empires of France and Spain: Louisbourg and Havana, 1700–1763*, Chapel Hill: University of North Carolina Press.
Ménard, Claude (ed.) 2000, *Institutions, Contracts and Organizations: Perspectives from New Institutional Economics*, Cheltenham: Edward Elgar.
Mendels, F. F. 1972, 'Proto-industrialization: the first phase of the industrialization process', *Journal of Economic History* 32: 241–61.
Merger, M., Barjot, D. and Polino, M. N. (eds.) 1998, *Les Entreprises et leur réseaux: hommes, capitaux, techniques et pouvoirs XIXe–XXe siècles*, Paris: Presses de l'Université de Paris-Sorbonne.
Meyer, Jean, and Acerra, Martine 1994, *Histoire de la Marine Française des origines à nos jours*, Rennes: Éditions Ouest-France.
Mingay, G. E. (ed.) 1989, *The Agrarian History of England and Wales, VI, 1750–1850*, Cambridge University Press.
Mitch, David 1993, 'The role of human capital in the First Industrial Revolution', in Mokyr (ed.), pp. 267–307.
Mitchell, B. R. 1975, 1981, *European Historical Statistics, 1750–1970*, London: Macmillan.
Mitchell, B. R. 1988, *British Historical Statistics*, Cambridge University Press.
Mitterauer, M. (ed.) 1974, *Österreichischer Montanwesen*, Vienna: Verlag für Geschichte und Politik.
Mokyr, Joel 1983, *Why Ireland Starved: A Quantitative and Analytical History of the Irish Economy, 1800–1850*, London: George Allen & Unwin.
Mokyr, J. (ed.) 1985, *The Economics of the Industrial Revolution*, Totowa: Rowman and Allenheld.
Mokyr, Joel 1990, *The Lever of Riches: Technological Creativity and Economic Progress*, New York: Oxford University Press.
Mokyr, Joel (ed.) 1993, 1999, *The British Industrial Revolution: An Economic Perspective*, Boulder, CO: Westview Press.
Mokyr, Joel 2000, 'The Industrial Revolution and the Netherlands: why did it not happen?' *De Economist* 148: 503–20.
Mokyr, Joel 2002, *The Gifts of Athena: Historical Origins of the Knowledge Economy*, Princeton University Press.
Morgan, E. Victor 1965, *A History of Money*, Harmondsworth: Penguin.
Morgan, Kenneth 2001, *Slavery, Atlantic Trade and the British Economy*, New York: Cambridge University Press.

Moriceau, J.-M. 1999, *L'Elevage sous l'Ancien Régime XVIe–XVIIIe*, Condé-sur-Noireau: SEDES.

Morineau, M. 1980, 'Budgets de l'État et gestion des finances royales en France au xviiie siècle', *Revue Historique* 264: 289–336.

Muldrew, Craig 1998, *The Economy of Obligation: The Culture of Credit and Social Relations in Early Modern England*, New York: St Martin's Press.

Munro, John H. 1997, 'The origin of the English 'New Draperies': the resurrection of an old Flemish industry, 1270–1570', in Harte (ed.), pp. 35–127.

Munroe, Arthur Eli (ed.) 1965, *Early Economic Thought*, Cambridge, MA: Harvard University Press.

Murphy, Antoin E. 1991, 'John Law's proposal for a bank of Turin (1712)', *Economies et Sociétés, Série Oeconomia* 15: 3–29.

Murphy, Antoin E. 1997, *John Law: Economic Theorist and Policy-Maker*, Oxford: Clarendon Press.

Musson, A. E. and Robinson, Eric 1969, *Science and Technology in the Industrial Revolution*, Manchester University Press.

Nash, R. C. 1997, 'The balance of payments and foreign capital flows in eighteenth-century England: a comment', *Economic History Review* 50, 1: 110–28.

Neal, Larry 1990, *The Rise of Financial Capitalism: International Capital in the Age of Reason*, Cambridge University Press.

Neal, Larry 1991, 'A tale of two revolutions: international capital flows 1789–1819', *Bulletin of Economic Research* 43: 307–37.

Neal, Larry 1994, 'The finance of business during the Industrial Revolution,' in Floud and McCloskey (eds.), vol. II, pp. 151–81.

Neal, Larry 2000, 'How it all began: the monetary and financial architecture of Europe from 1648 to 1815', *Financial History Review* 7, 2: 117–40.

Necker, J. 1791, *Sur l'administration de M. Necker par lui-même*, Paris.

Neeson, J. M. 1993, *Commoners: Common Right, Enclosure and Social Change in England, 1700–1820*, Cambridge University Press.

North, Douglass C. 1990, *Institutions, Institutional Change and Economic Performance*, Cambridge University Press.

North, D. C., and Thomas, R. P. 1973, *The Rise of the Western World*, Cambridge University Press.

North, Douglass C. and Weingast, Barry R. 1989, 'Constitutions and commitment: The evolution of institutions governing public choice', *Journal of Economic History* 49: 802–32.

Nugent, J. B. and Sanchez, N. 1989, 'The efficiency of the mesta: a parable', *Explorations in Economic History* 26: 261–84.

O'Brien, George 1918, *The Economic History of Ireland in the Eighteenth Century*, Dublin and London: Maunsel and Company.

O'Brien, Patrick K. 1967, 'Government revenue, 1793–1815: a study in fiscal and financial policy in the wars against France', D.Phil. thesis, University of Oxford.

O'Brien, Patrick K. 1982a, 'European economic development: the contribution of the Periphery', *Economic History Review* 35, 1: 1–18.

O'Brien, Patrick K. 1982b, 'In praise of new economic history', *Economia* 6, 1: 1–27.

O'Brien, Patrick K. 1983, 'Transport and economic development in Europe, 1789–1914', in O'Brien, Patrick K. (ed.) 1983, *Railways and the Economic Development of Western Europe, 1830–1914*, London: Macmillan, pp. 1–27.

O'Brien, Patrick K. 1985, 'Agriculture and the home market for English industry, 1660–1820', *English Historical Review* 100: 773–99.

O'Brien, Patrick K. 1986, 'Do we have a typology for the study of European industrialization in the nineteenth century?', *Journal of European Economic History* 15: 291–333.

O'Brien, Patrick K. 1988a, 'The costs and benefits of British imperialism, 1846–1914', *Past and Present* 120: 163–200.

O'Brien, Patrick K. 1988b, 'The political economy of British taxation, 1660–1815', *Economic History Review* 41, 1: 1–32.

O'Brien, Patrick K. 1989a, 'The impact of the Revolutionary and Napoleonic wars, 1793–1815, on the long-run growth of the British economy', *Review Fernand Braudel Centre* 12: 335–95.

O'Brien Patrick K. 1989b, 'Public finance in the wars with France, 1793–1815', in Dickinson (ed.), pp. 165–87.

O'Brien, Patrick K. 1991, *Power with Profit: the State and the Economy, 1688–1815*, Inaugural Lecture, University of London.

O'Brien, Patrick K. 1993, 'Political preconditions for the Industrial Revolution', in O'Brien and Quinault (eds.), pp. 124–55.

O'Brien, Patrick K. 1994, 'The state and the economy, 1688–1915', in Floud and McCloskey (eds.), vol. I, pp. 205–41.

O'Brien, Patrick K. 1996, 'Path Dependency, or why Britain became an industrialized and urbanized economy long before France', *Economic History Review* 49, 2: 213–49.

O'Brien, Patrick K. 1997a, 'The Britishness of the first Industrial Revolution and the British contribution to the industrialisation of the "follower countries" on the mainland, 1756–1914', *Diplomacy & Statecraft* 8, 3: 48–67.

O'Brien, Patrick K. 1997b, 'The micro foundations of macro inventions: The case of the Rev. Edmund Cartwright', *Textile History* 28, 2: 201–33.

O'Brien, Patrick K. 1998, 'Inseparable connections: trade, economy, fiscal state, and the expansion of empire, 1688–1815', in Marshall (ed.), pp. 53–77.

O'Brien, Patrick K. 1999, 'Imperialism and the rise and decline of the British economy, 1688–1989', *New Left Review* 238: 48–80.

O'Brien, Patrick K. 2000a, *The British Economy from Dominance to Decline*, Tokyo (mimeo).

O'Brien, Patrick K. 2000b, 'Mercantilism and imperialism in the rise and decline of the Dutch and British economies 1585–1815', *De Economist* 148, 4: 469–501.

O'Brien Patrick K. 2000c, 'Perspectives on global history: concepts and methodology. Is universal history possible?', *Proceedings. Reports, Abstracts and Round Table Introductions. 19th International Congress of Historical Sciences*, University of Oslo Press.

O'Brien Patrick K. 2001, 'Fiscal exceptionalism: Great Britain and its European rivals. From Civil War to triumph at Trafalgar and Waterloo', London School of Economics Working Paper, 65/01.
O'Brien, Patrick K., and Engerman, Stanley L. 1991, 'Exports and the growth of the British economy from the glorious Revolution to the Peace of Amiens,' in Solow (ed.), pp. 177–209.
O'Brien, Patrick K., Griffiths, T. and Hunt, D. 1991, 'Political components of the Industrial Revolution: Parliament and the English cotton industry, 1660–1774', *Economic History Review* 44: 394–423.
O'Brien, Patrick K., Griffiths, Trevor and Hunt, David 1992, 'Inventive activity in the British textile industry, 1700–1800', *Journal of Economic History* 52: 881–906.
O'Brien, Patrick K., Griffiths, Trevor and Hunt, David 1996a, 'Technological change during the First Industrial Revolution: the paradigm case of textiles, 1688–1851' in Fox (ed.), pp. 155–76.
O'Brien, Patrick K., Griffiths, Trevor and Hunt, David 1996b, 'Theories of technological progress and the British textile industry from Kay to Cartwright', *Revista de Historia Económica* 14, 535–55.
O'Brien, Patrick K., Griffiths, Trevor and Hunt, David 1998, 'The curious history and imminent demise of the challenge and response model', in Berg and Bruland (eds.), pp. 119–38.
O'Brien, Patrick K. and Heath, Daniel 1994, 'English and French landowners, 1688–1789', in Thompson (ed.), pp. 23–62.
O'Brien, Patrick K. and Hunt, Phillip A. 1993, 'The rise of a fiscal state in England, 1485–1815', *Historical Research* 66: 129–76.
O'Brien Patrick K. and Hunt, Philip A. 1999, 'England, 1485–1815', in Bonney (ed.), pp. 53–100.
O'Brien, Patrick K. and Keyder, Caglar 1978, *Economic Growth in Britain and France 1789–1914: Two Paths to the 20th Century*, London: George Allen and Unwin.
O'Brien, Patrick K. and Prados de la Escosura, Leandro 1992, 'Agricultural productivity and European industrialization 1890–1980', *Economic History Review* 45, 3: 514–36.
O'Brien, Patrick K. and Prados de la Escosura, Leandro 1998, 'The costs and benefits of European imperialism from the conquest of Ceuta, 1451, to the Treaty of Lusaka, 1974', in Núñez, C. E. (ed.) 1998, *Debates and Controversies in Economic History*, Madrid: 12th International Economic History Congress, pp. 9–69.
O'Brien, Patrick K. and Prados de la Escosura, Leandro 1998, 'The costs and benefits of European imperialism', *Revista de Historia Economica* 16, 1: 29–89.
O'Brien, Patrick K. and Quinault, Ronald (eds.) 1993, *The Industrial Revolution and British Society*, Cambridge University Press.
O'Driscoll, Gerald P., Holmes, Kim R. and Kirkpatrick, Melanie (eds.) 2001, *2000 Index of Economic Freedom*, New York: Heritage Foundation and the Wall Street Journal.

Ormrod, W. M., Bonney, Margaret and Bonney, Richard (eds.) 1999, *Crises, Revolutions and Self-Sustained Growth: Essays in European Fiscal History, 1130–1830*, Stamford: Shaun Tyas.

Overton, Mark 1996, *Agricultural Revolution in England: The Transformation of the Agrarian Economy: 1500–1850*, Cambridge University Press.

Pamuk, S. and Williamson, J. G. (eds.) 2000, *The Mediterranean Response to Globalization before 1950*, London: Routledge.

Pares, Richard 1936, *War and Trade in the West Indies, 1739–1763*, Oxford: Clarendon Press, reprinted London: Cass, 1963.

Pares, Richard 1938, *Colonial Blockade and Neutral Rights, 1739–1763*, Oxford: Clarendon Press, reprinted Philadelphia: Porcupine Press, 1975.

Parker, William N. and Jones, Eric L. (eds.) 1975, *European Peasants and Their Markets: Essays in Agrarian Economic History*, Princeton University Press.

Paulinyi, Akos 1974. 'Der technische Fortschritt im Eisenhüttenwesen der Alpenländer und seine Betriebwirtschaftlichen Auswirkungen 1600–1860', in Mitterauer, M. (ed.), *Österreichischer Montanwesen*, Vienna: Verlag für Geschichte und Politik, pp. 144–80.

Paulinyi, Akos 1986a, 'John Kay's flying shuttle: some considerations on his technical capacity and economic impact', *Textile History* 17: 149–66.

Paulinyi, Akos 1986b, 'Revolution and technology', in Porter and Teich (eds.), pp. 261–89.

Paulinyi, Akos 1987, *Das Puddeln*, Munich: Oldenbourg.

Persson, K. G. 1999, *Grain Markets in Europe 1500–1900. Integration and Deregulation*, Cambridge University Press.

Phelps Brown, E. H. and Hopkins, Sheila V. 1955, 'Seven centuries of building wages,' *Economica* 22: 195–206.

Phillips, Carla Rahn 1997, 'The labour market for sailors in Spain, 1570–1870', in van Royen *et al.* (eds.), pp. 329–48.

Phillips, Carla Rahn 2001, '"The life blood of the navy": recruiting sailors in eighteenth-century Spain', *Mariner's Mirror* 87: 420–45.

Phillips, Carla Rahn and Phillips, William D. 1997, *Spain's Golden Fleece. Wool Production and the Wool Trade from the Middle Ages to the Nineteenth Century*, Baltimore: Johns Hopkins University Press.

Pierenkemper, T. (ed.) 1992a, *Industriegeschichte Oberschlesiens im 19. Jahrhundert*, Wiesbaden: Steiner.

Pierenkemper, T. 1992b, 'Das Wachstum der oberschlesischen Eisenindustrie bis zur Mitte des 19. Jahrhunderts – Entwicklungsmodell oder Spielwiese der Staatsbürokratie?' in Pierenkemper (ed.), pp. 77–106.

Pierenkemper, T. 1994, 'Strukturwandlungen im System deutscher Motanregionen im 19. Jahrhundert – Saarregion, Oberschlesien und das Ruhrgebiet im Wachstumprozeß', in Wysocki (ed.), pp. 7–37.

Pijassou, R. 1980, *Un grand vignoble de qualité, Le Médoc*, Paris: Taillandier.

Plumpe, G. 1982, *Die württembergische Eisenindustrie im 19. Jahrhundert*, Wiesbaden: Franz Steiner Verlag.

Pollard, Sidney 1981, *Peaceful Conquest. The Industrialization of Europe, 1760–1970*, Oxford University Press.

Pomeranz, Kenneth 2000, *The Great Divergence: Europe, China and the Making of the Modern World Economy*, Princeton University Press.

Porter, Dale H. 1970, *The Abolition of the Slave Trade in England, 1784–1807*, Hamden: Archon Books.

Porter, Roy and Teich, M. (eds.) 1986, *Revolution in History*, Cambridge University Press.

Postan, M. M. 1950, 'Some agrarian evidence of declining population in the later middle ages,' *Economic History Review* 2: 221–46.

Postan, M. M. 1975, *The Medieval Economy and Society*, Harmondsworth: Penguin.

Pounds, N. J. G. 1990, *An Historical Geography of Europe*, Cambridge University Press.

Prados de la Escosura, Leandro 2000, 'International comparisons of real product, 1820–1990: an alternative data set', *Explorations in Economic History* 37, 1: 1–41.

Pressnell, L. S. 1956, *Country Banking in the Industrial Revolution*, Oxford: Clarendon Press.

Pressnell, L. S. (ed.) 1960a, *Studies in the Industrial Revolution*, London: The Athlone Press.

Pressnell, L. S. 1960b, 'The rate of interest in the eighteenth century', in Pressnell (ed.), pp. 178–214.

Price, M. 1995, *Preserving the Monarchy. The Comte de Vergennes, 1774–1787*, Cambridge University Press.

Price, M. 1997, 'Les Conseillers au contrôle general des finances à la fin de l'ancien régime: le cas de Jacques Marquet de Bourgade', in *L'Administration des finances sous l'Ancien Régime*, Paris: Comité pour l'histoire économique et financière de la France, pp. 65–80.

Price, Richard 1780, *An Essay in the Population of England, From the Revolution to the Present Time*, London: T. Cadell.

Prince, H. 1989, 'Changing rural landscape, 1750–1850', in Mingay (ed.), pp. 7–83.

Pritchard, James 1987, *Louis XV's Navy, 1748–1762: A Study of Organization and Administration*, Montreal and Kingston: McGill-Queen's University Press.

Pritchard, James 1995, *Anatomy of a Naval Disaster: The 1746 French Expedition to North America*, Montreal and Kingston: McGill-Queen's University Press.

Quinn, Stephen 1994, *Banking before the Bank: London's Unregulated Goldsmith-Bankers, 1660–1694*, Ph.D. thesis, University of Illinois at Urbana-Champaign.

Quinn, Stephen 2000, 'Follow the money: political economy, and the institutions of public finance in England, 1660–1700', mimeo.

Rapp, R. 1975, 'The unmaking of the Mediterranean trade hegemony: international trade rivalry and the commercial revolution', *Journal of Economic History* 35: 499–525.

Reis, Jaime 2000, 'How poor was the European Periphery before 1850? The Mediterranean vs. Scandinavia', in Pamuk and Williamson (eds.), pp. 17–44.

Reuss, C. *et al.* 1960, *Le Progrès économique en sidérurgie. Belgique, Luxembourg, Pays-Bas 1830–1955*, Louvain: Editions E. Nauwelaerts.

Ricardo, D. [1817] 1971, *On the Principles of Political Economy and Taxation*, edition by R. M. Hartwell, Harmondsworth: Penguin.

Richards, J. F. (ed.) 1983, *Precious Metals in the Later Medieval and Early Modern Worlds*, Durham: North Carolina Academic Press.

Richardson, David 1989, 'The eighteenth-century British slave trade: estimates of its volume and coastal distribution in Africa', *Research in Economic History* 12: 151–95.

Richardson, David 1991, 'Prices of slaves in West and West-Central Africa: toward an annual series, 1698–1807', *Bulletin of Economic Research* 43, 1: 21–56.

Richmond, Herbert W. 1920, *The Navy in the War of 1739–48*, 3 vols., Cambridge University Press.

Riden, P. 1977, 'The output of the British iron industry before 1870', *Economic History Review* 30: 442–59.

Riley, James C. 1980, *International Government Finance and the Amsterdam Capital Market*, Cambridge University Press.

Riley, James C. 1986, *The Seven Years War and the Old Regime in France: The Economic and Financial Toll*, Princeton University Press.

Riley J. C. and McCusker J. J. 1983, 'Money supply, economic growth and the quantity theory of money: France, 1650–1788', *Explorations in Economic History* 20: 274–93.

Ringrose, D. R. 1983, *Madrid and the Spanish Economy, 1560–1850*, Berkeley and Los Angeles: University of California Press.

Rodger, Nicholas A. M. 1986, *The Wooden World: An Anatomy of the Georgian Navy*, London: Collins.

Rodger, Nicholas A. M. 1992, '"A little navy of your own making": Admiral Boscawen and the Cornish Connection in the Royal Navy', in Duffy (ed.), pp. 82–92.

Rodger, Nicholas A. M. 1993, *The Insatiable Earl: A Life of John Montague, Fourth Earl of Sandwich, 1718–1792*, London: HarperCollins.

Romano, Ruggiero 1957, 'Documenti e prime considerazioni in torno alla "Balance du Commerce" della Francia dal 1716 al 1780', *Studi in onore di Armando Sapori*, Milan: Instituto Editoriale Cisalpino II, pp. 1,265–1,300.

Rose, M. R. 1965–6, 'Samuel Crompton (1753–1827), inventor of the Spinning Mule: a reconsideration', *Transactions of the Lancashire and Cheshire Antiquarian Society* 75: 11–32.

Rosenberg, N. 1976, *Perspectives on Technology*, Cambridge University Press.

Rosenthal, Jean-Laurent 1992, *The Fruits of Revolution. Property Rights, Litigation, and French Agriculture, 1700–1860*, Cambridge University Press.

Ross, S. 1965, 'Development of the combat division in eighteenth century French armies', *French Historical Studies* 1: 84–94.

Rostow, W. W. 1960, *The Stages of Economic Growth*, Cambridge University Press.

Roy, J.-A. 1962, *Histoire de la Famille Schneider et Du Creusot*, Paris: Marcel Rivière et Cie.

Ryan, A. N. 1985, 'The Royal Navy and the blockade of Brest, 1689–1805: theory and practice', in Acerra *et al.* (eds.), pp. 175–93.

Rydén, G. 2002, 'Responses to coal technology without any coal resources. Swedish ironmaking in the first half of the nineteenth century', unpublished paper, University of Uppsala.

Sacks, Jonathan 1999, *Morals and Markets*, London: Institute of Economic Affairs.

Sánchez Salazar, F. 1988, *La extensión de cultivos en España en el siglo XVIII*, Madrid: Siglo XXI.

Sandberg, L. G. 1979, 'The Case of the impoverished sophisticate: human capital and Swedish economic growth before World War I', *Journal of Economic History* 39: 225–41.

Sargent, Thomas and Velde, François 1995, 'Macroeconomic features of the French Revolution', *Journal of Political Economy* 103: 474–518.

Scherer, F. M. 1984, *Innovation and Growth: Schumpeterian Perspectives*, Cambridge, MA: MIT Press.

Schroeder, P. W. 1994, *The Transformation of European Politics 1763–1848*, Oxford University Press.

Scott, H. M. 1979, 'The Importance of Bourbon naval construction to the strategy of Choiseul after the Seven Years War', *International History Review* 1: 17–35.

Sen, G. 1984, *The Military Origins of Industrialization and International Trade Rivalry*, London: Frances Pinter.

Seybert, Adam 1818, *Statistical Annals . . .*, Philadelphia: Thomas Dobson & Son.

Shammas, Carole 1990, *The Pre-Industrial Consumer in England and America*, Oxford University Press.

Sheffield, Earl of 1790, *Observation on the Project of Abolishing the Slave Trade*, London.

Shepherd, Verene (ed.) 2002, *Working Slavery: Pricing Freedom*, New York: St Martin's Press.

Simpson, J. 1995, *Spanish Agriculture: The Long Siesta, 1765–1965*, Cambridge University Press.

Slack, Paul 1990, *The English Poor Law, 1531–1782*, Houndsmills: Macmillan.

Smith, Adam [1776] 1976, *The Wealth of Nations*, Oxford University Press.

Smith, Simon D. 1992, 'American colonisation and the terms of trade, 1700–1775', Economic History Society Annual Conference, Section 7, Leicester.

Snooks, Graeme Donald (ed.) 1994, *Was the Industrial Revolution Necessary?*, London: Routledge.

Sokoloff, Kenneth L. and Khan, B. Zorina 1990, 'The democratization of invention during early industrialization: evidence from the United States, 1790–1846', *Journal of Economic History* 50: 1–16.

Solow, Barbara L. 1985, 'Caribbean slavery and British growth: the Eric Williams hypothesis', *Journal of Development Economics* 17: 99–115.

Solow Barbara L. (ed.) 1991, *Slavery and the Rise of the Atlantic System*, Cambridge University Press.

Sombart, W. 1928, *Der Moderne Kapitalismus*, Munich: Duncker & Humblot.

Stamp, Dudley 1965, *Land Use Statistics of the Countries of Europe*, The World Land Use Survey, Occasional Papers no. 3, Bude, Cornwall: Geographical Publications Ltd.

Starkey, David J., 1990, 'War and the market for seafarers in Britain, 1736–1792', in Fischer and Nordvik (eds.), pp. 25–42.

Stein, Robert L. 1979, *The French Slave Trade in the Eighteenth Century. An Old Regime Business*, University of Wisconsin Press.

Stein, Robert L. 1983, 'The state of French colonial commerce on the eve of the Revolution', *Journal of European Economic History* 12, 1: 105–17.

Steinfeld, Robert J. 2001, *Coercion, Contract, and Free Labor in the Nineteenth Century*, Cambridge University Press.

Stewart, Larry 1992, *The Rise of Public Science: Rhetoric, Technology, and Natural Philosophy in Newtonian Britain, 1660–1750*, Cambridge University Press.

Stone, Lawrence (ed.) 1994, *An Imperial State at War: Britain from 1689 to 1815*, London: Routledge.

Swann, Julian 1995, *Politics and the Parlement of Paris under Louis XV, 1754–1774*, Cambridge University Press.

Sweet, Rosemary 1999, *The English Town, 1680–1840*, Harlow: Longman.

Taillemite, Étienne 1988, *L'Histoire ignorée de la Marine française*, Paris: Librairie Académique Perrin.

Tarrade, Jean 1972, *Le Commerce colonial de la France à la fin de l'Ancien Régime. L'évolution du Régime de 'l'Exclusif' de 1763 à 1789*, 2 vols., Paris: Presses Universitaires de France.

Temin, Peter 1997, 'Two views of the Industrial Revolution', *Journal of Economic History* 57, 1: 63–82.

Temin, Peter 2000, 'A response to Harley and Crafts', *Journal of Economic History* 60, 3: 842–46.

Terray, Abbé 1788, 'Mémoire présenté au Roi, vers la fin de l'année 1770, par M. l'abbé Terray', in Mathon de la Cour, C.-J. (ed.), *Collection des Comptes-rendus, pièces authentiques, états et tableaux concernant les finances de France depuis 1758 jusqu'en 1787*, Lausanne and Paris.

Thirsk, Joan 1961, 'Industries in the countryside', in Fisher (ed.), pp. 1–112.

Thirsk, J. 1967, 'Enclosing and engrossing', in Finberg (ed.), pp. 200–55.

Thirsk, Joan 1978, *Economic Policy and Projects: The Development of a Consumer Society in Early Modern England*, Oxford: Clarendon Press.

Thirsk, Joan (ed.) 1985, *The Agrarian History of England and Wales, V, 1640–1750*, Cambridge University Press.

Thirsk, J. 1997, *Alternative Agriculture. A History*, Oxford University Press, 1997.

Thomas, Brinley 1988, 'Was there an energy crisis in Great Britain in the 17th century?', *Explorations in Economic History* 23: 124–52.

Thomas, R. P., and Bean, R. N. 1974. 'The fishers of men: the profits of the slave trade', *Journal of Economic History* 34: 885–914.

Thomas, R. P. and D. N. McCloskey 1981, 'Overseas trade and empire 1700–1860', in Floud and McCloskey (eds.), vol. I, pp. 87–102.

Thompson, F. M. L. (ed.) 1994, *Landowners, Capitalists and Entrepreneurs: Essays for Sir John Habakkuk*, Oxford: Clarendon Press.

Thuillier, G. 1983, *La Monnaie en France au début du XIXè siècle*, Hautes études medievales et modernes, 51, Geneva: Droz.

Timmer, C. P. (ed.) 1991, *Agriculture and the State: Growth, Employment, and Poverty in Developing Countries*, Ithaca: Cornell University Press.

Toutain, J.-C. 1992, 'La production agricole de la France de 1810 à 1990', *Economies et Sociétés, Histoire quantitative de l'économie française*, no 11–12.

Toynbee, Arnold [1883] 1969, *Lectures on the Industrial Revolution in England*, London: David & Charles Reprints.

Toynbee, Arnold J. 1946, *A Study of History*, Oxford University Press.

Tracy, J. D. 1985, *A Financial Revolution in the Habsburg Netherlands: Renten and Renteniers in the County of Holland, 1515–1565*, Berkeley: University of California Press.

Tranter, N. L. 1994, 'Population, Migration and Labour Supply', in Aldcroft and Ville (eds.), pp. 37–71.

Turner, M. E., Beckett, J. V. and Afton, B. 2001, *Farm Production in England, 1700–1914*, Oxford University Press.

Turner, M. 1996, *After The Famine. Irish Agriculture 1850–1914*, Cambridge University Press.

Van der Ent, Leendert, Fritschy, Wantje, Horlings, Edwin and Liesker, R. 1999, 'Public finance in the United Provinces of the Netherlands in the seventeenth and eighteenth centuries', in Ormrod *et al.* (eds.), pp. 249–93.

Van der Woude, Ad and Schuurman, Anton 1980, *Probate Inventories: A New Source for the Historical Study of Wealth, Material Culture and Agricultural Development*, Wageningen, A. A. G. Bijdragen, No. 23.

Van Royen, Paul, Bruijn, Jap, and Lucassen, Jan (eds.) 1997, *'Those Emblems of Hell?': European Sailors and the Maritime Labour Market, 1570–1870*, St John's, Newfoundland: International Maritime Economic History Association.

Vauban, S. le Prestre, Maréchal de 1988, *Projet d'une dixme royale*, ed. J.-F. Pernot, Saint-Léger-Vauban.

Velde F. R. and Weir D. R. 1992, 'The financial market and government debt policy in France, 1746–1793', *Journal of Economic History* 52, 1: 1–39.

Vergé-Franceschi, Michel 1991, *Marine et Education sous l'Ancien Régime*, Paris: Centre National de la Recherche Scientifique.

Vergé-Franceschi, Michel 1996, *La Marine française au XVIIIe siècle: Guerres – Administration – Exploration*, Paris: Editions Sedes.

Vergé-Franceschi, Michel, 1997, 'Les Gérontes à la mer', in Buchet (ed.), pp. 253–69.

Vergé-Franceschi, Michel and A.-M. Graziani (eds.) 2000, *La Guerre de course en Méditerranée (1515–1830)*, Paris: Presses de l'Université Paris IV-Sorbonne.

Vial, J. 1967, *L'Industrialisation de la sidérurgie française 1814–1864*, Paris: Mouton.

Voltaire, Jean François Marie de 1947, *Candide, or Optimism*, Harmondsworth: Penguin.

Von Tunzelmann, G. N. 1978, *Steam Power and British Industrialization to 1860*, Oxford: Clarendon Press.

Von Tunzelmann, G. N. 1985, 'The standard of living debate and optimal economic growth', in Mokyr (ed.), pp. 207–26.

Wadsworth A. P. and Mann, Julia de L. 1931, *The Cotton Trade and Industrial Lancashire, 1600–1780*, Manchester University Press.

Wallerstein, I. M. 1974–91, *The Modern World System*, 3 vols., New York: Academic Press.

Ward, J. R. 1978, 'The profitability of sugar planting in the British West Indies, 1650–1834', *Economic History Review* 31: 197–213.

Watts, David 1987, *The West Indies: Patterns of Development, Culture and Environmental Change Since 1492*, Cambridge University Press.

Weatherill, Lorna 1988, *Consumer Behaviour and Material Culture*, New York.

Weber, Max 1958, *The Protestant Ethic and the Spirit of Capitalism*, New York: Scribner's.

Weber, W. 1976, *Innovationen im frühindustriellen deutschen Bergbau und Hüttenwesen, Friedrich Anton von Heynitz*, Göttingen: Vandenhoeck & Ruprecht.

Weingast, B. R. 1997, 'The political foundations of limited government: Parliament and sovereign debt in 17th- and 18th-century England', in Drobak, J. N. and Nye, J. V. C. (eds.), *The Frontiers of the New Institutional Economics*, San Diego and London: Academic Press, pp. 213–46.

White, Eugene 1995, 'The French Revolution and the politics of government finance, 1770–1815,' *Journal of Economic History* 55: 227–55.

White, Eugene N. 1997, 'L'Efficacité de l'affermage de l'impôt: la ferme générale au XVIIIe siècle', in *L'Administration des finances sous l'Ancien Régime*, Paris: Comité pour l'histoire économique et financière de la France, pp. 103–20.

White, Eugene N. 2001, 'France and the failure to modernize macroeconomic institutions', in Bordo and Cortés-Conde (eds.), pp. 59–99.

Williams, Eric 1944, *Capitalism and Slavery*, New York: Capricorn Books.

Williamson, J. G. 1984, 'Why was British growth so slow during the Industrial Revolution?', *Journal of Economic History* 44, 3: 687–712.

Williamson, J. G. 1985, *Did British Capitalism Breed Inequality?*, London: Allen and Unwin.

Williamson, Jeffrey G. 1987, 'Debating the Industrial Revolution', *Explorations in Economic History* 24: 269–92.

Wilson, Charles 1941, *Anglo-Dutch Finance in the Eighteenth Century*, Cambridge University Press, 1941.

Wysocki, J. (ed.) 1994, *Wirtschaftliche Integration und Wandel von Raumstrukturen im 19. und 20. Jahrhundert*, Berlin: Duncker & Humblot.

Woodward, Donald 1995, *Men at Work: Labourers and Building Craftsmen in the Towns of Northern England, 1450–1750*, Cambridge University Press.

Wordie, J. R. 1983, 'The chronology of English enclosure, 1500–1914', *Economic History Review* 36: 483–505.

Woronoff, D. 1984, *L'Industrie sidérurgique en France pendant la Révolution et l'Empire*, Paris: Ecole des Hautes Etudes.

Wright, J. F. 1999, 'British Government borrowing in wartime, 1750–1815', *Economic History Review* 52: 355–61.

Wrigley, E. A. 1967, 'A simple model of London's importance in changing English society and economy, 1650–1750', *Past and Present* 37: 44–70, reprinted in Wrigley (ed.) 1987, pp. 133–56.

Wrigley, E. A. 1985, 'Urban growth and agricultural change: England and the continent in the early modern period', *Journal of Interdisciplinary History* 15, 683–728.

Wrigley, E. A. (ed.) 1987, *People, Cities and Wealth*, Oxford: Basil Blackwell.

Wrigley, E. A. 1988, *Continuity, Chance, and Change: The Character of the Industrial Revolution in England*, Cambridge University Press.

Wrigley, E. A. 1991, 'Energy availability and agricultural productivity', in Campbell and Overton (eds.), pp. 323–39.

Wrigley, E. A. 1994, 'The classical economists, the stationary state, and the Industrial Revolution', in Snooks (ed.), pp. 27–42.

Wrigley, E. A. and Schofield, R. S. 1981, *The Population History of England, 1541–1871*, London: Edward Arnold.

Wrigley, E. A. and Schofield, R. S. 1989, *The Population History of England 1541–1871. A Reconstruction*, Cambridge University Press.

Wysocki, J. (ed.) 1994, *Wirtschaftliche Integration und Wandel von Raumstrukturen im 19. und 20. Jahrhundert*, Berlin: Duncker & Humblot.

Young, A. 1929, *Travels in France during the Years 1787, 1788 & 1789*, edited by Constantia Maxwell, Cambridge University Press.

Index